BLOWBACK

EAST-WEST CENTER
SERIES ON

CONTEMPORARY ISSUES IN ASIA
AND THE PACIFIC

Series Editor, Muthiah Alagappa

BLOWBACK

LINGUISTIC NATIONALISM, INSTITUTIONAL DECAY, AND ETHNIC CONFLICT IN SRI LANKA

Neil DeVotta

STANFORD UNIVERSITY PRESS

STANFORD, CALIFORNIA

2004

Stanford University Press
Stanford, California
© 2004 by the Board of Trustees
of the Leland Stanford Junior University

Printed in the United States of America
on acid-free, archival-quality paper

Library of Congress Cataloging-in-Publication Data

DeVotta, Neil.
  Blowback : linguistic nationalism, institutional decay, and
ethnic conflict in Sri Lanka / Neil DeVotta.
    p. cm. — (Contemporary issues in Asia and the Pacific)
  Includes bibliographical references and index.
  ISBN 0-8047-4923-X (alk. paper) —
  ISBN 0-8047-4924-8 (pbk. : alk. paper)
    1. Sri Lanka—Politics and government—1978– 2. Sri Lanka—
Ethnic relations—Political aspects. 3. Ethnic conflict—Sri
Lanka. 4. Tamil (Indic people)—Sri Lanka—Politics and
government. 5. Nationalism—Sri Lanka. 6. Sri Lanka—
Languages—Political aspects. I. Title. II. Series.

DS489.84 .D48 2004
323.15493'09'045—dc22   2003027044

Original Printing 2004

Last figure below indicates year of this printing:
13   12   11   10   09   08   07   06   05   04

Typeset by John Feneron in 10/12 Sabon

Dedicated to
WILMA W. GARDNER
and the memory of
KENNETH N. GARDNER

A Series from
Stanford University Press and the East-West Center

CONTEMPORARY ISSUES IN ASIA AND THE PACIFIC

Muthiah Alagappa, Editor

A collaborative effort by Stanford University Press and the East-West Center, this series addresses contemporary issues of policy and scholarly concern in Asia and the Pacific. The series focuses on political, social, economic, cultural, demographic, environmental, and technological change and on the problems related to such change. A select group of East-West Center senior fellows—representing the fields of political science, economic development, population, and environmental studies—serves as the advisory board for the series. The decision to publish is made by Stanford.

Preference is given to comparative or regional studies that are conceptual in orientation and emphasize underlying processes, and to work on a single country that addresses issues in a comparative or regional context. Although concerned with policy-relevant issues and written to be accessible to a relatively broad audience, books in the series are scholarly in character. We are pleased to offer here the seventh book in the series, *Blowback: Linguistic Nationalism, Institutional Decay, and Ethnic Conflict in Sri Lanka*, Neil DeVotta.

The East-West Center, located in Honolulu, Hawaii, and in Washington, D.C., is a public, nonprofit educational and research institution established by the U.S. Congress in 1960 to foster understanding and cooperation among the governments and peoples of the Asia-Pacific region, including the United States.

CONTENTS

TABLES

ACKNOWLEDGMENTS

This book was first conceived as a dissertation at the University of Texas at Austin, and I thank my dissertation committee—Robert L. Hardgrave, Jr., Sumit Ganguly, Zoltan Barany, Peter Trubowitz, and Robert Moser—for their constructive input. Two among these stand out: Bob Hardgrave, for being my longtime advisor and indefatigable critic, who diligently read through numerous drafts, and Sumit Ganguly, for being my biggest booster and dependable ally. Sumit introduced me to Muthiah Alagappa and is hence partly responsible for this book being published in the latter's series.

A number of persons made my research in Sri Lanka, the United States, and Canada easier by arranging (or trying to arrange) numerous interviews. For this I thank Godwin Fernando, T. D. S. A. Dissanayaka, John Gooneratne, Harold Sandarasagara, Kana Gnanachandran, and Ernest Corea. V. S. Sambandan, correspondent for *The Hindu* and *Frontline* magazine, deserves special mention in this regard, for not only have I benefited from his analyses of Sri Lanka's ethnic conflict, but it was through him that I met a number of politicians and diplomats. I appreciate all those who went out of their way to meet with me, and these include Sathivale Balakrishnan, Tyrol Ferdinands, Godwin Fernando, John Gooneratne, Bernard Goonatillake, Siri Hettige, Kathesh Loganathan, Jehan Perera, G. L. Pieris, M. D. D. Pieris, Gajan Ponnambalam, Suresh Premachandran, Paikiasothy Saravanamuttu, Kula Sellathurai, Dharmalingam Sidharthan, Usha and Bavan Sri-Skanda-Rajah, and Bradman Weerakoon. I must single out Jayadeva Uyangoda, for I have benefited immensely from our conversations and his willingness to share his immense knowledge of and insights into Sri Lanka's politics. There were some who would not go on record, and I especially thank them for sharing their experience and knowledge.

Chandra R. de Silva and Bruce Matthews provided useful comments on the final version of the manuscript, and Robert Rotberg read through both the penultimate and final versions and then volunteered to go over more material. Their labors have made what follows a much better book than it otherwise would have been, and I thank all three for their professional courtesy and support. I am also grateful to Susan Pharr for her advice and encouragement in the review and revision process.

The revisions to the manuscript were made at James Madison College, Michigan State University, when I worked there as a visiting assistant professor, and I thank the college for allowing me unlimited access to its resources. I am indeed grateful to Mohammed Ayoob, Michael Schechter, Norm Graham, and Sherman Garnett for their goodwill in various respects during my time at Madison.

I am especially indebted to Muthiah Alagappa and his team at the East-West Center and to the Stanford University Press for being committed to this project and encouraging me to complete it. Sharon Yamamoto and Elisa Johnston at the East-West Center and Muriel Bell, Carmen Borbon-Wu, and John Feneron at Stanford have been supportive and gracious from the outset. Their capacity for patient prodding no doubt comes from having dealt with dilatory authors. I hope that I was not among the worst of them. I am also grateful to Peter Dreyer, whose copyediting has made this a much better book.

There are a few paragraphs in this book that were previously published in my chapter in Michael E. Brown and Sumit Ganguly, eds., *Fighting Words: Language Policy and Ethnic Relations in Asia* (Cambridge, Mass.: MIT Press, 2003), and in an essay in *Pacific Affairs* 73, no. 1 (Spring 2000). I thank the MIT Press and the University of British Columbia for granting permission to reuse this material. I also thank the following for granting permissions to reproduce certain tables in this work: the *Daily News* for table 4, which originally appeared in "Mettananda on the Reasonable Use of Tamil," *Daily News,* July 14, 1958, p. 4; C. Hurst and Company (Publishers) Ltd., for table 7, which initially appeared in C. R. de Silva, "Education," in *Sri Lanka: A Survey*, ed. K. M. de Silva, p. 423; and the National Science Foundation in Sri Lanka for table 8, which initially appeared in C. R. de Silva, "The Politics of University Admissions: A Review of Some Aspects of Admission Policy in Sri Lanka 1971–78," *Sri Lanka Journal of Social Sciences* 1, no. 2 (December 1978): 105–6.

Finally, but most important, I thank my devoted wife, Sandhi. Her patience, understanding, and tolerance—especially when trying to negotiate my mood swings and frustrations—have set me a new standard for gauging spousal support and have indisputably made her the "better half" of us. Sandhi has long been, and remains, the cynosure of my life, and this book would not have been written without her unstinting encouragement and support.

I appreciate immensely the time and efforts all the above have expended on my behalf and happily acknowledge their contributions to this work. That said, I alone am responsible for all errors of omission and commission.

In 1988, Wilma W. Gardner and her family made a decision that opened a new world to me. What others and I have since achieved owes much to their munificence. I thank them and, as a show of everlasting gratitude, dedicate this book to Wilma and her late husband Kenneth N. Gardner.

Neil DeVotta
November 2003

PREFACE

A few years ago a professor of political science who had specialized in South Asia for nearly thirty-five years grumbled over not finding a book that theoretically and systematically covered Sri Lanka's ethnic conflict. He then asked if I could recommend a text that did so. I did recommend a few books rooted in different disciplines that dealt with the island's gruesome civil war, but we both agreed that there was "nothing out there" that sought to explain causally, and thereby especially satisfy political scientists, how and why a passive and nonviolent ethnic group ended up unleashing one of the twentieth century's most violent secessionist conflicts. This book has sought to fill that lacuna, and it relies on an institutional analysis to do so.

The book argues that the numerous ethnocentric practices successive Sri Lankan governments pursued from the mid-1950s on led to a milieu in which the island's institutions failed to deal dispassionately with the Tamil minority, and that the institutional decay that ensued helped mobilize disgruntled Tamil youth to seek a separate state. Nearly all those who have focused on Sri Lanka's postindependence politics recognize that making the majority community's Sinhala language the country's only official language in 1956 contributed to the Sinhalese-Tamil rivalry. What many fail to recognize, however, is the extent to which linguistic nationalism became the mechanism that precipitated institutional decay. As the book makes clear, the Official Language Act encouraged many hitherto marginalized Sinhalese to believe that the new policy would contribute to their socioeconomic upward mobility. Consequently, it also influenced much other ethnocentric legislation that sought to empower the majority community and fulfill the expectations the Official Language Act had generated. When rival Sinhalese politicians and their parties sought to outbid one another on who could better provide for their community, nearly always at the expense of the principal Tamil minority, the stage was set for institutional decay and separatist conflict. The world is now familiar with the atrocities committed by the ruthless Liberation Tigers of Tamil Eelam (LTTE), which is branded a terrorist group in numerous countries. What many people are not all that familiar with are the conditions that propelled the separatist LTTE to become the ogre it is today. This book should help on that score as well.

Focusing on institutions is crucial, given that Sri Lanka will most likely achieve peace and stability only if the island's Northern and Eastern Provinces obtain sufficient autonomy for the island's minorities to live with a sense of dignity, self-respect, and self-determination. While I have advocated a federal solution, I have eschewed playing the role of a constitutional engineer and delineating a federal arrangement that might best suit the country. Such a discussion is beyond the parameters of this book. That noted, I hope the book makes clear why devolution, irrespective of the arrangement utilized in the process, is an absolute necessity if Sri Lanka is to stay united and Tamils and Sinhalese especially are to coalesce as one polity.

My political science proclivities notwithstanding, the book is designed to appeal to a broad audience. Lay readers interested specifically in Sri Lanka's sad saga, and not in theoretical positions, may, however, want to skip chapter 1.

ABBREVIATIONS

CP   Communist Party
DDC   District Development Councils
DMK   Dravida Munnetra Kazhagam (Dravidian Progressive Front)
EPRLF   Eelam People's Revolutionary Liberation Front
EROS   Eelam Revolutionary Organization of Students
FP   Federal Party
IPKF   Indian Peace Keeping Force
JSS   Jathika Sevaka Sangamaya (National Worker's Union)
JVP   Janatha Vimukthi Peramuna (People's Liberation Front)
LRRP   Long Range Reconnaissance Patrol
LSSP   Lanka Sama Samaja Party (Lanka Equal Society Party)
LTTE   Liberation Tigers of Tamil Eelam
MEP   Mahajana Eksath Peramuna (People's United Front)
MoU   Memorandum of Understanding
PA   People's Alliance
PLOTE   People's Liberation Organization of Tamil Eelam
RAW   Research and Analysis Wing
SBAM   Sinhala Basha Arakshaka Mandalaya (Sinhala Language
        Protection Council)
SLFP   Sri Lanka Freedom Party
SU   Sinhala Urumaya (Sinhala Heritage)
TELO   Tamil Eelam Liberation Front
TNA   Tamil National Alliance

TUF	Tamil United Front
TULF	Tamil United Liberation Front
UF	United Front
UNF	United National Front
UNP	United National Party

BLOWBACK

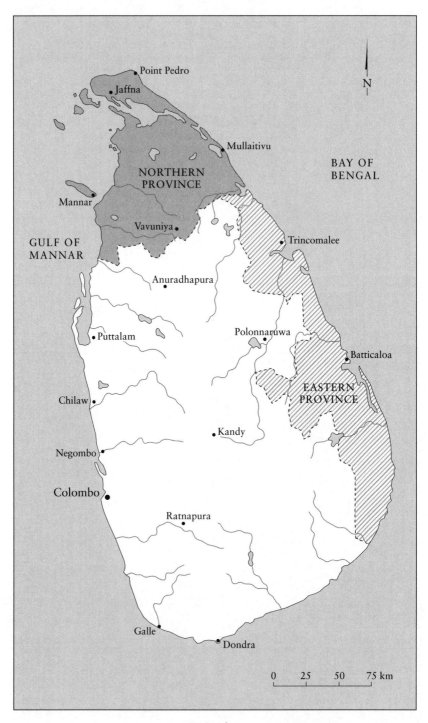

POINT PEDRO

Jaffna

Mullaitivu

BAY OF
BENGAL

NORTHERN
PROVINCE

Mannar

GULF OF
MANNAR

Vavuniya

Trincomalee

Anuradhapura

Puttalam

Polonnaruwa

Batticaloa

Chilaw

EASTERN
PROVINCE

Kandy

Negombo

Colombo

Ratnapura

Galle

Dondra

0   25   50   75 km

Sri Lanka

AN OVERVIEW

On July 24, 2001, exactly eighteen years after Sri Lanka's worst ethnic riots, thirteen rebels from the Liberation Tigers of Tamil Eelam (LTTE),
which is fighting to create a separate Tamil state in the island's northeast,
attacked the country's only international airport and the adjacent air
force base. In the six-hour battle that ensued, all thirteen rebels and seven
soldiers died, and twenty-six civilian and military aircraft were either totally destroyed or damaged, at a cost to the government of nearly U.S. $1
billion, further undermining Sri Lanka's sliding economy. Almost
overnight, international underwriters declared the entire island a war
zone and raised insurance premiums as much as 400 percent on all ships
and aircraft visiting the country. The opposition sought to topple the government, and the president suspended parliament to avoid that outcome.
This increasing political instability was related in no small measure to Sri
Lanka's twenty-year civil war between the majority Sinhalese and minority Tamils, which has killed approximately 70,000 people, displaced
thousands more, and forced nearly a million Tamils to flee the country.
For an island that was considered the postcolonial Asian country most
likely to succeed socioeconomically and democratically, Sri Lanka is no
doubt in a very sorry state. How does one explain theoretically why this
once liberal democracy unleashed a savage ethnic conflict and regressed
into a veritable "ethnocracy"?[1]

Theories of ethnic conflict typically focus on primordialist (historical
and biological), constructivist (sociological), and instrumentalist (elite
and rational choice) explanations, thereby underemphasizing how politics impacts intraethnic and interethnic relations. This study evaluates Sri
Lanka's "Sinhala-only" movement, which led to the majority Sinhalese
community's language being made the sole official language and facilitated ethnocracy and "ethnic outbidding."[2] Practiced over two decades,

ethnic outbidding and ethnocracy marginalized the island's minorities and especially undermined Tamils' confidence in the state's institutions. I argue here that institutional decay, facilitated by linguistic nationalism, mobilized the Tamils for ethnic conflict.[3] By focusing on linguistic nationalism as the mechanism Sinhalese elites used to achieve their preferences and also analyzing the ethnic outbidding culture and ethnocracy the Sinhala-only movement unleashed, this study stresses ethnic politics, while also taking into account primordialist, constructivist, and instrumentalist explanations. It attempts to answer the following questions: (i) Why and how did linguistic nationalism undermine Sinhalese-Tamil relations and influence ethnic conflict? (ii) Why do "ethnic entrepreneurs"[4] resort to ethnic outbidding and undermine impartial relations between a state's citizens and its institutions? and (iii) How is institutional decay related to group mobilization and violence?

When traditional societies—typically characterized by loyalty to family, clan, or village, where state sector employment and state-sponsored development are almost nonexistent and widespread illiteracy and mass dependence on subsistence agriculture are abundant—transform themselves into post-traditional or modern communities, there result complex interactions between community and state that are mediated through official and unofficial institutions. As Samuel Huntington has observed, "In a complex society community is produced by political action and maintained by political institutions."[5] When a polyethnic society's politics blatantly favors one group, thereby discriminating against others, those marginalized lose confidence in the state's institutions. The outcome may often be reactive nationalism, which if not carefully dealt with can easily lead to mobilization and conflict. As Jack Snyder has noted, ethnic nationalism "predominates when institutions collapse, when existing institutions are not fulfilling people's basic needs and when satisfactory alternative structures are not readily available."[6] The institutional decay that follows, especially if involving an ethnic group that is territorially based, may lead those marginalized to mobilize seeking redress. Depending on how the state or the majority group reciprocates, the aggrieved group may seek a separate existence. Herein lies the cause of Sri Lanka's ethnic conflict.

The civil war between the Sinhalese and Tamils in Sri Lanka is one of the deadliest and most protracted ethnic conflicts of our time. The two groups had, in the main, enjoyed cordial relations over two thousand years until the Sinhalese jettisoned a proposal to make Sinhala and Tamil the country's official languages and instead instituted Sinhala as the sole official language. The Official Language Act of 1956 led to ethnic riots in 1956 and 1958 and marked the beginning of postindependence Sinhalese-Tamil animosity. While the Sinhala-only movement and its association with Buddhism are generally recognized to have created animus between the ethnic groups,[7] the manner in which the Official Language Act and Sinhalese linguistic nationalism facilitated the ethnic conflict is not fully appreciated. This is because Sri Lanka's civil war dates from after the 1983 anti-Tamil riots and because other issues—namely, colonization, resource allocation, and education—have been overemphasized as major reasons for the rift in Sinhalese-Tamil relations.[8] Indeed, it is even argued that the language issue, while it led to emotive protests, was not the most salient reason for the Tamils' eventual quest for *eelam* (a separate Tamil state).[9] An encompassing evaluation supports a contrary view. The evidence suggests that the Sinhala-only movement and the Official Language Act of 1956 provided the catalyst for the numerous anti-minority policies and ethnocracy that followed, and that the institutional decay this generated over nearly two decades was what caused Tamil mobilization and the ongoing civil war. This was because the Official Language Act and the policies it inspired radically altered the rules of polyethnic coexistence.

The rules governing relations between state and polity in all societies are designed to ensure that those who make the rules can win most of the time. Polyethnic coexistence is attained when those who have the power to change the rules nevertheless consider minority aspirations and make an honest effort to operate amid compromise and conciliation. Thus, the challenge for a majority group is to attain its preferences without alienating the minorities. This is achieved if the minorities are made to feel that they too have a stake in the system. When minorities come to believe that the rules allow them to win some of the time, even if not as often as the majority community, they are likely to feel that the rules of the game are fair. The more this sense of fairness gets embedded, the more robust polyethnic coexistence will be. On the other hand, when a community can change the rules to its own advantage at will, disregarding minorities' aspirations, the latter will lose confidence in the country's institutions.

It is argued that institutions can significantly influence actors' strategies and their policy preferences,[10] and this study also suggests that Sri Lanka's institutions framed elites' preferences and influenced the policies they championed. While agreeing that Sri Lanka's elites operated instrumentally, the study argues that their decisions were influenced by interactions with various groups, as well as the island's institutional structures. Most Sri Lankan elites who manipulated linguistic nationalism and thereby engendered conditions conducive to creating the subsequent civil war were not communalists. Neither were they numbskulls. They certainly were not unpatriotic. Yet the fact remains that despite being cog-

nizant of the dangers of communalism and realizing that ethnic outbidding could unleash intolerance and conflict, these elites, influenced by the
extant opportunities and constraints, instituted rules, norms, routines,
and conventions geared toward creating an ethnocracy. Their rhetoric
clearly indicates that many strongly believed that ethnic outbidding and
the burgeoning ethnocracy might lead to the country's dismemberment,
but this did not lead them to cease their dangerous politicking.

The major reason politicians continued to practice ethnic outbidding,
despite knowing full well that it undermined polyethnic coexistence, was
because the institutional structure allowed them to do so and because
they realized that with others ever eager to replace them, there was much
to lose by not doing so. Like George Mallory, who when asked why he
relentlessly sought to climb Mount Everest retorted, "Because it is there,"
these ethnic entrepreneurs resorted to ethnic outbidding simply because
they could: the political structure did not preclude them from doing so or
punish them for the deleterious consequences. If anything, they stood to
be punished (by not being elected, or reelected) if they did not embrace
ethnic outbidding. The political structure thus encouraged the elites' instrumentalism and did not discourage or curb unprincipled and dangerous politicking. A related, and second, reason for ethnic outbidding was
political opportunism. Principled and far-sighted politicians would have
tried to reconfigure the island's political structure to ensure impartial
transactions between the state and all ethnic groups. But Sri Lanka's
politicians eschewed principle and instead sought to further their careers
by taking advantage of the political structure. A third reason Sri Lanka's
elites resorted to ethnic outbidding was because they underestimated the
adverse consequences it would have and overestimated their capacity to
deal with the fallout. A final reason was the Sinhalese elites' belief that
the Tamils had no option but go along with what their Sinhalese counterparts did. The Tamils' relative passivity during the first fifteen years after the Official Language Act was passed merely strengthened this view.

The analysis provided here differs from that championed by rational
choice institutionalists and locates itself amid the work done by historical institutionalists. Rational choice institutionalists contend that institutions operate as an intervening variable, and that one should therefore
pay more serious attention to individuals, their preferences, and how
those preferences are attained. Historical institutionalists, on the other
hand, argue that the institutional setting mediates political contests, and
that preferences are therefore "formed by the institutional context within
which they emerge and ought not be treated as fixed."[11] This is not to
suggest that institutions determine behavior. They do not. Rather, they
provide the context for action. The institutional structure can constrain,

inhibit, pressure, and influence, but it does not determine specific political action. Courageous and determined politicians can always reconfigure extant institutions or design new ones to overcome difficulties and elicit compromise. "Facing the same set of institutional hurdles, self-reflective actors can make creative decisions about how to proceed," Ellen Immergut observes.[12] The decisions made may backfire, of course, doing more harm than good in the long run. This is partly what makes focusing on context so important. It helps explain why politicians may unleash negative consequences in seeking to attain their preferences.

If courageous and determined politicians can make efforts to change the institutional structure so as to make it more conducive to stable relations between state and polity, spineless and unprincipled politicians may succumb to institutional pressures and eschew implementing the requisite change or back away from their commitment to change. In the case of Sri Lanka, the ruling politicians, having manipulated the institutional setting to gain power, sought to implement creative policies to quell ethnic tensions, but they were compelled to betray their rational beliefs and give up their own clear-cut preferences by pressures exerted from institutions both within and outside of the government. Successive governments were forced to back off from the Bandaranaike-Chelvanayakam Pact of 1957, the Senanayake-Chelvanayakam Pact of 1965, and the District Councils Bill of 1968 (any one of which might have smothered the smoldering ethnic fires) and instead embrace a communalistic line (see chapter 5). Understanding the strategizing of political actors (i.e., how their interests, values, and beliefs were reconciled) consequently requires knowledge of the context in which decisions were made.[13]

Explaining Sri Lanka's Ethnic Conflict: The Scholarly Context

In trying to explain Sri Lanka's ethnic conflict, some suggest that the country's heritage of two millennia of Buddhism, and the attendant indelible consciousness on the part of the Sinhalese of themselves as Buddhists, drove the ongoing Sinhalese-Tamil conflict.[14] Others hold that racial, class, and religious categories ascribed and accentuated under colonialism, and the divisions that these and other malpractices the British engendered, are primarily responsible for the island's current ethnic problems.[15] Still others merely place the blame on Sinhalese and Tamil elites for disregarding the need for conciliation and accommodation.[16] Thus the illiberal pro-Sinhalese 1972 constitution is also cited as "an immediate spur" that led to the quest for *eelam*.[17] Many also cite the island's proximity to the nearly sixty million Tamils in the Indian state of Tamil Nadu and infer that a minority complex based on regional security considerations underlies Sinhalese nationalism.[18] None of these primordialist, constructivist, instrumentalist, and geopolitical accounts explain why Sinhalese political elites eagerly embraced the linguistic nationalist movement in the postindependence era, notwithstanding that they had strongly opposed the Buddhist revival/nationalist movement in the immediate preindependence era. Furthermore, none of them explain the civil war itself, in that no account is provided of how the Tamils, who were stereotyped as career-oriented, intellectual, and passive, came to launch a deadly separatist conflict. A more overarching explanation is possible only if one examines the structural, political, and economic underpinnings of the conflict, as well as elite policies and politics over time.[19]

The Sinhalese, being around 74 percent of the population and controlling 80 percent of the electorate in a first-past-the-post-electoral system, determined which party gained power. As in postapartheid South Africa, the country's demography ensured that minority influence was locked out in all postindependence elections.[20] Some may argue that Sri Lanka's demography preordained Sinhalese dominance and ethnic conflict. This is debatable, because while demography and democracy guaranteed the Sinhalese majoritarian status, this need not have led to ethnocracy and ethnic conflict. Even assuming that Sri Lanka's demographic distribution made Sinhalese domination inevitable, what ultimately transpired went beyond what any self-respecting ethnic minority could tolerate; for within two decades after the Official Language Act was passed, the island had regressed to an illiberal, ethnocentric regime bent on Sinhalese superordination and Tamil subjugation. The point is that there is no reason to believe a large or relatively small disparity between groups will lead to conflict provided the extant institutional structure is conducive to ethnic elites favoring settlement and compromise. For example, despite Malaysia's demography approximating the ethnic breakdown in Sri Lanka,[21] that country's elites reached a settlement that explicitly favored the predominant Malays. This settlement has, in the main, led to ethnic quiescence in Malaysia, while Sri Lanka has grappled with a civil war. The outcome is all the more tragic given that Sri Lanka was said "to have the best chance of making a successful transition to modern statehood" when compared with the other "new Asian countries."[22]

Sri Lanka's 1978 constitution introduced proportional representation, but the country's ethnic composition ensured that the Sinhalese would continue to determine the party in power. Thus, for elites and their political parties, whose primary goal is attaining and maintaining power, acceding to the majority community's demands was a choice that was both strategic and rational. With the Tamils primarily voting for Tamil regional parties, the two major Sinhalese parties sought to corral the Sinhalese vote by competing with each other in the anti-minority stance adopted. The ethnocracy that eventuated produced institutional decay over two decades and led to Tamil mobilization and ethnic violence.

The Study

The contradictory ethnic positions taken by Sri Lanka's major political parties when in and out of power have been recognized,[23] but the fact that their outbidding was directly related to the anti-Tamil milieu spawned by the linguistic nationalist movement has not received systematic assessment. Indeed, no study has hitherto sought to examine theoretically how the ethnic conflict is related to institutional decay; and this despite many political scientists having emphasized how important impartial institutions are for maintaining polyethnic stability.[24] Even when discussing ethnic outbidding, scholars analyzing Sri Lanka have focused primarily on elites' instrumentalist shenanigans, without trying to identify the reasons for their machinations or how ethnic outbidding produced institutional decay, Tamils' marginalization, and ethnic conflict. This book seeks to account for these deficiencies in the literature. In the process, it goes beyond the numerous descriptive and limited accounts analyzing Sri Lanka's civil war and provides a causal explanation that is conceptual, empirical, and analytical. Conceptually, it clarifies and refines our understanding of the dialectic between majority rule and Sinhalese ethnonationalism; empirically, it tracks the historical antecedents leading up to the Sinhala-only movement and the ethnic outbidding and ethnocracy that the combination of Sinhalese ethnolinguistic nationalism and Buddhist nationalism unleashed; analytically, the study historicizes and theorizes the most radical and crucial period in Sinhalese-Tamil relations and evaluates how the Sinhala-only movement legitimated, enculturated, and habituated a superordinating ethnic culture that led to civil war. In doing so, it argues that while the primordialist, constructivist, and instrumentalist accounts are hardly irrelevant, by themselves they are no more than partial explanations.

It will be clear that the account presented in the following pages is both telescopic and panoramic, because while I have tried to elucidate Sinhalese-Tamil relations, especially during the twentieth century, my primary concern has been to elaborate on the linguistic nationalism evidenced by both groups and show how this led to institutional decay. Thus, ethnic and political relations between the groups during the twentieth century have been treated in a broad-brush fashion. On the other hand, the years between 1956 and 1961 have been accounted for in detail, given that Sinhalese linguistic nationalism and the Tamils' reactive nationalism were most jingoistic during this period. This is not to suggest that linguistic nationalism became insignificant or tepid thereafter. On the contrary, the Tamils especially clamored for their legitimate language rights until 1978, when the new constitution acknowledged Tamil as a national language. By then, however, the separatist movement had already taken shape among Tamil youth.

The study also focuses on Buddhist and ethnic elites: on how their influence on the electorate lay behind the strategic posturing of their respective communities' political elites, and how that in turn affected interethnic interactions and institutional decay. Special attention is paid to these elites' pronouncements, how their rhetoric was translated into policy—or, as was often the case, how their rhetoric undermined the government's sometimes accommodative ethnic policies—and how intraethnic competition led to ethnic outbidding and ethnocracy, which in turn were responsible for the institutional decay discussed here. I explain how ethnic outbidding created maestro ethnic entrepreneurs among Sri Lanka's political elites, and how such outbidding eroded impartial governance, because thereafter numerous governmental and nongovernmental institutions pursued policies conducive to Sinhalese socioeconomic and political upward mobility, while deliberately marginalizing the Tamil minority. Consequently, chapters 2–6 represent an analysis focused mostly on the history and policymaking process, while at the same time seeking to locate reasons for the actors' preferences and to elaborate on the strategizing that they resorted to.

The Sinhalese were not the only twentieth-century majority community to seek to impose their preferences using ethnocentric practices, but few ethnic groups have seen their policies rebound on them the way the Sinhalese have.

Ethnocentrism and Linguistic Nationalism

The impetus for separatism in most ethnonational struggles is sparked by ethnocentric practices initiated by the state or the dominant ethnic group. Ethnocentric regimes almost always deny minorities the opportunity for impartial political, economic, social, and juridical interactions with state institutions. The particularistic policies that inevitably ensue promote ethnic differentiation (whether officially calibrated or inadvertently), erode minority confidence in such institutions, exacerbate grievances, and radicalize minority sentiment against the government and/or the majority group. If the particularism is calculated to perpetuate minority subordination and the minority group is territorially based, what obtains may be a political milieu that facilitates nationalism and separatism.[25] By eschewing inclusive policies that could facilitate interethnic cooperation, states that encourage exclusivist and repressive policies effectively institutionalize nationalism among territorial groups. Ultimately, ethnocentric policies always highlight the differences between groups rather than promoting interethnic solidarity. Furthermore, the invidious policies themselves are often represented as mechanisms designed to ensure stability.

While religious nationalism extends back at least to the sixteenth century, linguistic nationalism is a post-1870 phenomenon.[26] This is, in the main, related to the different political and economic possibilities inherent in traditional communities and modern societies. Unlike traditional communities—which were primarily agrarian, distanced, and decentralized—modern or post-traditional societies—which are bureaucratized, centralized, and relatively industrialized and literate—facilitate resource accrual (e.g., employment, education, welfare benefits, government contracts) and increased interactions with official and unofficial institutions.[27] Thus, it is the inevitable proliferation of official and unofficial institutions in post-traditional societies that have made language an important entity for negotiating interactions and accruing resources and led almost all major ethnic groups to clamor for their languages being made official, even as dominant/majority communities have sought to prevent this.

Linguistic nationalism has consequently accentuated the ethnonational movements among Canada's Québécois, Belgium's Flemings and Walloons, Spain's Basques and Catalonians, France's Corsicans, Switzerland's French and German speakers, and India's Dravidian communities (in Tamil Nadu, Kerala, Karnataka, and Andhra Pradesh). Likewise, Algeria's Berbers, numbering nearly six million and constituting 20 percent of the population, have demonstrated for two decades seeking official recognition for their language. In Slovakia, Vladimir Meciar and the nationalists have made Slovak the state language, thereby deemphasizing Hungarian and Czech (despite the fact that Hungarian-speakers make up 11 percent of the population). The Chinese have likewise stopped providing university education in Uighur in Xinjiang Province, although over half the population are Uighur. In Belgium, the separatist Vlaams Blok party has called for a language test to be imposed to keep out francophone elements, thereby helping cast doubt on the future viability of the pact between Flemings and French-speaking Belgians that has hitherto enabled the two groups to coalesce. Indeed, the January 1993 Velvet Divorce that saw Slovakia separate from Czechoslovakia has encouraged separatist elements among both the Flemings and Walloons to the point where "linguistic communalism is the principal . . . cleavage in contemporary Belgian politics."[28]

The modern state is also a highly politicized state, and language has proved to be useful for ethnic elites seeking a symbolic, emotive, and practical mechanism with which to pursue identity politics.[29] Yet it is important to recognize that language, as an identity mechanism, is neither necessary nor sufficient for group mobilization. Thus, while discriminatory language policies may or may not be the catalyst for mobilization, they certainly can accentuate grievances and thereby exacerbate ethnic relations between groups. The end result, especially when territorial groups are marginalized along linguistic lines, is always the same: those mistreated lose faith in the institutions representing the state and eventually mobilize seeking better treatment, increased autonomy, or a separate existence.

When a majority community pursues linguistic nationalism hoping to attain superordinate status, what will likely ensue is an ethnocracy promoting particularistic interactions. The more particularistic interactions permeate institutions representing the state, the more likely those marginalized will rebel. This is especially so for territorially based minorities whose elites may easily use the very identity marginalized and manipulated by the majority community or state to mobilize in opposition. Minority protests along these lines can potentially unleash a violent spiral, making resolution of the conflict and reconciliation extremely difficult to achieve. Typically, when minority peaceful protests are suppressed and moderate leaders fail to deliver the requisite resources and opportunities to their constituents, a political vacuum develops, which extremist elements may attempt to fill. The initial small-scale violence these extremists resort to is often violently put down by the governing authorities. A retributive culture consequently takes hold, wherein minorities become radicalized and the majority-dominated police and paramilitary forces, in the name of security or revenge, become more repressive. This culminates in a common pattern of atrocities that deepens intergroup animosity and exacerbates violence. This general pattern was also more or less the case in Sri Lanka.[30] Consequently, the Tamil separatist movement is Sinhalese-inspired, given that the quest for *eelam* represents an extremist reaction to the ethnocracy Sinhalese elites instituted.[31] Of course, the LTTE has now taken this quest into the realm of terrorism. That should not blind us to terrorism's antecedents in Sri Lanka, however, especially if we seek to fully understand the island's civil war. For Sri Lanka's ethnocentric foundation was officially sanctioned soon after independence, when the United National Party, under D. S. Senanayake, denied citizenship rights to the country's Indian Tamils.[32] As will be made clear, the island's ethnocracy had already been fully and indisputably launched when the majority Sinhalese resorted to ethnic outbidding and made Sinhala the country's only official language in 1956.

Permissive Conditions for Ethnic Outbidding

The Sri Lankan case suggests that four interrelated conditions are especially necessary for ethnic outbidding to thrive: an uncompromising and
competitive political structure, bad leaders, socioeconomic grievances,
and territoriality.

Ethnic coexistence is most likely when the political structure encourages polyethnic coalitions, and ethnic outbidding is most likely when the
political structure encourages competition among ethnic parties.
Irrespective of the electoral system used, if the political structure pushes
groups to coalesce on an interethnic basis, then the divisions generated
will most likely be ideological rather than ethnic. It is thus recommended
that interethnic groups resort to vote pooling, because doing so will likely
vitiate the pressure to succumb to communalistic politicking.[33] Vote pooling will ensure that patron-client ties extend beyond one's own ethnic
group and encourage mutual dependence between voters and politicians.
On the other hand, a structure that allows a particular ethnic group to establish and change the rules of the game without input from those outside the group may eventually entice "communally based political entrepreneurs [to] seek to increase the salience of communal issues and then to
outbid the . . . multiethnic coalition."[34] More insidious, if each ethnic
group has more than one party, so that the outbidding taking place is not
just interethnic but also intraethnic, then "the centrifugal character of the
competition may so increase the distance between the positions of the
groups as to propel them toward violent outcomes, including secession."[35] It will be clear that this is what indeed turned out to be the case
in Sri Lanka, with the two main Sinhalese parties, the United National
Party and the Sri Lanka Freedom Party, vying for Sinhalese votes, even as
the Tamil Congress and the Federal Party sought to monopolize Tamil
votes. The Tamils' reactive nationalism did not require two Tamil parties
to make their case, and during much of the 1950s and 1960s, it was the
Federal Party that was most successful in garnering Tamil votes. But the
competition between the Tamil parties precluded a unified strategy being
formulated and emboldened the extremists among the Sinhalese, who
ratcheted up their anti-Tamil demands, which then motivated the politicians to try and deliver on those demands.

Michael Brown has observed that when it comes to triggering ethnic
conflict, "bad leaders are the biggest problem."[36] Political entrepreneurs
who let personal gain override patriotism typically disregard the long-
term (or for that matter even short-term) consequences their actions can
unleash, and they may consequently resort to ethnic outbidding to attain
their personal preferences. This is typically done in two ways. First, po-

litical elites magnify, if not manufacture, the dangers facing their ethnic community and use the sense of insecurity thereby generated to legitimize and bolster their support base, a strategy that was successfully executed during the 1990s by Yugoslavia's Slobodan Milosevic.[37] Second, such elites seek to further individual interests by positioning or commingling their preferences with the purported/constructed threats facing their ethnic group,[38] thereby enabling them to present themselves as their nation's saviors even as they pursue their instrumentalist designs. What needs to be recognized is that while the political structure can influence ethnic outbidding, principled leaders could still strive to create institutions that promote accommodation and conciliation between groups. Unfortunately, more often than not, these leaders' quest to attain power by any means takes precedence, and they become only too eager to outbid their opponents. This proclivity was best, albeit most vilely, exemplified by George Wallace who, having spurned the Ku Klux Klan's support and lost Alabama's 1958 gubernatorial election to John Patterson, proclaimed, "Well, boys, no other son-of-a-bitch will ever out-nigger me again."[39] As we shall see, this same mind-set dominated Sinhalese politicians, especially after S. W. R. D. Bandaranaike proved that an anti-Tamil platform could win elections. This indicates that while rules and laws can be redesigned to reconfigure a political structure inhibiting polyethnic stability, stable structures can also be destabilized by myopic and opportunistic elites. Variables such as the electoral system, ethnic population breakdown, and the political system—liberal democratic, quasi-democratic, or authoritarian—can all influence political elites' capacity to stabilize or destabilize interethnic relations, but the fact remains that it takes ethnic entrepreneurs to fashion, justify, and perpetrate ethnic outbidding.

Grievances, real or imagined, can also encourage ethnic outbidding. This is especially the case if the grievances concerned are economic in nature and there is a clear indication that a particular group benefits disproportionately. With all ethnic groups usually competing for scarce resources, disproportionately distributed benefits anger those who are relatively deprived and encourages politicking along ethnic lines. Politicians who want to break into the circles of power may use economic grievances to justify platforms that encourage ethnic outbidding, claiming that they want to "even the playing field" or empower the "sons of the soil." Resource allocation is often determined by the political structure. But those seeking a populist platform to attain power are bound to find conspicuous disparities between ethnic groups attractive, since this allows them to politicize ethnic relations by claiming that the system discriminates against their particular community or pampers other communities. Once such arguments have entered the political arena, political opponents seeking to stay in power need to either discredit them or embrace them in an effort to outbid their competition. This study makes clear both how Sinhalese politicians used linguistic nationalism as a mechanism to rectify extant economic disparities and how the political dynamics generated by this promoted ethnic outbidding and the subsequent institutional decay.

Finally, ethnic groups' territorial status may also influence ethnic outbidding. With the moderate Tamil quest for increased autonomy having now turned into an extremist struggle for independence, and Sinhalese ethnic outbidding designed to preclude such an eventuality, territoriality also features prominently in the Sri Lankan case. It should be axiomatic that while a territorially dispersed group may be discriminated against, a territorially concentrated group is much more easily targeted and manipulated for outbidding purposes, even though doing so might justify rebellion and separatism. Territorial groups typically command numerous ethnic markers (e.g., religion, language, customs, culture), and this makes differentiating and mobilizing along ethnic lines much easier. Degrees of development, resource allocation, and standards of living are all more easily gauged across regions and can be grist for the mill of elites seeking to promote an exclusivist agenda. Thus, while ethnic politics within and between territorialized groups will be influenced by resource allocation and the governmental structure, territoriality by itself represents an important variable influencing the ethnic outbidding process. But if territoriality may influence outbidding, that in turn can contribute to ethnonationalism among those being marginalized.

Explaining Ethnonationalism

Theories focusing on ethnonationalism may be placed into four overarching categories. The primordialist, constructivist, and instrumentalist approaches each offer unique perspectives, and one may trump another in explaining a particular conflict. In what follows, however, I argue that none of these hypotheses provides as encompassing an explanation as does the institutionalist approach.

For primordialists, ethnic identity is congenital and therefore immutable. Thus, the inherited language, culture, race, religion, pigmentation, and physiognomy are considered organizing principles that determine one's grouping, as well as the group's historical and societal experiences.[40] Primordialism's sociobiological strand claims that ethnicity, tied to kinship, promotes a convergence of interests between individuals and their kin group's collective goals. Consequently, even racism and ethnocentrism can be viewed as extreme forms of nepotistic behavior driven by feelings of propinquity and consanguinity.[41] Primordialists thus see nationalism as a natural phenomenon. The problem, however, is the theory's determinism, for it implausibly suggests that a sole independent variable (primordialism) dictates the outcome of various dependant variables. Another major shortcoming is the theory's inability to explain ethnicity's protean nature.

If primordialists view ethnicity and its potential for nationalism as being determined, constructivists see nationalism as an eighteenth-century ideological creation. Various constructivists have suggested that the desire to mobilize armies and improve military capabilities, industrialization and its failure to create a homogeneous cultural structure, standardized communication codes that made it possible to imagine and invent communities, and the arrogated and ascribed national character facilitating the nation-building process were some of the reasons that promoted nationalism.[42] The constructivist position is heavily Eurocentric, and it is questionable whether the claims made pertain equally to non-Western societies. While colonialism's divide-and-rule policies, census taking, the promotion of ascriptive identities, and codification procedures enhanced, if not created, cultural and ethnic distinctions in colonial societies, these processes by themselves hardly account for the nationalistic conflicts unleashed in the postcolonial era. If this is disregarded, it is because constructivists at times take a Utopian view of interethnic relations prior to industrialization and colonization. They thus fail to account for many cultures' "nationalistic" tendencies in the preindustrial, precolonial world.[43]

The advocates of an instrumentalist approach range from elite theorists, who focus on how elite tactics, pacts, and preferences influence policy,[44] to rational choice theorists.[45] The latter consider individual behavior to be a function of the interaction between an individual's sovereign preferences and structural constraints and conclude that whenever individual preferences are assumed to be known, are transitively ordered, and are temporarily stable, aggregate behavior may be predicted. While such a position accepts that certain individual preferences are idiosyncratic, it nevertheless holds that such idiosyncrasy is subsumed by the group's stated preferences.[46] Many ethnic groups operate within a strong, often historical, consciousness, which is in turn enhanced through multiple identities emanating from religion, language, and culture—none of which are easily bargained over and all of which contribute to instilling group norms, expectations, and even preferences. Thus, while rational choice theorists accept that it may be problematic to specify precisely an individual's preference under certain circumstances (e.g., situations with incomplete information), they nevertheless hold that the law of large numbers allows for an aggregate outcome to be more easily predicted.

If the Cold War's end, the subsequent gains in democracy, and the globalization onslaught have combined to promote significant homogenization in interstate relations and thereby made the rational choice paradigm more expansive,[47] the rise in ethnic conflicts has also enabled international relations scholars, whose expertise is the study of warfare, often explicated using rational choice assumptions, to segue into discoursing on ethnonationalism. While these international relations theorists have indisputably expanded our understanding of ethnonationalism, it is debatable whether the very same assumptions and conceptualizations they used to study interstate conflicts are equally profitable for studying intrastate conflicts. Despite the claim that ethnic conflict "can be studied with many of the same theoretical tools" used in the study of interstate wars,[48] there is no reason to believe that the causes promoting wars *between* states are identical to those promoting wars *within* states.

Ultimately, the fact remains that ethnic groups have no problem evoking ancient identities based on historical, ascriptive, or appropriated claims, despite the tenuousness of such claims. There is also no disputing that colonization and industrialization heightened ethnic consciousness and that the post–World War II era of modernization, coupled with the ongoing globalization phenomenon, have had an unsettling impact on ethnic groups, forcing many to seek security by drawing closer to their kin. Furthermore, there is much truth to the argument that humans behave instrumentally when mapping out their preferences and aspirations. Thus, despite their individual limitations, the primordialist, constructivist, and instrumentalist approaches need not be discarded. And while their distinctive theoretical positions preclude theoretical conflation, this is not to say that one cannot combine their insights to explain a particular group's struggles and aspirations. This study embarks from the standpoint that the institutional paradigm is the most useful, because it enables one to draw from the above approaches, affords a parsimonious explanation, exemplifies theoretical range, and deals with the very mechanisms (institutions) that need be structured, restructured, or reconfigured for conflicts to be resolved in deeply divided polyethnic states.

The Institutionalist Explanation

What I refer to as institutions are the official establishments that coalesce to create "the state"—the legislature, bureaucracy, judicial system, public education system, and the police and defense forces—as well as those

private establishments gaining legitimacy from and/or providing legitimacy to political elites representing the state. Institutions facilitate networks for individuals and groups to negotiate relations with the state,
given common interests, laws, rights, and aspirations. Such relations de-
marcate parameters for strategic behavior for elites and masses, lead to
repeated interactions promoting convergent expectations between the
state and the polity,[49] engender predictability, and cement rules, norms,
standards, and stability. Institutions gain legitimacy by structuring relations between the state and the polity "through systems of popular rep-
resentations, forms of interest mediation, and the delivery of public services to citizens."[50] While it is to be expected that individuals and groups
will attempt to maximize accruable benefits, the vigilant and competitive
nature of polyethnic societies requires their institutions to promote and
provide impartial interactions so as to preclude ethnic dissension. Thus,
if impartial interactions legitimize institutions, particularistic interactions
delegitimize them. By embedding rules of engagement, encouraging iter-
ated interactions, and thereby generating trust between strategic actors
regarding standard operating procedures, institutions enable cooperation
even amid uncertainty.[51] This is because "institutions are not only 'the
rules of the game.' They also affect what values are established in a society, that is, what we regard as justice, collective identity, belonging, trust,
and solidarity."[52] Consequently, institutional decay, especially in a polyethnic setting, ensues whenever the state's rule-making, -applying, -adju-
dicating, and -enforcing institutions eschew dispassionate interactions
with all constituencies and groups and instead resort to particularistic interactions. The more particularistic interactions permeate institutions
representing the state, the more likely it is that those marginalized will
mobilize in opposition. The more ethnically based such particularism is,
the more the state would likely regress toward an ethnocracy. And when
such an ethnocracy and its accompanying institutional decay forces those
dispossessed and discriminated against to retaliate by mobilizing along
ethnonational lines, more often than not, the stage will be set for ethnic
violence.

The Sri Lankan case fascinates, because while the country's demography, electoral system, and constitutional structure facilitated ethnic outbidding, scapegoating of minorities, and institutional decay, the overarching political structure also limited agency, since politicians realized that
not favoring illiberal norms and rules conducive to Sinhalese superordination was a sure way to commit political suicide. This was especially the
case during the 1950s and 1960s, when linguistic nationalism enabled
one to signify clear-cut ethnic allegiance. The ethnic outbidding instituted
during this period saw standard operating procedures designed to ensure

optimal benefits for Sinhalese Buddhists. But this effectuated an exclusivist agenda that systematically and blatantly marginalized the country's minorities and clearly indicated that egalitarianism and compromise were being jettisoned. Thus, elections were used to exclude rather than include the island's minorities, and public policies were sanctioned and patron-client ties promoted to win plaudits from Sinhalese alone. Practiced over two decades, a newly institutionalized ethnocracy dominated, subjugated, and marginalized the predominant Tamil minority so as to make many of the latter want to sever their association with the state and all its representative organs.

The Sri Lankan case also highlights that there are limits to what institutions can do, especially when demographics encourage politicians to disregard minority preferences. Lacking mechanisms to engender tolerance, compromise, civility, and egalitarianism, and saddled with constituents who demand immediate redress to their grievances, politicians may be tempted to resort to expediency, as opposed to principled bargaining. But whereas institutions can provide incentives for obeying or disobeying rules, the politics of expediency erodes the trust placed in institutions by undermining expectations of impartiality. Where there is no agreement on what the rules are and whether they were fashioned fairly, institutions responsible for enforcing the rules will lack legitimacy. On the other hand, institutional legitimacy is bolstered, the necessity for the institutions is acknowledged, and their rules are embedded only when there is general agreement that the rules being enforced are fair. Thus, institutions operating fairly influence the all-important sense of trust that needs to be maintained for engendering stable interactions between state and polity. In a polyethnic society, this fairness is attained when institutions representing the state, irrespective of its ethnic composition, act impartially. When a country's police force can be said to protect the innocent and prosecute the guilty, when its courts can be expected to mete out justice disregarding ethno-political affiliations, when its legislature can be counted on to pass laws without deliberately marginalizing or targeting groups based on ethno-racial categories, and when the state as a sovereign entity is recognized for embedding a culture that facilitates and encourages compromise, tolerance, and inclusiveness, then the entire polity is likely to trust its institutions as impartial mediators. There exists no perfect polyethnic society, which means that certain institutions representing the state may at given times operate in a biased or illegal fashion. One has to only consider racial profiling by the police, whether this is against African Americans in New Jersey and Maryland, those of Middle Eastern descent following the September 11, 2001, terrorist attacks, or some other group in another country, to realize that stereotypical beliefs can influence institutions to operate partially and unconstitutionally. That noted, however, if other official and unofficial institutions representing the state (i.e., the legislature, judiciary, and civil society organizations) condemn such practices and take the requisite measures to end them, trust between the groups discriminated against and the state will continue to increase, because the former will see that there are multiple outlets within the state to redress their grievances. This will ensure that institutional decay in its most egregious form is averted. On the other hand, whenever the most important institutions representing the state show clear-cut allegiances and favoritism when formulating policy and, for whatever reasons, seek to dominate some among its population along ethnic or racial lines, they are redrawing/creating rules that perpetrate partiality and undermine the trust reposed in the state. With the rules impacting elite and mass behavior thus tailored to engender partial gains for a particular group, and with this taking place within and across institutions, institutional decay may gradually set in. While those dispossessed or marginalized may seek to reinstate impartiality between the state and all sections of its polity, the fact remains that suboptimal institutions may persist for extended periods (especially if there are clear-cut beneficiaries who might lose out in an optimal structure).[53] "Rules leading to a sub optimal outcome may be continued in force for long periods of time because the distribution of benefits favors those who would be required to agree to a change," Elinor Ostrom observes.[54] But perpetuating a partial, suboptimal structure that conspicuously benefits a designated group only encourages those excluded to try and sabotage it, leading to dissension and conflict. The clash between those demanding and resisting change typically signifies institutional decay as far as the marginalized and change-seeking polity is concerned. Analyzing how such institutional decay led to Tamil mobilization and ethnic violence in Sri Lanka provides an instructive inductive example that may help us to understand other ethnic conflicts better.

Selective Definitions and Layout

Many authors alternate between "Sinhalese" and "Sinhala" when referring to Sri Lanka's majority community and their language. I use "Sinhalese" and "Sinhala" specifically to refer to the community and their language respectively. "Tamil," on the other hand, refers to both the predominant minority and their language. Given the multiple, and hence confusing, definitions permeating the literature on ethnicity and nationalism, it will be useful at this stage to distinguish some additional terms frequently used throughout this study. Despite a plethora of definitions of what constitutes a nation,[55] it is ultimately imperative for a nation to be associated with a particular territory,[56] and a nation is defined here as a group that believes it shares a common history, culture, and claims to a territory. A nation's identity is burnished through contact with other nations, often within a cultivated sense of enmity,[57] and this facilitates a "process of nationality-formation" whereby "objective differences between peoples acquire subjective and symbolic significance, are translated into group consciousness, and become the basis for political demands."[58] It must be recognized that while all separatist movements are (to various degrees) nationalistic, not all nationalistic movements are separatist. Thus, while "autonomy" refers to the devolution of power to regional entities, and "separatism" refers to a nation's quest to create a sovereign state, "nationalism" will be defined as "the rhetoric by which political actors describe, justify, and explain policies with reference to the interest of the 'nation' defined in ethnic terms."[59] Political and economic grievances and the subordination they impose are considered necessary, if not sufficient, for nationalism to be translated into autonomous or separatist movements.[60] Otherwise noted, the sense of marginalization that grievances elicit is what encourages groups to seek self-determination or secession. Finally, "elites" are defined "as persons who are able, by virtue of their strategic positions in powerful organizations, to affect national political outcomes regularly and substantively."[61]

In what follows, chapter 2 profiles Sri Lanka's polyethnicity and briefly introduces the historical antecedents that are so germane to understanding Sinhalese-Tamil identities and divisions. It further discusses the Buddhist revival/nationalist movement in the preindependence era, its limited impact on the Sinhala-only movement, and how the elites' stiff refusal to incorporate the Buddhist revivalist movement into the political arena was related to their polyethnic confraternity and a political structure that was devoid of multiparty competition in the immediate post-universal-franchise (i.e., post-1931) period. Chapter 3 evaluates linguistic nationalism among Sinhala and Tamil vernacular speakers and their political patrons, how and why recognizing both as official languages was eventually jettisoned, the ethnic outbidding that ensued thereafter, and the elites' decision to incorporate the Sinhala-only movement into the political arena. Chapter 4 discusses the events leading up to the Official Language Act and how its passage signified that the island had officially embarked on an ethnocentric trajectory. It delineates the passionate debates in parliament and how the Official Language Act led to the first ever anti-Tamil riots. The prescient warnings made by Sinhalese and Tamils opposing the act clearly indicate that the consequences stemming from this discriminatory legislation were foreseen, but the country's ethnic entrepreneurs, wedded to political opportunism amid a constraining institutional structure, preferred to conveniently overlook the mayhem they were enabling. Chapter 5 covers the first twenty years following the Official Language Act's passage. Sinhalese linguistic nationalism influenced an anti-Tamil milieu, which facilitated discriminatory legislation that stifled Tamils' higher educational and employment opportunities, legitimated rabid ethnic outbidding, unleashed institutional decay, and precipitated the extremist Tamil nationalist movement, leading ultimately to the use of military force against the northern Tamils and the clear realization on the Tamils' part that the Sinhalese were bent on subordinating the island's minorities. Chapter 6 discusses the post-1977 anti-Tamil violence, claims that the repression J. R. Jayewardene's regime perpetrated against all communities was related to the anti-Tamil practices of the previous two decades, delineates the major sources that contributed to institutional decay, discusses the internationalization of the conflict, and argues why linguistic nationalism should be considered the mechanism that led the country into civil war. Chapter 7 elaborates on the LTTE and explains why the conflict has resisted resolution. Finally, chapter 8 summarizes how institutional decay led to civil war, and why an institutional analysis provides the most complete account of the Sinhalese-Tamil imbroglio. It also discusses the lessons Sri Lanka has learned and calls for a devolved political structure that will make peaceful coexistence possible.

2

ETHNIC IDENTITIES AND POLITICS
BEFORE INDEPENDENCE

The late Isaiah Berlin astutely observed that nationalism "seems to be caused by wounds, some form of collective humiliation."[1] Sri Lanka's ethnic fratricide between the Sinhalese and Tamils is rooted in such wounds and feelings of mutual humiliation. Britain's divide-and-rule colonial practices had deliberately marginalized the Sinhalese Buddhists, and, conversely, the latter's postindependence policies methodically marginalized the Tamils. This chapter outlines the country's polyethnicity, briefly introduces the historical antecedents distinguishing the Sinhalese and Tamils, discusses the grievances colonialism imposed on the Sinhalese, elaborates on the religious nationalist movement prior to independence, details the electoral system during the period leading up to independence, and analyzes why religious nationalism before independence, unlike linguistic nationalism in the postindependence era, did not become part of Sri Lanka's political culture. Ethnic tensions and communalism notwithstanding, the country's socioeconomic status, party system, and constitutional and electoral arrangements made possible relatively fraternal interethnic relations, especially at the elite level, during the preindependence and immediate postindependence eras. This promoted false hopes, however, and had the effect of preventing the implementation of more creative, comprehensive, and specific minority safeguards.

General Overview, Historical Antecedents,
and Sinhalese Grievances

At 25,332 square miles, Sri Lanka (called Ceylon until 1972) is smaller than the Republic of Ireland in size but has nearly nineteen million people. The island was colonized by the Portuguese, Dutch, and British successively and gained its independence in February 1948. The fact that

TABLE I

Sri Lanka's Ethnic Composition in 1946, 1971, and 1981

Group	1946 Number	1946 %	1971 Number	1971 %	1981 Number	1981 %
Sinhalese	4,621,000	69.41	9,131,000	71.96	10,980,000	73.95
Sri Lankan Tamils	734,000	11.01	1,424,000	11.22	1,887,000	12.70
Indian Tamils	781,000	11.73	1,175,000	9.26	819,000	5.52
Sri Lankan Moors	374,000	6.52	828,000	6.52	1,047,000	7.05
Indian Moors[a]	36,000	0.53	27,000	0.21	—	—
Europeans[b]	5,000	0.08	—	—	—	—
Burghers and Eurasians	42,000	0.63	45,000	0.35	39,000	0.26
Malays	23,000	0.34	43,000	0.34	47,000	0.32
Veddhas[b]	2,000	0.04	—	—	—	—
Others	41,000	0.62	16,000	0.13	28,000	0.19

SOURCE: *Statistical Pocket Book of the Democratic Socialist Republic of Sri Lanka* (Colombo: Department of Census and Statistics, 1996), pp. 15–16.

[a]Included under others from 1963 onwards.
[b]Included under others for the year 1981.

Britain was able to transfer power to Ceylon peacefully and amicably, unlike in the case of many other colonies that attained independence after World War II, was mainly owing to the fraternal relations that prevailed among the country's polyethnic elites. The island gained universal suffrage in 1931—a commendable outcome, given that Britain itself had achieved similar status only three years earlier, when the voting rights of men and women were equalized—and has conducted elections regularly, through which the country's two major parties have alternated in power. Particularistic ethnic practices in the postindependence era, however, have ensured that Sri Lanka has ceased to be a genuine liberal democracy.

Polyethnicity

Sri Lanka is a plural society that is both polyethnic and multireligious. Indeed, the historical record suggests that the country has had a polyethnic culture over at least two millennia. According to the last all-island decadal census, taken in 1981—the ethnic conflict precluded a census in 1991, and the July 2001 census was not conducted in areas controlled by the LTTE—the island's ethnic composition was then nearly 74 percent Sinhalese, 12.7 percent Ceylon or Sri Lankan Tamils, 5.5 percent Indian Tamils, 7 percent Moors, and 0.6 percent Burghers, Malays, and Veddhas (see table 1). Statistics released by Sri Lanka's Central Bank in 1999 suggest that the country's ethnic composition had hardly changed: the ethnic breakdown then was Sinhalese, 74 percent; Sri Lankan Tamils. 12.6 percent; Indian Tamils, 5.5 percent; and Moors, 7.1 percent.[2]

The Indian Tamils, like their nineteenth-century indentured ancestors, who came to work primarily on tea plantations, are mostly settled in the central hills. Most of them were denied citizenship under laws passed in 1948–49, and their numbers were drastically reduced after two Indian governments agreed to relocate some Indian Tamils in India. Thus, by 1981, their population had declined to 5.5 percent from 11.7 percent in 1946. The 1978 constitution enfranchised many Indian Tamils, and those who were left out were granted citizenship in October 2003. While the group's overall economic position has markedly improved in the past two decades, these Tamils, who continue to sustain the island's important tea industry, remain the least educated and most marginalized group in Sri Lanka's class- and caste-conscious society. The island's separatist violence does not involve the Indian Tamils, and unless indicated otherwise "Tamils" is used here to refer to the Sri Lankan Tamils.

The ancestors of the Moors migrated primarily as traders from Malabar, India, and the rest of the Coromandel coast from the tenth century on. They are mostly concentrated along Sri Lanka's littoral, and their significant numbers in the Eastern Province, which the Sri Lankan Tamils claim as part of their traditional homeland, have led to tensions between Moors and Tamils in recent years. Islam dominates and defines the Moors' ethnic identity, but their language is Tamil, which is thus spoken by nearly 25 percent of the country's population.

The Burghers were originally Dutch settlers who worked for the Dutch East India Company, but the name later came to include those of other European and Euro-Asian ancestry. Despite the miscegenation that ensued among the Portuguese, Dutch, British, and Euro-Asians, an ascriptive divide was gradually generated to distinguish between those of Portuguese ancestry—called Portuguese Burghers—and the others—called Dutch Burghers—with the former being almost exclusively Catholic and the latter being almost exclusively Protestant. The Burghers became a dominant community during colonial times, given their over-representation in the bureaucracy and the august Ceylon Civil Service. When the British appeared resigned to granting Sri Lanka independence, those considered Dutch Burghers began emigrating to Britain and Australia (after the Australians came to consider the Burghers sufficiently white and waived the country's "whites-only" policy in their case). Never considered equal to the Dutch Burghers, the Portuguese Burghers became marginalized in postindependence Sri Lanka. Extensive miscegenation suggests that the Portuguese Burghers will soon cease to be a distinct cul-

TABLE 2

Sri Lanka's Population by Religion in 1971 and 1981

Religion	1971		1981	
	Number	%	Number	%
Buddhists	8,536,900	67.27	10,288,300	69.30
Hindus	2,238,700	17.64	2,297,800	15.48
Muslims	901,800	7.11	1,121,700	7.55
Christians	1,004,300	7.91	1,130,600	7.61
Other	8,300	0.07	8,300	0.06

SOURCE: *Statistical Pocket Book of the Democratic Socialist Republic of Sri Lanka* (Colombo: Department of Census and Statistics, 1996), p. 14.

tural entity in the island.

The Malays descend from Javanese mercenaries who accompanied the Dutch to Sri Lanka, while the Veddhas are what is left of the country's autochthonous peoples. Veddhas have intermarried with non-Veddhas and have adopted nontraditional customs, and this extremely small group faces a serious struggle to preserve its culture and traditions, despite the various efforts made to do so.

In terms of religion, approximately 90 percent of the Sinhalese are Buddhists, while approximately 90 percent of the Tamils are Hindus. The Moors and Malays are Muslims, while the Burghers are Christians, with the vast majority being Roman Catholic. The country's Christian population includes both Sinhalese and Tamils, but one rarely encounters a Sinhalese who is Hindu or a Tamil who is Buddhist. As shown in table 2, the 1981 census tabulated the country's religious composition as 69.3 percent Buddhist, 15.5 percent Hindu, 7.6 percent Christian, and 7.5 percent Muslim.

A Mythology of Conflict

Given that possession of a historical homeland helps solidify nationalism, it is hardly surprising that both the Sinhalese and the Tamils claim to be the island's original settlers. The Sinhalese claim that their Aryan North Indian ancestors were the first settlers to reach Sri Lanka's shores, almost 2,500 years ago, and point to a mythical account in the *Mahavamsa*, a historical chronicle written around the sixth century C.E. and updated during the thirteenth, fourteenth, and eighteenth centuries, to explain Buddhism's preeminence in Sri Lanka. According to the most popular account of this colonization myth, the founder of the Sinhalese race, Prince Vijaya, arrived on the island with seven hundred followers after his father drove him into exile.[3] The myth provides a fantastic ancestry for Vijaya by claiming a leonine progenitor. It also claims that Vijaya reached the island at the same time that Lord Buddha passed away, thereby introducing the notion that Sri Lanka was destined to be a Buddhist sanctuary.[4] Sinhalese who claim a longer history suggest a Sinhalese connection to the indigenous peoples and may brand Vijaya as nothing more than "a marauding pirate chased out of his country, with a set of rascals and never-do-wells, as bad as himself,"[5] but the Vijaya myth has been invoked often enough that most Sinhalese now accept it as indisputable history. And it is this that matters, not the account's dubiousness; for as Ernest Renan noted, "getting its history wrong is part of being a nation."[6]

The Tamils, on the other hand, claim that their Dravidian South Indian ancestors first settled the island. A commonsensical view suggests that if the ancestors of the Aborigines reached Australia over 40,000 years ago and determined settlers navigated the Pacific Ocean to reach America's western coast at least 13,000 years ago,[7] then it is highly unlikely that South Indians were unaware that a large island was situated just twenty-two miles across the shallow Palk Strait. "Dravidian infiltration into Ceylon must have been going on from the earliest historical times and probably before," the historian A. L. Basham argues.[8] Some even claim that only Dravidians settled the island, and that Buddhism and its Pali scriptures created an "ascriptive cleavage" dividing the Dravidians into Sinhalese and Tamils. "The Sinhalese, then, in terms of their origin, are not an Aryan people as popularly claimed, but Tamil people who adopted a language which developed from Pali, an Aryan dialect," according to Satchi Ponnambalam.[9] Or as a Tamil senator put it: "The Sinhalese man—people who have studied him closely say so—is really 90 per cent. a Tamil. Ethnically, culturally, historically and in every other way, we are all Tamil people with the only difference [being] that some are Tamil-speaking and some are Sinhalese-speaking."[10] These claims and counterclaims aside, there is little doubt that today's Sri Lankans are of utterly hybridized stock. From Sri Lanka's ruling elites to society's lowliest classes, miscegenation, conversion, and acculturation appear to have been common throughout centuries past, so that today's "Sinhalese and Tamil labels are porous sieves through which diverse groups and categories of Indian peoples, intermixed with non-Indians . . ., have passed."[11] Indeed, the Sinhalese and their elites did not object to, and often encouraged, intermarriage, provided that those joining the fold respected Sinhalese culture and did not seek to undermine Buddhism.[12] Thus, "the ease with which south Indian immigrants became Sinhalese points to the notion of Sinhalese identity as cultured and political rather than ethnic or racial."[13] Consequently, it appears that even the notion of being Ceylonese or Sri Lankan is a twentieth-century construct. Up to that point, Ivor Jennings writes,

[t]here were no Ceylonese; there were Burghers, Sinhalese (Kandyan and Low-country), Tamils, Indians, Moors, and Malays. Nor were these in any sense po-litical groups; they were not even social units, for the Sinhalese and the Tamils were collections of castes, while the unity of the Moors and Malays was the unity of Islam. . . . It is [thus] not an exaggeration to say that the Ceylonese as a people were invented in the present century.[14]

Not only does the Vijaya myth serve to bolster the claim that the Sinhalese were the island's original settlers, but the story of the Buddhist warrior king Dutthagamani (second century B.C.E.), also in the *Mahavamsa*, suggests that the Sinhalese and the Tamils are long-standing antagonists. The Dutthagamani account in the *Mahavamsa*, likely ex-trapolated from a historical event, but certainly embellished and dissem-bled, describes how the king, his army, and five hundred Buddhist monks battled and defeated the Chola king Elara, who had usurped power in the Anuradhapura kingdom. The *Mahavamsa* "glosses over facts and events which were inconvenient to . . . immortalising the honour and glory" of Dutthagamani and suggests that he unified a hitherto divided island, which was not actually the case.[15] The chronicle indicates that Elara was only one of thirty-two rulers Dutthagamani fought, and that many Buddhist rulers supported Elara, but Sinhalese elites have depicted the battle between Dutthagamani and Elara as a contest between valiant Sinhalese and Tamils.[16] For example, the scholar-monk Walpola Rahula says grandiloquently:

The entire Sinhalese race was united under the banner of the young Gamini [i.e., Dutthagamani]. This was the beginning of nationalism among the Sinhalese. It was a new race with healthy young blood, organized under the new order of Buddhism. A kind of religio-nationalism, which almost amounted to fanaticism, roused the whole Sinhalese people. A non-Buddhist was not regarded as a human being. Evidently all Sinhalese without exception were Buddhists.[17]

Yet as K. M. de Silva notes, "the facile equating of Sinhalese with Buddhist for this period is not borne out by the facts, for not all Sinhalese were Buddhist, while on the other hand there were many Tamil Buddhists."[18]

Manipulating historical myths and accounts by equating Sinhalese and Buddhism nevertheless provided ample fodder for opportunistic elites throughout the nineteenth and twentieth centuries. These elites showed no qualms about mixing folklore and religion to fashion a nationalistic ideology that powerfully reiterated and imposed the belief that Sri Lanka was the *Sihadipa* (the island of the Sinhalese) and *Dhammadipa* (the island ennobled to preserve and propagate Buddhism).[19] This led to the claim that "[f]or more than two millennia the Sinhalese have been inspired by the ideal that they were a nation brought into being for the definite purpose of carrying the torch lit by the Buddha."[20] Consequently, Walter Schwarz is right to observe that "[t]he most important effect of the early history on the minority problem of today is not in the facts but in the myths that surround them, particularly on the Sinhalese side."[21]

Religious Nationalism

Their disputable provenance aside, it is clear that the Sinhalese had developed a distinct consciousness of themselves as a people by at least the tenth century C.E. This consciousness was indubitably rooted in the Buddhist religion and its attendant culture, and the numerous invasions and brief occupation by the Cholas in the eleventh century helped consolidate Sinhalese group identity, but it was only after the island succumbed to "colonial rule that the Sinhalese consciousness underwent a radical transformation."[22]

As we have seen, the Portuguese, Dutch, and British colonized the island in turn. There is no gainsaying that Buddhism suffered enormously under these colonizers. The Portuguese were determined on converting the natives to Catholicism and committed major atrocities against Buddhist institutions and other local religions. The Dutch marginalized all religions, including Roman Catholicism, to promote the Dutch Reformed Church. The Portuguese and Dutch, however, only controlled certain coastal areas. With Buddhism thriving inland, there was no reason for Buddhists to feel that their religion was threatened. This was what ensued, however, after the British replaced the Dutch and eventually came to control the entire island. While the British differed from their predecessors in that they never oppressed the local religions, they nevertheless favored Christianity and made it a standard policy to provide economic and civil benefits to Christians, while neglecting the Buddhists' needs. Buddhism's marginalization was thus heightened under the British.

The Kandyan rulers in the south-central highlands were long viewed as Buddhism's benefactors and protectors, and they had preserved the Theravada Buddhist tradition and withstood Portuguese and Dutch attempts to conquer their kingdom. This Kandyan kingdom had epitomized a tolerance for other faiths that, in the main, was pervasive throughout the island until the Portuguese and Dutch introduced religious intolerance. Indeed, Catholic priests, when persecuted by the Dutch, "used the Kandyan kingdom as a springboard for their activities" in the island,[23] and it is arguable that the Catholic faith in Sri Lanka would not be as vibrant as it is today if it had not received such support. The Muslims, whom both the Portuguese and Dutch viewed as trading competitors, likewise received refuge within the Kandyan boundaries. Hindus, too, lived in peace and security among Sinhalese. Indeed, a number of Kandyan kings were Hindus who legitimated their rule by cultivating and protecting the island's Buddhist heritage. Sinhalese Buddhist tolerance of Christians did atrophy by the mid eighteenth century,[24] but open hostilities did not ensue until after the British conquered the Kandyan kingdom in March 1815. The British thus became the only colonizers to control the entire island and, by passing the Colebrooke-Cameron reforms of 1832, to unify it administratively. Acceptance of non-Sinhalese rulers, especially when the island was under European colonization, and the toleration of other faiths strongly call into question the idea that Sinhalese nationalism is primordial and stems from two millennia of Buddhist influence. If anything, the 1817–18 and 1848 Kandyan rebellions were the closest the Sinhalese came to displaying nationalistic tendencies. But neither rebellion was widespread, and the latter appears to have been primarily related to the British-sanctioned plantation economy, which encroached on peasants' subsistence agriculture; to taxation policies; and to Buddhism's marginalization.

It was standard practice for the island's kingdoms to support the Sangha (Buddhist clergy) by providing subventions and protecting Buddhist assets. The British agreed to follow suit under the Kandyan Convention of March 1815, but in the late 1840s, the Colonial Office caved into pressure from British evangelicals and reneged on its promises.[25] In so doing, the British not only unilaterally violated the rules of the game that had legitimized their governance but also shattered the trust the venerable Sangha had reposed in them. The rules agreed to by the 1815 Kandyan Convention obviously favored the British, but without utterly marginalizing the Buddhists. The decadence the new policy imposed on Buddhist monasteries, combined with the belief that the British had hoodwinked the Buddhists, influenced anti-British and anti-Christian hostilities. Two related issues galvanizing Buddhist antipathy toward the British were Christian proselytization and the British-sanctioned missionary education system, which threatened Buddhist monastic schools.

The Buddhists' initial reaction to the Christian missionaries was one of detached tolerance. Indeed, Christian missionaries were nonplussed by the hospitality the Sangha accorded them. Missionaries were given refuge in Buddhist temples and allowed to preach the Christian gospel to prospective converts. The missionaries were further perplexed when even traducing Buddhism hardly elicited angry and passionate reactions from the Sangha. As the Wesleyan missionary

Robert Hardy observed, "It is almost impossible to move them, even to wrath."[26] Hardy and his ilk had no doubts that the Sangha's passivity was due to carelessness, indifference, imbecility, and illiteracy.[27] It was only a matter of time before the monks proved them wrong.

The missionaries' zealous proselytizing efforts coincided with the glaring social and economic disparities between Christians and Buddhists, mainly engendered by pro-Christian colonial policies in the educational arena. While the Buddhist monastic schools were clearly inferior to the Christian missionary institutions, the deliberate marginalization of the former was a conspicuous example of colonial discrimination. When combined with the authorities' support for the missionaries, colonial misfeasance when dealing with Buddhist assets, and preferential treatment showered on Christians and Tamils, this led Buddhists to see the British as enemies.

Marginalizing the Sinhalese Buddhists, who were the majority and therefore the biggest potential threat to British rule, was consistent with Britain's divide-and-rule policies. This meant that the non-Buddhists and ethnic minorities came to be highly overrepresented in the bureaucracy, civil service, and primary and secondary educational institutions. In the Tamils' case, the arid, inhospitable northern agricultural terrain, coupled with a highly casteist society, had spurred many to seek governmental and other careers throughout the island. Thanks to American missionary and educational efforts in the north, many Tamils were competent in English. This mostly contributed to their overrepresentation in the colonial governmental and educational structures. Indeed, Tamils preferred government employment so much that it was said among them, "Even if your job involves looking after hens, let it be in the government's service." Given that British discriminatory policies toward the majority community greatly influenced Tamils' upward mobility, Tamil success soon became wormwood to the Sinhalese. Thus, the concurrent anti-Buddhist and prominority policies of the British may be seen as the backdrop to Sinhalese-Tamil divisions.

The Buddhists began systematically to mobilize against the missionaries by the 1860s and 1870s. In doing so, they generated a Buddhist revival, in which Buddhists combated Christian missionaries through public debates and printed material, tactics the missionaries had initially used themselves.[28] The 1883 Kotahena riots between Buddhists and Catholics are one example of Buddhists' newly assertive attitude toward Christians. The riots erupted when rumors spread that a Buddhist procession parading past the Roman Catholic cathedral in Kotahena, Colombo, on Easter Sunday carried "a cross with a monkey nailed to it and a statue resembling the Virgin Mary."[29] The British authorities quelled the riots, but such disturbances ominously portended the ethno-religious divisions that lay in store. Buddhist mobilization against Christian missionaries received a significant fillip when the Theosophists Colonel Henry Steel Olcott and Madame Helena Petrovna Blavatsky visited Ceylon in May 1880 and publicized Buddhist grievances against the British. Olcott eventually started numerous Buddhist schools to rival the Christian schools and designed the organizational apparatus that the Buddhists used to counter the missionaries. To some, the Buddhist revival became a platform for anti-British nationalism.

Anagarike Dharmapala: Patriot or Chauvinist?

The Buddhist scholar Anagarike Dharmapala was foremost among those who made religion a mobilizing marker. Dharmapala epitomized how folklore and myth could be brilliantly woven into religion to generate effective agitprop and delegitimize all those who were non-Buddhists. Anthony Smith has suggested that ethnic myths, when used for nationalistic purposes, typically incorporate four characteristics: they propound the belief that the group concerned is a chosen people and is therefore morally superior to others; they evoke the belief that the now depressed nation is destined to have its fortunes reversed; they ostracize outsiders to "the ethno-religious community" as having "no part in the sacred mission and its duties"; and they encourage apostates to return to the fold.[30] Dharmapala, by using chauvinistic oratory and religious and colonizing myths, evoked all four themes. He promoted a grandiose Buddhist history of Sri Lanka, inspired fear by suggesting that colonial rule threatened Buddhism with extinction, and claimed that Christians, Hindus, and the British were all responsible for Buddhism's decadence.

"Under the influence of the Tathagato's [Buddha's] Religion of Righteousness, the people flourished. Kings spent all their wealth in building temples, public baths, *dagobas* [pagodas], libraries, monasteries, rest houses, hospitals for man and beast, schools, [water] tanks, seven storied mansions, waterworks and beautified the city of Anuradhapura, whose fame reached Egypt, Greece, Rome, China, India and other countries,"[31] Dharmapala argued. He claimed that the Sinhalese, who were "the sweet, tender, gentle Aryan children of an ancient, historic race . . . [were now being] sacrificed at the altar of the whiskey-drinking, beef-eating, belly-god of heathenism."[32] He implored young Buddhists to "believe not the alien who is giving you arrack, whiskey, toddy, sausages" and instead urged them to "enter into the realms of our King Dutugemunu [or Dutthagamani] in spirit and try to identify yourself with the thoughts of that great king who rescued Buddhism and our nationalism from oblivion."[33] It was only due to Buddhism "that the Sinhalese have not met with the fate of the Tasmanian, the African savage, or the North American Indian," he declared.[34] "No nation in the world has had a more brilliant history than ourselves."[35] The golden Sinhalese Buddhist past could, he said, be recreated once the country had gotten rid of the infidels.

Dharmapala also realized that by propounding the belief that Buddhism and the attendant Sinhalese ethnicity and culture were superior to anything possessed by the Tamils and British, he could effectively shame those who had embraced Westernization. He thus ridiculed those Sinhalese who had sought to assimilate within the colonial structures: "A patriot's blood boils with indignation at the sight of the present Anglicized Sinhalese who loves neither his country nor nation. Fancy the descendants of Vijaya having names like Pereras, Silvas, Almeidas, Diases, Liveras."[36] Eagerly adopting the racist mentality the colonialists displayed toward Africans, Dharmapala added that "there is only one other idiotic and loathsome human group in the whole world who indulge in such bovine stupidity. That is the small Kaffir element in Africa who have embraced Christianity. The Sinhalese who follow European ways and those Christianized Kaffirs, both are found behaving in the same manner."[37]

Many have observed that the numerous South Indian invasions during the precolonial era, repeated colonization by Europeans, and living in close proximity to India's millions of Tamils have all combined to impose a minority complex on the majority Sinhalese.[38] Dharmapala epitomized this mind-set. "Ethnologically, the Sinhalese are a unique race," he claimed contradictorily, "inasmuch as they can boast that they have no slave blood in them, and never were conquered by either the pagan Tamils or European vandals who for three centuries devastated the land, destroyed ancient temples, burnt valuable libraries, and nearly annihilated the historic race."[39] His exasperation over the plight of his "historic race" sometimes led to comparisons between East and West and the lamentation that while "Europe is progressive, . . . Asia is full of opium eaters, ganja smokers, degenerating sensualists, superstitious and religious fanatics."[40] It was the British, he said, who gave "the Aryan Sinhalese poisons of opium and alcohol which are destructive for the continuance of the Sinhalese race."[41]

There can be little doubt that Dharmapala was articulating Sinhalese Buddhists' acute resentment of the injuries done to their religion by British colonialism, and one may even excuse his anti-Christian bombast as an appropriate response to the missionaries' anti-Buddhist stance. Yet his rhetoric, whether intended to do so or not, legitimated extremism and helped catalyze the chauvinism that followed. It was jingoist and exclusivist and showed no regard or tolerance for non-Buddhists. Indeed, Dharmapala manipulated the notions of *Sihadipa* and *Dhammadipa* to suggest that the island's non-Buddhists lived there under Sinhalese Buddhist sufferance.[42]

From an institutionalist standpoint, one can easily claim that the colonial structure the British superimposed discriminated against the Sinhalese Buddhists by seeking to institute rules conducive to that group's marginalization. But then colonial policy was typically predatory and arguably parasitic. Dharmapala's rhetoric suggests, however, that he was opposed more to the degrading position the Sinhalese Buddhists occupied than to prevailing hierarchy, whose discriminatory rules appeared to suit him only too well, provided the Sinhalese replaced the British as rulers. He consequently played a major role preparing the Sinhalese ideationally for the ethnocracy that lay in store.

Dharmapala managed the *Sinhala Bauddhaya*, a pro-Sinhalese Buddhist periodical, and he and the other contributors eagerly circulated chauvinistic and racist writings. When it came to vilifying non-Buddhists, Dharmapala and his acolytes displayed no qualms. For example, one writer characterized the Moors as "barbarians" when compared to the Aryan Sinhalese.[43] Dharmapala himself traduced Sri Lanka's Muslims as "alien people . . . [who] by Shylockian methods became prosperous like the Jews," saying, "the alien South Indian Muhammedan comes to Ceylon, sees the neglected illiterate villager, without any experience in trade, without any knowledge of any kind of technical industry and isolated from the whole of Asia on account of his language, religion and race, and the result is the Muhammedan thrives and the son of the soil goes to the wall."[44] It is no coincidence that the Sinhalese who perpetrated the 1915 anti-Muslim riots evoked these same themes to justify their violence.[45]

Dharmapala died in 1933, fifteen years before Sri Lanka achieved independence. The Buddhist movement he influenced remained relatively dormant during the interwar years—mainly because Sri Lanka's leading elites at the time were committed to a secular state—but his impact on Sinhalese Buddhist nationalists was pervasive. His powerful influence led many to shed Western clothing and adopt traditional Sinhalese attire and embrace Buddhism. Many also came to view their English names as obnoxious appellations and adopted Sinhalese names instead. Dharmapala influenced a network of anti-Christian *mahajana sabhas* (associations of the great masses), which emphasized the Sinhala language and the

Buddhist religion, and worked hard to regenerate traditional Sinhalese culture and values. While the lack of an anti-colonial nationalism, like that gaining force in India, made some consider the island's independence movement pseudonationalist, the anti-British Buddhist revival solidified by Dharmapala and his epigones nevertheless imposed a religio-nationalism that was partly responsible for the communalistic politics that followed.

Reasons for Religio-Nationalism

Five reasons could be cited as to why Buddhism, and not the Sinhala language, was emphasized when fashioning this nationalistic platform. First, nostalgic lamentation of Buddhism's decadence under the British made it a natural marker for mobilization purposes. Buddhism thus began to be equated with patriotism, so that loyalty to country and religion were deemed one and the same.[46] Related to this, and a second reason for religious nationalism, was the way the concepts "Buddhist" and "Sinhalese" soon became powerfully conflated, to the point where they began to be used interchangeably, and all true Sinhalese were thought to be Buddhists. With social divisions around the turn of the twentieth century that ran mostly along religious and caste lines, and with most Sinhalese Christians belonging to the lower castes and benefiting from the colonial order,[47] this emphasis on Buddhism helped maintain caste distinctions, while it was also reiterated that "to be truly Sinhalese was to be born Sinhalese, speak Sinhalese, and practice the Sinhalese religion, Buddhism."[48] Third, although English was essential to receive a quality education, be employed in the colonial bureaucracy, and attain socioeconomic upward mobility, the British hardly tried to suppress Sinhala or Tamil as vernacular languages. On the contrary, British administrators used both Sinhala and Tamil to promulgate their laws and edicts, published the *Government Gazette* in English, Sinhala, and Tamil, and, to a degree, promoted representation based on the regional language, thereby trying to rule using the local elites.[49] Even "Christian missionaries did not in any way discourage the use of Sinhalese and Tamil; on the contrary they learned one of these languages and produced the necessary books."[50] Language was thus not as useful an instrument as religion in denouncing the British and vilifying the minorities. While a small movement headed by some English-teaching secondary school teachers sought to use language as a mobilizing mechanism during the 1930s, they were strongly opposed by elites who clearly preferred the status quo and distrusted, even looked down upon, those not committed to Western norms.[51] A fourth reason why Buddhism was utilized for nationalist purposes was because government officials were almost exclusively recruited from the highest class and caste.[52] The low-caste and -class leaders of the Buddhist revival were thus noncandidates for the government bureaucracy and found Buddhism more useful than language for mobilization purposes, even while differentiating themselves from the country's dominant English-speaking, conservative Westernized elites. Finally, the dearth of industry, scarce employment opportunities in the state sector, an economy that was dependent on plantation and subsistence agriculture, and high illiteracy all relegated language to a less emotive status for mobilization purposes. What is especially important to recognize here is that while Buddhism and the Sinhala language were inextricably linked, and the latter clearly incorporated the burgeoning Sinhalese nationalism, Buddhism's emphasis over language in the precolonial era was also structurally induced. This was because the country's elites were not wholly dependent on the masses for their privileged positions until 1931, when universal suffrage was introduced. Prior to that, the fact that there were no political parties or organizations at the grassroots level meant the elites could conveniently disregard demands to incorporate Buddhism into the political arena even after universal suffrage was instituted.

Preindependence Electoral Politics and the Taming of Religio-Nationalism

Until universal suffrage was introduced, the franchise was limited to the highly educated, and the governor officially appointed ten of the sixteen council members of the Legislative Council that had been created in 1833, who were expected to act on his preferences. The Governor-in-Council was thus very much the executive power. The other six members of the council, called unofficial members, were nominated on a communal basis, with the Europeans getting three of the six seats and the Sinhalese, Tamils, and Burghers qualifying for a seat each. In 1889, the Kandyan Sinhalese and Muslims were also provided a seat each as unofficial members. This racial representation system heavily underrepresented the native population, and the numerous calls for reform led to the Legislative Council being repeatedly enlarged in 1912, 1921, and 1924.[53]

The islanders lacked political consciousness and political sophistication throughout much of the nineteenth century, and this was evident when transplanted British liberals clamored for elective representation, while the educated indigenes caricatured the masses as insignificant and indifferent and sought the vote only for those of their own class. Indeed, the 1875–1925 period saw campaigns for representation along religious and caste lines. For example, lower-caste Sinhalese castigated the British for only nominating persons from the high *goyigama* (farmer) caste and demanded that their fellows be represented in the council, even as both lower- and higher-caste Sinhalese clamored for the British to deviate from nominating only Christian Sinhalese. For their part, J. H. Broomfield writes, the British self-servingly viewed themselves as

a wise and benevolent body of rulers, keeping the peace between the irreconcilable races, religions, and castes of a huge subcontinent; a corps of dedicated men giving their knowledge and their energies to improve, however slowly, the material well-being of an ignorant but warmhearted and grateful people; protecting the weak and the downtrodden against the strong, minorities against majorities—a faction of order . . . in a factious society.[54]

The pervasive parochialism displayed by Sri Lanka's elites consequently enabled some crafty governors to manipulate caste and religious divisions to perpetuate a mostly nominative as opposed to a completely elective system.

Under a reformed electoral scheme that was instituted in 1910, communal representation was left in place, but Europeans, Burghers, and the so-called educated Ceylonese were allowed to vote for four additional members to the Legislative Council. Merely 1.8 percent of the population was enfranchised around this time.[55] The very first all-island election for the "educated Ceylonese" was held in 1912, and it saw high-caste Sinhalese and Tamils unite to elect a high-caste Tamil and defeat the lower-caste Sinhalese.[56] The Montagu Declaration of 1917, which proposed creating limited self-government for India, emboldened the island's elites, who thereafter asserted themselves more forcefully when demanding increased representation through an expanding franchise. Stating that "the infection of political reform had reached Ceylon from India,"[57] the governor gradually broadened democratic involvement by allowing for some unofficial members to be elected on a territorial basis. This heightened concerns along communal lines. For example, the Dutch Burghers protested against the Portuguese Burghers being included in the Burgher electorate, while the Tamils became alarmed that the more numerous "educated Sinhalese" would contribute to increased Sinhalese representation.

The Tamils, despite being a minority, had enjoyed parity of representation, and they consequently considered themselves and the Sinhalese to be the island's two "majority" communities. Sinhalese and British elites countenanced such thinking, whereby all other groups, excluding the Tamils, were classified as minorities. The gradually expanding franchise thus raised fears among Tamils that their "majority" status would become compromised. This turned out to be the case by 1920, when constitutional reforms introduced in June that year led to thirteen Sinhalese and only three Tamils being elected to the Legislative Council. The situation was exacerbated further when the Colonial Office stipulated that the new State Council would seat fifty elected members (out of a total of sixty-one), reducing Tamil representation to a mere 20 percent. The Donoughmore Commission, which introduced universal franchise and constitutional reforms, had argued that only by abolishing communal representation would "it be possible for the various diverse communities to develop together a true national unity."[58] Subsequent legislative representation, however, tilted toward Sinhalese dominance. Seeking to reinstate their status as one of the "majority" communities, the Tamils began to clamor for "fifty-fifty," or balanced representation, from the late 1930s to the mid-1940s.[59] This would have given the Sinhalese, who were around 70 percent of the population at this time, only 50 percent representation, and they and the Soulbury Commission, not surprisingly, opposed the arrangement. Having rejected the "fifty-fifty" formula, the Soulbury Commission accepted a compromise weightage formula designed by the Ceylon ministers. Recognizing that the minorities mostly lived in less populated areas, the ministers recommended that a parliamentary seat be allocated for every 75,000 persons and 1,000 square miles. The Soulbury Commission also allowed for six nominated members and five multimember constituencies, both being designed to shore up minority representation.[60] Voters in the multimember constituencies were accorded as many votes as there were candidates and allowed to cast all their votes for a single candidate if they so desired. Furthermore, the constitution designed by the Commission also permitted a Delimitation Commission for redistricting purposes.[61] Yet the island's demography was such that even this sort of tinkering did not prevent the Sinhalese from being an absolute majority in seventy-three constituencies and controlling "75 out of the 95 elected seats."[62]

Robert Dahl has suggested that it may be best to limit the majority principle whenever groups in a polyethnic society lack "political cooperation or mutual trust."[63] In hindsight, it is clear that the British should have insisted on explicit minority guarantees or a disproportionate representative system that circumscribed the potential for Sinhalese domination and promoted minority input in Ceylon's politics. But saddled with a predisposition to the plurality system and convinced that the putative interethnic comity between Sinhalese and Tamil elites was inviolable, the British failed to consider an alternative constitutional structure, electoral arrangement, or explicit, broad minority guarantees. They consequently promoted an "efficient" Westminster system that honored the one person, one vote principle as opposed to a "stable" system encouraging polyethnic coexistence. A "stable" system would have incorporated checks and balances and precluded majority tyranny. The "efficient" system the British helped impose, on the other hand, enabled the ethnic groups with the most votes and representatives to ride roughshod over the minorities. Their good intentions notwithstanding, the British thus inadvertently collaborated with their conservative Sinhalese counterparts to lay the groundwork for the majority tyranny that followed. Perhaps realizing this, Lord Soulbury later indicated that the British would have created more explicit minority guarantees had they better anticipated the potential for majority superordination. This, however, was a lame lamentation, especially given that Ponnambalam's fifty-fifty formula was based on such anticipation. Had the British overlooked Ponnambalam's communalistic rhetoric and given his demands due consideration, they would have realized the necessity for some other arrangement beyond their preferred unitary structure and the first-past-the-post electoral system.

The divisions beginning to take shape between Sinhalese and Tamils over representation in the immediate preindependence era remained latent, given politicians' continued emphasis on caste relations. The Ceylon National Congress, a polyethnic, elitist outfit dominated by the Low Country Sinhalese, was formed in 1919 and had the potential to achieve significant electoral reforms. Indeed, some hoped that it would replicate the revolutionary role played by the Indian National Congress. The emerging split between Sinhalese and Tamils was masked because the Ceylon National Congress often arranged for its members to be returned to the Legislative Council in uncontested elections, and personal rivalries, the members' conservative proclivities, and their benighted casteist preferences made the organization "relatively ineffective."[64]

The Ceylon National Congress nevertheless helped organize numerous *mahajana sabhas,* which conducted their activities in the Sinhala language and soon began to emphasize Sinhala and Buddhism when campaigning for their supporters. While such communalism did elicit the desired results in a few constituencies, it was prevented from gaining sway for at least three reasons. First, only about 4 percent of the population qualified to vote during the 1920s, and this hardly sufficed to sustain and spread even a movement based on such emotive issues as religion and language.[65] Second, the leading Sinhalese elites of the day, especially F. R. Senanayake and D. B. Jayatilaka, worked assiduously to counterbalance Buddhist nationalism and keep it out of the political arena, and this ensured that nationalists influenced by Dharmapala were marginalized for nearly a generation.[66] The 1915 Buddhist-Muslim riots made the elites want to reassure the British that they utterly disapproved of religious intolerance and were committed to a secular and liberal government, and this too contributed to their refusal to introduce religion into the political arena in the immediate preindependence era. Finally, and most important, there was "a complete absence of any party system among the elected representatives of the people,"[67] which ensured that the pro-Sinhala and -Buddhist forces lacked the institutional means to overturn the elites' preferences and dominance. Thus, even after the Donoughmore Constitution introduced universal suffrage, which the Ceylon National Congress and the leading elites disapproved of and the Tamils strongly opposed, the absence of competition along party lines blocked those who sought to catapult religion into the political arena. Individual politicians did try to use religion and other identity markers to their advantage during elections, and this was especially the case when voters had to choose among unfamiliar candidates. The Soulbury Commission noted that "the average peasant elector" was "influenced mainly by his personal knowledge of the candidate, and that when he finds himself unable to assess the qualities of a candidate who is a complete stranger to him, cries of race, caste or religion make a deeper impression upon him than they would in the ordinary concerns of his daily life."[68] But there never was a concerted attempt by any political group to manipulate religion for wholesale political gain.

To say that religion was not introduced into the political arena in an organized fashion is not to argue that religion was never an issue. If anything, there was a dichotomy in the way religion functioned in the political process, because some Sinhalese politicians differentiated between Buddhist and Catholic Sinhalese, even as their leadership worked hard to depoliticize religion. Consequently, while the emphasis on religion by individual candidates, especially during elections, meant that the hitherto marginalized Buddhists continued to gain increased representation, incorporating religion in a cohesive and systematic manner for ethnonationalist and jingoist purposes was eschewed. Some politicians used their caste and religious backgrounds in the 1931 and 1936 post-universal-franchise general elections, but they mostly did so to between Buddhists and Christians to differentiate themselves from fellow Sinhalese. A major reason for this was the absence of a party system.

The Absence of a Party System and Religio-Nationalism

One major reason a party system did not take hold during the preindependence era was because the country's conservative political elites, despite ethnic differences, enjoyed commendable camaraderie and considered themselves part of the indispensable educated ruling class. Sri

Lanka's feudal history was another important reason parties did not play a significant role in the preindependence era. The island's feudal heritage was reinforced by colonialism, and the concomitant patron-client ties that became embedded were due more to individual machinations than to any organizational structures such as political parties. Indeed, not even the dramatic rise in the number of voters in the 1936 election generated interparty competition; on the contrary, a significant number of candidates were elected without any opposition. The most important reason for there being no strong party system amid universal franchise was the governmental structure itself. The Donoughmore Constitution, which began operating in 1931, had instituted an executive committee system, whereby the legislature's members sat on committees overseeing the business conducted by the legislature and executive. Called "seven-tenths *swaraj*," this meant that seven committees located within the State Council, with the chairman of each executive committee holding a ministerial position and all the committee chairmen together forming the Board of Ministers, ran the government. As one scholar observed, this "Board of Ministers could give no lead because it was not politically homogeneous, consisted only of chairmen of committees and had responsibility for finance and the arrangement of business. Thus there was no 'Government' and no 'Opposition' but 58 independents whose votes were based on no consistent principles at all."[69] This arrangement, where individual members decided on particular issues in a clannish culture, was hardly conducive to generating parties. Indeed, "[t]he Donoughmore Constitution was established for a political system which had no parties, and therefore it discouraged parties."[70] The upshot was that there was no effective mechanism to organize and mobilize the mostly illiterate rural masses. This suited the leading politicians of the day, however, who, in true feudal fashion, preferred to control their political bastions and not be dictated to and disciplined by a party organization or grassroots mobilization. Most important, it meant that those who sought to catapult religion into the political arena failed to garner the requisite support for doing so. Indeed, the lack of a vibrant party system resulted in only two members belonging to a leftist party being "elected in any real sense as party men" throughout the Donoughmore Constitution era.[71]

The deemphasis on parties was clear given that the conservative United National Party (UNP) was not organized until April 1946, and its archrival, the Sri Lanka Freedom Party (SLFP), was not created until September 1951. Thus, the UNP was the only mainstream party during the 1947 election. Leftists had created the Trotskyist Lanka Sama Samaja Party (Lanka Equal Society Party—LSSP) in 1935, and the pro-Moscow Communist Party (CP) was formed in 1943, but they never really endeared themselves to a conservative and anti-communist electorate. In any case, the decorum the LSSP leaders and other factions exemplified enhanced elite compromise, so that the transfer of power from the British to the Ceylonese was, as already noted, a relatively smooth affair.

The impotent party structure was also obvious in the number of independents who contested elections, whose numbers declined as the party system strengthened. For example, while 181 out of 360 candidates who contested the 1947 election were independents, those figures dropped to 85 out of 303 and 64 out of 249 in 1952 and 1956 respectively. This decrease was especially significant in Sinhala-speaking areas, where the numbers of independents contesting elections dropped from 151 in 1947 to 41 in 1956.[72] This no doubt correlated with the competitive party politics that marked the 1956 elections. As for the Tamils, they had to wait until the Tamil Congress was formed in October 1944 before they could articulate their concerns over their community's dwindling influence.

What is important to recognize here is the influence the absence of a party system and grassroots mobilization had on comity among the elites in the preindependence era. The elites' overarching consideration, like that of political elites elsewhere, was to win and hold on to power and ensure that the patron-client ties they had cultivated remained robust. The executive committee system, through which the government operated under the Donoughmore Constitution, made the committee chairs kingpins and the other committee members dependable acolytes. It also enabled power and patronage networks to operate smoothly, especially since national demands on politicians remained minimal. Indeed, a major virtue of the executive committee system, as far as the politicians were concerned, was that it was hard to blame any one person, and impossible to blame a party, for the blunders committed. The system thus afforded influence, largesse, and power without demanding sufficient accountability. Promoting interethnic comity in this environment was hardly challenging. On the other hand, when the political opportunity structure was redesigned, the politicians also repackaged themselves, even at the expense of resorting to opportunistic and unprincipled politicking. Thus, ethnic outbidding and institutional decay ensued, not because the political elites experienced a metamorphosis or because their preferences changed, but because the political structure changed. The strategies the elites adopted were always designed to maintain their hold on power. If successfully holding on to power was made possible by being accommodative, tolerant, and conciliatory toward other ethnic groups, then the elites eagerly did so, because almost all were predisposed to peaceful coexistence. If winning office and hanging on to power called for being uncompromising, intolerant, and divisive, however, it became imperative to pursue ethnocentric policies. The politicians' goals were always the same—it was the means used to attain their preferences, not the preferences themselves, that changed. This explains why ethnic outbidding and institutional decay ensued.

It was the polyethnic English-speaking elites who articulated and legitimated the need for independence. The clamorous voices of the Sinhalese Buddhist nationalists do not appear to have been taken too seriously at the outset by either the British administrators or their English-speaking Sinhalese colleagues. This was partly due to the naïve belief, despite some evidence cautioning against such naïveté, that the relatively accommodative culture these elites promoted would hold sway over the communalists' primordialist and atavistic positions. Thus, the possibility that Sri Lanka's "brown Englishmen" might become maestro ethnic entrepreneurs once they became part of a party system and resort to the most insidious ethnic outbidding was never considered seriously. This is exemplified by the fact that in ruling on minority rights, the Soulbury Constitution merely stipulated that no government should favor a given religion or community over another. The optimistic belief that a Sri Lankan nationalism devoid of ethnic particularism could be nurtured was shattered less than a decade into the postindependence era, however, by Sinhalese extremists wielding the Sinhala language as a weapon. The culture of ethnic outbidding to which the language issue gave rise, the institutional decay that it concurrently generated, and the anti-minority sentiments and ethnocracy that it ultimately legitimated were the major reasons for Sri Lanka's twenty-year civil war.

3

FROM LINGUISTIC PARITY TO
SINHALA-ONLY

Scholarship suggesting that peoples belonging to the "Aryan race" spoke languages with common origins, coupled with claims regarding a Dravidian family tree, had promoted ethnolinguistic divisions between the Sinhalese and Tamils toward the latter half of the nineteenth century. Indeed, given his ceaseless propagation of the idea that the Sinhalese were racially of Aryan stock, Anagarike Dharmapala evidently fully exploited such ethnological contentions. All this permitted Sinhalese nationalists to claim that Sinhala was an ancient language. This constructed past dictated that the Sinhalese had always been Buddhist, "while their enemies who invade, create disruption and occupy their land are Tamil-speaking Hindus."[1] Not to be outdone, the Tamils also propagated accounts of a Tamil "classical age."[2] Some Tamils flaunted their classical pedigree and irresponsibly belittled the Sinhalese, and some even called for Sri Lanka to be merged with India. These pernicious claims and counterclaims were pervasive during the late 1930s, when the Tamils called for fifty-fifty representation, but they were employed mostly for purposes of identification in the preindependence era. The Sinhalese attempt to extract maximum utility from such constructions did not come until the Sinhala-only movement gained momentum after independence.[3]

The Sinhala-only language movement ensued when hitherto politically and economically marginalized Sinhalese forces coalesced to demand preferential treatment from the government. The movement's grievances were rooted in the "dual economy" that operated under British colonial rule, in which one sector "was a highly developed, organized, foreign-owned, capitalistic, plantation economy producing for export," while "the other was a tradition-bound, primitive, self-sufficing, subsistence peasant economy producing for domestic consumption."[4] This dual economy also created a class system, which, based on income and employment status, may be broken down into five strata: an upper class, upper-middle class, lower-middle class, working class, and peasantry. The first two groups coalesced to form the native elite stratum, Sri Lanka's "brown Englishmen."[5] According to Satchi Ponnambalam:

They had nothing in common with the ordinary people of the country and they stood as a class apart. In fact, to the people they were strangers. In terms of consciousness, ideologies, interests, dress, consumption patterns, and life-styles, they were in every sense British and wanted to remain so. They were educated in English, became early converts to Christianity, developed some degree of entrepreneurial spirit, acquired the skills of the Western masters, repudiated traditional values and customs, and became the local component of the ruling class with the establishment of internal "self government" in 1931.[6]

The ruling elites were not the only Anglophiles. All those aspiring to upward mobility sought to learn English, not necessarily to ape the British but because familiarity with the language was thought to improve one's employment possibilities. Apparently, there was even a tendency among those who had learned some English to thereafter look down on the vernacular languages: "their mother tongue has been despised by those who have acquired a smattering of English," one account noted.[7] The infatuation of certain youths with studying English even to a degree worried the British authorities. Although the latter believed that learning English would Westernize the indigenes and help consolidate British rule in Ceylon, they also realized that there were insufficient employment opportunities to accommodate everyone who learned the language, and that this might lead to a disgruntled cohort among the population. Thus, as early as the 1870s, British officials grumbled that some youths were turning their backs on the rice paddies and instead seeking "some small government post, the demand for which just now is far in excess of the supply."[8] Sri Lanka's language politics was initially launched against these vernacular bashers and especially the privileged, English-educated elite, who also monopolized scarce state sector resources. The initial agitation surrounding the language issue was midwifed by lower-class elites outside the political spectrum and was called the *swabasha* (self-language) movement.

The *Swabasha* Movement

The *swabasha* movement included both Sinhalese and Tamils who campaigned for their respective languages to replace English. It must be recognized that the *swabasha* movement was not designed to revamp the governmental structure. On the contrary, it was an attempt by the hitherto marginalized vernacular speakers to change the criteria by which the opportunities for socioeconomic upward mobility via education and gov-

TABLE 3

Percentage of Literates to Total Population Aged Five and Over, 1881–1946

Year	% literates	Average annual increase
1881	17.4	—
1891	21.7	.43
1901	26.4	.47
1911	31.0	.46
1921	39.0	.80
1946	57.8	.75

SOURCE: N. K. Sarkar, *The Demography of Ceylon* (Colombo: Ceylon Government Press, 1957), p. 203.

ernment employment were determined. The proponents of *swabasha* wanted the rules of the game tweaked so that they too could partake of the spoils.

English operated as an important link language between the ethnic communities, and an islandwide program that promoted it, even while accommodating the vernacular speakers' grievances, might better have served the country. Many realized that the vernacular languages hardly compared with English when it came to expanding students' academic horizons. As one member of Parliament noted: "It is true that we have a developed language, but what is the knowledge that we have in that language? Is it possible that in the near future we shall make available to the 100 per cent. swabasha educated students all the treasures of knowledge available to students of English? That would be like trying to empty the ocean with a bucket."[9]

But promoting English would have been contrary to the *swabasha* proponents' demands. In any case, a major practical barrier to such a policy was the dearth of competent English teachers. Many schools experienced difficulties recruiting sufficient English teachers in the mid-1940s, whereas qualified vernacular teachers were abundant.[10] These vernacular teachers had helped drive up standards of literacy (see table 3), but, as already noted, there were relatively few employment opportunities for the newly literate, and in that sense at least, the *swabasha* movement's demand to have Sinhala and Tamil replace English was amply justified. Thus, for both ideological and practical reasons, the policy eventually adopted sought to marginalize English.

For example, while the Education Ordinance of 1939 instituted a free education system, especially in denominational schools, and the island's literacy rate rose from 17 percent in 1881 to 65 percent in 1953,[11] only about 14 percent of this literate population actually knew much

English.[12] Even that figure was exaggerated, given that being able "to write a signature in English" was all it took to be considered "literate" in that language.[13] Those educated were eager to emancipate themselves from "rural life, from manual toil, from work which they [considered] . . . degrading."[14] But full emancipation required both an education and viable employment, and with no higher education provided in Sinhala or Tamil, the vernacular schools that proliferated in the 1940s, despite educating nearly 85 percent of the school-going population, were hardly equipped to promote social and economic upward mobility. According to S. W. R. D. Bandaranaike, who as prime minister from 1956–59 played a pivotal role in the country's language policies, "over ninety per cent. of the [state sector] jobs . . . are restricted to ten per cent. of the people who know English. In this land of ours, those ignorant of English are capable of obtaining much less than 10 per cent. of the Government jobs!"[15] Likewise, a Select Committee of the State Council, having studied the language issue, reported in 1946 that "[t]he present Government of this country is . . . a Government of the Sinhalese- or Tamil-speaking 6,200,000, by the English-speaking 20,000 Government servants, for the 400,000 English-speaking public."[16] The committee noted that "it is possible to attain the highest post in the island, amass wealth and wield influence, without learning a word of the national languages."[17] Indeed, the vernacular education that catapulted many Sri Lankans into the ranks of the "literate" proved insufficient for conducting even the most routine interactions:

Licenses, permits, and applications commonly had to be completed in English. Petitions and appeals to the government either had to be in English or were believed to stand a greater chance of favorable response if drafted in English. A Ceylonese making a complaint to the police had his statement recorded in English, which he was required to sign—before action could be taken. Court proceedings were conducted in English, probably to the frequent bewilderment of Sinhalese- or Tamil-speaking defendants undergoing trial in an incomprehensible language.[18]

One State Council representative complained: "Parties come before the Courts. The Judges are Sinhalese; the lawyers are Sinhalese; the parties are Sinhalese, but the whole proceedings are conducted in English. The result is that the lawyer argues the case in English, and the parties do not know what is being said about them."[19] Banking transactions in the vernacular languages were deemed illegal as late as 1953, and even parliamentary debates were conducted in English, with the speaker's permission being required in order to use Sinhala or Tamil.[20] Telegrams could not be sent in the vernacular languages until March 1956.[21] The *swabasha* movement thus recognized that the dominant status of English in the educational and governmental arenas was greatly responsible for socioeconomically marginalizing the burgeoning middle classes that spoke only Sinhala or Tamil. Consequently, it was not surprising that non-English speaking Sinhalese and Tamils clamoring for *swabasha* made education reform their foremost goal.

Sinhalese and Tamil legislators realized that having English as the sole official language was undermining the socioeconomic potential and marginalizing those speaking the vernacular languages, and they began gradually to support the *swabasha* proponents' demands. For example, in February 1926, A. Canagaratnam, a Legislative Council member from the Northern Province, moved a motion that cited the disparities between the English and vernacular media schools and called for "English, Sinhalese, and Tamil [to] be made language subjects in all schools, the mother tongue of the students being gradually adopted as the medium of instruction in all schools of all grades."[22] In March 1932, G. K. W. Perera, a Buddhist member of the State Council, also moved a resolution that called for its standing orders to be amended so that the vernacular languages could be used in the legislature, insisting that it was not appropriate "for people to come here and represent—to claim to represent—the interests of the people of this country if they do not understand the language."[23] No doubt emboldened by the universal suffrage instituted the previous year, Perera made it clear that "[w]e want to assert our elementary rights to carry out administration and legislation in this house . . . in the language the people understand."[24] With the *swabasha* movement gaining wide appeal in the 1930s, the Lanka Sama Samaja Party's Philip Gunawardene also introduced a resolution in 1936 calling for the courts and police to be allowed to keep records in the vernacular languages.[25] All this indicated that it was only a matter of time before the vernacular languages would reattain their rightful places in the island.

The excellent English education system instituted by American missionaries in the northern regions had taught many Tamils English. Indeed, by 1930, literacy in English in the Northern Province was second only to Colombo.[26] In 1911, 4.9 percent of Tamil males were considered literate in English, compared with 4.2 percent of Low Country and Kandyan Sinhalese.[27] The paucity of industry and agriculture in the northern regions, the prestige and security stemming from state sector employment, and the opportunity thereby for upward social mobility in the rigidly casteist Tamil society encouraged many northern Tamils to migrate south seeking a university education and governmental careers. Tamils consequently became heavily overrepresented in the elite Ceylon Civil Service, the judicial service, and higher education. Two years prior to independence, for example, Tamils made up 33 percent of the civil service and 40 percent of the judicial service.[28] They also accounted for 31 percent of the students in the university system. In the medical and engineering fields, Tamils numerically equaled the Sinhalese. Such overrepresentation diminished the appeal of the *swabasha* movement for upperclass and upper-caste Tamils, and the movement to replace English with the vernacular languages was thus Sinhalese-led. Some Tamils did mobilize to encourage *swabasha* reforms—the Jaffna Youth Congress and Teachers Association forcefully supported the switch to *swabasha*, for example —but such support soon fizzled out when Sinhalese nationalists, apparently agitated over the Tamils being overrepresented in the coveted civil service, began to adopt a communalist posture and demanded that *swabasha* mean Sinhala-only. This demand was the first real indication that the informal rules governing Sinhalese-Tamil coexistence could be undermined provided there was sufficient support among the country's majority for doing so. What is important to recognize is that the socioeconomic structures that encouraged government employment, given the security and prestige such employment afforded during an era of economic scarcity, were a major reason for the call for Sinhala-only. Writing to the secretary of state for the colonies, Governor Andrew Caldecott noted:

The Public Service looms far too prominently in the thoughts and attentions of the Islanders. Employment under Government provides a social cachet which approaches almost to that of a ruling caste. [One] . . . result is the desire of every parent to see a son get a Government job, and intense jealousy if that job falls to somebody of a different family, caste, or race. . . . I have no doubt whatever that a great deal of the communalism that is so unfortunately rampant derives directly from competition and jealousy about Government appointments.[29]

This rising communalism was correlated with the increasing numbers of Sinhalese joining the educated stratum. For example, while the 1911 census indicated that a higher percentage of Tamils were literate in English than Kandyan and Low Country Sinhalese, the overall literacy rate among Low Country Sinhalese was nearly 2 percent higher than overall literacy among the Tamils.[30] Ten years later, the 1921 census again noted this difference, observing: "The Ceylon Tamils were ahead of the Low Country Sinhalese in English literacy, though they were behind them in literacy generally."[31] With the Sinhalese becoming increasingly literate and their socioeconomic aspirations rising commensurately, it was merely a matter of time before their perception of the Tamils as dangerous competitors hardened.

The Tamils fully recognized that, given the significant Sinhalese majority, Sinhala would inevitably dominate in the bureaucratic and educational arenas. Consequently, between 1938 and 1940, the Hindu Board of Education introduced Sinhala as a compulsory subject in northern schools, and the Jaffna Youth Congress called for Sinhala and Tamil to be made compulsory subjects throughout the island. The anti-English position of the Jaffna Youth Congress, coupled with the clamor for independence from the British, even forced many Tamil politicians to boycott the 1931 State Council elections in Jaffna. Support for the mandatory study of Sinhala and Tamil was also voiced in the State Council. R. S. S. Gunawardana, a Sinhalese representative, noted, for example, that "it would be a happy day for this country if in Sinhalese schools Tamil was made compulsory, and in every Tamil school Sinhalese was made compulsory, and both sections understood each other's languages."[32] But the Sinhalese realized that Tamil was not essential to their upward mobility and displayed no enthusiasm for acquiring another vernacular language. This disregard for Tamil was accentuated by future prime minister and president J. R. Jayewardene when he introduced a resolution in June 1943 that included a call for Sinhala to be made the only official language.

The State Council and the Sinhala-Only Proposal

Jayewardene's motion to make Sinhala the country's only official language, which the *Ceylon Daily News* called a "politically fascinating proposal,"[33] read as follows:

That with the object of making Sinhalese the official language of Ceylon within a reasonable number of years this Council is of opinion—

(a) That Sinhalese should be made the medium of instruction in all schools;

(b) That Sinhalese should be made a compulsory subject in all public examinations;

(c) That Legislation should be introduced to permit the business of the State Council to be conducted in Sinhalese also;

(d) That a Commission should be appointed to choose for translation and to translate important books of other languages, into Sinhalese;

(e) That a Commission should be appointed to report on all steps that need be taken to effect the transition from English into Sinhalese.[34]

Three amendments, by C. W. W. Kannangara, V. Nalliah, and T. B. Jayah respectively, were moved in response to Jayewardene's motion:

(1) That paragraph (a) of the motion be deleted and the following new paragraph (a) be inserted: "That the medium of instruction in schools should be the mother tongue."

(2) That the words "and Tamil" be added after the word "Sinhalese" wherever the word "Sinhalese" occurs.

(3) That paragraphs (a), (b), (c), and (d) of the motion be deleted and that the words "and Tamil" be added after the word "Sinhalese" occurs.[35]

Jayewardene subsequently supported the motion to include Tamil with Sinhala, but he did so voicing concern over India's Tamils in Tamil Nadu. He said he intended "that Tamil should be spoken in the Tamil-speaking provinces, and that Tamil should be the official language in the Tamil-speaking provinces." However, he feared that Sinhalese, "spoken by only 3,000,000 people in the whole world would suffer, or may be entirely lost in time to come" if the Tamil language were afforded parity of status. He added: "The influence of Tamil literature, a literature used in India by over 40,000,000 and the influence of Tamil films and Tamil culture in this country, I thought might be detrimental to the future of the Sinhalese language; but if it is the desire of the Tamils, that Tamil should also be given an equal status with Sinhalese, I do not think we should bar it from attaining that position."[36] In expressing this concern about India's Tamils, Jayewardene showed the Sinhalese to be a majority community with a minority complex and provided fodder for the burgeoning extremists demanding a Sinhala-only policy. "The Member for Kelaniya [Jayewardene] does not seem to have been very clear in his own mind whether he wanted to enhance national unity or accentuate communal differences," the *Ceylon Daily News* observed.[37]

Jayewardene's Sinhala-only motion and its eventual incorporation of Tamil also evidenced that the extant institutional structure was one geared to promoting polyethnic compromise and coexistence. With a party system yet to be organized, grassroots groups still to be mobilized, and the Board of Ministers, as opposed to two party factions, dictating the agenda, politicians could be pressured by their counterparts to overlook demographic disparities and be more accommodating. It is easy being principled when there is no benefit to being unprincipled, and the political structure at this juncture certainly encouraged principled accommodation. The institutional setup may consequently be said to have coerced, or at least influenced, Jayewardene and his backers to accommodate the Tamil language. In light of this, however, it is all the more disappointing that nearly fifteen years later, the British did not insist on a constitutional structure that encouraged fair play and stability but instead promoted an efficient Westminster clone that was well suited to minorities' subordination.

When Jayewardene's motion was debated, the State Council's members were by and large divided into three groups—those who preferred to have Sinhala made the sole official language, those who preferred or were willing to have both Sinhala and Tamil made official languages, and those who insisted that it was imperative that English continue to be the official language. The first camp included the future prime minister Dudley Senanayake, who proclaimed that he, "without any fear of being called communal, without any communal motive whatsoever, would like to have the original motion in its unadulterated form." How, Senanayake asked, had the Tamils been able to "tolerate English all this time as the official language . . . [when they were not willing to] give that same measure of tolerance to our own language, Sinhalese?"[38] Some in this camp shared Jayewardene's concern that Sinhala would become a "dead language" if English were made "free and universal" and hence clamored for Sinhala to be made the only official language.[39] The second camp acknowledged that language was an emotive and cultural marker and showed a willingness to accommodate Tamil. S. W. R. D. Bandaranaike observed, for example, that "there is no question that one of the most important ingredients of nationality is language, because it is through the vehicle of language that the aspirations, the yearnings and the triumphs of a people through the centuries are enshrined and observed."[40] This group realized that "just as much as the Sinhalese language has a fairly important literature behind it, . . . the same can be said of the Tamil language, which is the language of a considerable section of the people of this country."[41] They consequently supported linguistic parity. As was to be expected, the British and Burgher nominated members and some Tamils (e.g., G. G. Ponnambalam) wanted English to be one of the official languages. "Practically in every country throughout the world the English language is spoken and for this country now to think of throwing that language out and denying the people the right to learn English . . . is, to my mind, a most retrograde step," the Burgher nominated member G. A. H. Wille observed.[42] This third group realized that Sinhala would eventually be declared an official language, given the large Sinhalese majority, but worried about the communalism evoked by the Sinhala-only proposition. They therefore preached gradualism and accommodation. "It is very unfortunate that we have to speak out . . . as the tendency in this debate is to emphasize communal feeling, to make us feel that an attempt is being made to place Sinhalese in a predominant position. I say that that will come about in the natural course of events, but let us not force the pace," Wille said.[43] G. G. Ponnambalam strongly opposed Jayewardene's initial motion, saying: "It is merely one of the first steps that one would take to advance the theory of one race, one religion, one language."[44] He added: "When a whole world war is being fought to kill this canard of a superior race, or a Herrenvolk in Europe, we do not want a 'Herrenvolk' in Ceylon and the language of the 'Herrenvolk' to be imposed upon the other sections of the people of this country."[45] Ponnambalam saw English as a link language and consequently wanted its continuance: "The practical position is this: as long as there are two or more races inhabiting this country, professing different religions and speaking different languages, we must have a common language. Let our own languages be given a position of complete equality with the common language."[46] Ponnambalam was partly responding to those Sinhalese who were trying to downplay ethnic distinctions between the Sinhalese and the Tamils and thereby promote homogeneity. For example, B. H. Aluwihare, a Sinhalese State Council member, had argued that Tamils in the northern Jaffna peninsula were not pure Tamils, because "if you read the history of this country, you will find that most of the Jaffna Tamils are, not half-baked, but more baked Sinhalese . . . We [Sinhalese also] had the closest association with the Tamils. I am pretty certain if you scratch a good many of us, you will probably find Tamil blood underneath."[47] Acknowledging such commonality in a milieu of burgeoning communalism was commendable, but in this instance it was invoked to promote acculturation and assimilation, and that was anathema to the Tamils.

Jayewardene had evoked the grandeur of Sinhala to justify his motion:

We have one of the most ancient languages of the world. For 2,400 years Sinhalese has been spoken, has been written . . . When Socrates was speaking Greek, Sinhalese was a spoken language; when Cicero was delivering his Latin orations, Sinhalese was a spoken language; both these languages are now dead, but Sinhalese still lives. When Chaucer was writing his ancient English, Sinhalese was still a spoken language. Chaucer's English is now forgotten except at examinations, but Sinhalese is still spoken.[48]

It is instructive that Jayewardene did not acknowledge Tamil, which by all accounts is considered much older than Sinhala. "It is also known that 5,000 years ago when those who are today supposed to be progressive and civilized nations had not developed an exact grammar or syntax, Tamil was spoken and was a living language," G. G. Ponnambalam later observed.[49] Jayewardene also made it clear that he wanted to "displace English" from its 125 years of dominance "as the official language of the country," because "over 80 per cent. of our schools educate our children in Sinhalese and Tamil, while only about 6 or 7 per cent. of the children are given an English education . . . . [Ultimately], the vast majority who go through the Sinhalese and Tamil schools must always be in the position of hewers of wood and drawers of water."[50] Jayewardene added: "It is not because we do not love English that we want to get rid of it; it is not because we love Sinhalese more; it is because we love our people more that we want the national language as our official language."[51] Yet by introducing a resolution that called for Sinhala to be the sole official language, Jayewardene had clearly indicated that he and those who supported his initial resolution were willing to marginalize the minorities. Jayewardene was right to note that change was needed and needed fast, but this was best achieved by accommodating the other languages. As G. A. H. Wille observed, Jayewardene's motion merely sought "to create disruptive feelings among the different communities."[52]

Jayewardene's motion was ultimately amended to include both Sinhala and Tamil, and this was possible because the ruling Sinhalese elites, in the main, preferred a gradual transition to *swabasha*. In adopting this gradualist approach, however, they misgauged the sentiments and frustrations of the Sinhalese lower and middle classes. Their subsequent volte-face on the language issue merely evidenced this. For example, the Ceylon National Congress, which was fast becoming a Sinhalese and Buddhist body, called in 1939 for both Sinhala and Tamil to be declared official languages, and the Select Committee on Official Language Policy appointed in September 1945 recommended that both Sinhala and Tamil be made administrative languages by January 1957. Yet, in October 1953, the chairman of the Official Languages Commission, Arthur Wijeyewardene, added a rider to the commission's final report suggesting that "the replacement of English by Swabhasha would have been very much easier if instead of two Swabhasha Languages as Official Languages one alone had been accepted in terms of the motion introduced by Mr. J. R. Jayewardene in the State Council on June 22, 1943."[53] Wijeyewardene, like many proponents of a Sinhala-only policy, appears to have held that linguistic parity was nonessential, because the Sinhalese made up over 70 percent of the population. It was only a matter of time before opportunistic politicians adopted the language issue for electoral gain.

Toward a Sinhala-Only Policy

At the end of September 1954, the United National Party's brash and abrasive prime minister, Sir John Kotelawala, visited Jaffna to a rousing welcome and while there publicly agreed with the one-time Youth Congress leader and Hindu College principal Handy Perinbanayagam that both Sinhala and Tamil should be made official languages. He said that he was willing to amend the constitution to ensure that this happened. Sinhalese nationalists immediately upbraided Kotelawala. Some leading Buddhist priests called his comments "ridiculous," saying that linguistic parity would make the Sinhalese a minority in their own country.[54] A number of senior Buddhist priests started to voice concern regarding their more vociferous colleagues, but it was becoming clear that the nationalists and extremist bhikkhus (Buddhist monks) were determined to merge forces and clamor for Sinhala to be made the sole official language.

Approximately three weeks later, the prime minister visited Jaffna again and promised the Jaffnese that he would stick by all the promises he had made them. Thoroughly impressed by the reception he received, Kotelawala proclaimed that never before in the history of Ceylon had a Sinhalese been afforded such a hospitable reception by the Tamils and that "he loved the Jaffna people more than the Sinhalese."[55] However, when Sinhalese nationalists mounted a campaign that once more castigated him for his comments in Jaffna, Kotelawala, who continued to advocate parity, insisted that he had said nothing about amending the constitution. In hindsight, it is clear that Kotelawala's accommodative pronouncements in Jaffna and the anti-parity movement it influenced among Sinhalese extremists marked the turning point at which the call for a Sinhala-only policy gained the ascendance. Hitherto, there had been a patina of civility associated with the Sinhala-only campaign; following Kotelawala's trip to Jaffna, this civility was replaced by sulfurous communal rhetoric. Indeed, in later years, Bandaranaike and others responsible for instituting a Sinhala-only policy conveniently referred to Kotelawala's trip as the event that catalyzed Sinhalese opinion against linguistic parity.

With the *swabasha* movement reaching fever pitch, the UNP government announced in January 1955 that it "accepted the principle that Sinhalese and Tamil should be the official languages and that they should progressively become the media of instructions in schools."[56] It also proposed that civil service personnel be trained in Sinhala and Tamil; that a translation and compilation bureau be organized; that the clerical service examination in English be scrapped in 1962, and that it instead be given in the vernacular languages, starting in 1958; and that examinations in all subjects (excepting science and mathematics) for the senior school certificate be held in *swabasha*, starting in 1957. The National Languages Commission on Higher Education had been organized to advise the government on the transition to the vernacular languages, and some of its members called for special *swabasha* inspectors to be appointed to ensure that all schools followed the government's new directives.

When parliament debated the *swabasha* bill in January 1955, all except two speeches were in Sinhala, leading the *Ceylon Daily News* to observe that "the lucid and chaste dignity of the speeches . . . demonstrated that the Sinhalese language was both an adequate and graceful means of disputation to those skilled in the art of debate."[57] Members had spoken in Sinhala before—Bandaranaike was the first to do so in July 1948 during a debate on the budget—but the fact that many members now resorted to their vernacular (and provided a summary in English for those not versed in the language) indicated that there was solid support among the Sinhalese for incorporating Sinhala as an official language. What was less clear was the extent to which Tamil was to be accommodated.

The parliamentary debates on the *swabasha* bill focused mostly on the language or languages to be used in education, but the crux of the matter was how the changes implemented would affect the Sinhalese and Tamil communities' economic fortunes. With various Sinhalese leaders and Buddhist monks calling for a Sinhala-only policy, Tamil leaders and parliamentarians also started to adopt an intransigent stand. C. Suntharalingam, the parliamentarian for Vavuniya, who became a vocal supporter of the idea of a separate Tamil state, offered an amendment in June 1955, for example, that in part stated that anti-Tamil discrimination was leading "to disharmony among the people, and is causing grave disaffection to the extent of creating a strong desire for the formation of a separate independent State . . . of Tamil speaking peoples in Ceylon within the Commonwealth."[58] Claiming that "[t]here is something in the Tamil language which expresses thought in such a way as to make for accuracy and advancement," Suntharalingam argued that "no Tamil at any time will agree to the Tamil language being slighted."[59] Frustration and anxiety over the Sinhalese nationalists' agenda promoted hyperbole among Tamil politicians, and Suntharalingam exemplified this to the extreme. "Tamils are now worse off than they were under the British," he declared.[60] The aroused passions and attendant rhetoric also provided signals about the dangers ahead, as when Suntharalingam warned that "[w]henever the Sinhalese and Tamils lived together in peace there was prosperity in the land. . . . But whenever they quarreled and fought the people who went under, I am sorry to say, were the Sinhalese . . . . Remember, from city to city you went because you were defeated and your capital cities sacked. Whenever the Tamils and Sinhalese fought the Tamils always triumphed in the long run."[61]

The polemics and dubiousness notwithstanding, such rhetoric was pernicious for at least two reasons: it both reinforced Sinhalese nationalists' demands for a Sinhala-only policy, while emboldening some Tamils to resort to extremist demands themselves, and undermined Tamils' confidence in the state apparatus.

Reflecting the tensions in parliament and the country, the National Languages Commission itself soon fractured, with the minority members Canon R. S. de Saram, A. W. Mailvaganam, and E. O. E. Pereira boycotting meetings. Those members who thereafter represented the commission, Arthur Wijeyewardene, L. J. de S. Seneviratne, N. J. Wijesekera, G. P. Malalasekera, and L. H. Mettananda, were proponents of a Sinhala-only policy, and it was hardly surprising when, in May 1955, they recommended that whereas the post-1959 university entrance examinations ought to be conducted in all three languages, only one *swabasha* language should be offered at the university level after 1962. In August, this majority cabal recommended that the island jettison parity and instead institute one national language, because they believed that the ensuing monolingual milieu would eventually facilitate "mutual amity, goodwill and nationhood"![62] In doing so, this majority group masked their communal bias by pretending that they were being practical. They claimed that the difficulties that would inevitably arise in duplicating staff and providing the requisite textbooks for a two-language curriculum made a one-language policy the most workable. With Arthur Wijeyewardene having called, as chairman of the Official Languages Commission, for only one language to be made the state language, and especially with Malalasekera and Mettananda resorting to pro-Sinhala agitprop, there was no doubt as to what this one language was going to be. "We are not imbeciles to imagine that it will be Tamil," one Tamil politician exclaimed.[63]

Rather than providing advice to the government, as most commissions typically do, the National Languages Commission's pro-Sinhalese and -Sinhala majority even adopted activist stands designed to force the government's hand on the language issue. They recommended, for example, that the national languages be put into use immediately for purposes of administration; that the government establish a *swabasha* research institute; that a new Department of National Languages be created to replace the Official Languages Bureau; that the island's elite university at Peradeniya operate only in Sinhala after 1962; and that a new university be built in Jaffna to accommodate Tamil students. There was no opposition to the majority's views, since the minority members, having disagreed over the draft report the majority faction had dictated, boycotted the commission's meetings. The Sinhala-only forces, however, eagerly embraced the commission's claims to legitimize their demands.

These demands inevitably took on an anti-Tamil tone, while effectively linking the Sinhala language with Buddhism. One prominent southern Sinhalese claimed that the government was so utterly biased toward the Tamils that the latter had arrogated to themselves "fifty times more [resources] than they deserved."[64] Persons belonging to some Sinhalese associations threatened to fast to death if Sinhala were not made the official language, and a number of public resolutions were passed demanding the same outcome. L. H. Mettananda, wearing his other hat as general secretary of the ultranationalist Lanka Jatika Bala Mandalaya (which roughly translates as Lanka National Activist Forum), threatened to launch a countrywide satyagraha campaign if the government refused to make Sinhala the only official language. Senior Buddhist priests and their acolytes were almost always associated with such organizations or spoke at these pro-Sinhala functions, thereby legitimating the nationalists' claims. The rhetoric these monks adopted was similar to that used by Anagarike Dharmapala, for they inculcated fear into the Sinhalese that linguistic parity would extinguish Sinhala, even as they warned politicians not to disobey their wishes. "The Tamils whose language is spoken by millions are preparing to wipe out the Sinhalese language," the monks claimed.[65] "If parity of status is granted to both Sinhalese and Tamil then in no time the Sinhalese language will disappear from our island."[66] These extremist bhikkhus asked the Tamils to accept Sinhala as the only official language and claimed to be prepared to shed their priestly robes to join in the Sinhala-only struggle.[67] As far as symbolism was concerned, such claims were ironic, given that the bhikkhu's saffron robe commanded more attention and influence than laymen's clothes. Yet, that revered monks could put a pro-Sinhala policy ahead of their religion also indicated the emotive power commanded by language and the lengths to which some of the island's Buddhist clergy would go to achieve their particularistic designs.

Two primary concerns galvanized the Tamils against a Sinhala-only policy. The first of these was that such a policy would marginalize their community socioeconomically. Suntharalingam indicated what had to be on many Tamils' minds when he some time later noted: "We do not worry about Tamil language and Tamil culture but we do worry about Tamils enjoying jobs in this country, about Tamils enjoying positions as citizens of Ceylon and not as slaves of Ceylon. We will not have Tamils as Sinhala slaves in Ceylon. We never had them before and you will never have them hereafter."[68] The second concern was the fear that if Sinhala was made the dominant language, Tamils would eventually be forced to assimilate into the Sinhalese community. With many Tamils along the coastal areas having acculturated into the Sinhalese community to the extent that some Sinhalese lower castes were considered to be wholly of Tamil stock, there was a historical context for such fears. Claims in parliament that "[w]e [the Sinhalese] want to absorb you into our community,"[69] whether made seriously or in jest, merely reinforced Tamils' fears, which ethnocentric pronouncements by G. P. Malalasekera and his ilk further exacerbated. For example, in a three-part article in the *Ceylon Daily News*, Malalasekera proclaimed that "a single language is more conducive to the . . . assimilation of minority communities . . . into a larger society with a common virile culture."[70] Such "a composite culture . . . will result in a homogenous state," he claimed, forcing "those foreigners who do not wish to make Ceylon their permanent home . . . gradually [to] leave this country. Those that remain will learn the language and be absorbed into the community."[71] Such pronouncements by educated and respected Sinhalese merely hardened some Tamils' belief that a conspiracy was under way to strip them of their distinct culture. It was in reacting to such fears that G. G. Ponnambalam warned that "one century of English education from the finest English masters has not converted a single Tamil into an Englishman, but one decade of the imposition of the Sinhalese language on the Tamil race will convert the Tamils in everything but name into Sinhalese." Ponnambalam averred that "a long-suffering and indulgent people will be stirred to their very depths and will rise in resistance against this attempt at genocide. Far better would it be for us to accept the parting [of the] the ways here and now, and pursue our different paths."[72] And Suntharalingam argued: "Sir, the Sinhalese are not a race; they are a linguistic group. And if Tamils start studying Sinhalese, they become Sinhalese too. I do earnestly hope that every one of my posterity will be dead before the occasion ever arises when they are made to call themselves Sinhalese."[73]

The Tamil quest for parity was strongly supported by some Sinhalese, with those belonging to the Lanka Sama Samaja Party and the Communist Party especially standing out in this regard. In October 1955, the LSSP and CP even conducted raucous meetings in Colombo Town Hall calling for linguistic parity, only to have proponents of a Sinhala-only policy, ably assisted by bhikkhus, break up both meetings. That same month, the LSSP's N. M. Perera moved a motion supporting parity in the legislature, while Buddhist monks protested his doing so outside parliament. The motion specifically called for "the Ceylon (Constitution) Order in Council . . . [to] be amended forthwith to provide for the Sinhalese and Tamil languages to be state languages of Ceylon with parity of status throughout the island."[74] Perera chastised his colleagues for not advocating parity outside of parliament, berated the UNP for not moving faster to establish linguistic parity throughout the island, and he quoted extensively from the State Council debates in May 1944 to remind members that many among them had supported parity at that time. Perera referred to the twenty-pound garland the Jaffnese had placed on the prime minister when he visited the Northern Province in September 1954 and lambasted him by saying, "I do not know whether he was overwhelmed by those garlands or inebriated by the warmth of the welcome he was given there," but the promise he had given the Tamils was "the only correct thing he has done in his life so far as the political future of this country is concerned."[75] Perera urged his colleagues to satisfy the minorities so "that they will not be treated as pariahs, that they will not be treated as outcasts, that they will be given equal status, that they will have the fullest rights to live as human beings in this country."[76] The numerous arguments made against linguistic parity were, he averred, undermining the island's unity.

The Tamils had protested against the various government-sponsored colonization programs whereby thousands of Sinhalese peasants were transplanted from the densely populated Southern and Western Provinces especially to the Eastern Province, which the Tamils considered part of their historic homeland. These concerns had led some Tamils, headed by S. J. V. Chelvanayakam, to organize the Federal Party, which called for the extant unitary state structure to be replaced by a federal structure. Concerns over linguistic parity had made the Tamils more vociferous when demanding regional autonomy, because they realized that a devolutionary arrangement would preclude their language being subordinated to Sinhala in at least the Northern and Eastern Provinces and also halt the Sinhalese from continuing to colonize these traditionally Tamil areas. Most Sinhalese strongly opposed any devolution, because they believed it would lead to the country's dismemberment. The LSSP's Perera, however, called upon the government not only to provide the Tamils with parity but also to accommodate them within a federal structure. Alluding to the over 40,000,000 Indian Tamils in Tamil Nadu, he argued that lacking linguistic parity and federalism, "the other alternative left for the Northern and Eastern Provinces . . . [is to] break away and join somebody else."[77] Perera was among the few Sinhalese to see how Tamil aspirations were intertwined with language and territory and warned that to disregard legitimate Tamil concerns would "be disastrous for the welfare of this country, [for] we shall have a perpetual division of the country, we shall never get a united Ceylon and we shall have a tremendous amount of bloodshed."[78]

While claiming that he and the government stood for linguistic parity, the prime minister disregarded Perera's motion as an "election stunt" and refused to support it.[79] Despite Kotelawala proclaiming support for linguistic parity, it became clear toward the end of 1955 that the UNP would need to make a profound decision as to how to combat Bandaranaike and the opposition, who were now demanding a Sinhala-only policy. Dudley Senanayake, the previous prime minister, who was D. S. Senanayake's son and begrudged Kotelawala his leadership of the government, also proclaimed his support for a Sinhala-only language policy. Senanayake argued that parity was impracticable and threatened to leave the UNP and "make an appeal to the country" if the government did not reach a "satisfactory decision" on the language issue.[80] While some Sinhalese UNP members went around arguing that the government was less for the Sinhalese and more for the Ceylonese, they were few and far between. Thus, N. M. Perera was right to question why no UNP parliamentarian had strongly voiced his support for parity outside parliament. Some Tamil members ensconced in the UNP—for example, the Kayts representative A. L. Thambiayah, Minister of Posts and Broadcasting S. Natesan, and acting Minister for Transport and Works V. Kumaraswamy—continued to repose faith in the party and went around reiterating that the UNP would never stand for a Sinhala-only policy. Kumaraswamy was among the most vocal in this regard, and it is noteworthy that by early November 1955, even he was being tentative in his comments. Suggesting that the UNP would have betrayed the Tamils if it denied them linguistic parity, Kumaraswamy said: "No self-respecting Tamil in Ceylon will accept Sinhalese as the only State language. If our Sinhalese brethren do not treat us with equality, honour and dignity we have no other course open to us but to secede and form our own government."[81]

Bandaranaike's Sri Lanka Freedom Party, together with all the other parties, had embraced linguistic parity during the 1952 election campaign. The year before that, the SLFP's position on language was stated as follows:

It is most essential that Sinhalese and Tamil be adopted as official languages immediately so that the people of this country may cease to be aliens in their own land; so that an end may be put to the iniquity of condemning those educated in Sinhalese and Tamil to occupy the lowliest walks of life and above all [so] that society may have the full benefit of the skill and talent of the people, the administration of Government must be carried on in Sinhalese and Tamil.[82]

By 1955, however, it was clear that the language issue would feature prominently in the forthcoming election, and the SLFP officially adopted a Sinhala-only policy in December that year. By that month's end, UNP members were confidently predicting that their party would also adopt a similar position. The Muslims, who spoke the Tamil language, had briefly supported linguistic parity, but by mid-November 1955, the All Ceylon Muslim League and the All Ceylon Moors' Association agreed to accept Sinhala as the only state language, provided due recognition was given Tamil and English. With their one-time Muslim allies agreeing to a Sinhala-only policy and with the government equivocating on linguistic parity, a number of Tamil parliamentarians and Tamil ministers of state resigned from the Government Parliamentary Group. The Tamil-speaking members in the House and Senate thereafter sought to move a resolution at the UNP's forthcoming language policy session calling for "two separate independent states of equal status or the setting up of a federal form of government in two autonomous states."[83] The UNP's Working Committee refused to include the resolution and instead recommended that Sinhala alone be made the island's official language. By the time the

UNP unanimously voted on February 18, 1956, to make Sinhala the only official language of Ceylon, fourteen Tamil-speaking members had left the party in protest. Even though new elections were not due until the following year, John Kotelawala asked the governor-general to dissolve parliament the same day the UNP adopted a Sinhala-only platform, claiming that a new mandate with what he hoped was a two-thirds majority would enable him to incorporate the one-language policy through a constitutional amendment. S. W. R. D. Bandaranaike countered that all he needed was a simple majority to ensure that Sinhala was made the official language. Given that the UNP had a significant parliamentary majority yet did not seek to institute a Sinhala-only policy, Bandaranaike claimed the party was not seriously committed to the Sinhala language. Soon thereafter Kotelawala promised that he too would make Sinhala the official language whether he had a two-thirds majority or not: "Whatever my majority my first resolution in parliament will be the 'Sinhalese only' motion. And if you have one drop of Sinhalese blood in your veins, I know my request will not go unheeded."[84] It was the beginning of Sri Lanka's culture of ethnic outbidding.

S. W. R. D. Bandaranaike and the Politics of Opportunism

While the emotive support the Sinhala-only movement engendered caught the country's elites off guard, some, such as S. W. R. D. Bandaranaike, recognized that the erupting pro-Sinhala sentiments could be manipulated for political gain. Bandaranaike was a cabinet member in the ruling United National Party when he feigned frustration at the pace of reforms and bolted to the opposition benches in July 1951.[85] He mainly changed sides having realized he would not succeed the country's first prime minister, D. S. Senanayake. Bandaranaike sincerely believed he was better qualified to replace Senanayake, and he no doubt was among the most intelligent and eloquent members in parliament. But Bandaranaike was also vain and opportunistic. The scion of a wealthy, aristocratic family whose progenitors had displayed no qualms over converting from Hinduism to Buddhism to Roman Catholicism to the Dutch Reformed Church to Anglicanism to gain favor with the ruling powers of the day,[86] Bandaranaike, who himself became disenchanted with Christianity and converted to Buddhism, soon sought to make himself the paladin of the Sinhala-only movement. In this he contrasted with D. S. Senanayake, who, despite being prejudiced against the Indian Tamils, opposed making the vernacular languages official, because he believed that doing so would complicate Sinhalese-Tamil relations. In discussing educational policy, for example, Senanayake made it clear that whatever the island chose as "the medium of instruction we must ensure that Sinhalese, Tamils, Muslims and Burghers shall be able to serve in any part of Ceylon."[87] Rather, it appears that Senanayake wished his countrymen to be multilingual, for in one of his memorandums, he noted that "our essential task is to create a nation . . . [where] our people speak not one language but two or perhaps three."[88]

Writing in the mid-1950s, Sir Ivor Jennings, advisor to D. S. Senanayake, vice-chancellor of Colombo's university, and arguably the most astute observer of the island's politics during the 1950s, gauged "an undercurrent of opinion," which he described as follows:

It is aggressively nationalist and aggressively Buddhist. In language policy it is anti-English; in religion it is anti-Christian; in foreign policy it is anti-Western; and in economic policy it is both anti-capitalist and anti-socialist. Socially, it might be described as anti-Colombo, because it consists primarily of English-educated young men from the provinces, the sons of small cultivators, minor officials, shop-keepers, and the lower middle-class groups generally. It dislikes the cosmopolitan airs of the products of the big Colombo schools, who dominate Colombo society. It is not a political movement, but it is politically important because it has the support of the Buddhist Sangha, or priesthood, of the teachers in the Sinhalese schools, and of the *vedarala* or practitioners of indigenous medicine, all of whom have strong political influence in the villagers.[89]

What Jennings was partly describing was what became known as the Pancha Maha Balavegaya (Five Great Forces), consisting of the *ayurveda* physicians, bhikkhus, farmers, teachers, and laborers, and it fell to Bandaranaike to manipulate the Sinhala-only sentiments these aggrieved, ambitious, and troublesome groups espoused and thereby create a political movement. In the mid-1930s, Bandaranaike had organized the Sinhala Maha Sabha (Great Sinhalese League), a latent communalistic outfit that he was to use at opportune moments. The Sinhala Maha Sabha was an element within the UNP until Bandaranaike merged it into the Sri Lanka Freedom Party, which he formed two months after crossing over to the opposition benches. Though promoted as a centrist party, the SLFP was a leftward leaning, pro-Buddhist entity, and in organizing the party's grassroots base, Bandaranaike appealed to the Sangha (Buddhist clergy) and the Sinhalese Buddhist masses. His efforts paid little dividends in the 1952 election, when the SLFP contested fifty-nine seats but won only nine, but they helped catapult him to power in the 1956 election. It is instructive that Ivor Jennings could write in 1954 that Bandaranaike was unlikely single-handedly to topple the extant UNP government.[90] This is perhaps not surprising, given that two years prior to that, in 1952, another observer claimed that while the Federal Party was reinforcing communalism in clamoring for federalism, "In general, however, communalism is declining in significance as a political factor, while economic and social issues are gaining importance as determinants of lines of political cleavage."[91] What these observers did not realize was the extent to which communalism could be powerfully implemented to manipulate a nation's economic and social grievances. In demonstrating this, Bandaranaike not only won power in 1956 but also unleashed a spiral of events that eventuated in civil war.

The 1956 General Election

There can be little doubt that Bandaranaike cared sincerely about society's disadvantaged and believed that Sri Lanka's potential was realizable only provided those marginalized were integrated into the country's socioeconomic processes. The *swabasha* movement was seen as a step in that direction, and Bandaranaike maintained the need for both Sinhala and Tamil to replace English even after leaving the UNP. His position was hardly unique in the early 1950s, given that the leftist parties, the UNP, and "even bhikkhus, Sinhala writers, and teachers—people who might have been expected to seek preferment for Sinhala alone—tended to appeal on behalf of Tamil as well."[92] By late 1954, however, anti-Tamil and anti-Christian sentiments had coalesced, invigorating the Sinhala-only movement, and this led Tamil politicians to make combative noises as well. Thus, for example, G. G. Ponnambalam thundered:

No amount of patronising talk from any quarter will lull us into a feeling of security. Nor should those in authority be misled into thinking that exhibitions of poltroonery by small sections prove the absence of dissatisfaction. . . . Let it not be thought that a great and proud race will agree to play second fiddle in this country. I now find myself a more determined advocate of Tamil nationalism.[93]

The Mahajana Eksath Peramuna (People's United Front, or MEP), which was the coalition Bandaranaike cobbled together for the 1956 election, was infested with jingoists, and its opportunistic leader reversed positions and became a vociferous proponent of a Sinhala-only policy. In May 1944, when the State Council debated J. R. Jayewardene's motion to make Sinhala the official language, Bandaranaike had argued that it "would be ungenerous on our part as Sinhalese not to give due recognition to the Tamil language." He added: "If the object is that it is rather awkward to have more than one official language, I would like to point out that other countries are putting up with more than two official languages and are carrying on reasonably satisfactorily."[94] Promoting linguistic parity, Bandaranaike observed: "It is necessary to bring about that amity, that confidence among the various communities which we are all striving to achieve within reasonable limits. Therefore, . . . I have no personal objection to both these languages being considered official languages; nor do I see any particular harm or danger or real difficulty arising from it."[95] Ten years later, in April 1954, when a newspaper mistakenly reported that he was against Sinhala being made the official language, Bandaranaike responded in a letter, saying: "It is stated that I said that I would never make Sinhalese the State language. The word 'only' has been omitted. What I said was that neither I nor my Party [the SLFP] are in favour of Sinhalese only being made the official language of the country but that both Sinhalese and Tamil be made official languages."[96] By 1955, however, Bandaranaike was inebriated with the desire to become prime minister. He thus manipulated the existing, self-imposed minority complex of the Sinhalese and repeatedly portrayed the language issue as a "life and death struggle,"[97] claimed that UNP leaders supported parity only because they were traitors to their race and language, and argued that parity would spell disaster for the Sinhalese, because it would enable the Tamils to use "their books and culture and the will and strength characteristic of their race . . . [and] exert their dominant power over us."[98] Bandaranaike showed no qualms about commingling communalism with the bogus, and what he subsequently came up with was wholly in tune with the fear psychosis developed by Anagarike Dharmapala. For example, Bandaranaike argued that to grant "parity to both Sinhalese and Tamil will only lead to the deterioration of Sinhalese which may disappear from Ceylon within 25 years."[99] He also claimed that the UNP and those Tamils who had left the party had made a secret pact, that the two groups would consequently remerge after the election, and that all this was designed to prevent Sinhala alone from being made the national language. Using imaginary secret pacts as a bogey to vilify the opposition soon turned out to be a common practice among both Sinhalese and Tamil parties.

Though wallowing in communalistic rhetoric was antithetical to his core liberal proclivities, vanity had deluded Bandaranaike into thinking that the chauvinists he was manipulating could be tamed after obtaining power. Such chutzpah was based on his belief that the emotive Sinhala-only demands would dissipate once the Sinhala-only legislation was passed, and that he could thereafter seek to accommodate Tamil. Bandaranaike appears at least to have believed that he could eventually inveigle his Tamil counterparts into accepting a language policy short of parity, because the Tamils were themselves divided and their options rather limited. Consequently, the SLFP manifesto put out in September 1955 endorsed a Sinhala-only position but also noted the need for Tamil to be used for administrative and educational purposes in the Northern and Eastern Provinces.

In resorting to chauvinistic rhetoric, Bandaranaike was well assisted by numerous lay Buddhists and activist bhikkhus, who together organized emotive and impressive processions demanding a Sinhala-only policy. Such bhikkhus anathematized the Tamils as "parasites," argued that linguistic parity was undemocratic and unjust, since 80 percent of Ceylonese spoke Sinhala, and claimed that the failure to institute a Sinhala-only policy "would be the death-knell of the Sinhalese."[100] These monks evidenced no desire for compromise and instead suggested that Sri Lanka was for the Sinhalese only. For example, one leading monk thundered: "The Dravidians want parity or Tamilnad. We will give them neither. This country belongs to the Sinhalese. We can't give even an inch of it to the Tamils."[101] Other monks claimed that not just Sinhala but Buddhism too would disappear if parity was instituted. While the prime minister and some leading monks spoke against these activist monks' incendiary rhetoric, there was no silencing the extremists in the Sangha.

Indeed, the Sinhala-only movement gave prominence to the so-called political bhikkhu. One of these, Walpola Rahula, argued that the separation of church and state was a calculated Western construct to emasculate the masses, and that "from the earliest days the Sinhala monks, while leading the lives of bhikkhus, were in the forefront of movements for the progress of their nation, their country, and their religion."[102] By using the Dutthagamani account and linking the Sangha's activism to patriotism, Rahula argued that historically "both *bhikkhus* and laymen considered that even killing people in order to liberate the religion and country was not a heinous crime" if motivated by "religio-patriotism."[103] In campaigning for a Sinhala-only policy, the ubiquitous bhikkhus primarily operated under the Eksath Bhikkhu Peramuna (United Buddhist Front), which became a political umbrella organization for a Sangha divided along caste lines, but many also became active through the numerous *sangha sabhas* (bhikkhu associations). "Here were the best election agents any politician could wish for—12,000 men whose words were holy to over 5,000,000 people, campaigning for the downfall of the Government, zealously and, what is more, gratis," one contemporary observed.[104] These bhikkhus were joined by other powerful groups such as the Young Men's Buddhist Association, the Theosophical Society, the Ayurveda Sangamaya (Congress of Indigenous Medical Practitioners), the Bhasa Peramuna (Language Front), and the Lanka Jatika Guru Sangamaya (Sinhalese Teachers' Association), the latter two uniting Sinhala language teachers, educators, poets, and writers.

The 1956 election coincided with the Buddha Jayanthi, the 2,500th anniversary of Lord Buddha's death, and the Sinhala-only forces adeptly manipulated the enthusiasm surrounding this event by emphasizing the unique Sinhalese religio-linguistic identity and promoting the belief that as inheritors of the *Sihadipa* (the island of the Sinhalese) and *Dhammadipa* (the island ennobled to preserve and propagate Buddhism), the Sinhalese were entitled to make Sinhala the island's sole national language. The year 1956 also saw the Buddhist Commission publish *The Betrayal of Buddhism*, which highlighted Buddhism's decline under colonialism and indicted the postindependence UNP governments for failing to remedy the situation. The Buddhist Commission's demands included amending Article 29 of the constitution, which provided for minority rights; making the island a republic; nationalizing private schools; banning horse racing; terminating the services Catholic nuns provided in government hospitals; and substituting the Buddhist Poya holiday for Sundays.[105] All combined, this Sinhalese Buddhist tsunami soon forced the UNP also to resort to communalistic rhetoric.

John Kotelawala had repeatedly said that he and the UNP would not budge from linguistic parity. In June 1955, for example, he had said: "I can assure you—and I have said it not once but many times—that the U.N.P., of which I am the head, have accepted the principle that both Sinhalese and Tamil will be the languages of this country. We have said so, and we propose to put it into practice."[106] Kotelawala had also magnanimously observed that the Sinhalese should realize that "we lose nothing by being fair by the Tamil-speaking people who wish to preserve their culture and their language quite as intensely as we want to preserve ours."[107] He further indicated that he knew about the dangers of manipulating communalism and was therefore committed to linguistic parity: "Those of you who start this communal racket do not know what it means. I have myself seen this communal racket work in India. I saw enough bloodshed there. But I can assure hon. Members of this House that as long as this Government exists and as long as I am head of the U.N.P. the principle we have adopted will be maintained to the very end."[108] A month later, during a prize-giving ceremony at a Colombo school, Kotelawala said: "Bilingualism, and even trilingualism, should . . . be encouraged as far as possible if the communal harmony which we pride ourselves in having today is to be preserved for the future."[109] Once he had opted for a Sinhala-only policy, however, the prime minister asserted: "I want Sinhalese to be the official language of the country as long as the sun and moon shall last."[110] Indeed, as polling day approached, it was hard to distinguish Kotelawala from Bandaranaike, for the prime minister had fully embraced the latter's rhetoric. "If the country chooses parity, then in the years to come your children will be speaking Tamil," he was quoted as saying. "His name and mine will be no more. I say this because parity would mean equality where every child would have the option for qualifying for professions in either language. Tamil has a more prolific literature and as such will gain precedence and finally kill the Sinhalese language."[111]

Why did Kotelawala change his stripes and advocate what he and any average educated Ceylonese knew was utter claptrap? He did so for the same reason that Bandaranaike did, which was the craving to win or hang on to power. Kotelawala and Bandaranaike were both rightly considered liberal democrats, and yet here they were resorting to the most shameful communalism and ethnic outbidding. That acknowledged, there can be little doubt that both would eagerly have eschewed communalism if the political structure had allowed them to attain their goal without resorting to ethnocentric politicking. All their pronouncements prior to the 1956 election campaign make this amply clear. But with grassroots groups and nationalists mobilized to demand special treatment and a constitution that provided no checks and balances to prevent marginalizing the minorities, Kotelawala, like Bandaranaike, saw no choice but to try to convince the majority community he was most suited to ensure Sinhalese superordination. Ergo, he too turned to communalism and ethnic outbidding.

For at least three reasons, however, Kotelawala lacked the legitimacy Bandaranaike commanded as the proponent of a Sinhala-only policy. First, while Sinhalese Buddhist extremists had doubted Bandaranaike's resolve to be their standard-bearer, the fact remained that Kotelawala and the UNP had embraced a Sinhala-only policy after Bandaranaike and the SLFP had committed to it. Second, both Kotelawala and the UNP were widely seen as favoring English speakers and Christians, and this was resented by the rural Buddhist masses the SLFP had cultivated. Finally, and most important, Kotelawala had compromised himself by not passing Sinhala-only legislation prior to dissolving parliament, even though he could have done so with a two-thirds majority. The UNP had fifty-four members in parliament even after its Tamil members had quit the party in protest, and this number combined with the sixteen opposition members who had pledged their votes for a Sinhala-only policy was ample for passing a Sinhala-only act with a two-thirds majority. Kotelawala instead dissolved parliament, seeking a two-thirds UNP majority to institute a Sinhala-only policy, whereas Bandaranaike had promised to make Sinhala the official language in twenty-four hours by simple majority. Kotelawala did change tunes toward the end of the campaign, claiming that he would guarantee a Sinhala-only policy even if the UNP were reelected with a simple majority, but by that time Bandaranaike and the MEP had successfully smeared their opposition for waffling on the language issue.

The 1956 election was the first to indicate that the country lacked strong norms that could withstand political opportunism, and the ethnic outbidding practiced by the UNP and SLFP especially evidenced this. It is clear that it was the political structure that coerced the politicians into perpetrating their divisive rhetoric. Yet the lengths to which they went to outbid their opponents also indicate that the harmony among Sri Lanka's elites that the British had been so impressed with was fragile. The ethnic outbidding for which the 1956 election set a precedent subsequently became deeply ingrained and the bane of Sinhalese-Tamil relations. Indeed, not only did the two major parties outbid each other on the Sinhala-only issue, but individual politicians, more concerned about getting into parliament than about being identified with a party's social and economic principles, eagerly switched sides if guaranteed a spot on the ballot. Thus, the UNP recruited some SLFP members the party believed were favored to win certain constituencies, while the SLFP in turn nominated some UNP members whose candidacies had been rejected by the UNP.

Sri Lanka's elections have consistently generated high voter turnout, and the electorate in general is viewed as politically sophisticated. This noted, the 1956 election was easily the most closely followed up to then. This was evident, for example, in the higher number of newspapers sold during the election as compared to those sold before the election.[112] Election meetings were also well attended, with the Sinhala-only issue especially influencing rural voters to believe that they were close to generating a revolution. The significance of all this was not lost on Bandaranaike, who repeatedly observed that he and the MEP would indeed unleash a revolution if elected.

The year 1956 was thus key to Sinhalese-Tamil relations. As already observed, interethnic politics had turned communalistic by around the late 1920s, when it became clear the Donoughmore Commission's reforms (1928–31) would provide universal suffrage to Sri Lanka and eradicate the communal electorates that had enabled the Tamils to wield a disproportionate influence in the legislature. Property and educational qualifications, combined with communal electorates, had allowed the Tamil elites in the National Assembly to function on an equal footing with their Sinhalese counterparts. The Donoughmore constitution changed that. Indeed, the All-Ceylon Tamil Congress's attempt to get the Soulbury Commission to endorse a "fifty-fifty" representation scheme in the mid-1940s was a clear signal that Tamil elites recognized that universal suffrage had made them and their community a marginalizable minority. Given the rabid anti-Tamil rhetoric, the fact that neither the UNP nor the SLFP fielded Tamil candidates or campaigned in the Northern and Eastern Provinces, and given especially the absence of Tamils from the postelection cabinet, the 1956 election was the first to vindicate such fears.

It needs to be noted that the Tamils themselves failed to unite. On the contrary, they resorted to ignominious factionalism and vilified one another. Those who left the UNP after the party embraced a Sinhala-only policy sought to create a United Front, but the now ascendant Federal Party (FP) opposed this. The FP was organized in 1949 after some members left the Tamil Congress because they opposed the party's leader, G. G. Ponnambalam, joining the UNP Cabinet. The FP had called for a federal form of government within a united Ceylon, whereas those Tamils who operated within the UNP trusted their party to accommodate Tamil concerns and hence favored the extant unitary structure. The UNP's Sinhala-only volte-face led its estranged Tamil politicians to propose "the creation of a Tamil state which will offer to federate with the Sinhalese state on terms of complete equality if acceptable to both nations or elect to remain independent."[113] This group sought to organize a United Front that included the FP, but the latter contended that it was against any project to dismember the country. The FP was after more autonomy for the Sri Lankan Tamils and never contemplated compromising the country's sovereignty. Some Sinhalese nonetheless tried to blacklist the party as a threat to Sri Lanka's territorial integrity. That said, the FP at this juncture could afford to take the high ground against its Tamil counterparts, who were now trying to disassociate themselves from the UNP's perfidy, while the FP stood untarnished. FP members were right to divine that the main reason most ex-UNP Tamils wanted to establish a United Front was so that they could be returned to parliament at the FP's expense. The party's Executive Committee consequently demanded that the ex-UNP Tamils not contest the upcoming election if the United Front was to become a reality. When the party soon thereafter adamantly opposed using a single list of nominations, these other Tamil politicians assailed it, and all hopes for a United Front were shattered. Some among these ex-UNP Tamil politicians thereafter claimed that the FP had agreed to a secret pact with the UNP to join the latter after the election, even as others claimed that the secret pact had been reached with Bandaranaike's SLFP. G. G. Ponnambalam argued that a federal Sri Lanka would make Tamil only a regional, as opposed to a national, language, and that the FP's agenda threatened the Tamils' right to islandwide linguistic parity. On a different level, lower-caste Tamil groups, strenuously protesting against the rigid casteist practices among the northern Tamils, threatened to vote for Sinhalese candidates if their higher-caste fellows did not immediately eradicate the humiliating indignities their groups faced (e.g., segregated temple worship and discrimination in employment). With such factionalism dominating the Tamil community, there was even less incentive for the two major Sinhalese parties to reevaluate their ethnic outbidding tactics.

Ultimately, the 1956 election represented the triumph of linguistic nationalism. The way the Sangha and the nationalists manipulated the Buddha Jayanthi clearly proved that religion was never excluded from the rhetoric promoting the Sinhala-only movement. Nevertheless, "the dominant issue that drove it [the election] forward was that of language. Religion—which is to say Buddhism—ran in a close second."[114] Three issues need to be stressed here. First, while Buddhism was never relegated to insignificance, language was allowed to subsume religion, because it expedited the Sinhalese community's quest for upward mobility. "Linguistic nationalism had an appeal which cut across [even] class interests, and . . . evoked as deep a response from the Sinhalese working class as it did among the peasantry and the Sinhalese educated elite," K. M. de Silva observes.[115] Second, emphasizing language precluded intra-Sinhalese divisions, whereas emphasizing Buddhism in the preindependence era had led to Sinhalese Christians being vilified and marginalized. Indeed, ethnic differentiation along linguistic lines has become so ingrained that commonalities among Tamil and Sinhalese Christians, for example, are now disregarded, while Sinhalese Buddhists and Christians, their religious differences aside, have coalesced as a common sociopolitical unit.[116] Finally, the surge in ethnolinguistic nationalism in postindependence Sri Lanka clearly coincided with increased centralization, bureaucratization, and modernization and the state-sponsored educational opportunities afforded to thousands of youths.

The Nexus Between Linguistic Nationalism and Development

Linguistic nationalism, unlike religious nationalism, is a recent phenomenon. As already noted, this is, in the main, related to the different political and economic possibilities inherent in traditional communities and post-traditional or modern societies.[117] While traditional communities are primarily agrarian and decentralized, modern or post-traditional societies are typically bureaucratized, centralized, and relatively industrialized, necessitating increased interactions with both official and unofficial institutions. Language becomes the most important medium when negotiating among these institutions, and it is thus more significant for post-traditional societies. This certainly was the case in postindependent Sri Lanka, but it is best briefly to contrast some salient features in the pre- and postindependence eras to highlight this point.

The Portuguese and Dutch presences in Sri Lanka hardly altered do-

mestic economic relations, and the vast majority of people continued to
rely on subsistence agriculture. The British introduced an export-depen-
dent plantation economy centered primarily on tea, rubber, and coconuts,
but Sri Lanka's industrialization thrust did not begin until the late 1950s.
In 1900, out of a population of about 3,500,000, only around 20,000
were being educated in English schools, while 150,000 were being educated in vernacular schools.[118] The literacy rate in 1921 was 39.9 percent,[119] but most of those considered literate had attended vernacular
schools and had only received "basic instruction for living in a community with very limited horizons."[120] These resource-starved vernacular
schools eschewed a modern, scientific curriculum and were not even considered secondary schools, despite the fact that 84.7 percent of the
school-going population was enrolled in such institutions in 1931.[121]
Thus, while Sinhalese recruitment into the civil service did not increase
significantly until the 1920s and 1930s, which meant that the Tamils and
Burghers were overrepresented there, state sector employment was not as
salient an issue as it would be during the 1950s. The best secondary institutions were Christian and primarily catered to the elites and upper-
middle-class strata. It was graduates of these Christian schools who
helped staff the lower and mid-level ranks of the civil service, but it was
not until the 1880s that the first Sri Lankans were hired. There were no
technological institutes in the island "till well into the twentieth century,"[122] a university college was not created until 1921, and a full-
fledged university was not established until 1942. The country's "gain-
fully occupied" population in 1921 was 62.4 percent, of which the
majority engaged in agriculture and fishing.[123] The caste system circumscribed societal relations, and intra-Sinhalese divisions along caste and religious lines were more acute than the ethnic divisions that were beginning to take shape. This socioeconomic milieu was hardly conducive to
making language a mechanism for mobilization, and it is no coincidence
that the anti-British mass movement in the preindependence era was fashioned primarily using religion.

This is not to suggest that language was unimportant to the Sinhalese
community, or that some literati did not seek to utilize Sinhala as a mobilizing mechanism. For example, James D'Alwis, a nineteenth-century
Sinhalese aristocrat who worried that Sinhalese culture was endangered
because colonialism marginalized the vernacular languages, devoted his
life to resuscitating the Sinhala language. C. Don Bastian, a journalist,
Piyadasa Sirisena, a novelist, and John de Silva, a dramatist, had likewise
used their talents during the preindependence period to generate enthusiasm and provide pride of place to the Sinhala language. And Munidasa
Cumaratunga, a prominent educator who claimed that the Sinhala lan-

guage was derived from an ancient Hela civilization rooted in Ceylon, sought to use the Hela movement to demand a respectable place for Sinhala. Indeed, Cumaratunga even went so far as to demand that only those who promised to speak exclusively in Sinhala should be elected to the State Council. Not only was Cumaratunga unsuccessful in his attempts, but he became estranged from many prominent linguists and bhikkhus, who campaigned against him and his movement. Thus, while the island was not devoid of linguistic nationalists who used their Sinhala writings to generate a valuable literary and ethnic consciousness in the preindependence period, its traditional societal structure precluded these literati from using language to mobilize as powerfully as they might have in a post-traditional society.

Sri Lanka in the mid-1950s was such a post-traditional society for a number of reasons: population growth, coupled with free education, had provoked heightened expectations from the government at a time when the state was the most significant employer; nearly twenty-five years of experience with the suffrage had led to numerous grassroots movements that sought to use elections to channel scarce resources to their hitherto neglected communities, even as politicians and parties were becoming cognizant of how pork barrel politics and patron-client ties could be used for corralling electoral support; a vibrant labor movement headed by leftist parties was at the forefront of manipulating liberal democracy's accoutrements and demanding labor reform and increased representation in governmental institutions; and a general welfare program had increased living standards. Indeed, the social and welfare programs instituted by the British and Sri Lankan elites in the 1930s were designed to offset the threat posed by the leftist/Marxist elements represented by the labor movement. One such program was the so-called rice subsidy. The public's dependence on this rice subsidy was so acute that when the UNP government under Dudley Senanayake increased the price of rice, it led to a Marxist-inspired *hartal*, or violent protest, and the prime minister's resignation in October 1953.

In 1940, the population had numbered roughly six million, with nearly 650,000 students educated in the vernacular and another 100,000 in English.[124] In 1945, despite the state not being well positioned to provide employment for this burgeoning group, the government mandated compulsory education for the first five grades. Consequently, the numbers being educated kept rising, but employment opportunities failed to improve commensurately. All this combined meant that by 1956, the overwhelmingly rural and predominantly Sinhalese electorate was also a politically driven electorate that depended on and demanded special treatment from the government. Language was the key indicator of who was to receive such treatment, and the April 1956 election enabled the Sinhalese to coalesce around their linguistic identity.

Besides enabling the Sinhalese to use linguistic nationalism to ensure a system of ethnic favoritism, the 1956 election was the first to make it clear how the country's constitutional structure had limited the choices facing politicians in their attempt to get elected or reelected by a predominantly Sinhalese electorate. Indeed, the demographics coupled with the absence of any checks and balances protecting minority rights made it possible for ethnic and nationalist institutions to influence politics to the point where they could more or less blackmail the island's politicians. Buddhist and nationalist groups thus dared their political elites to go against their wishes. Lacking any incentives to muzzle the extremist forces, most politicians joined the Sinhala-only bandwagon, in the process resorted to chauvinism and ethnic outbidding, and thereby unleashed the inevitable institutional decay that would justify the Tamil quest for separatism. To place blame on the political structure is not to absolve the island's elites for their opportunistic and unprincipled behavior. That noted, merely to vilify the country's maestro ethnic entrepreneurs without paying due regard to the institutional structure that incited their actions is to misunderstand, perhaps even overlook, why they sanctioned ethnic outbidding and institutional decay.

The end result of the 1956 election was a landslide electoral victory for S. W. R. D. Bandaranaike's Mahajana Eksath Peramuna. The MEP's victory was such that fifty-one of its sixty candidates were elected to parliament, while only eight out of seventy-six UNP candidates were elected. The FP fielded fourteen candidates and ten won seats in parliament, making the party the Tamils' leading representative. Bandaranaike had campaigned on the slogan "Sinhala-only, and in twenty-four hours," and once elected, there was no reneging on the substance of this promise.[125] But fulfilling it amid the untrammeled passions and firebrand rhetoric of both Sinhalese and Tamils shattered relations between the two communities.

4

THE OFFICIAL LANGUAGE ACT OF 1956

Ellen Immergut has noted that since institutions are crafted by humans, they "can be transformed by politics." Consequently, new or redesigned laws could reform a society's standard operating practices, "thereby causing citizens to think more about the common good and less about their personal possessions."[1] The Official Language Act of 1956 was unfortunately not a law designed for the common good. On the contrary, its goal was to enhance the majority community's socioeconomic possibilities, while imposing relative deprivation on the minorities. There is no doubt that language reform was necessary, but rather than being a law that took into account the interests of all groups, the Official Language Act simply imposed Sinhalese preferences. It was clear from the outset that the Official Language Act had the potential to change the political opportunity structure radically. The administrative changes required to implement the act were not adopted overnight; instead, they were authorized, typically, by way of notices in the *Government Gazette,* over the next few years. But the emotive protests demanding a Sinhala-only policy, the act's subsequent passage, amid severe rioting, and the positive and negative consequences envisioned by Sinhalese and Tamils respectively guaranteed that significant changes along ethnolinguistic lines were in store, and that these changes were bound to affect relations between the ethnic groups adversely.

At its most fundamental level, the Official Language Act exemplified a radical change in policy implemented by the Sinhalese for the benefit of the Sinhalese. Granted, the attendant politics were dictated by the majoritarian principle. The illiberal nature of the act suggested, however, that its sponsors expected the will of the majority to be the will of all. No law is likely to pass with complete consensus, and this is especially so in a polyethnic society. But provided the laws passed entail a degree of fairness, even those objecting to their passage will likely respect them until they are able to change the offending rules using established constitutional and legal precedents. Sri Lanka's political structure ensured, however, that it would be impossible to change the Official Language Act without support from the very Sinhalese lawmakers who had enacted it in the first place.

Even while campaigning for a Sinhala-only policy, some members of the Sinhalese elite realized that some form of explicit recognition of Tamil was crucial to interethnic stability. Indeed, the events that immediately followed the 1956 election indicate that Bandaranaike's clear preference was to accommodate Tamil. He was obliged to back off from doing so, however, by extremists in the Sangha who were opposed to even token accommodation. Clearly, if ethnic outbidding between the country's major parties was a logical tactic in winning power, accommodating the Tamils was also logical, even in the context of a Sinhala-only policy, and that was what Bandaranaike would have preferred to see happen after he became prime minister. But the very political structure that had led to ethnic outbidding in the first place now exerted sufficient pressure on him and others to cause them to jettison their rational preferences and adopt a more extremist stance in order to hold on to power. Bolder statesmen might have stood by their convictions and fought on principle. They might have failed in the process, but the increasingly beleaguered Tamil minority would have applauded their efforts and continued to put their trust in the state. But with Sinhalese politicians disinclined to compromise, Sinhalese extremists became further radicalized, while indignant Tamil leaders fought back with divisive rhetoric that contributed to interethnic animus and laid the groundwork for institutional decay and separatism.

Feeling Betrayed

With both the Mahajana Eksath Peramuna and the United National Party having promised to institute a Sinhala-only policy if elected, there was no doubt in anyone's mind that Bandaranaike would quickly make Sinhala the country's only official language. However, the extent to which the Sinhala-only policy would be imposed, and with what impact on the minorities, was far from clear. Sinhalese leaders argued that the effect would be minimal, while Tamil leaders predicted the worst. This noted, the Tamils had every reason to feel that the Sinhalese elites were betraying them.

At the turn of the twentieth century, Tamil elites stood at the forefront in challenging the British to institute a more representative political system, with the inimitable brothers Ponnambalam Ramanathan and Ponnambalam Arunachalam playing significant roles. The Montagu Declaration of 1917, which proposed limited self-government for India, influenced the founding of the Ceylon National Congress in 1919 by Ponnambalam Arunachalam, who intended it to replicate the Indian National Congress and fashion a Ceylonese nationalism that promoted interethnic unity. His brother Ramanathan had "braved the enemy submarines," as a member of parliament later put it, to travel to England and defend the Sinhalese position in the aftermath of the 1915 Sinhalese-Muslim riots. At a time when many Sinhalese leaders were in British custody for their supposed involvement in the riots, Ramanathan's defense of the Sinhalese, described in his book *Riots and Martial Law in Ceylon, 1915*, was a testament to interethnic harmony among the country's elites. Ramanathan even urged the Sinhalese to take pride in their language, saying: "If you do not speak your language on public platforms, in railway carriages and in drawing rooms you will not stand up for your national institutions, then I say none of you deserves to be called Sinhalese. The nation will be ruined and we must await with trembling knees the early destruction of the Sinhalese language."[2] Despite the tensions created over universal suffrage and the fifty-fifty campaign, Tamil leaders had also banded together with their Sinhalese counterparts and promoted a united front when seeking independence from the British. Thus, "the transfer of power took place so efficiently that the ordinary citizen did not even realize that it had happened."[3]

In promoting a united front, State Council member George E. de Silva proclaimed: "On behalf of the [Ceylon National] Congress, and on my own behalf, I give the minority communities the sincere assurance that no harm need they fear at our hands in a Free Lanka. We want not only a Free Lanka, we want a free, united and democratic Lanka."[4] In trying to dispel Tamils' fears about an overbearing Sinhalese majority, Francis Molamure pleaded: "I would ask . . . the Tamil community . . . to give us a fair chance; to give us a trial. . . . After all, let them see when we have more power in our hands whether the majority community is going to, as they say, dominate over them or whether it is going to be fair to them."[5] A Tamil State Council member reciprocated: "Let us accept this so that we may not stand in the way of the freedom of the Ceylonese people, and let us accept their assurances at their face value and have confidence in the majority community and see that they do not do any injustice to us."[6] With Tamil sentiment coalescing around such views, D. S. Senanayake, soon to be the island's first prime minister, promised: "I can assure these [minority] communities that every Sinhalese here is worthy of the trust placed in him and will not disgrace our ancestors. We shall see that that good feeling is fostered . . . to the best of our ability." Speaking on behalf

of the Sinhalese, Senanayake further promised that "whether they [the minorities] were against me or whether they were against anyone else, I say that we, the Sinhalese, will show that we are worthy of our race."[7] Trust can be a fickle and frangible commodity, and it therefore does not guarantee expected outcomes, especially in prickly polyethnic settings, but the Tamils' trust in D. S. Senanayake and other Sinhalese luminaries enabled them to accept the Soulbury Constitution of 1946, which merely stipulated that all ethnic groups were to be treated impartially. Specifically, Article 29(2) of the Soulbury Constitution stated:
No law shall—

(a) prohibit or restrict the free exercise of any religion; or
(b) make persons of any community or religion liable to disabilities or restrictions to which persons of other communities or religions are not made liable; or
(c) confer on persons of any community or religion any privilege or advantage which is not conferred on persons of other communities or religions; or
(d) alter the constitution of any religious body except with the consent of the governing authority of that body: Provided that, in any case where a religious body is incorporated by law, no such alteration shall be made except at the request of the governing authority of that body.[8]

Now, less than a decade after independence, these flimsy minority guarantees were being disregarded, and Tamils in the Northern and Eastern Provinces boycotted the country's Independence Day celebrations on February 4, 1956, and flew black flags to protest the Sinhalese attempt to create a Sinhala-only policy. Their sense of betrayal was voiced by G. G. Ponnambalam, who asked his parliamentary colleagues,

Is this . . . that great freedom that the Tamils . . . fought for with the Sinhalese to obtain, to wrench, from the British? Is this all that independence is to mean to the Tamil community? That from white masters we are to turn to a lot of brown masters, from masters who crossed the seas . . . to an indigenous brand of masters permanently settled in this country?[9]

The Tamils' sense of betrayal hardened when the MEP made Sinhala the official language and Sinhalese extremists sought to suppress peaceful Tamil protests against the Sinhala-Only Act with violence.

Hints of Ethnocracy

Within days after the MEP came to power, the English programming on Radio Ceylon was reduced by two hours. A number of ministers in the government also began displaying their office name boards in Sinhala only, and officials in some predominantly Sinhalese districts announced that they intended to operate on a Sinhala-only basis. Despite the radicalism such acts evoked, there was reason to believe that Prime Minister Bandaranaike would not compromise on his intent to accommodate Tamil in a Sinhala-only milieu. He indicated as much in his first press conference approximately a fortnight after the election. Furthermore, when the Government Parliamentary Group became dissatisfied with the draft of the Sinhala-only bill that was circulated and appointed a committee to make recommendations on the bill to the cabinet, Bandaranaike, during his second press conference as prime minister, reiterated that both the MEP and the SLFP were committed to the "reasonable use of Tamil" and any other language in use (i.e., English) and promised that this Sinhala-Only Committee would give serious consideration to accommodating the minority languages. With no Tamil in the cabinet for the first time, Bandaranaike also announced that the committee would meet with Tamil parliamentarians who had accepted the Sinhala-only principle to determine how the Tamil language could be accommodated. Bandaranaike made it clear that in his mind, "the real, sane and sound solution" to the language issue was to create regional councils that would ensure the "reasonable use of Tamil."[10] He likewise magnanimously encouraged the Sinhalese to be "reasonable" when dealing with the Tamils. Indeed, when during a meeting with parliamentary colleagues, one member protested that the MEP might lose support if it tried to accommodate the Tamil language, Bandaranaike retorted that being unreasonable toward the minorities was a sure way to lose the entire country.[11] Thus, there is no gainsaying the fact that Bandaranaike was aware of the dangers of a Sinhala-only policy, and some of his statements on devolution also make it clear that he believed that a quasi-federal structure was necessary to pacify the Tamils. The reality, however, was that he lacked both the decisive predisposition and an electoral mandate to provide either; and this became evident when the Sinhala-Only Committee, which included Bandaranaike, decided not to incorporate a clause permitting Tamil and English to be used to correspond with government officials for "religious, business and unofficial purposes" into the Sinhala-only bill, "on the ground that it was redundant."[12]

The loquacious Bandaranaike was prone to self-promoting palaver, and he made numerous statements asking the people to trust him, because he was fully capable of solving the language conundrum. Each such pronouncement further polarized both the Tamils and Sinhalese extremists. The Tamils felt that Bandaranaike, having achieved power on a Sinhala-only policy, was now trying to hoodwink them into demobilizing their anti-Sinhala-only protests, while the extremist Sinhalese suspected that the prime minister was preparing to renege on his most important election pledge. Bandaranaike, however, believed that he would ultimately present a bill that would satisfy both parties, and he suggested that "there would be greater friendliness amongst the peoples, and their differences would be solved" once the Sinhala-only legislation was introduced.[13] He may have wanted to indisputably signal his commitment to reconciling Tamil grievances, but if this was indeed the case, the master manipulator of the Sinhala-only movement had thoroughly misread the extremist forces he had coddled.

Bandaranaike, who became prime minister on April 12, 1956, had promised to introduce a Sinhala-only bill in parliament on May 2, but this was not done until June 5. Throughout this period, Bandaranaike hoped to strike a compromise that would satisfy the Sinhalese without completely marginalizing the Tamils. He was thus seeking to institute a law that many, if not most, Tamils would have found tolerable, for that would have broadened its legitimacy on an all-island basis. Rules, conventions, and laws that are completely rejected by a specific and significant section of the population may nonetheless be implemented and their acceptance obtained through coercion. But the injustice inherent in such laws encourages protests and agitation. With politicians often being least qualified to divine what consequences will stem from their actions, it is always preferable to ensure the most possible support for especially controversial policies, and this was what Bandaranaike was hoping to achieve.

Bandaranaike had repeatedly stated that he would institute a Sinhala-only policy in twenty-four hours, and the delay in doing so caused the extremist Sinhala-only forces to passionately criticize the prime minister and his government. These forces made it clear that Bandaranaike had come to power only because they had supported the MEP on the Sinhala-only issue, that both the prime minister and his government were therefore obligated to them, and that Bandaranaike was delinquent for not expeditiously fulfilling his campaign promise. When Bandaranaike sought to appease the minorities by hinting that a Sinhala-only policy would not preclude them from conducting day-to-day transactions with the state in their respective languages, he drove the Sinhalese extremists into paroxysms of rage. For example, L. H. Mettananda, a pro-Sinhala member of the National Languages Commission and a thoroughbred Buddhist ideologue, but not a member of parliament, proposed his own Sinhala-only bill, which opposed accommodating Tamil, saying: "If the Tamil-speaking minority is given the legal right to communicate with the Government in their own language, the Tamil language will automatically become an official language. This is what the Communists and communalists want."[14] By citing the communists, Mettananda sought to vilify the leftist MPs and their parties who favored linguistic parity and some form of devolution; in citing the communalists, he was attacking Tamils who clamored for federalism or linguistic parity. It was a ploy that a number of Sinhalese parliamentarians also used when trying to justify their preference for Bandaranaike's Sinhala-only bill. The communalist label was ridiculed by A. Amirthalingam, the Tamil member from Vaddukoddai, who commented: "While the desire of the Sinhalese to make the whole country their own, to thrust their population into our territory, is considered nationalism, the desire of the Tamil-speaking people to protect their land, to be allowed to live in their own territory as they have done from time immemorial, is considered communalism."[15] S. J. V. Chelvanayakam added: "We who protest are sometimes regarded as communal. Those who inflict all this . . . injustice on the Tamil-speaking people are called national."[16]

Despite Mettananda not being a member of parliament, many in the MEP's Parliamentary Group began opposing Bandaranaike's desire to accommodate Tamil, because they saw it as breaking the party's most significant election pledge, and they advocated adopting Mettananda's bill instead. That members of parliament could disregard their prime minister's position and embrace the radical recommendations of an unelected ideologue shows how much Bandaranaike had underestimated the Sinhala-only extremists. This and other events further pressured Bandaranaike to capitulate to the extremist forces he had manipulated to attain power. For example, F. R. Jayasuriya, a university lecturer and a founding member of Bandaranaike's SLFP, began a hunger strike outside parliament, claiming that if the government's Sinhala-only bill was passed in its draft form, it would "only lead to Ceylon becoming part of Madras in six months."[17] For Jayasuriya and his Sinhala-only colleagues, the prime minister's plan to allow Tamil to be used in Sinhalese areas was worse than granting parity itself. Jayasuriya, who suggested that Bandaranaike was coddling prominent Tamil politicians in an attempt to appease them on the language issue, consequently made two demands: (1) "That Sinhala only be made the official language throughout the island," and (2) that Tamil "be used by local bodies, if they so choose, for their local administrative purposes" in the Northern and Eastern Provinces.[18] Bandaranaike's initial reaction was to belittle Jayasuriya's tactics, claiming that the latter's press statements were not merely "false but preposterous, absurd and even mischievous."[19] Yet the quicksilver prime minister soon sent cabinet ministers to negotiate and commiserate with Jayasuriya. Bandaranaike himself thereafter met with Jayasuriya, helped him halt the hunger strike with a glass of orange juice, and agreed to have him address the Government Parliamentary Group.[20] As a leftist member of parliament later noted: "It was the biggest concession to communalism when [Bandaranaike] gave a glass of orange juice to Mr. Jaya-suriya."[21]

Bandaranaike fancied himself as a troubleshooter, and by inviting Jayasuriya to address the Parliamentary Group, he may have been seeking to burnish his image as an indispensable conciliator. In doing so, however, he inadvertently proved that when it came to the language issue, the prime minister was a mere marionette, while Jayasuriya, Mettananda, and the other Sinhala-only extremists were the puppeteers. Allowing Jayasuriya to address the Parliamentary Group was unprecedented, and some parliamentarians opposed it. But the fact that the prime minister felt constrained to let Jayasuriya do so exhibited how beholden Bandaranaike's government was to the Sinhala-only radicals. Indeed, the Parliamentary Group, influenced by Jayasuriya's speech, bowed to the extremists' demands and deleted two clauses from the Sinhala-only bill that would have allowed local boards to use Sinhala and Tamil for business purposes and enabled public servants to sit for examinations in those languages. Thereafter, Bandaranaike sought to save face by arguing that drafting the bill in its simplest form was the most practical thing to do, given the manifold complications surrounding the switch to a Sinhala-only policy. Yet, with the bill saying nothing about accommodating Tamil, and the clauses dropped being those opposed by the extremists, it was clear the prime minister had capitulated to the communalists' demands. It would not be the first time Bandaranaike had done so, and with each such instance, he and the others representing the government clearly showed that what was gradually being instituted was an ethnic-based particularistic regime that was marginalizing the country's minorities and undermining their confidence in the state's institutions.

More important, Bandaranaike's political behavior also indicated that while his anti-Tamil campaign rhetoric was primarily instrumental, he had underestimated how constrained he would be when implementing all his preferences. Part of this was perhaps due to his immense vanity and affected chutzpah. But part was perhaps also due to his not fully understanding the structural constraints he would face in a milieu dominated by Sinhalese extremists and political bhikkhus who especially enjoyed immense influence. The irony here is that while Bandaranaike was among the very first Sinhalese politicians to realize that the emerging political structure was conducive to manipulating Sinhalese Buddhist nationalism, he failed adequately to grasp that this very political structure that made ethnocentric rhetoric and ethnic outbidding an effective strategy would constrain his capacity to practice even limited compromise

With the MEP determined to introduce Sinhala-only legislation, the Federal Party began to clamor more vociferously for a federal state.

Having won ten of the sixteen constituencies it had contested in the Northern Province, the FP felt that it had a mandate to lead the Tamil protest. Non-FP Tamil politicians derided the party and its leader, Chelvanayakam, however, and the call for a federal arrangement was said to be impractical, especially given that this might potentially jeopardize the livelihoods of thousands of Tamils living in the southern, and predominantly Sinhalese, areas. Although they occasionally came together across party lines to address public meetings, the antipathy between the Federalists and the other Tamil elites, notably G. G. Ponnambalam, was such that the latter would have said anything to delegitimize the Federalists. A fully united Tamil front at this stage might not have been sufficient to persuade the Sinhalese leadership to act any differently, but it would certainly have generated more pressure on the government. With Tamil politicians sniping at one another, however, there was even less pressure on the government to accommodate the minority position.

The Tamils' divisions did not prevent their politicians from resorting to pyrotechnics and encouraging protest movements when opposing the Sinhala-only bill. For example, G. G. Ponnambalam urged the Tamils and their leaders to resist the Sinhala-only legislation by refusing to communicate with the government in Sinhala, by not teaching or conducting Sinhalese classes in Tamil areas, by avoiding learning Sinhala to work in government institutions, and by boycotting the legislature until the Sinhala-only bill was withdrawn. Despite opposing federalism, Ponnambalam even began suggesting that the Tamils might need to embark on a self-determination movement,[22] which most Sinhalese construed to mean a separatist movement. Chelvanayakam, too, made it known that the Tamils had no choice but seek "Federalism or Separatism" in the absence of parity,[23] and the Federal Party announced that it would hold its convention in Trincomalee, with party delegates and supporters marching from all parts of the island to the convention site. For C. Suntharalingam, the Tamils had three options. The first was to do nothing, which would be unconscionable. The second option was to seek federalism, but in doing so, he said, Chelvanayakam resembled "a lady who wants to be married to a person who does not want to be married to her." The third option, and his own preference, was to campaign for an independent Tamil state. "We [the Tamils] were in turn under the dominion of the Portuguese, Dutch and the English, and we shall not tolerate any foreign domination by the Sinhalese. We shall resist to the bitter end," he thundered.[24] Suntharalingam was the most precipitous among the Tamil politicians. His firebrand rhetoric was unrealistic in the 1950s, but in time to come, many of his threats would unfortunately become reality.

For example, in opposing the government's Sinhala-only policy, he noted that he was not averse to resorting to violence, and he repeatedly said that if marginalized to extremes, the Tamils would have no choice but embrace violence: "We are here . . . not to declare war. That stage will come; certainly it will come."[25] This was contrary to the views held by the Federal Party and many other Tamils, who preferred to counter the discriminatory legislation with nonviolence, yet two decades later, marginalized and frustrated Tamil youth began mobilizing to fight one of the world's most gruesome civil wars. In opposing the Official Language Act, Suntharalingam also predicted: "In the same Buddha Jayanthi Year [the 2,500th anniversary of the death of Buddha, celebrated in 1956] there may be other blood baths throughout the country."[26] Barely five weeks later, the first anti-Tamil riots ensued and brought about that bloodbath.

The 1956 Anti-Tamil Riots

The FP had called on Tamils to resort to satyagraha (peaceful protest) against the Sinhala-only bill, and Tamils in the Northern and Eastern Provinces responded to the call. As the FP had also organized a satyagraha demonstration on the premises of the House of Representatives on the day the Sinhala-only bill was to be introduced, a number of delegations from the Northern and Eastern Provinces traveled to Colombo to participate. When the government decided to close the parliamentary debate to the public and barricade the building, the satyagrahis decided to congregate outside the parliamentary complex. Their plan was to meditate and fast from sundown to sunset to protest the Sinhala-only legislation. The Sinhala Basha Arakshaka Mandalaya (Sinhala Language Protection Council), or SBAM, had threatened to counter the FP's protest with one of its own, and L. H. Mettananda had likewise indicated that Sinhalese protestors would meet force with force. Mettananda, like many Sinhalese politicians, had undergone a metamorphosis on the language issue. In 1942, he had written: "Tamils and Sinhalese have lived together in Ceylon for 2000 years. We are brothers. It is our duty to learn each other's language; every Sinhalese must learn Tamil and every Tamil must learn Sinhala. That is how we can bring about national unity."[27] By 1956, however, he had arguably become the craftiest Sinhalese bigot. He wrote glib articles defending the right to a Sinhala-only policy but urged the Sinhalese to embrace Buddha's teachings and eschew violence, even though his speeches tacitly encouraged it. Whatever the reason for this paradox, his followers appeared more enamored by his rhetoric than his writings, and Suntharalingam consequently ridiculed him, saying: "Mr.

Mettananda is now engaged in quoting the Buddha as the devil quotes the Scriptures."[28] In countering the FP's call for satyagraha, Mettananda announced that the SBAM had plans to activate a massive boycott of Tamil lawyers, doctors, Tamil-owned movie theaters, and tobacco and cigar products from the Northern and Eastern Provinces. He further threatened that a couple of leading newspapers, including a Sinhala newspaper, would be boycotted because their shareholders were mostly Tamil and even claimed that the forthcoming boycott would prevent Tamils buying or renting property.[29] That Mettananda, one of the country's leading educators and a member of the National Languages Commission, could resort to such vitriol indicated linguistic nationalism's capacity to arouse emotions. Mettananda and K. M. P. Rajaratna, the bigoted junior minister of posts, also accused the FP of colluding with the Americans to try and divide the country, just as, they claimed, the Americans had divided Korea and Vietnam. There was nothing too fanciful when it came to mobilizing the Sinhalese against the FP and those opposing the Sinhala-only legislation, and Mettananda and his ilk had no qualms about resorting to dirty tricks and outright threats. A leading bhikkhu closely associated with the MEP even warned that if the Tamils attempted to prevent the Sinhala-only bill from becoming law, they would be driven to Jaffna and never allowed to return to Colombo.

With communal passions running high and Mettananda, the SBAM, and others threatening to undermine the FP's satyagraha protest, Bandaranaike was aware that events could turn dangerous. He consequently tried to get Chelvanayakam to cancel the satyagraha demonstration. The whole purpose of conducting satyagraha protests is to nonviolently call attention to a perceived injustice, however, and the FP and its supporters saw no reason to cancel the event. Thus, on June 5, 1956, approximately two hundred Tamils assembled on Galle Face Green across from parliament, where they were soon attacked by Sinhalese protesters, led by Junior Minister Rajaratna.[30] The satyagrahis were beaten and pelted with stones; at least one Tamil was thrown into the nearby Beira Lake, and another had an ear "bitten and torn off." The protest was therefore called off by 1:00 P.M.[31] Some Tamils were hospitalized, and among those wounded were members of parliament. The police, in the main, stood by as passive observers, having been given explicit orders not to intervene unless they themselves were attacked.

Bandaranaike sought to pacify the Sinhalese crowd outside parliament, saying: "I will give you the Sinhalese language. Give me one thing. Co-operate with me and go home peacefully."[32] When the crowd failed to disperse, the police used fire hoses to prevent them from entering parliament, where debate on the Sinhala-only bill had begun. Mettananda, who addressed the counterprotestors gathered on Galle Face Green, asked the Sinhalese not to be afraid of the Tamil satyagrahis and urged them to boycott Tamil businesses. Whether this was intended to be a veiled communication sanctioning mayhem or not, these rioters thereafter fanned out across the city and resorted to massive anti-Tamil looting and violence. That night, Bandaranaike told his coalition members, "People say I have no backbone, but now I will show them my strength."[33] Yet by then numerous Tamil establishments had been attacked and looted and many Tamils had been assaulted throughout Colombo. While the Sinhala-only bill continued to be debated over the next few days, the riots spread to many parts of the country, and the parliamentary debate was interrupted on a number of occasions when Tamil members read out telegrams from various outposts in the Eastern Province where Tamils were being assaulted and murdered. The worst violence ensued in Gal Oya, a Sinhalese colonization settlement in the Eastern Province, where transplanted Sinhalese hoodlums took possession of government vehicles and explosives and terrorized and killed dozens of Tamils. The government underreported the violence in Gal Oya, which perhaps helped prevent further violence. However, word soon got out regarding what had actually transpired in Gal Oya and caused the thunderstricken Tamils to seriously question what their future was going to be in a Sinhala-only Ceylon.

The security forces were praised for their conduct during the riots, but both Tamils and some Sinhalese expressed concern that no serious attempts were made to detain those responsible for perpetrating mayhem. This was hardly the case. The police had in fact arrested over one hundred persons during the first two days of the riots, and the security forces had even opened fire on three occasions to quell the rioting. Police also opened fire on a Tamil protest rally in Batticaloa, killing two people.[34] Yet the numbers arrested were paltry relative to the numbers that activated the riots, and the Tamils were justified in feeling angry that hardly any of the Sinhalese who had sparked the violence outside parliament were arrested. Indeed, some Tamils complained that the police had arrested some of their wounded fellows while making no effort to arrest the Sinhalese who had inflicted the wounds. The degree of violence caused Suntharalingam to claim that much of the looting and rioting had been done with the police force's connivance. Suntharalingam even accused the prime minister of having connived at "these acts of hooliganism."[35] Whether such accusations were justified or not, Suntharalingam was simply saying what many in his community believed; the Tamils were coming to doubt that the security forces could be trusted to operate in an impartial fashion. Discrimination by the state's institutions was, in fact, only to be expected, given that the government itself was now disregarding the minority protections afforded by the constitution. Ponnambalam noted:

The history of civilization does not record anything more dark, anything more gloomy than . . . the marshalling of forces and machinery of a Government to enforce one language, the language of one nation upon another. The only parallel in the past has been where at the point of the sword after military conquest the language of the conquerors willynilly has been adopted or forced upon an unwilling conquered race."[36]

The discriminatory language legislation being debated in parliament, the anti-Tamil riots, and (what to Tamil minds at least was) the partial treatment meted out to those involved in the riots undermined Tamils' confidence in the country's governing institutions. Senator Nadesan lamented that "people who preached racial hatred were not brought to book" and added: "I do not think there was in the history of this country ever a time when a Government stood discredited in respect of the preservation of law and order as this Government stands discredited today."[37]

Soon after the satyagrahis were attacked and debate on the Sinhala-only bill had begun, a Tamil politician called attention to the stoning of one of his fellows by the Sinhalese mob outside parliament, only to hear Bandaranaike sarcastically remark, "Honourable wounds of war."[38]

Bandaranaike little realized that he had helped legitimate and entrench a jingoistic Sinhalese Buddhist culture that would eventually provoke a full-scale ethnic war. The first engagements occurred both inside and outside the country's parliamentary complex. In parliament, Tamil politicians, supported by some far-sighted Sinhalese colleagues, passionately defended their language and warned that the Sinhala-only bill would do irreparable harm to relations between the island's two largest ethnic groups. Meanwhile, outside, riots, primarily in Colombo, Batticaloa, Trincomalee, and Gal Oya, led to approximately 150 Tamils being killed and generated harrowing memories for many Tamils.[39]

The Sinhala-Only Bill in Parliament

When Bandaranaike presented the Sinhala-only bill to parliament, G. G. Ponnambalam sought to argue that the bill violated Article 29 of the Soulbury Constitution and was therefore unconstitutional. With Bandaranaike and the MEP determined to pass the bill, and the Speaker having already ruled that a two-thirds vote was unnecessary for it to become law, Ponnambalam's argument, while not without merit, merely delayed the inevitable. This did not, however, prevent the Tamil representa-

tives and their leftist Sinhalese colleagues from eloquently and passionately defending the Tamil language and demanding federalism on a linguistic basis. Tamil was said to be "like Latin, Greek and Sanskrit"; it
was "a living and virile language spoken by over 40 million people."[40]
No sooner had the bill being introduced, than Suntharalingam too ques-
tioned its constitutionality and asked:

Can we . . . follow the ancient usage of the House of Commons—a usage that has
now unfortunately become obsolete—take this Bill, tear it to pieces, trample it
down and kick it right to the end of the aisle? I would do it if I felt that the authority on Parliamentary procedure did not say that that usage was obsolete, for
it would be a kick administered in the proper place, in the proper quarters.[41]

Tamil legislators claimed that the bill would extinguish the Tamil language in Sri Lanka and the Sri Lankan Tamils. Sinhalese legislators justified it on grounds that parity would lead to the "suppression of the
Sinhalese and their entire disappearance from this country."[42] Such hyperbole aside, there is little question that the Tamils were the aggrieved
party. About thirty years prior to this time, Karl Vossler, a German
philosopher of language, had compared religion with language to emphasize the latter's far-reaching powers, writing:

Tolerance of national languages is a still later, tenderer flower of human culture.
Once that insight has been gained, therefore, intolerance on this point is an even
greater idiocy. If I grudge my neighbor his religious beliefs, and hammer my own
into his skull, I shall at any rate be able to excuse myself on the ground that I believe my own to be the only ones that lead to salvation, that his lead to damna-
tion, and that I want to save his soul. But if I throttle my neighbour's mother
tongue in order to impose my own on him, what excuse can I have except that of
conceit, which is made no better by the fact that it is a national conceit? For my
neighbour's language is his inner eye, his form of thought, with all its potentiali-
ties of expression, his spiritual childhood and future. To everyone who has understood this, all repressive measures directed against a language must seem like
crimes against the budding life of their spirit.[43]

Tamils' reaction to the Sinhala-only bill clearly mirrored Vossler's
analysis, and there were primarily four interrelated reasons why they opposed the bill. The first was concern about the impact it would have on
the medium of instruction in schools and on employment opportunities
for the non-Sinhalese. It was obvious that a Sinhala-only policy would
have a radical effect on minorities' future employability, especially in the
state sector. With the bill's passage, Suntharalingam complained, "the
Sinhalese would hold all jobs from top to bottom and the Tamils would
hold the scavenging and latrine cooly jobs."[44] With some Sinhalese, including the minister of education and many bhikkhus, intimating that

they intended to lobby the new government against providing any employment to Tamils until Sinhalese unemployment was addressed, Tamils had every reason to fret about the adverse consequences the legislation might have on their community.

Tamils also opposed the bill because they feared assimilation. Many Tamils believed that there was a Sinhalese conspiracy to make Tamils into Sinhalese. Comments made by Sinhalese in the press, the House of Representatives, and the Senate merely aggravated these concerns. Senator Palipane, for example, defended the Sinhala-only policy by saying that King Dutthagamani, having defeated the Tamil King Elara, had thereafter built "a single, united nation absorbing the concourse of Tamils who were in the armies. There were Tamils in the armies of the Sinhalese king as well. All . . . were absorbed into one nation."[45] Another Sinhalese senator suggested: "The people in the north and the east should co-operate with the Sinhalese people and they should study the Sinhalese language. I know that the people in the north and the east are cleverer than the Sinhalese-speaking people."[46] These comments might have been made in passing, but they reinforced the insecurity among the Tamils, who were well aware that historically many lower-caste Tamils who had settled along the island's littoral had assimilated into the Sinhalese nation. "The imposition of Sinhalese as the sole official language of this country must inevitably and inexorably put an end, even if that is not your real objective today, to the Tamil nation and the Tamil people as such," Ponnambalam averred; "the direct result of this Bill would be . . . the creation of one nation, the homogenising of the population into a Sinhalese-speaking population."[47] Senator S. R. Kanaganayagam, however, was more defiant: "Do not think that once you have passed that Bill, hey presto! every thing will be alright and every Kandiah and Subramaniam will thereafter be Sinhalese?"[48]

Another reason Tamils opposed the bill was their deep-seated fear that it was merely a prelude to other discriminatory legislation. "A government which is capable of perpetrating a piece of legislation of this type is also capable of doing worse than this," Senator Kanaganayagam said.[49] And Senator Nagalingam noted that the Official Language Act was "looked upon by well-meaning people as not an end but as a means. . . . This weapon is being forged with a view to further discrimination."[50] With bhikkhus demanding increasing influence within the government and insisting, along with some Sinhalese elites, that much more needed to be done to enable the Sinhalese to regain their rightful superordinate position, which had been undermined by British colonialism, the Tamils' fears were justified. Indeed, the belief that the island was inexorably heading toward a Sinhalese ethnocracy was starting to take hold among the Tamils, and Sri Lanka's history over the next two decades proved that they were right to harbor such concerns.

The fourth reason Tamils opposed the Sinhala-only legislation was, however, the most important, and it dealt with the cultural and intellectual connection to their language. Ponnambalam passionately argued:

Language is the basis of one's culture, of one's nationality. It is the mirror of the genius of a people. . . . I look upon the denial of equality of status to one's language as almost a challenge to one's history, to one's past, to one's culture and to one's civilization. Language itself is a spiritual matrix in which one's culture lives and moves and has its being. Deprived of that matrix there can be no progress, either spiritual or otherwise.[51]

The Tamils' angry reactions to the Official Language Act were above all based on this cultural inheritance, and on the belief that in violating the trust reposed in them by their ethnic counterparts during the struggle for independence, the Sinhalese were acting perfidiously. A member of parliament lamented:

You [Sinhalese] have promised us all these years that Tamil and Sinhalese would receive equal status; you have lulled us into that belief; you have got us to acquiesce in your policy and asked us to work with you; you have got independence and everything else after we have fought for it together; and now when you are in this position you ask us to get out and give us a good kick—as we were actually given on the 5th and 6th of this month. This, I say, is political treachery of the worst type.[52]

The passionate defense of Tamil and the vociferous opposition to the Sinhala-only legislation were not mere reactions rooted in instrumentalism; they were based on the sense that the Tamils and their language were being betrayed. Ponnambalam said:

I hope it will go down throughout the ages, that I would sooner see my son and my son's son starve than that once again they should have to learn another language to keep their body and soul together. If that is all the association that thousands of years has brought us, if that is all the result of the association we were told we were building up as a nation, let us here and now acknowledge the parting of the ways. . . . You cannot or will not compel, either directly or indirectly, the sons and daughters of the Tamil nation to acquire another language to keep their bellies full or half full.[53]

Ponnambalam was adamant that there should not be another Tamil "generation rise to learn another language of another master."[54] If there had not been a move to make Sinhala the only official language, he said, Tamils would willingly have learned Sinhala to further their prospects. This certainly was the case during the 1930s, when northern Tamils expressed an interest in learning Sinhala. That interest, however, was discontinued when the *swabasha* movement became a Sinhala-only movement. The LSSP's N. M. Perera noted that "the minorities were studying Sinhalese of their own accord. Every school in Jaffna was teaching Sinhalese. When I visited schools in Jaffna the Tamil children proudly recited Sinhalese verses. Tamil public servants in various departments were having special classes and studying Sinhalese. Now everybody has stopped it."[55] Ponnambalam was therefore right when he said: "A true nation could have been welded by making both languages the only official languages. Any hope of a bilingual nation has now been blasted for ever."[56]

Suntharalingam and Ponnambalam were not the only ones passionately defending their language. P. Kandiah, the member of parliament from Point Pedro, who was allied with the Communist Party, gave voice to what many Tamils were perhaps feeling during this time:

When you deny me my language, you deny me everything that I, as a Tamil national of this country, have and can have. You present me with a decision, which you have arrived at in your wisdom, that I and my people should cease to exist, should cease to be. You will not be surprised, therefore, if I refuse to efface myself until with your superior strength, not of logic, not of reason, but of might and weapon, you remove me and my people from the face of this fair land. There is no people servile enough to suffer without resistance the rape of their language, the dearest thing of their lives.[57]

In winding up his speech to the House of Representatives, Kandiah adopted a defiant note:

You will never crush the spirit of a people fighting for its existence. You will never make it forget its history; you might [make] a tribe forget its history, because it does not have much of it, or an individual to forget its past; but not a mass of people with a common, great culture, from which has flown down the centuries some of the finest creations of culture. Outside the battles of the working class for its rights and its life, I cannot think of a fight more righteous or ennobling than the one which the Tamil people are today beginning for their language.[58]

Senator S. R. Kanaganayagam warned that as a result of the passage of this legislation, the Tamil population "for the next so many years . . . will resent the slight on their language, will, for generations, remember the deliberate insult hurled at them, and they will be a source of danger to the integrity of the country."[59] Senator Nagalingam spelled out the danger even more explicitly:

The Tamil-speaking people may appear to be poor worms today, unable to act with immediate results, but I am certain that unless parity of status is granted to them and they are conceded the right to carry on their affairs in their own language, they will somehow find the means of establishing a separate State of their own in this country. I have no doubt about it.[60]

And Senator Nadesan, a Tamil moderate who often criticized Suntharalingam's pyrotechnics in the House of Representatives, passionately denounced the bill and asked, "If this is not tyranny . . . what is tyranny?"[61] With no control over the MEP's agenda or any capacity to thwart it, V. A. Kandiah, the member for Kayts, pleaded: "Please do not divide Ceylon; please do not harm Ceylon. If you persist in this measure, if you implement this Bill, you will go down to history as members of a party which has done the greatest harm to the unity and prosperity of this country."[62]

Some far-thinking leftist Sinhalese MPs who recognized that the Sinhala-only bill had the potential to divide the country beyond repair seconded the Tamils' sentiments. N. M. Perera, for example, pleaded: "Children that are born will live to curse us for having ruined this country. It is in that spirit that I appeal to the Government to take this Bill back, to reconsider their policy."[63] But Bandaranaike and the MEP had come to power by promising a Sinhala-only policy and now had to implement it. "Not even hydrogen bombs can prevent Sinhalese becoming the official language of Ceylon," Mettananda gleefully proclaimed.[64] Consequently, the Official Language Act, No. 33 of 1956, making Sinhala the "one official language of Ceylon," was passed after fifty-two hours of debate early in the morning on June 15, 1956. The vote was sixty-six in favor to twenty-nine opposed, which was just two votes shy of a two-thirds majority. Eager to prove that their pro-Sinhala and -Sinhalese credentials were in no way second to those flaunted by the governing coalition, all the UNP members joined their MEP counterparts to vote for the legislation (see appendix A). On July 6, 1956, the bill also passed in the Senate, by a vote of nineteen to six. The Official Language Act's passage in both houses was the first signal that Sri Lanka had now officially embarked on a particularistic trajectory. It made it powerfully clear that if the Sinhalese parties joined forces, they could ride roughshod over the Tamils, even while claiming that they were operating democratically and constitutionally. To act legally is not necessarily to act reasonably and morally, and the ethnic outbidding the Official Language Act unleashed was unreasonable, if not immoral. As Giovanni Sartori has noted, if ethnic "outbidding becomes the rule of the game," then "somebody is always prepared to offer more for less, and the bluff cannot be seen." What thereafter ensues "is no longer a situation which allows the survival of a political system based on competitive principles. Beyond certain limits, the politics of over-promising and outbidding is the very negation of competitive politics."[65]

The day after the Official Language Act passed the Senate, the *Government Gazette* published Notification No. 10,949, which declared that "where any language or languages has or have hitherto been used for any official purpose such language or languages may be continued to be so used until the necessary change is effected."[66] The languages referred to were, of course, Tamil and English, and the UNP soon started claiming that in publishing Notification No. 10,949, the government had invalidated the Official Language Act and duped the Sinhalese. "Racial riots and hatred were caused by this Bill, innocent citizens killed, property damaged and tension created which has not yet subsided," J. R. Jayewardene declared. "Why was this farce enacted at all if the Premier had any idea of rendering this Bill ineffective? Bloodshed and racial bitterness would have been avoided if he had disclosed his intention."[67] The MEP and UNP were both committed to making Sinhala the only official language, and it is unlikely the events that followed the language bill's introduction in parliament would have been different if it had been the UNP, as opposed to the MEP, that had carried out this promise. But having lost the election to Bandaranaike and the MEP, Jayewardene and the UNP were now determined to do anything to undermine the government. They were also resolved never again to let the MEP outbid them on the ethnic front. Jayewardene's feigned compassion for those who had suffered during the riots was intended to position the UNP to outbid the MEP on the language issue, which it would adeptly accomplish the following year.

Toward the end of the parliamentary debate, the LSSP's Colvin R. de Silva noted that unless the government changed course, the act's passage meant that "two torn little bleeding states may yet arise out of one little state."[68] And the CP's Pieter Keuneman claimed that whereas the Official Language Act had already led to communal riots, "Ten years from now it will be several times worse. This Bill is heading straight for the division of the country. . . . Every order and regulation under it will be a cause for further strife."[69] And Suntharalingam warned: "You are hoping for a united Ceylon. It is a simple matter, Mr. Prime Minister. Do not fear, I assure you [that you] will have a divided Ceylon."[70]

5

INSTITUTIONAL DECAY

THE CONSEQUENCES OF THE
OFFICIAL LANGUAGE ACT, 1956–77

Three salient points should be recognized so as to fully comprehend Tamil reaction to the Official Language Act and the impact of post-1956 language policies on the movement seeking *eelam*. First, language, as a communication medium, helps promote intra- and intergroup interactions by enabling and enhancing identity within a group, even while selectively encouraging distance and hostility between groups. The distance and hostility are best manipulated if the language concerned is territorial or the dialect is isoglossal, thereby creating geographic demarcations and also differentiating between distinctive speech patterns. Territoriality is also important for ethnolinguistic nationalism, because language, as an identity construct enhancing mobilization, is especially likely to accrue salience if the ethnolinguistic group is concentrated and not dispersed. Indeed, a territorially dispersed group would most likely incorporate the dominant *ethnie*'s language for economic and political gain, thereby eroding the capacity to mobilize along ethnolinguistic lines. On the other hand, a territorially concentrated group would likely coalesce to fight for its language rights, if not to seek an ethnic divorce, as a distinct cultural entity. As India's Linguistic Provinces Commission observed, given that country's experience, this was because "language . . . represented culture, race, history, individuality, and finally a subnation."[1] It is thus hardly surprising that the Tamils, as a group with historical claims to a homeland and a linguistic heritage than spans millennia, resorted to emotive protests to maintain their linguistic independence when the Sinhalese created a Sinhala-only language policy.

Second, given that assimilation and group upward mobility are expedited by linguistic homogeneity, a dominant community may find it attractive to impose a national or official language policy. But doing so automatically depresses the socioeconomic possibilities of the group not fluent in that language and promotes a "quasi-hegemonic language regime."[2] If Ernest Gellner was right in his observation that "shared language and culture" ultimately define ethnonationalism,[3] then such "quasi-hegemonic language regimes" may operate as catalysts for separatist movements. By automatically shutting off those not fluent in the official language and curtailing, if not precluding, their educational and employment opportunities, such policies may be used as a mechanism to inhibit or control minority groups' socioeconomic upward mobility. When the affected individuals and groups experience "failure to obtain a status or dignity commensurate with their educational achievements" and have "to settle for low-status and often unprofessional employment ill-matched to their professional diplomas,"[4] anger and frustration set in. This "blocked mobility" inevitably stokes ethnic discord. Discriminatory language policies accentuate ethnic differentiation and make it possible to use the minority identity marker (i.e., language) as a mechanism for mobilization purposes.

Paul Brass has argued that "assimilation," as opposed to "political differentiation," will most likely "occur when social change in a cultural group is slow enough for its members to be absorbed gradually into another, dominant cultural group." Thus, the "conditions for political differentiation are created when social mobilization outpaces assimilation."[5] Depending on group size, miscegenation over a significant period can reduce clear-cut ethnic identities, but few, if any, groups seek to be assimilated. Whereas conciliation and accommodation facilitate coexistence, attempts to dominate often encourage ethnic differentiation, reactive nationalism, violence, self-determination, and secession. This is especially the case if the group is territorial and has claims to a distinct cultural heritage, as in the case of the Tamils in Sri Lanka.

Third, when a majority community pursues linguistic nationalism to attain superordinate status, particularistic ethnic interactions will likely ensue. The more one ethnic group benefits, the more likely those marginalized will rebel. Small-scale violence will soon follow, and over time, the governing forces will become more repressive, while those marginalized turn more aggressive. As the security forces widen their dragnet and innocent civilians are apprehended, tortured, and even killed, many will gravitate toward the rebels and boost their numbers. By then, the institutions representing the state will probably have become irrelevant to minority needs, since they primarily operate to ensure the dominant community's interests. This irrelevance and the attendant institutional decay will completely marginalize the moderate forces and legitimize the quest for separatism. Such are the antecedents to ethnic mobilization, and this general pattern was more or less what happened in Sri Lanka.[6]

Tamil Protests Against the Official Language Act

The Tamil protests that accompanied the Official Language Act's passage were unprecedented. When the bill was introduced on June 5, 1956, Tamils flew black flags on their businesses and homes in the Northern and Eastern Provinces, satyagraha protests took place at numerous locations, students wearing black armbands or ties marched through the streets, while others fasted in protest, prayers were offered at temples, "shops and schools were closed, lawyers stayed away from the courts, and bus services were stopped and a day of mourning was observed."[7] Crowds paraded the streets and denounced the government, especially after it became known that the satyagrahis outside parliament had been assaulted. The timely intervention of some Tamil leaders and calls against reciprocating anti-Sinhalese violence in the Northern Province ensured that the angry protests did not turn riotous. The Tamils' determination to eschew violence, even while not relenting on their demands for linguistic parity, was illustrated by the Federal Party's E. M. V. Naganathan, who warned: "Any attempts at cowardly reprisals will bring nothing but dishonour to a great and peace-loving but determined Tamil-speaking people who will not be intimidated or black-mailed into surrender on a matter which they consider to be the very soul and life of their nation."[8]

No sooner had the Official Language Act passed in the House of Representatives than Bandaranaike sought to pacify the minorities and condition the Sinhalese to compromise with the Tamils. Appearing before the Sri Maha Bodhi, a most holy Buddhist shrine in Anuradhapura, he proclaimed: "Let it not be said, to the eternal disgrace of Buddhism as well as Ceylon, that the Sinhalese, the chosen people of the Buddha, have done harm and injury to our Tamil brothers. To the non-Sinhalese and non-Buddhists I say 'Bear with us, have faith in us, and join hands with us, so that united we can lead our land to peace, prosperity and success.'"[9] The obvious hypocrisy here was that it was partly Bandaranaike's chauvinistic rhetoric and ethnocentric actions that had contravened and undermined almost all that he was now promising to restore. On the other hand, it was also clear that the prime minister recognized that the Tamil language had to be accommodated in some manner.

Tamils characterized the Sinhala-only legislation as leading to an era of "apartheid" that relegated them to subject status.[10] As Naganathan noted, the Official Language Act was "tantamount to a declaration that henceforth the Sinhalese-speaking people alone are the masters and rulers of this country and the others must accept subject status under them, because it goes without saying that a country is ruled in the language of its masters."[11] Tamils subsequently mobilized throughout the island to counter the discriminatory legislation, and the Federal Party organized a convention in Trincomalee and asked participants to march to the convention site from various points in the north and east. Sinhalese extremists wanted the government to ban the march and convention, but Bandaranaike ultimately decided to let the events take place. Tamil leaders had warned that the convention would be conducted "no matter what [Bandaranaike] might do," and the prime minister wisely decided to avoid a showdown with the FP. But with Sinhalese extremists now used to having the ruling politicians bray to their every whim and fancy, Bandaranaike's decision was viewed as a defeat for their forces. Consequently, the chauvinistic K. M. P. Rajaratna, parliamentary secretary to the minister of posts, broadcasting and information and the junior minister who had led the Sinhalese mob against the satyagrahis outside parliament, resigned his office and his membership in the Government Parliamentary Group to protest Bandaranaike's unwillingness to proscribe the FP's march to Trincomalee. Rajaratna's main gripe was that the prime minister had promised him that the FP's march would be banned but had thereafter reneged on his word. There is no reason to gainsay Rajaratna's claim, given that Bandaranaike was predisposed to being all things to all people.[12] Yet, the fact that an influential member in the government could protest like this over an ethnic party's right to conduct a democratic exercise against an anti-democratic bill shows how deep-seated anti-Tamil sentiments were even in official quarters.

The FP's convention was held successfully, and the party made four primary demands. First, it called for the unitary state structure to be jettisoned and for a federal constitution that provided autonomy for the Northern and Eastern Provinces to be instituted in its place. The FP argued that the two and a half million Tamil speakers were "gravely undermined by reason of their helpless dependence on the goodwill of six million Sinhalese people," whose parties could attain power without contesting a single Tamil constituency (as was the case with the MEP during the 1956 election), and that a federal arrangement on a linguistic basis would preclude such Sinhalese dominance.[13] Thus, it also demanded linguistic parity throughout the country. The convention further demanded that Sinhalese colonization in traditional Tamil homeland areas be halted and, finally, that Indian Tamils denied citizenship under statutes passed by the UNP government in 1948–49 be made citizens. The irony in this last demand was that some northern Tamil representatives, submitting to their benighted casteist and communalistic proclivities, had supported their Sinhalese counterparts' denial of citizenship to many Indian Tamils born and bred in Sri Lanka. At that time, S. J. V. Chelvanayakam, who opposed disenfranchising the Indian Tamils, had warned that a government that could deny a group their citizenship rights might one day just as easily deprive the Tamils of their language rights.[14] With this now having come to pass, both Chelvanayakam and the FP were convinced that a federal state along linguistic lines was the only way to preserve both the Tamils' self-respect and the country's territorial integrity.

There was, however, an element of communalism to the FP's demands, in that it was seeking linguistic parity throughout the island but sought to deny Sinhalese the right to settle in what were traditionally considered Tamil areas—and this despite thousands of northern and eastern Tamils having relocated to the predominantly Sinhalese south to earn a livelihood. Yet, part of the FP's argument against Sinhalese colonization was rooted in the fact that successive governments had allocated resources disproportionately to favor transplanted Sinhalese settlers, while deliberately marginalizing the Tamils' needs in the Northern and Eastern Provinces. Thus, from the FP's standpoint, the party was not guilty of a double standard in asserting that the Tamils had a right to linguistic parity, but that the Sinhalese had no equivalent colonization rights; on the contrary, it was forced to clamor for federalism and its other demands because the unitary constitution had deprived Tamils of both equal language facilities and resources for settling their lands.

The FP made a crucial decision when it threatened to launch a nonviolent campaign if the party's demands were not met by August 20, 1957. The Sinhalese feared, however, that a federal constitution would be a first step toward dividing the country, and Sinhalese nationalists and extremist bhikkhus immediately began defaming the Tamils. One prominent bhikkhu said that the only reason the FP made such threats was because the Sinhalese were too lenient. Threatening the deportation of all Tamils in the south to the north, he declared: "If we accede to this demand for Federalism we will see the end of the Tamil race [because] they exist with our assistance."[15]

Anagarike Dharmapala had most effectively propounded the notion that the island's minorities were dependent on the Sinhalese Buddhists' sufferance, and now his epigones and heirs, the extremist bhikkhus and their nationalist allies, adopted the same stance. Many politicians had realized that the political bhikkhus not only shamed Buddhism but might destabilize the country's politics, and that some monks faked patriotism out of ulterior motives. "These bhikkhus are young politicos who have singularly little to do with the teachings of Buddha. Though they wear the saffron gown of the priest by day, they are in fact interested only in political power and the pursuit of women," Sir John Kotelawala said.[16] But such monks had joined the lay extremists to catapult Bandaranaike to power, and this meant that Bandaranaike was captive to their dictates and preferences.

The Sinhalese fear that a federal structure might divide the country was understandable, given that the island's Tamils shared a sociocultural bond with over forty million Tamils in India's Tamil Nadu state, and that Chelvanayakam and others had briefly flirted with the idea of incorporating the Tamil parts of Sri Lanka into India. It also did not help that Ponnambalam Arunachalam, who founded the Ceylon National Congress, had called for a federal arrangement between Ceylon and India in 1918, and that some "less responsible politicians" in South India had made speeches about India being destined to pursue a policy of Manifest Destiny.[17] Yet Indian leaders had made it clear that they opposed such an arrangement and discouraged the island's Tamil leaders from broaching the issue.

The FP's official name was Ilankai Thamil Arasu Kadchi, or Tamil Federal Freedom Party. There was, however, some disagreement as to whether *arasu* meant "sovereignty" or "separate state," and many nationalist Sinhalese had used the word's ambiguity to argue against devolution. Chelvanayakam explained that *Thamil arasu* referred to a Tamil state, and that by this the FP meant a Tamil state within a federal arrangement, but such assurances were ignored by Sinhalese radicals, who were merely interested in exaggerating the island's security concerns to whip up anti-Tamil sentiments. Thus, the two-year period 1956–58 saw Tamil fears over their future under a Sinhala-only regime, coupled with the determination of Sinhalese extremists to prevent any compromise over the language issue, lead to inflamed communalist passions. "People who have never been communalists have become communalists and those who have been moderates have become extremists while extremists have become incorrigible fanatics," one parliamentarian noted.[18]

Groping for a Compromise

The MEP's election manifesto had promised the "reasonable use of Tamil" in a Sinhala-only milieu, and this took on increased urgency after the FP threatened to launch a major satyagraha campaign if its demands were not met by August 1957. With no clear definition of what "reasonable use" meant, Bandaranaike grappled with trying to reach a compromise that was acceptable to the Tamils as well as the Sinhalese extremists. In mid-March 1957, the prime minister announced a vague three-point

scheme that he believed would enable the reasonable use of Tamil and as-
suage the minorities in general. This scheme included regional councils
geared toward some decentralization, constitutional amendments that
would guarantee fundamental rights to all citizens, and the use of Tamil
within the framework of the Official Language Act. The FP objected to
all the clauses of the scheme, since they hardly addressed the party's four
demands. They especially saw the last clause as a gimmick, arguing that
it did not make much sense to say Tamil would be accommodated within
the framework of the Official Language Act, which had given Sinhala
alone official status and invalidated all other languages.

Toward the end of April 1957, Bandaranaike presented four underlying principles whereby to accommodate the reasonable use of Tamil: (i)
Tamils were to have the right to be educated in their mother tongue; (ii)
Tamils would be allowed to sit for public service examinations in Tamil,
but would be required to learn Sinhalese within a certain period; (iii)
Tamils could correspond with state institutions and expect to receive
replies in Tamil; and (iv) local authorities in Tamil areas would be vested
with the power to transact business with the central government in
Tamil. Sinhalese nationalists turned furious especially about the third
principle, since they believed that it more or less allowed for linguistic
parity. For example, F. R. Jayasuriya, the university lecturer who had embarked on a death fast to ensure a Sinhala-only policy, wanted there to be
a propaganda campaign to make Tamils aware of how generous the
Sinhalese had been in allowing Tamils to work in the civil service, and
how ungrateful it would be of the Tamils to demand further concessions.
Bandaranaike's four principles were also ridiculed by J. R. Jayewardene,
who declared: "Having destroyed the unity that existed in this country
for generations, Mr. Bandaranaike now seeks to emasculate the 'Sinhala
Act' through fear of the civil disobedience movement in the Northern and
Eastern Provinces. It seems that one has only to puff and blow at Mr.
Bandaranaike for him to withdraw."[19] Jayewardene, Dudley Senanayake,
and the UNP quite rightly indicted Bandaranaike and his government for
the ethnic violence the Official Language Act had unleashed, but a UNP
government would likewise have had to institute a Sinhala-only policy
and would most likely have replicated the extant anti-Tamil milieu. The
UNP now conveniently vilified Bandaranaike, but doing so had less to do
with concerns about the Tamils or the island's ethnic stability than with
the party's thirst for power at any cost. C. Suntharalingam gave voice to
what many Tamils had by now come to believe when he noted that no
"safeguard is safe with Sinhala political opportunists vying for the
Ceylon Prime Ministerial top-hat!"[20] Yet it must be noted that the Sinhalese political opportunists were well complemented by Tamil political op-

portunists. Suntharalingam and Ponnambalam were prominent among the latter.

There can be no doubt that both Suntharalingam and Ponnambalam sincerely believed that their ethnic community had been betrayed, but better statesmen would have better attuned to the opportunities and constraints facing Bandaranaike and the MEP and tried to reach a compromise with the government, placated the Sinhalese community so that its extremists were marginalized, and promoted a united Tamil front that would have strengthened the Tamils' hand, even as it eschewed communalism. On the contrary, Ponnambalam and Suntharalingam resorted to astringent rhetoric and demanded naïve solutions that no Sinhalese politician could at that stage deliver. Ponnambalam kept demanding linguistic parity, even as he vilified the Federal Party for seeking a federal solution. The call for parity was principled, but it was not practical. No legislation that explicitly undermined the Official Language Act was going to get through parliament, and any Sinhalese politician who tried to repeal or even weaken the act was destined to ruin his and his party's prospects. The only Sinhalese mavericks who supported parity were the Marxists, but they too would soon show a preference for eschewing principle and staying in power rather than embracing principle and being driven from power. One member of parliament noted: "Who is the Prime Minister, I dare to ask, in the present situation who can now go back and tell the people 'Scrap the Sinhala Act.' I would like to meet the man who is going to be Prime Minister, who can go before the country and say, 'Scrap the Sinhala Act because the Federal Party is threatening satyagraha.'"[21]

Ponnambalam equated linguistic parity with equality. Suntharalingam brandished a passionate radicalism and demanded a separate state. In an open letter that he addressed to Bandaranaike, Suntharalingam declared:

[T]he Tamils of Ceylon have been tricked and betrayed! I now hold the view that if one scratches a Sinhalese politician today, one uncovers a cut-throat or a traitor, or both! I . . . tell my fellow Tamils not to trust . . . any Sinhalese Government. . . . They must go all out and save themselves and their posterity from Sinhalese treachery and Sinhala colonialism and establish in the first instance an independent Tamil Illankai [state].[22]

The majority of Tamils might have sympathized with Suntharalingam's rhetoric, but with thousands making a livelihood in the south, few favored separatism as a solution to the language question. This is not to say that Suntharalingam lacked support. "The Tamils must be prepared without any mental reservations to form their own Government," V. Kumarasamy, a former member of parliament, argued. "In other words, they must secede from the Sinhalese, whether it means even a war of independence. The writ of the Sinhalese Government must be made to have no effect in Tamil areas. A parallel Government must be formed, so that we may lead our own way of life without neglecting our own language."[23] These calls for a separate Tamil state provided ample fodder for Sinhalese nationalists and made Bandaranaike's attempt to pacify the Tamils harder, because these captious and bigoted extremists cited such statements as proof that any compromise with the Tamils would only facilitate the country's dismemberment. Ultimately, the quandary for the Tamils was that their most eloquent and prominent leaders were fractionalized, with Ponnambalam denouncing Chelvanayakam for demanding federalism, Suntharalingam vilifying Chelvanayakam in particular for not demanding secession, and Chelvanayakam chastising both Ponnambalam and Suntharalingam for not realizing that with secession hardly an option, and a legislature dominated by Sinhalese, who were in no way dependent on Tamils for getting elected, Tamils could only accomplish self-determination within a federal structure.

As the date for the satyagraha campaign approached, some Tamils and Sinhalese claimed that the FP was more concerned about federalism than about the plight of the Tamil language, but the party's leaders reiterated that the Tamil language would be secure only within a federal structure. As early as 1947, Chelvanayakam had noted percipiently that there might be a movement afoot to make Sinhala the only official language: "The Tamil language is in danger of being annihilated. The Sinhalese leaders are plotting to make Sinhala the only official language in the country, and to relegate Tamil to the Northern and Eastern Provinces and make it a purely local language."[24] The reactive nationalism that the Sinhala-only movement had engendered was what galvanized Tamil support for the FP, and the party realized that failure to address the language issue was tantamount to committing political suicide. But the FP also knew that a federal structure was more beneficial, since it would empower the Tamils with regard to language, employment, and colonization within the Northern and Eastern Provinces. Bandaranaike himself had advocated federalism in his previous political incarnation:

If they consider past history they would see that these communities, the Tamils, the Low Country Sinhalese and the Kandyan Sinhalese have lived [side by side] for over a thousand years and have not shown any tendency to merge. They preserve their customs, their language and their religion. He would be a very rash man who would pin his faith on the gradual disappearance of these differences. . . . In Ceylon, each province should have complete autonomy. There should be one or two assemblies to deal with the special revenues of the island. A thousand and one objections could be raised against this system, but when objections were dissipated some form of federal government would be the only solution.[25]

The problem now, however, was that the Sinhalese in general and the Sinhalese nationalists in particular were adamantly against federalism and wedded to the extant unitary structure. Indeed, numerous delegations of Buddhist monks and Sinhalese nationalists kept meeting with the prime minister seeking reassurance that the government would not vitiate the Sinhala-only policy and the unitary structure. The Sinhala Bhasa Peramuna (Sinhala Language Front) also kept heaping pressure on the MEP government by resorting to hunger strikes and demanding that Bandaranaike withdraw the four-point program he had announced to counter the FP's demands. K. M. P. Rajaratna and F. R. Jayasuriya were among those who launched a hunger strike, and they only relented when a bhikkhu emissary assured them that the governor-general's speech from the throne would not contain any reference to Bandaranaike's "four points." The UNP continued to apply pressure on the government as well, with J. R. Jayewardene thundering: "The time has come for the whole Sinhalese race, which has existed for 2,500 years, jealously safeguarding their language and religion, to fight without giving quarter to save their birthright."[26] To Bandaranaike's chagrin, he now found himself buffeted from all sides. The UNP was resorting to ethnic outbidding to undermine his government; the nationalists were demanding that he withdraw his four-point program for the reasonable use of Tamil and thus questioning his authority; and the FP was making him look ineffective by threatening to destabilize the northeast. He consequently warned that the likes of Rajaratna and Jayasuriya were "very dangerous to the nation, as they are trying to deny the Tamils the rights they should enjoy. They are trying to bring about the collapse of this government with the help of the FP."[27] But such warnings had no impact on the Sinhalese extremists, because they believed they controlled the MEP's agenda. The extremists' confidence, the opposition's outbidding tactics, and the Tamils' demands further proved that Bandaranaike had failed to comprehend how severely the political structure would constrain his preferences.

With Sinhalese nationalists demanding that the FP's satyagraha campaign be banned, and many believing that if carried out, it might symbolically undermine the government's authority over the northeast, Bandaranaike sought to follow a policy of intimidation and adjuration to put pressure on the FP. He claimed that satyagrahis could be charged with treason and also announced that the SLFP had enlisted 100,000 blue shirt volunteers (blue being the party's color), who, if called upon, would assist the police and the army. At the same time, he appealed to the FP to abandon the satyagraha campaign. Bandaranaike's boasting of a force of 100,000 blue-shirted volunteers conjured up images of German and Italian fascism, and the FP derided the prime minister's scare tactics and vowed to carry on the satyagraha campaign even if its members were arrested and charged with treason.

The Bandaranaike-Chelvanayakam Pact

The FP's determination to conduct its satyagraha campaign until the government acceded to its demands and the tensions surrounding the impending event caused the party to suggest negotiations with the prime minister, even though it resolutely rejected Bandaranaike's four-point program. This opening culminated in discussions between Bandaranaike and FP leaders and led the latter to cancel the satyagraha campaign, due to begin on August 20. The decision was announced on July 25, just a day before the party's convention in Batticaloa. The FP's preference to have an agreement with the prime minister before the convention began had led to expedited discussions between the two groups, and the end result was the Bandaranaike-Chelvanayakam (B-C) Pact of July 1957. Under the B-C Pact, the Tamils agreed to drop their demands for linguistic parity, together with their plans for the satyagraha campaign, while the Sinhalese agreed to recognize Tamil as a minority language. This would have allowed Tamil to be used for all administrative purposes in the Northern and Eastern Provinces. Furthermore, in order to deal with Tamil demands for autonomy, it was agreed that regional councils would be created to deal with education, agriculture, and Sinhalese colonization of Tamil areas.

Two issues contributed to the misinformation surrounding the B-C Pact and assisted the disinformation being spread by those against compromising on the language issue. First, while the meetings between the prime minister and the FP were publicized, the details were not made public. Indeed, Chelvanayakam even had those of his members who were involved in or privy to the discussions swear to secrecy until the talks were completed. Second, with the FP members having to attend their convention in Batticaloa and there being insufficient time to discuss the requisite minutiae, the parties postponed issuing a joint statement. This meant that those against the agreement got a head start distorting the B-C Pact. With no official version, many received the subsequent disinformation as gospel.

Associated with this were the comments made by FP members during their convention. The B-C Pact was no doubt an honorable compromise, but the FP had fully capitulated on the language issue, agreed to an arrangement that fell short of federalism, and received no guarantees regarding the disenfranchised Indian Tamils, although it attained some control over colonization. For example, the month before he agreed to the B-

C Pact, Chelvanayakam had opposed regional councils as a solution, dismissing them as "glorified local bodies. They owe their existence not to the Constitution but to a piece of legislation, and a regional council is subordinate in function to the Government of the country. We do not consider regional councils in any way an appropriate alternative to federalism."[28] A federal setup was a structural arrangement—in this case, a call for a structural rearrangement—and Chelvanayakam was right to seek a constitutional change. Yet in trying to avert an impasse, the FP had now agreed to create regional councils. Perhaps seeking to downplay the degree to which the party had compromised, the FP's leaders made self-congratulatory and Pollyanna-ish pronouncements regarding colonization and a future Tamil homeland, even as they passed resolutions that claimed inter alia that the FP was determined to achieve "an Autonomous Tamil linguistic state or states within the framework of a Federal Union of Ceylon" and "Parity of status for the Tamil language with Sinhalese throughout Ceylon" (see appendix B).[29] Indeed, the FP leaders claimed that the B-C Pact laid the foundation for a federal state and was a stepping-stone toward attaining all the party's goals.

The FP leaders' comments that the B-C Pact was a temporary agreement designed to buy time until the party's four demands could be instituted contravened the MEP leaders' statements that the pact had ensured that the FP and the Tamils had embraced Sinhala as the island's sole official language. No sooner had the FP's resolution and the speeches at the Batticaloa convention been publicized than the B-C Pact's opponents went around arguing that they were right to claim that the FP meant to create a federal structure as a precursor to dividing the island. This also allowed them to accuse the prime minister of having dissembled over his agreement with the FP. Mettananda accordingly asked the prime minister to "unlock his tongue and disclose to the country what his arrangement has been with the Federal Party." He lamented that Mr. Bandaranaike had signed off on a future Tamil Raj. Manipulating the near racist attitudes of some Sinhalese toward the Indian Tamils, Mettananda further warned that "the colonization schemes of the North and the East will be the mustering points of thousands of illicit immigrants and the colonies will be the spring board for the ultimate overthrow of the Sinhalese by the Tamils."[30]

What the FP and the Sinhalese extremists preferred not to fully disclose was that the agreement appeared to suggest that while colonization would be overseen by the regional councils, the councils themselves would be under parliamentary control. This suggested that while the B-C agreement as advertised would have allowed the FP to have a significant say in who qualified to colonize the northeast, parliament could technically veto the regional council's preferences. Bandaranaike reiterated this and noted that colonization would come under the minister of lands, not the FP. He also repeatedly noted that prior to negotiating the B-C Pact, he and the FP had agreed that there was to be no compromise on Sri Lanka's unitary structure and the Sinhala-only policy. Bandaranaike further crowed that his diplomacy averted the instability that would have ensued from a satyagraha campaign in the northeast: "In this period of peace I, with the power of the spoken word, won over the Federalists. If I did not do this, what would have been the result? Thousands would have been massacred in a bloody war."[31] Never the man to shy away from political puffery and ever eager to embellish his deeds, Bandaranaike even claimed that his agreement with the FP could be characterized as "one of the greatest victories a leader had achieved in the last hundred years."[32] His sycophants readily endorsed the prime minister's arguments. These smarmy lackeys claimed that Bandaranaike deserved the Nobel Prize for solving such an intractable problem and one, parodying Winston Churchill, observed that "never in [the] history of human life was so much owed by so many to one man."[33] "The Prime Minister's achievement in averting a national disaster by peaceful negotiation was an achievement worthy of a 'bodhisatta' [sic]" (a Buddha-to-be), W. Dahanayake, the MEP's education minister, even suggested.[34] Such panegyrics notwithstanding, by the time Bandaranaike and the FP had issued two joint statements regarding the pact and regional councils (see appendix C), it was the extremists' message that had taken root.

Tamils who clamored for linguistic parity or secession, and who therefore opposed the B-C Pact, resorted to rhetoric that only worsened the situation. G. G. Ponnambalam claimed, for example, that the Federal Party had "deliberately and in cold blood and without any misapprehension and misunderstanding whatsoever stabbed the trusting Tamils on the back."[35] For Ponnambalam, the B-C Pact represented "a complete and abject surrender of the cherished fundamental right of the Tamil people to live on terms of equality, dignity and self-respect with the Sinhalese in the whole island" and was also "a tragic betrayal of the economic future of Tamil youth for generations to come in the matter of employment." He had no doubt that the FP's capitulation was a "pathetic effort to save face before the gigantic bluff of its threat of civil disobedience was called," and that the FP was now complicit in creating "a local version of apartheid."[36] Ponnambalam even argued that the pact was "an agreement with the Federal party leaders and not with the Tamil people."[37] Other Tamils branded the pact "ignominious," because it relegated their "community to a very subordinate and inferior position in an apparently free country."[38] Suntharalingam derided it as a "most contemptible capitulation of the Tamil cause"[39] and admonished "the Tamil leaders and their followers of this generation [to] realize . . . that they will prove to be traitors to their past history, to their language, to their culture and to their self-respect if they do not man, woman and child as one rise up to conserve their birth rights and their human rights."[40] Suntharalingam denounced the FP, saying that despite the party's claim that the pact was a first step toward federalism, "I think this is a step backwards; this is not a step forwards. Until you entered into this so-called agreement you were a forward, fighting people. By this agreement you are a backward, running-away people—cowards!"[41] For Suntharalingam, the B-C Pact was nothing more than a "Bloody-Cut-throats' Agreement," and he vilified both the FP and the prime minister. His vitriol was on full display in parliament, as indicated by the following altercation with Bandaranaike after Suntharalingam had accused him of leaving the UNP "like a rat":

> *The Hon. S. W. R. D. Bandaranaike:* You damned low scoundrel, you say that outside this House and I will rub your dirty face in the dust. There is a limit to abuse of this nature, even from a low and despicable man of your nature who is not accepted by your own community. You are a disgrace to the community which you represent and the other Tamils. You damned bloody mongrel that you are. How long are we going to put up with such a low despicable person who, I do not think, any Tamil will accept as his leader.
>
> *Mr. Speaker:* The Hon. Prime Minister must contain himself. He will get an opportunity of replying. Order, please!
>
> *The Hon. S. W. R. D. Bandaranaike:* Damned low scoundrel. We have been putting up with a lot of this for seven or eight hours, most despicable charges made against us, against the Sinhalese race as a people. I certainly do not believe that they are the views of responsible Tamils. There is a limit to this kind of thing. Let the hon. Member realize that. . . .
>
> *Mr. Suntharalingam:* As long as those words remain not withdrawn, I shall continue with my remarks. In 1951 the Hon. Prime Minister left the Cabinet like a rat and then proceeded in his own way to disturb the peace and concord of this country only to wear the Prime Minister's top hat—and he speaks like a mongrel. He has had his genealogy traced to the "Feringhee" [a derogatory term for those with Portuguese ancestry].[42]

Such impassioned rhetoric did not merely undermine the decorum the country's legislature was respected for; it also emboldened the extremists on both sides. The irony was that Ponnambalam, Suntharalingam, and others claimed that the FP had betrayed the Tamils by negotiating the B-C Pact, even as Sinhalese radicals and the UNP claimed Bandaranaike had betrayed the Sinhalese by doing likewise.

While still giddy over becoming prime minister, Bandaranaike had told an interviewer: "I have never found anything to excite the people in quite the way this language issue does."[43] Yet by now it was clear that people, both Sinhalese and Tamils, had gotten so hyperexcited over the language issue that some were talking about an impending civil war, and Bandaranaike realized that the B-C Pact provided the best chance to pacify the Tamils without compromising his position with the Sinhalese. "We are proud of being Sinhalese," he declared. "We like to preserve and to foster those things that matter to the Sinhalese. We are not prepared to deny the same position to others, for that will not be in keeping with one's conception of either justice or equity. That is what we are trying to do." He added: "Nationalism in a narrow way only creates hatreds and ill-feeling amongst people . . . and all this must now cease. We are not out in the quest of creating a Herrenvolk in this country."[44] It was also clear to many that the Tamils by now harbored legitimate grievances and that, especially given the past Sinhalese-Tamil camaraderie, they had reason to feel betrayed. "We have taken the language issue before the people and created a division which is going to be eternal, which is going to be to the eternal disgrace of our people," one Sinhalese parliamentarian admitted. "We are letting down a race, a people who have helped us in our fight for freedom."[45]

In October 1955, by which time Bandaranaike had crowned himself king of the Sinhala-only movement, he had said: "I think it is quite possible to declare Sinhalese the official language . . . and to give due recognition to the Tamil language in the legislature, in the administration and in education. It can be worked out without causing any hardship or difficulty."[46] And soon after the B-C Pact had been publicized, the prime minister criticized Sinhalese who opposed it, saying:

> The attitude of some of the extremists on the Sinhalese side can only be justified if they say that the Tamils have no place in Ceylon, and if they remain here at all they can only do so on such conditions as the Sinhalese choose to lay down, and that they are here as slaves or semi-slaves under the Sinhalese. While not having the courage openly to adopt that attitude, they adopt a position with regard to the language issue . . . which is nearly conformable with such an attitude.
>
> If on the other hand the position is that the Tamils are also fellow citizens with the Sinhalese and have the right to live here with self-respect and the rights and privileges of citizens, then it is necessary, while safeguarding the legitimate rights of the Sinhalese, to recognize the legitimate rights of the Tamil citizens.[47]

The B-C Pact, to a significant extent, provided the opportunity for the prime minister to reverse the attitudes perpetrated by the Sinhalese extremists and also rectify the ethnocentric milieu his opportunistic pronouncements during the election had legitimated. But if the pact represented a commendable compromise between Sinhalese and Tamils during a period of rabid communalism, it also enabled the opposition UNP, supported by the omnipresent Sangha and Sinhalese nationalists, to resort to ethnic outbidding and traduce the pact. Thus, the militant Eksath Bhikkhu Peramuna (United Buddhist Monks' Front), Sinhala Jatika Sangamaya (Sinhala National Association), Sri Lanka Sangha Sabha (Sri Lanka Sangha Association), Sinhala Bhasa Peramuna (Sinhala Language Front), and the Tri Sinhala Peramuna (Tri Sinhala Front) all claimed that Bandaranaike had "sold the rights and heritage of the Sinhalese to the Tamils," demanded that the B-C Pact be abrogated, and threatened to conduct their own satyagraha campaign if Bandaranaike refused to accede to their dictates.[48] The UNP's Working Committee also issued a statement claiming that the B-C Pact effectively abrogated the Official Language Act. The party's logic was simple. If Tamil became the official language of the Northern and Eastern Provinces, then Sinhala would cease being the official language throughout the island. Ergo, the Official Language Act would have been negated. The UNP's Dudley Senanayake consequently claimed that the B-C Pact would ensure that the "majority race is going to be reduced to a minority" and that "Ceylon would in no time be a state of India." He added: "I am prepared to sacrifice my life to prevent the implementation of the Bandaranaike-Chelvanayakam Agreement, which is a racial division of Ceylon under the guise of the Regional Council System and is an act of treachery on the part of the Prime Minister."[49] It was no secret that Senanayake and J. R. Jayewardene were competing to lead the UNP at this time, and it is perhaps not surprising that each now sought to outdo the other and solidify his credentials on the anti-Tamil front, even as they both vilified Bandaranaike.

After agreeing to include Tamil as an official language in the State Council in May 1944, J. R. Jayewardene had pleaded that "we want the Tamils . . . to co-operate with us to make Sinhalese and Tamil the official languages in this country."[50] At that time, Jayewardene astutely observed: "It is the universal franchise that has brought the English-educated and the masses together, and it is the impulse created by the use of the universal franchise . . . which will ultimately make Sinhalese and Tamil the official languages of this country."[51] He further opined:

Language . . . is one of the most important characteristics of nationality. Without language, a nation stands a chance of being absorbed or of losing its identity. With language, it has a chance of living for centuries. It is because of our language that the Sinhalese race has existed for 2,400 years. . . . This House, I am sure, will vote with me that English should be deposed from its position as the official language of the country and Sinhalese and Tamil, the ancient languages of our people, spoken by over 80 to 90 per cent. of our people, should be made the official language[s] of Lanka.[52]

In January 1955, Jayewardene reiterated the Sinhala language's ancient status and emphasized that having "Tamil and Sinhalese as official
languages of Ceylon and as the media of instruction is in keeping with
our heritage and with modern psychological education."[53] Indeed, two
days before the Sinhala-only legislation was introduced in parliament,
Jayewardene again indicated that parity might be a better option, saying:

No Government should and could make Sinhalese the official language by tram-
pling down the language rights of over a million of the permanent residents of the
country. It cannot thrust [in]to the wilderness the cherished languages of these
people. The doors of the public services should not be closed to the thousands of
youth who did not know Sinhalese for no fault of their own. *Surely that was the
way to sow the seeds of a civil war* [emphasis added].[54]

Such common sense was utterly disregarded a year later when
Jayewardene, eager to become the UNP's leader, organized a protest
march against the B-C Pact from Colombo to Kandy and thereby showed
that the ethnic card could be played in both inter- and intraparty machinations.[55]

Sinhalese jingoists and extremist bhikkhus ably assisted these ethnic
entrepreneurs. F. R. Jayasuriya vilified the B-C Pact, for example, saying:
"The Prime Minister has performed the last act of treachery against the
Sinhalese people. The bitterest enemy of the Sinhalese would not have
done any worse."[56] A leading bhikkhu said that Bandaranaike was "trying to ruin our race."[57] Another bhikkhu warned that the Sinhalese were
destined to occupy a position worse than that of slaves if the pact were
not abrogated, and that he and his saffron-robed colleagues would therefore "tear up that agreement to pieces and throw it in the face of the
Prime Minister." He vowed that the agreement with the FP would only be
implemented over the monks' dead bodies and warned that just as the
bhikkhus had helped Bandaranaike become prime minister, they could
also remove him from power if they wanted to.[58] Such intimidating
rhetoric catalyzed opinion against the B-C Pact. More important, it
shows how the Tamils were being used "as whipping horses for contending Sinhala political factions"[59] and how political, social, and religious
groups had coalesced to undermine Tamil confidence in the country's
governmental and nongovernmental institutions alike.

The "Anti-*Sri*" Campaign

In late March 1958, forty state-owned and -operated buses were
transferred north with the Sinhala letter *sri* marked on their license
plates. A recent directive by the minister of transport and works,
Maitripala Senanayake, under the Motor Transport Ordinance was

responsible for the letter's use on all vehicles. At a time when linguistic nationalism was raging in both communities, the Tamils inevitably viewed this as another Sinhalese attempt to dominate all minorities. As the FP's C. Vanniasingam argued, being forced to use the Sinhala *sri* in Tamil areas was akin to been told: "'Instead of the British master, you now accept the Sinhala master: the Sinhalese are today the rulers, you are the ruled.' That is how we at least understand the imposition of the Sinhala 'Sri' on us."[60]

As early as November 1956, G. G. Ponnambalam had condemned the government's decision to use the Sinhala *sri* letter on all vehicles and encouraged Tamils to protest the law by using the Tamil equivalent of the letter. Tamils, especially in the Northern Province, had actively protested against the *sri* letter as early as January 1957, when so-called anti-*sri* satyagrahis prostrated themselves before the Jaffna prison superintendent's *sri*-marked vehicle demanding that he substitute either the Roman letter used hitherto or the Tamil letter *shri* for the Sinhala *sri*. The FP had protested against using the Sinhala *sri* on vehicles in Tamil areas and even conducted a civil disobedience campaign. The Tamil *shri* was substituted for the Sinhala *sri* and Roman letters on many Tamil-owned vehicles, with exceptions being made for government officials and Sinhalese traveling in Tamil areas, and the FP's members of parliament were the first to change the letter on their license plates. Doing so violated the law, but FP leaders and their supporters had carried on their campaign in front of the police, who avoided arresting anyone. Only around twenty vehicles were involved in the FP's first anti-*sri* campaign, most of which belonged to Tamil political leaders. The aim was to protest a law that symbolically imposed the Sinhala language on Tamils, and FP leaders claimed that their civil disobedience campaign had achieved this goal. The prime minister, on the other hand, characterized the enterprise as a failure and warned that the government would take stern action against those who broke the law in the future. This did not deter the many Tamils who boycotted buses belonging to the Eastern Bus Company, until it agreed to change its license plates, and picketed against Tamils who had failed to put a Tamil *shri* on their vehicles. Some tension ensued when certain Sinhalese in the Eastern and North-Central Provinces retaliated by painting the Sinhala *sri* on Tamil businesses, but the initial anti-*sri* campaign took a back seat when the parties began discussing Bandaranaike's plans for the reasonable use of Tamil. The license plate issue was catapulted back to prominence, however, after the government dispatched the forty Sinhala *sri*-numbered buses to the Northern and Eastern Provinces.

The government had not prosecuted anyone for using the Tamil *shri* on vehicles. When Bandaranaike visited Batticaloa, even he, perhaps inadvertently, traveled in a car with Tamil lettering on its license plate. All this had led Tamils to believe that the government was resigned to looking the other way as some among them flouted this particular law. Thus, when the Ceylon Transport Board sent the new Sinhala-lettered buses to the northeast and the minister of transport threatened to deal severely with those who tampered with them, the Tamils were provoked. The FP felt especially insulted, given that party leaders had met with the minister of transport and thought that he had agreed not to send Sinhala-lettered buses to the northeast. According to the FP, the minister had indicated that the issue would be satisfactorily solved after regional councils were instituted, given that these councils would thereafter be responsible for registering all vehicles. The minister, Maitripala Senanayake, said, however, that while he had discussed the matter with FP leaders, he was also beholden to protect the people's interests, and given that there was a scarcity of state-owned buses in Tamil areas, he had sent the new buses to accommodate the Tamils' needs. That a member of the MEP would go out of his way to ensure Tamils' needs and comfort by doing exactly what they had campaigned against was deemed ludicrous, and the FP consequently began a campaign to efface the Sinhala *sri* from all buses and substitute the Tamil letter. The FP's Naganathan announced that "the Sri campaign had . . . become the acid test of the Tamil-speaking people's determination to resist the political domination of the majority linguistic group over them and it is a token of their irresistible resolve to be free and equal citizens with their Sinhalese brothers in this their common motherland."[61] Some Sinhalese in parliament suggested that the Tamils were overreacting, given that the new law was merely symbolic. The FP's Amirthalingam argued:

If this is such a minor matter why do the Sinhalese people worry so much about it? No, it is not such a minor matter. The Hon. Minister of Labour said that the letter "Sri" is only a symbol. I agree, but as far as the Tamil people are concerned the Sinhala "Sri" is certainly a symbol of their eternal slavery in this country, a slavery which every self-respecting Tamil is not prepared to tolerate in his territory."[62]

Amirthalingam added:

I say in all humility as a member of the great Tamil race which has held its own against all intruders at all times of history that even if only one Tamil man is left in this Island he will fight to the bitter end and to death to assert our rights. We will fight for equality of status with the Sinhalese people and never accept this stamp of inferiority.[63]

While the Tamil letter had hitherto, in the main, been pasted on license plates, the new FP campaign began tarring the Tamil *shri* over English and Sinhala lettering. Soon thereafter the Sinhalese retaliated by smearing tar over Tamil lettering on street signs, commercial boards, buses, public buildings, and vehicles with English lettering. On April 1, 1958, the pro-*sri* or anti-anti-*sri* campaign, as it came to be called, spread to many areas, with the All Ceylon United Bhikkhu Association and K. M. P. Rajaratna leading the crowds. Some Buddhist monks eagerly participated in effacing Tamil and English signs, and even the prime minister's Cadillac, displaying a "Left Hand Drive" sign in Sinhala, Tamil, and English, was tarred.[64] Tamil leaders had conducted their anti-*sri* campaign in an organized manner and ensured that little vandalism was perpetrated, and only a few Sinhalese shops in the north had their Sinhala board names effaced. The pro-*sri* campaign that transpired in the south, however, was an utterly mobbish affair:

Barebodied, sarongs held shoulder high displaying genitals unashamedly, armed with tar-pails and brushes and brooms they shrieked through the streets of Colombo tarring every visible Tamil letter on street signs, kiosk name boards, bus bodies, destination boards, name plates on gates, and bills posted on walls. They were armed with ladders to reach roof level where necessary.[65]

Their activity was so thorough that Ponnambalam only mildly exaggerated when he later noted, "Six hours, and the whole of Ceylon could not see a Tamil letter."[66] The police were ordered not to intervene, and the mob consequently ran amok with utter impunity: when they ran out of Tamil signs, some among them turned to tarring anyone they could find who looked Tamil. According to a Tamil member of parliament, Tamils "had the Sinhala 'Sri' painted on their foreheads, on their faces, and a lady was forced to take her jacket off and the Sinhala 'Sri' was painted on her back."[67]

When a band of bhikkhus, amid all this, parked themselves outside the prime minister's residence and refused to budge until the B-C Pact was abrogated, Bandaranaike used the bus controversy in Jaffna to cave in. The B-C Pact's death knell was indisputably signaled when Bandaranaike "tore up a copy of the pact in front of the assembled monks who clapped in joy."[68] Bhikkhu leaders demanded, however, that Bandaranaike guarantee the pact's abrogation in writing, and the prime minister wrote a statement that said the B-C Pact was "null and void." Ten years earlier, a member of parliament had mocked Bandaranaike's quicksilver predisposition by saying, "When God created Mr. Bandaranaike, He gave him the necessary organs, except the backbone."[69] If Bandaranaike's vacillation over the B-C Pact especially vindicated such a comment, the ethnic animosity consequently generated also highlighted the extents to which the language issue had undermined interethnic relations. Just before the Official Language Act was introduced in parliament, a Tamil senator complained about the bhikkhus' excessive influence in politics, saying, "this is not a people's Government but a priests' Government. They give the orders, and whether those orders are right or wrong we execute them."[70] That certainly turned out to be the case with regard to the B-C Pact. As James Manor's excellent biography of Bandaranaike has noted, the prime minister was hardly sympathetic to the extremist demands made by the nationalists and by some in the Sangha, but he was a weakling "in the face of pressure from [these] Sinhalese bigots."[71] Thus, while the country's political structure no doubt constrained Bandaranaike from implementing his preferences, his weak and indecisive character was also a major reason for his pandering to the extremists.

Bandaranaike had met with his ministers the day he abrogated the B-C Pact, and they jointly decided that Sinhala *sri* numbered buses would be sent all over the country, including the Northern and Eastern Provinces, full police protection would be provided for the buses operating in the northeast, and the country's laws would be strengthened so that those effacing license plates could be prosecuted more effectively. Tamils had protested the Sinhala-numbered license plates, because they saw their imposition as culturally domineering. In that sense, the anti-*sri* campaign was an extension of the Tamils' protest against the Official Language Act. But the B-C Pact's abrogation and the government's determination to assertively impose a pro-*sri* policy now starkly proved that the Sinhalese were indeed the superordinating group. Concomitantly, it made it clear that the island's governments could not be trusted to protect Tamils' rights or eschew treating them in a subordinating fashion, even in areas where Tamils were the dominant group. "The sri affair is a petty thing," the FP's Naganathan commented. "The sri campaign is not a means to an end nor an end in itself, but merely resistance to the first Sinhala only law imposed on the Tamil-speaking people."[72]

At least with regard to the Sinhala-only policy, it was clear that Bandaranaike was following through on a campaign promise, no matter how divisive and egregious that promise was. In this instance, the prime minister had reversed course merely because he could not muster the courage even now to take a principled stand. Bandaranaike shamelessly blamed the FP for his volte-face in abrogating the B-C- Pact and repeatedly assured the Tamils that he alone would treat them fairly. The FP indicated publicly that it was not surprised by Bandaranaike's perfidy, but party leaders worried in private that the FP had been compromised.

Suntharalingam was the Tamils' most obstreperous Cassandra, and in opposing the B-C Pact, he had issued the FP a warning: "I do not wish it to be recorded that the Tamils allowed themselves to be fooled or tricked or betrayed a second time by Prime Minister Bandaranaike."[73] Suntharalingam had also taunted the prime minister by saying: "Can a leopard change its spots? Can Prime Minister Bandaranaike fail in his perfidies?"[74] The radical stance of Tamil extremists like Suntharalingam had now been vindicated. Sinhalese extremists had once again successfully undermined the possibility of renewed Sinhalese-Tamil unity, and the moderate FP had been made to look naïve and fatuous. All leading Tamil politicians embraced defiance soon after the B-C Pact was abrogated, but there was little consensus among Tamils as to how to respond. Ponnambalam claimed the Tamils had lost nothing, because the B-C Pact had been a great "catastrophe" to begin with. Suntharalingam thundered: "Instead of riding in Sinhala Sri buses as slaves, they [Tamils] should prefer to walk as free men with their heads erect. When a similar insult was offered to the negroes in some States in America, they brought the whites to their senses in double quick time by using their own feet and by boycotting the buses."[75]

The FP sought to reapply pressure on the government by calling for a nonviolent campaign. The party continued to conduct campaigns that painted over the Sinhala *sri* lettering on vehicles, and some passengers refused to pay the fare when traveling on *sri*-numbered buses. Now, however, FP leaders and their supporters were arrested, and they were released only on bail. Such defiance notwithstanding, it was soon clear that these civil disobedience campaigns were impotent affairs, given that they could not sway the majority community's politicians, who were not dependent on or interested in creating patron-client ties with Tamil voters. While no doubt useful to highlight Sinhalese ethnocentrism and intransigence, these campaigns also, to an extent, distracted from the larger issues facing the Tamil nation. The most fundamental issue was the degree to which Tamils' status within the state had suffered since the UNP and MEP embarked on their ethnic outbidding crusade, and how matters could be rectified in a democracy that was clearly moving toward becoming an ethnocracy. The events that followed highlighted the extent to which the state considered Tamils a dispensable minority, how marginalized they had consequently become, and why many began to believe that their only recourse was to secede, using violence if need be.

The 1958 Anti-Tamil Riots

Soon after the B-C Pact was abrogated, a train carrying delegates to a Federal Party convention in Vavuniya (on May 23) was derailed and its Tamil occupants were beaten. The accompanying anti-Tamil riots in Colombo and other areas saw hundreds murdered and thousands displaced. Sinhalese living in the north were also attacked and forced to relocate south.[76] Although the train derailment was the immediate cause galvanizing the riots, the anti-Tamil climate generated by the Official Language Act was more broadly culpable. Bandaranaike sought, however, to blame the Tamils for the riots. D. A. Seneviratne, a one-time mayor of Nuwara Eliya, had been murdered on May 22. No one was certain who had done it or what the motive was, but when Bandaranaike addressed the country over the radio on May 26, he claimed that Seneviratne's killing was responsible for the anti-Tamil rioting in various places. The implication was that a Tamil had murdered Seneviratne, and that this had sparked the mayhem. Thereafter Sinhalese thugs justified even more anti-Tamil violence to avenge Seneviratne's killing. A frightened and flummoxed Bandaranaike avoided taking decisive action himself and instead asked the governor-general, Sir Oliver Goonetilleke, to impose a state of emergency four days after the riots had begun. By making his irresponsible, perhaps calculated, statement about Seneviratne, Bandaranaike was complicit in lengthening the riots. But at least publicly, he showed neither remorse nor a sense of responsibility for his actions. To do so would have required him to show remorse for passing the Official Language Act as well, and neither Bandaranaike nor the Sinhalese extremists were willing to take the blame for the ethnic mess they had wrought.

Donald Horowitz has argued that three conditions are especially conducive to causing riots: rioters must harbor a sense of moral justification for committing violence, they must be confident that they can run amok with impunity, and they must believe that their opponents are competing with them for benefits and resources that are rightfully theirs.[77]

These conditions were most certainly obtained during the 1958 communal riots. First, rhetoric using the Dutthagamani and Vijaya stories had inculcated the belief among many that the island was a Buddhist preserve, to be superintended by the Sinhalese, and that their community was therefore duty bound to resort to whatever measures were necessary to protect the Sinhalese Buddhists' dominant status. With the activist bhikkhus justifying violence to ensure that the country remained *Sihadipa* and *Dhammadipa,* and the Tamils easily caricatured to be undermining that goal, the rioters who attacked Tamils felt they were fully justified in their actions. Indeed, with the political bhikkhus who had taken the lead inciting anti-Tamil sentiments, many goondas (thugs) became monks, because wearing the venerated yellow robe allowed them to move about freely and avoid arrest. "Monks were ordained in Polonnaruwa in those few days faster than ever before in the history of *Upasampada,* the Buddhist ordination ceremony," Tarzie Vittachi wrote.[78] These miscreants showed no guilt over defiling the sacred saffron robe. On the other hand, there was no reason to harbor much guilt, given that the extremist bhikkhus, by their indulgence in fecund racist rhetoric and anti-Tamil actions, had already defiled their habiliments. The UNP had also published a number of accounts that repeatedly called upon the patriotic Sinhalese to "kill" and "murder" Tamils to prevent the country from being divided, and there can be no doubt that some among the rioters were influenced by such propaganda.

Second, the anti-Tamil climate that the Official Language Act had generated allowed Sinhalese nationalists and thugs to commit mayhem with impunity, and they took to looting, murdering, and raping in a frenzy. "When a Government, however popular, begins to pander to radical or religious emotionalism merely because it is the loudest of the raucous demands made on it, and then meddles in the administration and enforcement of law and order for the benefit of its favourites or to win the plaudits of a crowd, however hysterical it may be, catastrophe is certain," Vittachi astutely observed.[79] The CP's Pieter Keuneman noted that Tamils "had lost confidence in the machinery of the state to protect them,"[80] and Chelvanayakam lamented: "When Government after Government despises the Tamil people and carries on a policy that relegates them to a disgraceful, inferior, position in this country, is it not natural for the masses to take the cue from the Government and descend to such levels as have been exhibited during the past few weeks?"[81] Indeed, disregard for law and order took root as soon as the MEP attained power. On the day the victorious government entered the House of Representatives, its supporters stormed the chamber, running over representatives' desks and chairs, and many even took turns sitting in the Speaker's chair. When the State Council debated J. R. Jayewardene's motion to make Sinhala the island's only official language in 1944, one member had suggested that "we would not like the Sinhalese language to be the language of the State Council, because we are afraid of the vulgar mob who will come here and take our places."[82] Now, a dozen years later, the mob had certainly descended on them, for never before had such an unruly spectacle been witnessed in the country's parliament. When the police tried to intervene against the crowd, Vittachi notes, they were ordered: "'Let the People have their way.' The crowds jeered and hooted at the police. Inspectors and constables looked on shamefacedly while they got their first glimpse of the *Apey Aanduwa* [Our Government] mentality in action."[83] This mentality also saw parliamentarians barge into police stations and demand that their arrested minions be summarily released, thereby paying scant regard for the island's laws and conventions. Indeed, it was soon made clear to opponents and the security authorities that those associated with the government were above the law. Consequently, those inciting the

1958 riots did so with a clear feeling of impunity. The Official Language Act and the pro-*sri* campaign, coupled with the emasculated state response, had especially inured the anti-Tamil radicals, and they now went about perpetrating the worst atrocities ever visited on the Tamils. "The mob was certain that the police would never shoot and their experience of the past two years during which the politicians had publicly denounced the police and taken the side of the crowd, right or wrong, increased the fears of the police."[84] In those rare instances when the police did fire on the rioters, they and their parliamentary representatives castigated the police for "shooting Sinhalese." The message communicated to the police was that this was a government of Sinhalese for the Sinhalese, and that they consequently had no business muzzling its supporters, no matter how atrocious their actions. At Kurunegala, K. M. P. Rajaratna even incited the crowd saying: "There are 10,000 policemen. Kill them all: then we can deal with the Federalists. They are the only people who are standing in our way."[85] Even a Sinhalese member of parliament observed: "So many people participated in these riots with a feeling of complete immunity, with the feeling 'Our Government would not act against us.'"[86]

Finally, with the FP demanding federation and the government having agreed once to a pact that would have controlled, if not banned, Sinhalese colonization, those who rioted in the Sinhalese colonies in the northeast rightly realized that the Tamils, if successful in their designs, would undermine their socioeconomic upward mobility. The Tamils had therefore to be taught a lesson, and it was unlikely the Sinhalese would ever have a more opportune moment for teaching it. This was clearly the sentiment among many Sinhalese businessmen as well, who tried to manipulate the prevailing disturbances for economic advantage. They did so by burning down their Tamil competitors' businesses or merely forcing the latter to leave the area. In some areas, leaflets were passed around exhorting Sinhalese to end the Tamils' economic influence in the south. Some suggestions on how to do so included: do not talk to Tamils, do not buy from Tamil shops, do not go to Tamil restaurants, do not consult Tamil doctors, do not employ Tamil lawyers, do not rent or sell houses, shops, or land to Tamils, do not work in Tamil houses or shops, do not go to see Tamil films, and so on.[87]

While significant anti-Tamil violence took place in Colombo and some suburbs, the worst violence took place in the colonization areas, where Sinhalese employees from the Land Development Department and the Irrigation Department, using government vehicles to transport themselves, went about raping and murdering Tamils and looting their property. The need to assert themselves against Tamil colonists or Tamils in general was related to the insecurity most Sinhalese colonists felt, given their transplanted status and the FP's attempts to ban such Sinhalese colonization. Many village headmen had come under political pressure to relocate some of their villagers to the colonization settlements, and they had conveniently gotten rid of troublemakers in this way. Prisoners granted early release upon the promise that they and their families would colonize government settlements also joined these undesirables.

Sinhalese nationalists, including bhikkhus, lost no time in fanning the flames of communalism. They distributed leaflets encouraging the Tamils' marginalization and even demanded that many leave their occupations and homes. One leaflet read in part:

All Sinhalese employees are . . . urged to be in readiness to disobey, defy and ignore any order or request made by any Tamil Officer placed in authority. This must be done collectively. The campaign will go on until Sinhalese is made the sole official language in the length and breadth of Sri Lanka.

Sinhalese men in whose veins run Aryan blood must stand united to defy and exterminate our common enemy—the Tamil. These wretched and ungrateful blood-suckers who have been and are living on our charity from time immemorial are even scheming to destroy us. Look at the Tamil cooly. He is allowed to come here and earn a living. In his own country [India] he is starving and eats rotten carcasses. He is ignored and despised by his own 40 million Tamil blood-brothers. What is he trying to do now? He wants to own our country. . . . Show no mercy to those most ungrateful parayahs. They are parasites. Sparrow hawks. A Tamil is a Tamil. In Malaya, Burma, and in our own dear land the problem is the same. They come as discarded beggars and when treated kindly out of sympathy they bite the hands that feed them. Why cannot the boastful, arrogant 40 million Tamils who own half a continent, if they have anything called self-respect, recall these blood-brothers, sisters and mothers to be cared for by others? Low-bred scum of God's creation.[88]

The anti-Tamil riots were primarily against the Ceylon Tamils. But as evidenced by the quotation above, the nationalists used the resentment many Sinhalese harbored toward the Indian Tamils to blur the distinction between the two groups. Furthermore, the FP had taken up the Indian Tamils' cause, demanding citizenship for them, and Sinhalese nationalists feared that if the FP were successful, the two Tamil groups combined would represent an even greater threat to their community's dominant political and economic status.

This time around, the Tamils in the northeast did not act passively. Instead, some gangs in the Jaffna Peninsula went about burning Sinhalese property and forcing Sinhalese out of their homes. Tamil rioters also tried to destroy the Naga Vihare (Buddhist temple) in Jaffna town, but timely action by the police prevented this. Rioters did succeed a few days later, however, in completely destroying the Nagadipa temple in Nainativu.

The government kept this secret and went about rebuilding the temple in record time. As Vittachi noted, "if its destruction had not been kept a tight secret, all the vigilance and guns of the armed services would not have prevented a wholesale massacre of the Tamils."[89] Ultimately, the anti-Sinhalese riots in Jaffna forced over two thousand Sinhalese to leave the Jaffna Peninsula. This number did not compare to the over ten thousand Tamils evacuated in Colombo alone, but the number of Sinhalese living in Jaffna was small compared to the large numbers of Tamils who had settled in and around Colombo. All reports indicate that no Sinhalese were killed in Jaffna, but the fact that thousands in the north and south were forced to leave clearly showed that the 1958 riots were the worst communal riots the country had faced up to that point in time. Bandaranaike noted as much when he addressed the SLFP's Working Committee in July, but he failed to take the blame for not bringing the situation under control much earlier. When the riots were debated in parliament, N. M. Perera rightly noted that he and the LSSP had "pointed out that you were, in June 1956, really sowing dragon's teeth and that you would harvest a monster that would try to swallow you up in the end. Is that not what has happened today?"[90] But there was no eliciting any acknowledgement that Bandaranaike and the MEP were in the wrong. Instead, the prime minister and party leaders went about proclaiming that the island belonged to both the Sinhalese and Tamils and that the people could always trust the MEP to be fair to all communities! Bandaranaike even had the gall to claim that "if the U. N. P. Government had been returned the position in this country would have been ten times worse and there would have been bloody revolution here before this."[91] Suntharalingam, however, minced no words when accusing the prime minister: "Owing to the Hon. Prime Minister's failure, he has turned out to be a murderer."[92] Suntharalingam added: "If any day the history of these times is written by an impartial historian, he will place on record that the partition of Ceylon had its origin in your dirty communalist careerism."[93] Even Ponnambalam, who was no doubt a communalist, but whose communalism was rooted in the demand for equality, warned: "Believe me you will not impose Sinhalese on the corpses of Tamils. You will drive them and it will not be a question of a federal state or an autonomous state in a federal union, it will be a complete truncation, a complete separation."[94]

The 1958 riots were brought under control only after the governor-general ordered the army and navy to ruthlessly impose their authority. The official death toll was placed at 158, which the UNP's Dudley Senanayake justifiably claimed was a "big lie." Tamil parliamentarians argued that at least 2,000 Tamils were killed.[95] Somewhere from 300 to 400 would perhaps be more accurate.[96]

Bandaranaike shamelessly claimed that while the killings and subsequent military action were "regrettable," he had nevertheless "succeeded in restoring peace and order and safeguarding the lives of nine million people."[97] The FP and Jathika Vimukthi Peramuna (National Liberation Front), a chauvinistic Sinhalese party, were banned soon after the riots, and their leaders were placed under house arrest for nearly three months. The ban on the parties was not lifted until the end of October. By now it was crystal clear to the Tamils that they were an utterly defanged minority community in a country that was fast being transformed into an ethnocracy. In this budding ethnocracy, Tamils were dispensable, and the state showed an undisguised preference for the majority community. Such partiality was made clear soon after the 1958 riots, when the prime minister made a point of visiting the Thurstan Road camp housing Sinhalese who had been forced to evacuate Jaffna but did not go to the nearby Royal College camp housing Tamils.

The Tamil Language (Special Provisions) Act

All politicians recognized that the 1958 riots were linked to the MEP's Official Language Act. Just as the anti-*sri* campaign was an extension of the Tamils' opposition to the act, the 1958 anti-Tamil riots were influenced by relations between the communities since the discriminatory legislation was passed. With the FP leaders under house arrest, the MEP presented a draft bill on the "reasonable use" of Tamil, which was eventually passed as the Tamil Language (Special Provisions) Act, No. 28 of 1958 (see appendix D). This allowed for Tamil to be used in schools, the universities, during public service examinations, and for all administrative purposes in the Northern and Eastern Provinces, and for those educated in Tamil to communicate in that language with government departments and local bodies in the northeast.

Those non-FP Tamils left in the House opposed the bill, which they considered subservient. Tamil fears about assimilation were merely reinforced by comments by certain Sinhalese legislators along the lines of "no doubt . . . in ten years' time my Tamil friends in the North will beat some of our boys down South in Sinhalese when they sit for examinations."[98] Tamils believed that the government's proposal to allow "reasonable use" of Tamil was merely a gimmick, and in any case, the bill did not adequately address their grievances. "Do I want your permission to speak Tamil to my children?" Ponnambalam demanded. "Do I want your per-

TABLE 4
Government Staff Posts Held by Sinhalese and Tamils, 1957

	Sinhalese	Tamil	Others	% of staff posts held by Sinhalese	% of staff posts held by Tamils
Accountants Service	56	109	5	33	64
Audit Office	10	24	1	29	69
Income Tax Office	39	30	9	50	38
Census and Statistics	4	10	1	27	67
Government Analyst	8	12	2	36	54
Rural Development	6	6	—	50	50
Survey Department	27	28	3	47	48
Irrigation Department	50	64	4	42	54
Marketing Department	9	9	1	47	47
Department of Health	486	386	49	53	42
Ministry of Labour	12	16	2	40	53
Dept. of National Housing	4	2	3	44[a]	22[a]
Registrar of Companies	—	3	—	—	100
Department of Industries	8	13	—	38	62
Public Works Department	62	64	11	45	47
Department of Government Electrical Undertakings	26	26	12	41	41

SOURCE: *Ceylon Daily News*, "Mettananda on the Reasonable Use of Tamil," July 14, 1958, p. 4.
[a]Percentages for Department of National Housing were changed, since these calculations were erroneous.

mission to sing my songs in Tamil, to pray to my gods in Tamil, to speak to any man I come across in Tamil? Reasonable use of Tamil, if that is what it means, is an insult added to the injuries we have already suffered."[99]

The transition to a Sinhala-only milieu was heady, and many Sinhalese expected immediate changes. They were consequently disappointed when these did not materialize as quickly as they had hoped or prove as significant. For example, to the chagrin of Sinhalese nationalists, the Civil List for 1957 indicated that Tamils continued to be disproportionately represented among government managerial personnel (see table 4). Employment featured prominently in both communities' calculations. "Nadars, Nalliahs and Suppiahs used to comprise eighty per cent of our doctors, lawyers, engineers, and scientists. Within two years there will be an end to that and Somapalas, Leelawathies and Gunapalas will monopolise these professions," the minister of education, W. Dahanayake, boasted, for example, to a southern audience.[100]

Only three months after the worst ethnic riots in the country, both some in the government and many outside it were still indisposed to accommodating the Tamil language, even in this flimsy form. The opponents of the bill included not only chauvinists bent on humiliating the

Tamils but the many who begrudged the Tamils their overrepresentation in the civil service and felt that this legislation would do nothing to reduce, or would even increase, their share of government jobs. C. R. Beligammana, the representative for Mawanella and parliamentary secretary to the minister of local government and cultural affairs, voted against the bill and was immediately expelled from the Government Parliamentary Group. The representative for Welimada, Mrs. K. M. P. Rajaratna, whose husband was among the most notorious Sinhala-only bigots, broke down sobbing and then tore the bill to pieces in protest. With all Tamil representatives present in parliament opposing it, and the opposition and the UNP boycotting the debate to protest the ongoing emergency rule, there was little doubt, however, that the bill would pass in the House of Representatives. This it did, by a vote of forty-six to three.

Bandaranaike's Assassination

In August 1958, defending his decision to pass the Tamil Language (Special Provisions) Act, and with the leaders of the Federal Party under house arrest, Bandaranaike had lamented: "Every kind of opprobrious epithet has been flung at me. Sinhalese anonymous letters have come to me [saying] that I have been a traitor to the Sinhalese people. From the Tamil point of view I have simply ruined the Tamil race. All types of things have been said. They are all wanting to bump me off."[101]

His foreboding proved accurate: the chauvinistic forces he had manipulated to attain power had turned against him. In September 1959, a bhikkhu, Talduwe Somarama, following orders from a leading monk, Mapitigama Buddharakkitha, shot Bandaranaike in his official residence, and the prime minister died soon thereafter in hospital.

The tragedy of Bandaranaike's premiership was that even though he sincerely cared for the lower classes, wanted their lives enriched, and therefore unleashed a near revolution to ensure that the common people were fully mobilized to create their own government and also benefited from it, he did so by dividing the country ethnically. He had persuaded himself that the extremists could be muzzled once he was in power, but they turned out to be intractable and made insatiable demands on him. A more principled man would have eschewed scapegoating the country's dominant minority, even while trying to rectify the legitimate grievances the Sinhalese harbored. But this would have been the hard route and would most likely have not guaranteed him the premiership. Bandaranaike therefore took the easy, albeit unprincipled, path that gradually began corroding the country's institutions and laying the foundation for a separatist movement. In making use of communalist chauvinism to become the country's prime minister, he had created a political climate of "rowdyism and lawlessness,"[102] and he himself ultimately fell victim to it.

The emotional Tamil protests against the Official Language Act, the attendant anti-Tamil riots, the divisive rhetoric emanating from both sides, and Tamils' rampant disenchantment with the state should have prompted the government to conciliate the minorities. Instead, the language issue was used to marginalize the Tamils and benefit the Sinhalese. The rabid anti-Tamil rhetoric that preceded the March 1960 and July 1960 elections shows, moreover, that Sinhalese politicians had no qualms about continuing their ethnic outbidding. This especially turned out to be the case under Bandaranaike's widow, Sirimavo.

Toward Sinhalese Dominance and Tamil Separatism

"In Solla's [S. W. R. D. Bandaranaike's] time Sirima presided over nothing fiercer than the kitchen fire," according to a Bandaranaike relative.[103] It was a time when, to the general applause of civilized opinion, women in many parts of the world were overcoming barriers and becoming empowered. Ironically, however, the growing antipathy between Sinhalese and Tamils might have been reversed had Mrs. Bandaranaike stuck to her "kitchen fire." For as one author observed, "it could be said with no exaggeration that it was the widow [Sirimavo] who was the mother of Tamil militancy!"[104]

Supported by party leaders, this political novice was catapulted from the kitchen to the premiership, becoming the world's first woman prime minister in July 1960. Where her husband had vacillated and sought to accommodate the Tamils for opportunistic reasons, Sirimavo Bandaranaike, whether out of inexperience, ignorance, or a deliberate disregard for Tamil concerns, consistently eschewed ethnic compromise and instead pursued an agenda that further poisoned relations between the Sinhalese and Tamils.[105] Mrs. Bandaranaike was a woman of limited education and "had not the foggiest idea of how to run a government," *Time* magazine said.[106] She relied completely on Felix Reginald Dias Bandaranaike, the pugnacious yet likewise inexperienced nephew of S. W. R. D. Bandaranaike, who became her finance minister and the government's chief spokesperson in the House of Representatives, while Mrs. Bandaranaike initially took shelter in the less hostile Senate.

Ethnic outbidding was deeply entrenched in Sri Lanka by the time of S. W. R. D. Bandaranaike's assassination, and in the March and July 1960 elections, the UNP and the SLFP vied to persuade Sinhalese voters that they were best equipped to ensure Sinhalese dominance. Mrs.

Bandaranaike campaigned as a "weeping widow" in both elections, backed by film footage of S. W. R. D. Bandaranaike and his recorded speeches. The UNP complained that she seemed to "produce tears to order." A 1951 constitutional amendment had increased the number of elected members in the House to 151 (from the previous 95), and in the March 1960 election, the UNP secured 50 seats, while the SLFP garnered 46. With the FP winning 15 of the 19 seats it contested, the party became the key to a coalition government. The FP made four demands on Dudley Senanayake, who was now the prime minister, as a condition for supporting the UNP: for regional councils that controlled colonization and irrigation within their areas; for Tamil to be recognized as the official language in the northeast, and for facilities to be provided for Tamil to be used in other areas; for changes to the country's citizenship laws as they applied to Tamil-speakers; and for Indian Tamils to be allowed four appointed members until their citizenship rights could be negotiated. Senanayake refused these demands, and the UNP lost a vote of no confidence in April, which led to the parliament being dissolved and a new election scheduled for July.

The more or less acephalous SLFP nominated Mrs. Bandaranaike to lead the party in the July election, which also saw the LSSP, the Communist Party, and the Jathika Vimukthi Peramuna resort to no-contest pacts with the SLFP in order to ensure that the UNP was defeated. The LSSP, which had hitherto advocated parity, even switched to a Sinhala-only language policy. When Mrs. Bandaranaike and other SLFP leaders met with Chelvanayakam and assured him that they would accommodate the Tamils' grievances once in power, along the lines S. W. R. D. Bandaranaike had wanted to, the FP encouraged Tamils outside the northeast to vote for the SLFP in the July election. The UNP retaliated with what was by now the opposition's standard role, claiming that the SLFP and the FP had made a secret pact that would divide the country. Dudley Senanayake thereafter went around claiming that if he had agreed to the FP's demands, he "would have become the most treacherous man in history." He refused to betray the Sinhalese nation, he said, "even if I am given a kingly crown with [the] right to rule the whole world."[107] But Mrs. Bandaranaike's lachrymose campaign invoking her husband's memory, coupled with the no-contest agreements with the leftists, won her the premiership. The SLFP captured seventy-five of the ninety-eight seats it contested, while the UNP was reduced to a mere thirty seats in parliament. The SLFP's support came mostly from rural areas, where the party won two-thirds of its seats.[108] The need to cater to the fears and aspirations of rural Sinhalese voters, who were the key to winning elections, was never lost on the party, and Felix Dias Bandaranaike was speaking for the entire SLFP when he gratefully admitted a few years later that "there are no considerations which stand higher than the need to preserve the rights of the Sinhalese people."[109]

When the election ensured that the SLFP had a majority to govern on its own, Mrs. Bandaranaike cavalierly disregarded the unwritten promises made to FP leaders. She thereafter pursued policies that further marginalized the Tamils and complicated Sinhalese-Tamil relations. Indeed, it is difficult to overemphasize how blatantly Mrs. Bandaranaike's governments disregarded Tamils' rights. For example, her first government refused to provide scholarships for doctors, engineers, and scientists to do postgraduate work abroad unless they were fluent in Sinhala. Given that Sinhala was unnecessary for pursuing such studies, Tamils rightly claimed that the government was systematically seeking to undermine their upward mobility.[110] In the 1960s and early 1970s, Mrs. Bandaranaike used her influence to ban Sri Lanka's Dravida Munnetra Kazhagam (Dravidian Progressive Front, or DMK), an insignificant group named after the significant and influential Tamil Nadu political party, and she also banned the importation of Tamil films, magazines, and newspapers, and denied entrance visas to Tamil movie stars and Tamil Nadu's chief minister.[111] While the DMK in Tamil Nadu sympathized with and supported Sri Lanka's Tamils, and while Sri Lanka's leaders had legitimate concerns regarding this, such actions displayed a blatant disregard for Tamil cultural preferences.[112] As the FP's Amirthalingam complained, this was "an attempt to cut off the Tamil-speaking people in this country from the cultural life, from the development of the Tamil language and from the Tamil people of South India. I think these are all directed towards one end and that is making this country purely a Sinhalese country; making the Tamil-speaking people first of all slaves and then assimilate and destroy them altogether."[113] Amirthalingam's hyperbole aside, there was little doubt by the mid-1960s that Mrs. Bandaranaike was determined to impose the Sinhala-only policy on the Tamils. Indeed, the above actions were benign when compared to her other anti-Tamil policies.

In November 1960, the government presented and soon thereafter passed the Language of the Courts Act, which was designed to promote and expand the use of Sinhala in all courthouses. The FP's Working Committee decided to cease discussing the language issue until the government amended this bill and made provisions for Tamil to be used in the courts in the northeast. The bill did not even mention Tamil, leading M. Balasunderam, the representative for Kopai, to say:

They [the Sinhalese] are moved by that patriotism, that Sinhala-only patriotism, and they think they can ignore the Tamils, their language, even their very existence. They think that by not mentioning Tamil they can wipe off the face of the earth the Tamil race and their language. Remember that the [Tamil] race and the language have withstood the vicissitudes of time and circumstance in a manner that compels admiration. If this little Minister of Justice thinks that by not mentioning Tamil he can finish the Tamils once and for all, he is hugging an illusion.[114]

The government's obstinacy in this regard only confirmed that Sirimavo Bandaranaike and other Sinhala-only extremists were obsessed with imposing their language, if needs be forcibly, on the Tamils. Indeed, it often appeared that the Bandaranaike duo, Sirimavo and Felix, only craved kudos among the Sinhalese and were willing to completely marginalize the Tamils in the process. For the Tamils, the notion that the Northern Province, where nearly 98 percent of the population was Tamil-speaking, now had to gear itself up to litigate in Sinhala was considered ludicrous and tyrannical. The FP's Naganathan thus vociferated: "The language of a people is the soul of that people. When the soul departs you are left with a corpse. If you take our language under this Bill, what remains of us? A stinking corpse. Is that your policy, to take away our very life and create in this country a stinking corpse? That is the policy of the Government as exhibited in this Bill."[115] The Tamils now felt betrayed again. For, only six months after the SLFP had sought to form an alliance with the FP and promised to address the Tamils' grievances, Mrs. Bandaranaike and her government had passed an act that further confirmed their community's subordinate status. "We will have to undergo very great pain and our wives, children, brothers and mothers will have to suffer untold misery," Naganathan said. "The attitude of the Government shows only one thing—that the Tamil-speaking people and religious and other minorities have no future."[116]

In August 1958, the Tamil Language (Special Provisions) Act had been passed under S. W. R. D. Bandaranaike's government, but as a result of the political flux engendered by his assassination, the regulations needed to implement the bill were not approved. Once she had come to power, however, Mrs. Bandaranaike's government rigorously imposed the Sinhala-only policy. Government officials not proficient in Sinhala were denied bonuses and salary increases; all public servants hired in the post-1956 period were given three years to learn Sinhala or forfeit their jobs; and, most chafing to the northern Tamils, Sinhalese public servants were transplanted north to ensure that the government apparatus in Tamil areas operated in the Sinhala language. Throughout all this, no effort was made to implement the Tamil Language Act. On the other hand, a well-calibrated government policy was under way to hire Sinhalese into the government service. Consequently, while 30 percent of the Ceylon Administrative Service, 50 percent of the clerical service, 60 percent of engineers and doctors, 40 percent of the armed forces, and 40 percent of the labor force were Tamil in 1956, those numbers had dropped to 20 percent, 30 percent, 30 percent, 20 percent, and 20 percent respectively by 1965. By 1970, they had plummeted to 5 percent, 5 percent, 10 percent, 1 percent, and 5 percent respectively.[117]

The government kept reiterating that the Tamils needed to be patient, and that it was not anti-Tamil, even as Mrs. Bandaranaike and her minions worked assiduously to relatively deprive them. "It is cruel and heartless for Madam Prime Minister to preach patience to a people who are being kicked about by the puny poltroons in the Public Service, whose actions are indirectly being blessed by Members of the Government," M. Sivasithamparam, the Tamil representative for Uduppiddi, declared.[118] When an education commission recommended that Sinhala be taught as a second language to students in the northeast, efforts were made to implement this expeditiously. "The Tamil-speaking people have been clamouring and agitating for a Tamil university since 1956, but that has been denied to us," Amirthalingam complained. "But the Hon. Minister of Education says that even if one Tamil child wants education in Sinhala it is his duty to provide for such education. And he wants to send two thousand Sinhalese teachers [to the Northern and Eastern Provinces]."[119]

The country's mission schools had benefited immensely from discriminatory British policies, and Buddhist leaders had long viewed these institutions as proselytizing centers. These schools continued to rely on government financing in the postindependence era, even though they admitted relatively few non-Christians. Mrs. Bandaranaike acceded to Buddhist organizations' demands and nationalized these mission schools in 1961. Excepting some (mostly Roman Catholic) schools that chose to stay private, all of them were brought under government control. That the linguistic nationalist movement influenced the nationalization of the schools was clear when all schools, both private and government-controlled, were forced gradually to cease English-medium instruction, so that by the mid-1970s, English was taught only as a second language—notwithstanding that once they were at university, students read for their examinations in Sinhala, Tamil, or English. Nationalizing the schools by and large affected both Sinhalese and Tamils equally, but it was an unmitigated disaster for the country's excellent denominational schools.

The Military in the Northern Province

The Official Language Act of 1956 took effect on January 1, 1961, and on February 20, 1961, the FP launched a satyagraha campaign to prevent the Sinhala-only law and the Courts Act from taking effect in the northeast. The satyagrahis blocked the entrances to most public buildings, the FP set up a postal system and issued its own postage stamps, and the general administration of the Northern and Eastern Provinces was brought to a standstill for nearly two months. When the government finally intervened in mid-April, the military brutally attacked the satyagrahis. The government also imposed emergency rule, detained the FP's leaders for over six months, and banned the party for a year. This meant that the FP was not able to conduct political meetings or publish any literature. Tamils arrested under the emergency regulations were, moreover, denied bail and held without trial. When Tamils complained that their civil liberties and rights were being violated, Felix Dias Bandaranaike suggested that a little dictatorship was not a bad thing if it ensured order in the country.[120] Bandaranaike was merely twenty-nine years old when he entered parliament, but Mrs. Bandaranaike had made it clear that she was "going to lean heavily on Felix. He is very intelligent, though young."[121]

The emergency rule imposed on the northeast allowed the military to operate brutally with impunity, and Tamils soon viewed the military as an occupation force. When the military was stationed in the Northern Province during the 1958 riots, Ponnambalam had admonished the government to "not add to the incubus, the horrible burden that the Tamils have to bear. Do not make it appear that you will rule with the Military, because he who rules by force does not rule at all."[122] This advice was disregarded, and SLFP leaders justified the military's overreaching as unavoidable. During subsequent years, Tamils were ordered about and searched in humiliating fashion, beaten, and stoned by soldiers passing by in military vehicles, and Tamil women were occasionally raped, so that by the mid-1960s, the army especially was seen as a Sinhalese occupation force. The army and navy personnel stationed in the Northern Province served "no useful purpose, except to increase the price of toddy," Chelvanayakam complained. "They go about in search of toddy and having drunk toddy they go about in army vehicles and assault men and molest women."[123] The government claimed the military's presence in the Northern Province was necessary to halt illegal immigration from South India, but most Tamils believed, like Amirthalingam, that the military was "also there to beat us down occasionally."[124] Amirthalingam added that "if the Government pursues this line, persists in this attitude, the inevitable consequence will be a division of the country. The Tamil-speaking people are not going to lie down, they are not going to surrender without a fight."[125] But such warnings fell on deaf ears. The propensity to placate and favor Buddhist Sinhalese at the expense of Christian Sinhalese, too, led to an attempted coup in 1962, most of the officers implicated in which turned out to be Christians.[126]

With both the UNP and the SLFP pandering to the chauvinists, resorting to ethnic outbidding, and passing discriminatory laws, the country's various institutions also began marginalizing the Tamils. This was mostly evident among the police and defense forces, whose domineering tactics when dealing with the Tamils were not confined just to the northeast. Tamils throughout the country were soon exposed to petty indignities that undermined their confidence in the security forces and the government. Most Tamils recognized that the milieu created by the Sinhala-only legislation was responsible for the humiliations they were now experiencing, but Sirimavo Bandaranaike's policies especially encouraged the police and security forces to harass Tamils. "If the policy is Sinhala only, it means that Tamils do not count," the FP's E. M. V. Naganathan said. "And if the police make a distinction between a Sinhala imperialist and a Tamil subject, it is because your laws are wrong. I do not blame the police if they happen to be rude to a Tamil."[127] Naganathan further observed that the security forces' discriminatory treatment of Tamils was "a reflection on society; it was a reflection on the Government. Their policy makes these poor policemen to behave like thugs."[128] By the mid-1960s, many Tamils, especially those living in southern areas, were also receiving responses from the government in Sinhala to correspondence in English or Tamil. That such correspondence was understood in the language in which it was written but nevertheless replied to in Sinhala shows that there was a coordinated effort being made by the state to impose the Sinhala language on the minorities. The insouciant arrogance that Mrs. Bandaranaike and her government displayed when dealing with the Tamils was especially made possible by the way the island's electoral system enabled the Sinhalese to elect approximately 80 percent of the representatives to parliament. The Soulbury Commission, having calculated future representation along communal lines, had ruled that "of the 95 elected seats, 58 would go to Sinhalese candidates and 37 to the minority candidates (Ceylon Tamils 15, Indian Tamils 14, Muslims 8), making, with the six nominated seats, a minority representation of 43 in a House of 101."[129] Yet by the time Mrs. Bandaranaike came to power, there were only twenty-nine representatives of minorities in a House of 151 members. As Amirthalingam noted, "they [the Soulbury commissioners] said that it would be 37 in a House of 95, and we have today 29 in a House of 151!"[130] Ponnambalam's Tamil Congress had disagreed with the Soulbury Commission and argued that its constitution was unlikely ever to lead to there being more than 29 out of 101 seats for the minorities,[131] but it was now clear that they had actually overestimated minority representation. The Citizenship Acts passed in 1948–49 and Sinhalese colonization were mostly responsible for this decline in minority representa-

tion, but the fact remains that Sinhalese overrepresentation in the legislature allowed the Sinhalese parties, and especially Mrs. Bandaranaike and her government, to ride roughshod over Tamils' preferences. Naganathan complained:

> You duped us into accepting the Constitution. You solemnly declared before the Soulbury Commission that there would be equality in all matters, that you would accept Tamil and Sinhala as equal languages, that you would accept the Tamils as equal partners. Today the cry is that the Buddha Sinhala should rule, all others be damned.[132]

Because of this overrepresentation of the Sinhalese, governments had "prostituted democracy and made it a meaningless term as far as the minorities in this country are concerned" Amirthalingam lamented. Reinforcing Naganathan's comments, he added: "It is this horrifying travesty of representative Government giving the Sinhalese majority an overwhelming weightage which has resulted in the surrender of every major political party to chauvinism in order to capture power."[133]

Tamil Grievances over Resource Allocation and Colonization

Aggravating Tamil grievances were various governments' discriminatory policies regarding resource allocation and colonization. For example, successive governments deliberately avoided allocating resources to Tamil areas and sometimes even unscrupulously shelved internationally sponsored development projects in these areas. When development projects were occasionally commissioned in the north and northeast, they were designed mainly to benefit Sinhalese colonizers.[134] The government's selectivity could be viewed as highly rational, however, for to develop the Tamil areas would bring them closer to self-sufficiency and perhaps inadvertently promote future designs of secession. On the other hand, such policies clearly smacked of discrimination, and the Tamils justifiably construed them as yet another governmental attempt to keep them dependant on their ethnic nemesis.

Successive governments continued to resettle large numbers of Sinhalese in areas Tamils considered their historic homeland. Independent land clearance by peripatetic swidden farmers had once been common in these regions, but the clearance and land development projects advocated by Sinhalese elites, beginning around the mid-1930s, and intensifying after independence, were undoubtedly aimed at creating Lebensraum for the Sinhalese. As far as Tamils were concerned, the resettlement polices had two fundamental aims: first, to dilute the region's ethnic concentration so that Tamil electoral representation was curtailed, and, second, to delegitimize claims regarding a distinct Tamil geographical entity. Colonization

in disputed territories succeeded so well that by the 1960s, the government could create an entire new district in the Eastern Province that was nearly 80 percent Sinhalese. This Amparai district was carved out of the Batticaloa district, where Tamils had been a majority even at independence.

The resettlement policies inevitably became a political thorn in the sides of successive Tamil parties. For the Sinhalese, however, the appeal of peasant resettlement was engendered by pangs of primordialism, a sense of necessity, their Buddhist religion, and territorial insecurities. In the first instance, the Sinhalese pointed toward their ancient civilization in the Anuradhapura region, in the North Central Province, and claimed ancestral rights of occupation, although Sinhalese bureaucrats also referred to high population density in the west and south to justify Dry Zone resettlement. The widespread belief that Sri Lanka was *Sihadipa* and *Dhammadipa*, the island of the Sinhalese who were ennobled to preserve and protect Buddhism, also contributed to the zeal for resettlement. Related to all these justifications was—and is— fear of the Tamils in India's Tamil Nadu. This has led to a minority complex in this majority community. "We are carrying on a struggle for national existence against the Dravidian majority," Sinhalese believe. "If the Tamils get hold of the country, the Sinhalese will have to jump into the sea."[135]

The Senanayake-Chelvanayakam Pact

The SLFP, which from its inception was a pro-Sinhalese Buddhist party and under Mrs. Bandaranaike treated the Tamils with supercilious arrogance, was defeated in the March 1965 election and thereafter resorted to chauvinistic and racialist propaganda to put the UNP-led coalition that succeeded it in power on the defensive on language and ethnic issues. The UNP captured sixty-six seats in the 1965 election, while the SLFP managed to win only forty-one. The FP won thirteen seats, and the Tamil Congress won three. The UNP government that was subsequently formed under Dudley Senanayake was called a "National Government" because it relied on the FP, the Tamil Congress, and five other minor parties to maintain a majority in parliament. The FP argued that "this is a National Government as opposed to a communal Government which we had during the last nine years,"[136] but the SLFP rightly raised the question of the ethnic outbidding tactics the UNP had hitherto championed and put the latter on the defensive. Apropos of the UNP's alliance with the FP, Felix Dias Bandaranaike commented:

The U. N. P. hates the Tamils when it is convenient for them . . . [and] call those who associate with them "betrayers"; but when it suits them and when

they are hard pressed they remember national unity as a great objective. When the U. N. P. finds things difficult because of them [the FP], they condemn them and decry them; when the U. N. P. cannot survive without their help, the highest motives of national unity begin to inspire the Hon. Prime Minister.[137]

Putting words in the prime minister's mouth, Bandaranaike taunted Senanayake saying: "Had I become Prime Minister with 80 seats, I would have been for Sinhala only; but because I did not get enough seats, I am a little bit Tamil also!"[138] Bandaranaike could easily have said as much about his own party, given that the SLFP had sent an emissary to negotiate an alliance with the FP after the 1965 election.[139] Ultimately, what his comments and the UNP's alliance with the FP showed was that the main Sinhalese parties were willing to work with Tamil politicians only whenever they needed the latter's support to attain power, and that they condemned such support whenever it was given to their opponents. This not only promoted Sri Lanka's culture of ethnic outbidding but also encouraged false hopes among the Tamils, who kept believing that every alliance or potential alliance would finally rectify their grievances.

The UNP and FP leaders had agreed to what came to be called the Senanayake-Chelvanayakam (S-C) Pact of 1965 (see appendix E) to ensure the latter's support for the government, but the agreement was not publicized. The S-C Pact, if implemented as agreed to, would have recognized the Northern and Eastern Provinces as Tamil-speaking, amended the Language of the Courts Act of 1961 so that both Sinhalese and Tamil could be used in all courts, and given Tamils first preference when colonizing Tamil areas, but placed district councils under the central government's authority. It turned out, however, that Dudley Senanayake had equivocated regarding the S-C Pact, because he later told Chelvanayakam that he had hoped that the UNP and FP would come to trust each other sufficiently to make implementing the pact meaningless![140]

The SLFP's Felix Dias Bandaranaike and Sirimavo Bandaranaike, however, used the agreement to traduce the UNP and FP alliance, claiming that the UNP had promised the Tamil leadership to undo the Sinhala-only policy. Felix Dias Bandaranaike argued that the Sinhala-only policy would be doomed if district councils were established, because the UNP depended on the FP to stay in power and would therefore not stop the central government becoming subordinated to district councils. He noted that the SLFP opposed allowing Tamil to be used for administrative purposes in the Northern and Eastern Provinces and threatened that, should such a policy be instituted, the party would do its "level best to set aside that settlement some day when we come back into power."[141] Bandaranaike further warned the government that the SLFP would not tolerate "lip service to Sinhala in the Northern and Eastern Provinces. We want some reasonable assurance that we are really going to have one country. Give all the guarantees you want to the Tamil language. . . . But ensure that Sinhala will be taught to the Tamil people, at least to the children who are to be born from now onwards."[142] It was such assimilationist rhetoric that most frightened the Tamils, and it did not help that Mrs. Bandaranaike went about saying things like: "The day is not far away when Ceylon will be overrun by Tamils."[143] The fact that M. Tiruchelvam, a leading member of the FP, was the minister of local government only served to reinforce these SLFP claims. "On every single issue, when the Hon. Tiruchelvam chooses to sneeze you all must get pneumonia," Felix Dias Bandaranaike taunted the government.[144] It made no difference that Tiruchelvam had announced publicly that the national government would never alter the Official Language Act. The goal of the SLFP was to vilify the Tamils and disparage the UNP.

All the Sinhalese politicians had to do, if they doubted the mess they had wrought by resorting to ethnic outbidding on the language issue, was to look to their neighbor India; for when linguistic nationalism had threatened to sunder that country, the far-sighted leadership of Jawaharlal Nehru had embraced accommodation and effectively smothered South India's ethnolinguistic fires. India's constitution, which came into force in 1950, stipulated that Hindi would replace English as the country's official language (Article 343) and also mandated that English continue as the language of administration for another fifteen years only. The commendable English standards and paucity of Hindi speakers in the south made the idea of this future language switch exceedingly unpopular there. The linguistic nationalism that this provoked in southern India—expressed in slogans such as "Hindi never, English ever!"—led to rioting against the central government.[145] In seeking to tame this reactive southern nationalism and preempt the secessionist clamor, the central government gradually initiated ethnolinguistic demarcation and devolution, with Nehru assuring the southerners that their states could retain English "as an alternative language as long as the people require it." Consequently, India's internal borders were modified to create states such as Andhra Pradesh for Telugu speakers, Karnataka for Kannada speakers, Maharashtra for Marati speakers, Kerala for Malayalis, Tamil Nadu for Tamilians, Gujarat for Gujaratis, and Haryana for the Punjab's Hindi speakers. States were also created along ethnoregional lines, thereby absolving the central government from dealing directly with intraethnic squabbles. Sri Lanka's Sinhalese politicians were so involved in trying to attain and hold on to power, however, that they disregarded this instructive example and instead continued to exacerbate interparty and interethnic relations.

The regulations for implementing the Tamil Language (Special Provisions) Act of 1958 were finally approved in January 1966, but the Tamil Language (Special Provisions) Regulations of 1966 (see appendix F) were bitterly opposed by the SLFP, LSSP, and the Communist Party. The two Marxist parties had originally vociferously supported linguistic parity, suggesting that not all Sinhalese politicians were unprincipled, but to avoid political marginalization, the LSSP and the CP had by the time of the March 1965 general election switched tactics and climbed on the ethnic outbidding bandwagon. As Felix Dias Bandaranaike sarcastically noted, the LSSP's N. M. Perera might have been among the most vocal when advocating linguistic parity in the past, but "he is 100 per cent against parity now; he is 100 per cent against religion being the opium of the masses now; he is 100 per cent for Mrs. Bandaranaike now; he is 100 per cent against revolution now; he is 100 per cent against district councils now."[146] Trying to combine their anti-capitalist ideology with their newly embraced communalist sentiments, the Marxists claimed that the UNP and FP were part of an American-sponsored conspiracy designed to expand the imperialist designs of the United States in Asia. The irony, of course, was that the Marxists opposed American colonialism, as they called it, in South East Asia while eagerly advocating a form of cultural colonialism in Tamil areas of Sri Lanka, and the FP's Naganathan inquired appositely why Pieter Keuneman and the other leftists were so dogmatically anti-colonialist when it came to Vietnam but nonetheless sought "to impose Sinhala colonial rule on us, the Tamil-speaking people."[147]

The anti-Tamil sentiments that had coalesced among the opposition persisted once the UNP was in power. Consequently, when Dudley Senanayake and the UNP sought to approve a flimsy devolutionary scheme through the District Councils Bill of 1968 and thereby appease the Tamil politicians allied with the UNP, even that was vehemently opposed by the SLFP, which was ably backed by the Sangha, Sinhalese Buddhist nationalists, and Marxists. The Muslims, who had by now come to fear Tamil dominance over their Eastern Province settlements, now joined the opposition. Some UNP backbenchers also protested the agreement. The collective pressure forced the UNP to abandon its decentralization plans, which led the FP to withdraw from the government. Consequently, like Bandaranaike before him, Senanayake once more jettisoned the opportunity to placate the country's Tamils, for the politics of ethnic outbidding mandated that ethnic entrepreneurs embrace political opportunism and chauvinism, not principled positions conducive to polyethnic coexistence and stability. The grand irony in this political tragicomedy was that the UNP, which had virulently opposed S. W. R. D. Bandaranaike's plans for devolution, had tried to implement something remotely akin to the B-C concordat, only to be opposed by the SLFP and Bandaranaike's widow, who purported to pursue the "Bandaranaike revolution." When combined with the Marxists' somersault on the language issue, the entire episode of the approval of the District Councils Bill highlighted how far Sri Lanka's politicians and parties had regressed to wallowing in an ethnic outbidding culture. The only consistent entities throughout this were the extremist bhikkhus and the Sinhalese nationalists. They alone clamored unrelentingly for a primarily Sinhala-speaking, Sinhalese Buddhist Sri Lanka in which the minorities lived at the majority community's sufferance.

The United Front: A Sinhalese Ethnocracy

A Sinhalese ethnocracy was made easier to achieve when the United Front (UF), consisting of the SLFP, the LSSP, and the Communist Party, rode to a landslide victory in the May 1970 election, winning 115 out of the 151 elected seats. The UNP was reduced to merely 17 seats, while the FP and Tamil Congress captured 13 and 3 seats respectively. In the early 1960s, Mrs. Bandaranaike had proclaimed that the island's fortunes rested in the hands of "angels and my late husband."[148] She now claimed that "Bandaranaike dead is mightier than Bandaranaike alive" and began what by all accounts must rank as the most damaging rule the island has experienced, both economically and ethnically. On the economic front, the autarkist and dirigiste policies her government instituted, coupled with its nationalization program, made the island an economic basket case. On the ethnic front, she utterly disregarded Tamil grievances and instead implemented policies that took only the Sinhalese Buddhists' preferences into consideration.

This is best shown in the constitution of the First Republic of Sri Lanka, which was enacted in May 1972. This new constitution declared Sri Lanka "a Unitary State," gave "Buddhism the foremost place" and made it the state's duty "to protect and foster Buddhism," instituted Sinhala as the "Official Language of Sri Lanka," and mandated that the regulations drafted under the Tamil Language Act of 1958 were "subordinate legislation." It also abrogated the Soulbury constitution's minority safeguards. Many Sinhalese were dissatisfied that the island never developed an anti-colonial nationalism like India and viewed the Soulbury constitution, under which the British monarch continued to operate as the nominal head of state, as a colonial artifact. They thus embraced the new constitution as an autochthonous nationalist document. The new constitution encompassed almost all that the Sinhalese nationalists had clamored for, even as it further alienated the Tamils. The Marxists within the United Front had often appeared ready to accommodate some of the Tamils' demands, but Mrs. Bandaranaike and Felix Dias Bandaranaike opposed any compromise. Indeed, the irony was that it was the LSSP's Colvin R. de Silva, once among the most eloquent Sinhalese championing linguistic parity, who oversaw the constitution's design as the minister of constitutional affairs. The LSSP's leaders "had reconciled themselves in the sunset of their lives to abandoning the vision of world revolution and settling cosily for the three portfolios that Mrs. Bandaranaike had given them,"[149] and they thus indicated no qualms about foisting this illiberal and ethnocentric constitution on the country.

A constitution is a country's most important institution, for it lays out the laws structuring the governing process. A constitution makes clear what the state stands for and structures the relations between the state and polity. It thus provides a blueprint of how the institutions of government should interact with one another and with the masses they were designed to serve. A constitution that fails to take into consideration all citizens' aspirations will not only lack legitimacy but will also undermine the patriotism of those marginalized. Sinhalese politicians might have manipulated the Soulbury constitution to discriminate against the Tamils, but at least the document itself was seen as well intentioned by the latter. No doubt the Soulbury constitution failed to fashion mechanisms precluding the tyranny of the majority, but Tamils in general were more inclined to blame unscrupulous politicians (both Sinhalese and their own), not the constitution. The United Front's 1972 constitution, however, was clearly a document written by the majority community for the majority community. It had taken Sri Lanka less than twenty-five years after independence to regress from a liberal democracy to a near ethnocracy.

The new constitution and the anti-Tamil policies that followed were to some extent related to the April 1971 insurrection by the Maoist Janatha Vimukthi Peramuna (People's Liberation Front, or JVP), made up of disgruntled young Sinhalese, because the government thereafter sought to bolster its legitimacy by even more radically catering to the Sinhalese Buddhists' needs.[150] For example, when the UF government in 1973 selected 100 personnel for the administrative services, 94 were Sinhalese. The other 6 positions went to 4 Tamils and 2 Muslims.[151] Besides the radical anti-Tamil hiring practices now made conspicuous within the state sector, the government and especially the Bandaranaike duo continued their Sinhalese-centric policies in the university arena as well. Indeed, their anti-Tamil measures were so far-reaching that A. Jeyaratnam Wilson has called them "harbingers of Tamil nationalism."[152]

Until 1971, university entrance had been based on merit, and Tamil students were constantly overrepresented, especially in scientific disci-

TABLE 5

Sri Lanka's Population, 1871–1968

Year (census)	Total (thousands)	Density per sq. mile (number)
1871	2,400	95
1881	2,760	109
1891	3,008	119
1901	3,566	141
1911	4,106	162
1921	4,498	178
1931	5,307	210
1946	6,657	263
1953	8,098	320
1963	10,582	418
1966[a]	11,439	457
1967[a]	11,703	468
1968[a]	11,964	478

SOURCE: *Statistical Pocket Book of Ceylon* (Colombo: Department of Census and Statistics, 1969), p. 21.
[a]Provisional mid-year estimates.

TABLE 6

Life Expectancy at Birth in Sri Lanka, 1920–1962

	1920–22	1946	1953	1962
Males	32.7	43.9	58.8	61.9
Females	30.7	41.6	57.5	61.4

SOURCE: *Statistical Pocket Book of Ceylon* (Colombo: Department of Census and Statistics, 1969), p. 27.

plines. There were at least two reasons for this. The first had to do with the influence on the Tamils of the excellent schools that American missionaries had created in the Northern Province, as well as the fact that throughout the 1960s, teaching in English continued in secondary institutions, notably in the sciences. The second reason Tamils were overrepresented in the sciences was that successive governments, especially Mrs. Bandaranaike's governments, had effectively excluded hiring Tamils in the state sector, which meant that Tamils were forced to seek professional employment. The island's population had increased by 3 million between 1901 and 1946, and it went up by another 6 million between 1946 and 1971, creating a veritable "youth bulge."[153] As tables 5 and 6 indicate, this rapid population growth was related to a high birth rate and high life expectancy. Not surprisingly, the numbers registered in primary and secondary schools also rose, from 867,000 in 1945 to 2,244,000 in 1960, and to 2,700,000 in 1970.[154]

TABLE 7

University Admissions in Sri Lanka, 1945–1973/74

Year	Total sitting	Total admitted	% admitted
1945	754	289	38.9
1950	1,443	438	30.3
1955	2,061	658	32.0
1960	5,277	1,812	34.3
1965	31,350	6,359	20.3
1969/70	30,445	3,457	11.3
1973/74	36,236	3,533	9.7

SOURCE: C. R. de Silva, "Education," in *Sri Lanka: A Survey*, ed. K. M. de Silva (London: C. Hurst, 1977), p. 423.

Thus, the problem facing the Sinhalese politicians was that the Sinhala-only policy, coupled with this "youth bulge," had led to large numbers of Sinhala-educated students clamoring to gain a university education, even as the state's capacity to accommodate them kept shrinking (see table 7). Cross-regional research suggests that increased education is correlated with ethnocentrism.[155] This is especially likely to be the case during periods of economic scarcity, and it is not coincidental that anti-Tamil and anti-Sinhalese sentiments had increased by the early 1970s.

The second Sirimavo Bandaranaike government (1970–77) sought to overcome this blocked mobility by introducing various ethnic "cut-off" points for university entrance. This new standardization system mandated that Tamil students score over twenty points higher than their Sinhalese counterparts in engineering, medicine and dentistry, and physical science to gain university admittance.[156] The system was changed to one based on district quotas in 1974, but the upshot was that Tamil entrance to the universities plummeted. For example, in 1969, Tamil students were represented as follows in some of the most prestigious disciplines: engineering 48.3 percent, medicine 48.9 percent, agriculture 47.4 percent, and veterinary science 39.8 percent. By 1975, the respective numbers had fallen to 14.2 percent, 17.4 percent, 23.5 percent, and 29 percent.[157] Consequently, while Tamils made up 39.8 percent of the students taking science-based courses in 1969–70, their numbers had decreased to 19 percent in 1975 (see table 8).

The numbers in 1977 meant the Tamils were, as a percentage of their population, still overrepresented in the universities, but the way Mrs. Bandaranaike's government curtailed Tamil representation vindicated Tamil fears that the Sinhalese authorities were hell-bent on marginalizing them. The results stemming from the government's Sinhalese-centric policies were starkly clear by the mid-1970s. For example, while the

TABLE 8

University Admissions to Science-Based Courses of Study, 1970–1977

Year entered	Total no.	Tamils		Sinhalese	
		No.	%	No.	%
1969/70	792	315	39.8	457	57.7
1970/71	955	337	35.3	579	60.6
1971/72	1,069	389	33.6	680	63.6
1973	1,177	347	29.5	793	67.4
1974	1,403	294	20.9	1,058	75.4
1975	1,411	268	19.0	1,101	78.0
1976	1,395	362	25.9	994	71.3
1977	1, 485	350	23.6	1,089	73.3

SOURCE: C. R. de Silva, "The Politics of University Admissions: A Review of Some Aspects of the Admission Policy in Sri Lanka, 1971–1978," *Sri Lanka Journal of Social Sciences* 1, no. 2 (Dec. 1978), pp. 105–6.

TABLE 9

Two Months' Median Income in 1963 and 1973
by Community

Community	1963 median income (Rs)	1973 median income (Rs)
Kandyan Sinhalese	164	376
Low Country Sinhalese	199	425
Ceylon Tamils	198	385
Indian Tamils	118	180
Moors and Malays	259	470
Others	467	633
All communities	165	360

SOURCE: Central Bank of Ceylon, *Survey of Sri Lanka's Consumer Finances, 1973* (Colombo, 1974), pp. 84–85.

Kandyan and Low Country Sinhalese saw their per capita incomes increase by 24 percent and 18 percent respectively between 1963 and 1973, Ceylon Tamils and Indian Tamils saw their per capita incomes decrease by 28 percent and 1 percent respectively during the same period.[158] A look at the rise in Sinhalese median income between 1963–73, as indicated in table 9, further reinforces the point.

Tamil leaders had protested that the United Front's constitution denied Tamils "even their basic minimum rights" and called for an amended constitution that provided linguistic parity. They threatened to conduct a nonviolent struggle and promised to boycott the State Assembly, but by now it had become amply clear that the Tamils were unlikely to attain any gains utilizing political processes. With no bill of rights in the 1972 constitution to alleviate Tamil concerns, minority rights deliberately undermined, and all major Sinhalese Buddhist preferences constitutionalized, Sri Lanka had segued into an ethnocracy masquerading as a secular and liberal democracy. When combined with decreasing Tamil university enrollment and state sector employment, the dearth of private sector opportunities for upward mobility, mainly owing to the government's economic policies, and the military's ham-handed practices in the north, it is hardly surprising that Tamil youth began to turn radical.[159]

By the early 1970s, a mostly Sinhalese military had developed a notorious reputation for heaping unremitting indignities on the Tamils, who were taunted, shamed, and beaten on a regular basis. Tamils' complaints against the security forces elicited no response from the government. S. W. R. D. Bandaranaike had, especially during and immediately after the anti-Tamil riots, developed a reputation for writing back to the Tamil leaders and promising to look into their complaints, but he often did not follow through on his promises. Mrs. Bandaranaike, however, rarely bothered to reply to the letters Chelvanayakam and other FP leaders sent her. Indeed, the government even refused to discipline policemen who attacked the Fourth International Tamil Conference in January 1974, despite an independent commission having condemned the police for killing nine Tamils.[160] Chelvanayakam had consistently claimed that surrender and violence were not options, and that the best way to overcome the anomie facing the Tamils was "the method India adopted under the guidance of Mahatma Gandhi—the Gandhian method."[161]

Mrs. Bandaranaike's secretary from 1970–77, M. D. D. Pieris, argues that the main reason the prime minister failed to seriously deal with Chelvanayakam and the FP, and was forced to "place the ethnic issue on the back burner," was because she was preoccupied with numerous other important issues, such as dealing with the fallout of the 1971 JVP insurrection, crafting a new constitution, nationalizing the island's estates and pursuing land reform, trying to repatriate some of the Indian Tamils to India, and dealing with the food and fiscal crises facing the country at this time.[162] Yet it was Mrs. Bandaranaike's addlebrained policies during this time that foisted many crises on Sri Lanka, and none of these issues, in any case, explain why she reacted to the Tamils' entreaties with Olympian indifference. Furthermore, it is ironic that the prime minister could not find time to deal with the most pressing issue of the day, which was Sinhalese-Tamil animus, but instead found ample time to institute legislation and pursue ethnocentric practices that exacerbated the ethnic divide.

Chelvanayakam believed that just as Gandhi's satyagraha campaigns had ultimately influenced the British to accommodate the Indians' demands, the Tamils' nonviolent movement could likewise force Sinhalese politicians to accommodate their justified demands. Ho Chi Minh, by colorfully noting that Gandhi "would long since have entered heaven" had he tried his tactics in a French colony,[163] clearly indicated that satyagraha campaigns could only succeed in states where the governing authorities felt restrained by liberal ideals. The Tamil representative for Nallur, E. M. V. Naganathan, had grasped this as early as 1956, when he was beaten outside parliament by the Sinhalese mob opposing the Tamil satyagrahis. "I . . . was walking along when the howling mob came and beat me up," Naganathan recalled. "At the time [when] I was on the ground some people tried to trample me, I believe, on my vital parts. Then I felt that this was not a place for satyagraha."[164] By the early 1970s, many Tamils had become especially convinced that resorting to satyagraha was meaningless against successive Sinhalese governments that did not respect fundamental civil liberties, displayed no qualms about using violence to suppress peaceful protests, and were determined to create a Sinhalese ethnocracy. They were thus more likely to identify with Suntharalingam, who soon after the 1958 riots argued that the FP's policy demanding a federal state and "their methods of ahimsa and satyagraha, have brought horror on the Tamils. Wherever the Tamils exercised their elementary right to protect their person and property by force if necessary, they were safe. Wherever they were shackled down by satyagraha, they were slaughtered."[165]

Consequently, Tamil youth, many of whom had been forced to forgo educational and employment opportunities given the pro-Sinhalese policies instituted over the past fifteen years, especially began demanding that their leaders take a more uncompromising stand. The fact was that despite struggling for nearly twenty years to have the Tamils' language and other claims realized, the FP's moderates had attained little. The moderate Tamil parties forged a fissile coalition in May 1972, but the belated unity of this Tamil United Front (TUF) appears to have been dictated more out of frustration and as a way to appease the increasingly disgruntled Tamil youth than by any strategic design.[166] By 1972, even Chelvanayakam had begun to make demands that went beyond federalism and smacked of a more radical self-determination. Thus, in October that year, he argued: "In view of the events that have taken place, the Tamil people of Ceylon should have the right to determine their future, whether they are to be a subject race in Ceylon or they are to be a free people."[167] This was certainly in line with the radicalism that was afoot, especially in the Northern Province. For example, in 1972, Tamil leaders had contemplated protesting the government's anti-Tamil actions by boycotting the legislature. When they reversed course and decided to participate in the State Assembly, hundreds of Tamil youths invaded an All Ceylon Tamil Congress meeting and demanded that the politicians carry out a boycott. As the *Ceylon Daily News* judiciously recognized, Tamil politicians might have threatened to boycott parliament for propagandist reasons, but "[a] movement of militant youth rooted in the soil of Jaffna and nourished by material frustration, a feeling of humiliation and bitterness, could be another kettle of fish."[168]

The TUF's Youth League had been preceded by the FP's Tamil Ilainar Iyakkam (Tamil Youth Movement) and Tamil Manavar Peravai (Tamil Students' Union). Tamil youth grew increasingly restless and radical as time passed and moderate Tamil politicians had nothing to show for their cooperation with successive Sinhalese governments. Unrequited violence against a territorially based ethnic group is uncommon, and by the late 1960s, young Tamils were bracing themselves to retaliate against the government. But all concerned disregarded them. Felix Dias Bandaranaike claimed that Tamil leaders manipulated the youth to put pressure on the government, saying:

Their leaders are setting up their own Federal Party Youth League, telling them to put up a show of protest. . . . The Federal Party Youth Leaguers say, "Let us secede and demand Tamilnad." This is absolute nonsense. This is all set up internally by their own people. Their own leaders go and tell the youth leaguers, "Please, now kick up a row, otherwise we will not be able to save face." It is good organization. But we do not mind so long as the basic interests of the Sinhalese people are not going to be hurt in the process. And they cannot be hurt because the Federal Party can do nothing now.[169]

Some Tamil leaders, like Amirthalingam, eventually came to believe that they could manipulate their youth to exert pressure on the government, but just like the government, they underestimated the radical resolve of the youth movement. The pressure these young Tamils ultimately imposed on Tamil politicians forced the moderate Tamil United Liberation Front (TULF), formed after the Federal Party, the Tamil Congress, and the Ceylon Workers Congress (which represented the Indian Tamils) joined forces, to issue the May 1976 Vaddukoddai Resolution (see appendix G). The resolution emphasized that the Tamils were "a nation distinct and apart from the Sinhalese" and declared: "This convention resolves that restoration and reconstitution of the Free, Sovereign, Secular Socialist State of TAMIL EELAM based on the right of self-determination inherent to every nation has become inevitable in order to safeguard the very existence of the Tamil Nation in this Country." Successive Sinhalese governments, it charged, had deprived the "Tamil nation of its territory, language, citizenship, economic life, opportunities of employment and education." The Vaddukoddai Resolution thus "represented a shift from the struggle for equality to an assertion of freedom, from the demand for fundamental rights to the assertion of self-determination, from the acceptance of the pluralistic experiment to the surfacing of a new corporate identity," Neelan Tiruchelvam noted.[170]

It is plausible that the call for *eelam* was a gimmick to marginalize the burgeoning Tamil militant youth movement. On the other hand, it perhaps was an extremist political gesture designed to force the Sri Lankan government to compromise and grant the Tamils increased autonomy. Whatever the case, *eelam* galvanized many extremists and young Tamils, so that by July 1977, when the UNP under J. R. Jayewardene attained power, Tamil youth had begun to target progovernment politicians, assassinate police constables, and rob numerous banks to fund their incipient rebellion. "The militant youth in the Jaffna district were raised in an environment of continuous conflict with the Government. Since 1956 the boycott of schools, the picketing of Government offices, hoisting black flags and performing satyagraha was a way of life for them," T. D. S. A. Dissanayake observed.[171] These youths had become inured to radicalism and refused to tolerate the indignities and domination their elders had suffered since the passage of the Official Language Act. H. L. Seneviratne correctly notes that the Sinhala-only policy promoted a climate "for the subversion of democratic institutions . . . [which then led to] terror, anomie, and the violent call for a separate state."[172] In that sense, the Sinhala-only movement and the Official Language Act of 1956 represent the birth pangs of Sri Lanka's ethnic conflict. Consequently, Tamil separatism can be said to be Sinhalese-inspired, given that the rebels' ongoing quest for *eelam* represents an extremist reaction to the particularistic policies, institutional decay, and anti-Tamil violence the Sinhalese helped institute.

6

FROM LINGUISTIC NATIONALISM
TO CIVIL WAR

By the time elections were held in July 1977, there was little doubt that the UNP under J. R. Jayewardene would be comfortably elected. What was not expected was the party's landslide victory, in which, although it received just over 50 percent of the votes, it won 141 out of the 168 seats in parliament, while the SLFP was reduced to just 8 seats. Not a single Marxist candidate won election in 1977. The Tamil Congress and the FP had merged to form the Tamil United Liberation Front (TULF), and under A. Amirthalingam, the party won 18 seats, becoming the opposition. Jayewardene had promised to accommodate Tamil concerns and also to junk the SLFP's highly unpopular economic shibboleths. Many Tamils consequently voted enthusiastically for the UNP. The more than two-thirds parliamentary majority it garnered also enabled the UNP to pass the constitution of the Second Republic of Sri Lanka in August 1978, replacing the 1972 constitution.

This new constitution introduced a presidential system, replaced the hitherto first-past-the-post-electoral system with proportional representation and preferential voting, and explicitly provided for some minority rights, but it gave the president dictatorial powers. By counting voters' second and third preferences if no candidate obtained a majority during presidential elections, the voting system also enabled minorities to have a greater impact on the election process, even as it sought to avoid the disparities hitherto experienced between the number of votes a party polled and the number of seats it won. The dictatorial powers they acquired notwithstanding, Jayewardene and the UNP showed no sign of wanting to accommodate the Tamils, and this despite the increasingly militant youth movement in the north. One may, in hindsight, argue that the massive majority the UNP obtained through the 1977 election actually hindered accommodating or co-opting the looming separatist movement. While the new constitution did make Tamil a national language, it failed to fully acknowledge that the reactive linguistic nationalism of the Tamils had now metamorphosed into a separatist movement; it therefore made no attempt to accommodate the Tamils' territorial concerns.

The 1978 constitution still tilted toward favoring the Sinhalese, and in that sense, it was hardly an ethnically impartial document. It maintained the state's unitary structure, thereby ensuring that Tamils would continue to occupy a subservient position in their relations with all subsequent Sinhalese governments. Thus, while the constitution changed, and while the new document provided numerous minority guarantees, the political structure remained the same as far as interethnic relations were concerned. The anti-Tamil milieu that the Sinhala-only policy had created had become so established that many Tamils doubted whether the few constitutional clauses encouraging polyethnic coexistence would have any effect. Ultimately, not only did the doubting Tamils turn out to be right, but under Jayewardene the government reached the apogee of institutional decay. Arguably, many clauses of the 1978 constitution were conducive to polyethnic coexistence, but the government's unwillingness to resolutely put these provisions into practice, and, in many instances, its blatant violations of the most fundamental freedoms enshrined in the document, undermined whatever promise it contained. This goes to show that it is one thing to design institutions and quite another to ensure that they function as intended. In a real sense, institutions that codify promises that are then not kept are even more insidious than not having the requisite institutions to begin with.

The UNP's landslide victory ushered in a new economic and political era for Sri Lanka. With aid from Western countries, the International Monetary Fund, and the World Bank, the victorious government jettisoned the previous regime's autarkic, dirigiste policies and instead adopted large-scale irrigation and infrastructure development and structural adjustment reforms. The UNP's legitimacy in office almost immediately became tied to the structural adjustment program's success, which engendered three outcomes that had adverse ramifications especially for Sinhalese-Tamils relations. First, it influenced the UNP to resort to illiberal governance so as to ensure stability, even as Tamil rebels operating principally in the Northern Province were becoming increasingly more daring in challenging the state. Second, it forced the government to adopt pro-Western foreign policies that alienated India at a time when politicians in Tamil Nadu were heaping pressure on the Indian central government to support Sri Lanka's beleaguered Tamils. Third, structural adjustment mandated that the government dismantle food subsidies, privatize government-owned industries, curtail the state-employed workforce, reduce tariffs, deregulate financial markets, and liberalize foreign trade.

The latter policies especially allowed for cheaper and superior imports, which quickly marginalized many Sinhalese entrepreneurs who had thrived as a result of their access to scarce resources under the monopolistic quotas imposed between 1970 and 1977, while their hitherto restrained Tamil counterparts began using their ties with India to gain economic ascendance in a relatively free market. With numerous chauvinists ensconced in the UNP, it did not take long before anti-Tamil violence erupted once more.

Illiberal Democracy and Post-1977 Anti-Tamil Violence

Sri Lanka represents a classic case of how a state may eschew constitutional liberalism, which incorporates the rule of law, limited government, free and fair elections, impartial interactions with all ethnic groups, and the freedom of assembly, speech, and religion, and yet appear to be a functioning democracy.[1] Indeed, it is the abuse of democracy's messy accoutrements—such as universal suffrage, popular elections, party politics, and elite competition—that is chiefly responsible for the weakening of a country's norms and institutions.[2] If two turnovers of power between opposition parties make for a consolidated democracy,[3] Sri Lanka had achieved that status by 1960. On the other hand, when evaluated against the more classical definition, which requires that rules governing democratic participation in the polity be institutionalized and respected by all, so that illiberalism and authoritarianism are precluded,[4] it becomes clear that the ethnic particularism and outbidding that had dominated the country's politics since the passage of the Official Language Act had undermined democratic consolidation.[5] The UNP governments under J. R. Jayewardene, however, took repression to new heights.

Whereas the Bandaranaikes' illiberal policies specifically marginalized the Tamils, and the Sinhalese lower and middle classes, the main beneficiaries, supported those policies, the UNP's post-1977 illiberal practices targeted all those who were thought to stymie the government's agenda. The over two-thirds parliamentary majority the UNP commanded enabled it to ride roughshod over its opponents and make a mockery of constitutional government, and the party did so with alacrity under Jayewardene's leadership. For example, the government used UNP trade unionists belonging to the Jathika Sevaka Sangamaya (National Worker's Union), or JSS, and thugs associated with the party's leadership to harass and beat anyone that opposed its economic policies. The JSS was nothing more than a fraternity of goondas run by Cyril Mathew, an inveterate Sinhalese bigot who was also the minister of industries and scientific affairs. Those targeted included members and supporters of the SLFP and

Marxist parties, Buddhist and Christian clergy who dared oppose government policy, and student unionists and non-UNP trade unionists. It did not matter whether those opposing government policy did so peacefully and lawfully, and the police frequently looked the other way, since the thugs and their political patrons had threatened them as well. The goondas usually traveled about in state-owned vehicles to make it clear that they operated under the government's imprimatur and attacked protestors and picketers with stones, clubs, knives, swords, and occasionally with bombs as well. Even luminaries in Sri Lankan society were not spared, if and when they protested against the government. For example, Vivienne Gunawardena, a left-leaning women's activist, was beaten for protesting outside the U.S. Embassy. When the Supreme Court ruled in her favor, the UNP government paid the requisite compensation and then promoted the officer responsible for assaulting her. The government's thugs thereafter harassed the three Supreme Court justices who had ruled against the police officer by parading outside their homes and causing damage to their properties. When another police officer was fined for unconstitutionally seizing leaflets from Pavidi Handa (Voice of the Clergy), a group comprised of Buddhist and Christian clergy who peacefully opposed the government, he too was promoted, and the cabinet decided to use government funds to pay his fine. E. R. Sarachchandra, a highly renowned professor of Sinhala literature and theater and a one-time ambassador to Paris, and many other well-known literati were also beaten by JSS goondas for participating in a meeting criticizing the government. Despite some of the goondas being identified, none were arrested.[6] In November 1957, Jayewardene had criticized and cautioned the S. W. R. D. Bandaranaike government for what he feared was a nod toward authoritarianism. In retrospect, his words turned out to be a prophetic assessment of his own illiberal rule two decades later:

I do not think that those who belong to democratic parties and lead them, such as Mr. S. W. R. D. Bandaranaike[,] would consciously wish to convert our democracy into a dictatorship. But what often happens is that in individuals who attain to positions of political power, the human desire to retain that power predominates. The unpopularity which comes to those who are in power . . . makes them seek to buttress their position, by the taking of undemocratic measures. The more their unpopularity grows, the more they seek to retain power in this way. [Consequently,] the more undemocratic do their actions become.[7]

The repression Jayewardene and his cabinet so arrogantly indulged in was, ironically, an extension of the illiberalism practiced against the Tamils since the 1950s. The unconstitutional, extrajudicial, and ethnocentric policies that successive governments had instituted against the Tamils since S.W.R.D. Bandaranaike's premiership were tolerated, if not ardently supported, by most Sinhalese, since it was their community that reaped the benefits. What the Sinhalese failed to realize was that repression cannot be compartmentalized so as to affect only one ethnic community, and that eventually its odious influence would affect the entire country.[8] The power-hungry Jayewardene may inadvertently have ensured that his fellow Sinhalese got their comeuppance for supporting repression of the Tamils, but his policies also broadened, deepened, and internationalized the ethnic conflict and adversely affected the entire island.

The new constitution that the UNP enacted introduced a complex electoral system that combined proportional representation with preferential voting. Besides being designed to favor the UNP in future contests, the constitution also gave the president almost dictatorial powers,[9] and Jayewardene bragged that the only thing he could not do as president was turn a man into a woman and vice versa. Once he was president, Jayewardene collected undated letters of resignation from all UNP ministers, which ensured that there was little dissent from his preferences.[10] Taking her cue from Indira Gandhi, Sirimavo Bandaranaike had postponed parliamentary elections for two years, from 1975 to 1977. Jayewardene initiated a presidential commission to examine Mrs. Bandaranaike's actions, which led to her civic rights being suspended until 1987. This barred Mrs. Bandaranaike from running for president and campaigning for her party, conveniently precluding Jayewardene's most effective opponent from challenging him in the October 1982 presidential election. The most egregious parliamentary maneuver Jayewardene and the UNP perpetrated was to pass the Fourth Amendment in December 1982, which extended the party's rule via a referendum as opposed to parliamentary elections. This enabled the UNP to extend its parliamentary majority of more than two-thirds for another term by simple electoral majority. In September 1956, while articulating the opposition's role in a democracy, Jayewardene had argued that the "freedom of opposition presupposes several other freedoms. Freedom of speech and writing, freedom of meeting, and the freedom of the judiciary. These are the essential democratic freedoms, without which there can be no Democracy." He added that "without an Opposition these liberties will wither away. It is the duty of the Opposition to use and to develop them."[11] By 1982, however, Jayewardene was intoxicated by the idea of absolute power and said: "We are contesting the election to win and at a time most favourable to us. We intend . . . to demolish and completely destroy the opposition politically. After that I say to you, roll up the electoral map of Sri Lanka. You will not need it for another ten years."[12] Seeking to minimize opposition in the referendum, the UNP instigated legal proceedings against numerous SLFP members and enticed others to switch parties. All this, coupled with election fraud, enabled the party to win the referendum.

A constitution's legitimacy requires that it be seen to operate impartially and for the betterment of all citizens concerned. The 1978 constitution Jayewardene and the UNP imposed on the country scarcely did this. The Jayewardene government was able to use its parliamentary majority of more than two-thirds to pass sixteen amendments to the constitution between 1978 and 1988, notwithstanding that it had received only a little more than 50 percent of the votes cast in the 1977 general election. In almost every case, the primary purpose in passing these amendments was to ensure the UNP's viability and Jayewardene's megalomaniac aspirations, not the country's betterment.

Jayewardene had come to power promising a *dharmistha* (righteous) society, which was interpreted to mean "clean government, ethical conduct in public life, respect for the rule of law, the independence of the judiciary, and freedom of the press."[13] Throughout the 1977 election campaign, Jayewardene borrowed Buddhist terminology to expound his vision of the genuinely liberal democracy this *dharmistha* society would be. Yet no sooner had he solidified his grip on power than opportunism led him to further undermine the island's already anemic political institutions and more deeply entrench its repressive regime. There is no evidence that Jayewardene was complicit in the mayhem Cyril Mathew's JSS perpetrated, and the question is therefore debatable. It is, however, indisputable that the violence took place with his connivance. Jayewardene was certainly responsible for the impunity under which the country's goondas and other destabilizing forces operated. He was consequently also to blame for the worst anti-Tamil violence, because it was these very same goondas and politicians whose violence Jayewardene condoned to buttress his rule that ultimately oversaw the pogrom unleashed on the Tamils.

The 1977 and 1981 Anti-Tamil Riots

Notwithstanding that many Tamils voted for J. R. Jayewardene and the UNP in 1977, the election took place amid heightened ethnic tensions, chiefly because of the TULF's separatist platform and the violence being committed by young Tamils in the Northern Province, which was often reported in doomsday fashion, especially by the Sinhala press. Combined with insidious rumors, this enabled Sinhalese politicians of all parties to ratchet up their rhetoric about the threat facing the Sinhalese and Sri Lanka. The Sinhalese were also nonplussed that a separatist Tamil party was now the country's legitimate opposition, and some mistakenly believed that this would facilitate the country's dismemberment.

Merely three weeks after the UNP won the elections, Jayewardene boasted that depending on what the Tamils wanted, he was willing to give them war or peace. His comments were repeatedly aired over the government-owned radio stations and no doubt contributed to the August 1977 anti-Tamil riots, which killed nearly a hundred Tamils. The ferocious nature of the riots is evident from the fact that even Sinhalese hospital personnel went about attacking their Tamil superiors and Tamil patients.[14] The riots began in the Jaffna Peninsula and were initiated by police and armed forces, who appear to have been influenced by the anti-government actions perpetrated by disgruntled northern Tamil youth, and by UNP nationalists eager to demonstrate their fervent pro-Sinhalese spirit. (This is not to suggest that thugs belonging to the SLFP and other parties did not participate in the riots; they did in some areas.) UNP politicos like Cyril Mathew spouted chauvinistic rhetoric in parliament even as their party tried to introduce a new constitution that partly sought to accommodate Tamils' grievances. The following May, the government proscribed the Liberation Tigers of Tamil Eelam and other rebel groups bent on secession. The Prevention of Terrorism Act, originally passed as a temporary measure in 1979, was made a permanent law applicable throughout the island in July 1982. The act was meant to eradicate the terrorism perpetrated by Tamil rebels; it instead made terrorists out of the security forces, who were empowered to arrest, imprison, and hold all suspected subversives incommunicado for eighteen months without trial. The new law explicitly contravened the International Covenant on Civil and Political Rights, to which the country was a signatory, and led to many young Tamils being abused and tortured, which merely deepened their determination to secede. With the police and security forces in the Jaffna Peninsula also continuing to harass, beat, and rape Tamils with impunity,[15] Tamil rebels stepped up their violent acts.

The UNP had arguably assembled one of the brightest and ablest cabinets in Sri Lanka's history, yet it refused fully to grasp the dangers stemming from the burgeoning Tamil rebellion. If anything, its actions were geared to alienating the Tamils even further. For example, the most important and expensive development project the UNP launched once it came to power was the Accelerated Mahaweli Program, which would have developed 320,000 acres of hitherto undeveloped land. Not only was the program designed to benefit predominantly Sinhalese areas, or areas that Sinhalese were well positioned to colonize, but when it was scaled back, the projects that were eliminated were those that would have benefited Tamils in the Northern Peninsula. And this was done despite the original plan having deliberately avoided areas populated by Tamils in the Eastern Province. Indeed, in some areas, the military was used to evict Tamils and replace them with Sinhalese.[16]

One reason that Jayewardene was unwilling to compromise with the Tamils (especially in devolving power to the Northern and Eastern Provinces) was because he believed that instability in the north suited the UNP's fortunes. The party commanded over a two-thirds majority in parliament, and this gave it the capacity to pass constitutional amendments in a partisan and even whimsical fashion. Thus, the more unrest there was in the northeast, the easier it was for Jayewardene and the UNP to justify autocratic rule.[17] Jayewardene was an ardent admirer of Singapore's Prime Minister Lee Kuan Yu and believed that an iron hand was necessary both to institute much-needed economic reforms and to put down the Tamil rebellion. He sought to achieve this by further compromising the country's already flawed democracy and taking an uncompromising stance. In doing so, however, he further vindicated the radical Tamils' claim that they could never trust a Sinhalese leader to treat their community fairly and legitimated the destabilizing activities Tamil youth were resorting to in the northeast.

Violence perpetrated by Tamil rebels and government forces during the June 1981 District Development Councils[18] elections in Jaffna also led the latter to burn down the Jaffna Municipal Library, which destroyed nearly 100,000 ancient and rare documents and convinced Tamils that some Sinhalese were determined to annihilate their culture. "On the Buddhist side it was an unparalleled act of barbarism, since rarely in Sri Lanka's recorded history (and perhaps even in the larger history of Buddhism) was there an example of book burning of this magnitude," Gananath Obeyesekere writes.[19] No action was taken against the perpetrators, perhaps because it was well known that it was government-sponsored goondas who had burned the library. The library burning was followed by intermittent anti-Tamil riots throughout July and August of 1981, with the government's supporters playing a major role in the mayhem. Just as in 1958, the rioters were confident that they could act with impunity. This was especially the case during the 1980s, given that the same miscreants involved in anti-Tamil violence were also those the UNP used to browbeat and assault its opponents. The worst anti-Tamil riots, however, took place in July 1983, after the LTTE ambushed and killed thirteen soldiers in the north.

The 1983 Anti-Tamil Riots

The 1983 riots were a watershed in Sinhalese-Tamil relations. While the riots correlated to a significant extent with the economic changes that ensued from Sri Lanka's post-1977 structural adjustment reforms, they were more intense than the anti-Tamil riots of 1977 and 1981. The open market reforms allowed a large number of Tamils to use their ethnic and business connections with Indians to become upwardly mobile. Thus, if the pre-1977 era had seen Sinhalese heavy and small industrialists, shop-keepers, and traders using their ethnic identity to procure quotas, li-censes, and general access to scarce resources, the open market reforms allowed Tamils to become successful traders and industrialists in their own right. The subsequent prosperity catapulted previously lumpen Tamil groups into the middle- and upper-class strata, while their Sinhalese counterparts, unable to compete with the cheap and superior imports inundating the marketplace, were stripped of their status as "captains of the industry."[20]

Economic transitions especially create uncertainty, amid which ethnic cohesion is likely to be strengthened.[21] This is especially true if one group articulates its grievances and relative deprivation as resulting from the doings of a rival group. Such grievances then lead to chauvinism and the racialization of politics, which is what occurred during the 1983 riots. Marx may have been right in claiming that the lumpenproletariat lacked class consciousness, but that is not to say that the lumpenproletariat can-not be galvanized along ethnic lines by using such emotive issues as lan-guage, religion, and culture. As has already been noted throughout this book, ethnic rhetoric allows for doing just this, and it is thus not coinci-dental that the relatively deprived Sinhalese bourgeoisie was able to uti-lize the destabilizing tendencies of the Sinhalese lumpenproletariat in en-suring that the Tamil entrepreneurial classes were more or less wiped out in the 1983 riots. "Two weeks ago Tamils owned 60 percent of the wholesale trade and 80 percent of the retail trade in the capital. Today that trade is gone," the *Economist* reported.[22] "[T]he majority Singalese observed that more than half of 'their' new industries were Tamil-owned—and . . . burnt down the Tamil factories."[23]

The 1983 riots took place in two stages. The first mostly targeted Tamils' property, with the rioters looting and burning. The second stage, which ensued after a rumor was spread that the LTTE was in Colombo to avenge the anti-Tamil violence, targeted Tamil persons as well and was the most horrifying: "Cars were stopped and this time if Tamils were in the cars they were burned inside them, petrol was poured over people and they were set alight, people were also burned in their houses, and were hacked to death."[24] The 1983 riots marked the climactic moment in the institutional breakdown caused by the impact of Sri Lanka's postin-dependence language policies on religion, education, employment, colo-nization, and resource allocation. Indeed, the systematic and virulent vi-olence unleashed during the 1983 riots made them a veritable pogrom. The Sinhalese lumpenproletariat may have rioted in order to loot, but

those who led the rioters sought to ensure that Tamil goods and properties were destroyed. In at least one instance, Minister of Industries Cyril
Mathew, whose once prosperous political clientele had now become economically marginalized, led the rioters himself. The political organization
against the Tamil entrepreneurial classes was especially evident when rioters were baldly transported in government vehicles and provided with
electoral registration forms to pick their targets. In some instances, the rioters were accompanied by extremist bhikkhus. Sinhalese nationalists,
chauvinist politicians, the ruling party's goondas, and extremist elements
in the Sangha, all aided and abetted by the security forces, wreaked
havoc. Tamil businesses and homes were looted and burned, thousands
were made refugees, and between 400 and 2,000 Tamils were murdered.[25] The country's maximum-security jail at Welikada became an
abattoir when Sinhalese prisoners and their Sinhalese guards murdered
two groups of Tamil prisoners, numbering thirty-five and seventeen, on
successive days. President J. R. Jayewardene neither imposed an immediate curfew nor addressed the nation over radio and television until three
days after the riots. When he did finally face the country, Jayewardene
spoke against separatism but evinced "not a syllable of sympathy for the
Tamil people or any explicit rejection of the spirit of vengeance."[26] And
"[a]fter two days of violence, and the murder of 35 Tamils in a maximum-security jail, the only editorial in the government-run newspaper
was on 'saving our forest cover.'"[27] Neither Jayewardene nor his cabinet
ministers bothered to visit any of the nearly 70,000 Tamils made home-
less by the riots, many of whom were housed in schools in Colombo and
throughout the interior. That the security forces had killed nearly sixty
Tamils in Jaffna immediately after the LTTE's attack was also kept a secret, although this revenge attack against civilians, had it been publicized,
might have mitigated the genuine anger many Sinhalese felt over the thirteen soldiers' deaths. When Lalith Athulathmudali, the country's minister
of trade, addressed the nation, he too seemed more concerned about paci-
fying the nationalist Sinhalese than the aggrieved Tamils: "A few days
ago, my friends, I saw a sight which neither you nor I thought that we
should live to see again. We saw many people looking for food, standing
in line, greatly inconvenienced, seriously inconvenienced."[28] Given that
many Tamils were hiding (most often with courageous Sinhalese friends
and neighbors) to save their lives, the comment was little short of mon-
strous.

One major reason Jayewardene did not take immediate action to quell
the violence was because, like Bandaranaike during the 1958 riots, he
was terrified by the way the riots had spread. And, also like
Bandaranaike, he was averse to admitting that he had failed to act expe-

ditiously, and that his very own party colleagues were partly responsible for much of the violence.[29] Therefore, rather than indicting the UNP politicians and racist bhikkhus who formed the anti-Tamil vanguard in some locales, Jayewardene blamed "Naxalite [i.e., Maoist] forces" bent on toppling the government and banned three political parties.[30] But it was clear to everyone that the very goondas Jayewardene had tolerated and tacitly supported to implement his repressive rule were the main perpetrators of the July 1983 anti-Tamil riots. As the TULF's Amirthalingam noted:

The Tamil people do not believe that the left parties had any hand in the attack on the Tamil people. . . . The attack on the Tamil people is pure ethnic violence planned well ahead and executed with ruthlessness by forces close to the Government—the same forces that attacked the strikers in July, 1980; attacked Professor Saratchandra and others at the meeting at the Buddhist congress hall and demonstrated before the houses of the judges. These forces include the armed forces for whom Mr. Cyril Mathew always holds a brief in Parliament.[31]

About two weeks prior to the riots, Jayewardene told the London *Daily Telegraph:* "I am not worried about the opinion of the Jaffna [Tamil] people. . . . Now we can't think of them. Not about their lives or their opinions of us."[32] While it is debatable whether presidential insouciance emboldened the anti-Tamil elements responsible for the riots, such comments were certainly indicative of the institutional decay facing the Tamils. Ultimately, the president's dilatory response, his carefree reaction to the orgiastic anti-Tamil violence, and the numerous official and nonofficial institutions that coalesced to systematically attack the Tamils drove thousands abroad and created the first Tamil refugee wave, which soon became the financial linchpin of the Tamil quest for *eelam*. Equally important, Tamil youths fled north by the thousands and almost overnight transformed a marginal separatist movement into a redoubtable rebel force.

Major Sources of Institutional Breakdown

Sri Lanka's political structure encouraged ethnic outbidding, and its political elites thus figured prominently among those who contributed to institutional breakdown, but Buddhist monks, various Sinhalese Buddhist organizations, and Sinhalese Buddhist nationalists also bore significant responsibility for the course of events. The Sangha and nationalist scholars eagerly misconstrued and reinvented Sinhalese history, folklore, and mythology, thereby promoting both Sinhalese grievances and cultural nationalism. Furthermore, by positioning the Buddhist clergy as protectors of Theravada Buddhism, and the island of Sri Lanka as the designated sanctuary for Buddhism under the Sinhalese, these groups created a milieu that demanded Sinhalese ascendancy and dominance. For a Sinhalese government to eschew these demands was tantamount to committing political suicide.

If "ideas" are incorporated as an institutional construct, as is common in the institutionalist research paradigm, then such ideational institutions, as articulated by the Buddhist clergy and nationalist organizations, were part of the standard operating procedures of Sri Lanka's postindependence sociopolitical landscape, leading to powerful political slogans such as "Buddhism Betrayed" and "Sri Lanka for the Sinhalese." The institutional breakdown was thus legitimated, if not orchestrated, using the resources and ideational constructs and influence of Sinhalese Buddhist organizations. Embedded over decades, that influence permeated both state and private institutions, so much so that even the once impartial judiciary, the armed forces, and private organizations, from business establishments to sports clubs, were soon schooled in a pro-Sinhalese, pro-Buddhist mentality.

The institutional breakdown was most starkly highlighted by the security forces' actions during the 1983 riots. While the security personnel had to be encouraged to act during the 1977 riots and were openly slow to intervene during the 1981 riots, they either aided and abetted the rioters or merely stood by in 1983. This was in contrast to the general discipline, impartiality, and professionalism imputed to the forces and was particularly contrary to their conduct in the 1950s, when they had been highly regarded by even northern Tamils. This high regard had extended to Sinhalese policemen as well. Indeed, quite often lower-caste Tamils had preferred to deal with Sinhalese policemen, as opposed to fellow Tamils, "whenever or wherever caste was a factor," because the former were seen as detached and dispassionate.[33] Such perceptions of dispassion and professionalism had disappeared by the 1960s, when the police and army came to be viewed as part of the anti-Tamil Sinhalese vanguard.

It was the pro-Sinhalese and pro-Buddhist institutions that initially propagated divisive ethnic politics. The mechanism used to achieve this was the Sinhala language. The electoral system, constitutional structure, and the country's demographics were no doubt conducive to generating demands that favored the Sinhalese and marginalized the Tamils. Yet those seeking to institute a Sinhalese ethnocracy needed an issue to mobilize around, and the call for a Sinhala-only policy provided an overarching mechanism for doing so. What ultimately needs to be recognized is that if the success of this Sinhalese upward mobility was effectively generated through the manipulation of state institutions, then the relative deprivation effectively imposed on the Tamils was in turn a gross failure of these very institutions, designed to promote equality and impartiality.

Ensuring the implementation of divisive policies also meant controlling and emasculating the judiciary. The 1972 constitution granted the legislature power over the judiciary, and this led the government to coerce and dismiss certain justices and promote those supportive of governmental policies. As already noted, such control and coercion were especially rampant during the post-1977 UNP era, when justices ruling against the government's preferences, ethnic or otherwise, had to face state-sponsored goondas shouting threats outside their offices and homes. If such practices were undemocratic, they were nevertheless considered essential for stability and, from an ethnic standpoint, for the government's legitimacy in the eyes of the majority. But the very rationale justifying such actions encouraged a milieu that in turn promoted an institutional culture negating minority rights. Ultimately, a host of institutions, both governmental and private, acted in unison to dismantle the Tamils' advantages. Referring to the discriminatory legislation imposed on the Tamils, the Federal Party's Naganathan had noted as early as December 1960: "You cannot build a Government on such petty and rotten foundations and actions. You will be crushed. . . . Is this the rotten foundations on which they are going to build their future? To placate the mob, to enjoy a moment's popularity with the mob they will do anything."[34] The 1983 riots exemplified how rotten the state's institutions had become and the disastrous impact this had on the Tamils and the country.

The Internationalization of Sri Lanka's Civil War

Sri Lanka's major parties, like most political parties, distinguish themselves ideologically. Consequently, while the UNP has been pro-Western and pro-market, the SLFP has historically supported leftist/communist regimes, encouraged welfare policies, and shown a penchant for state-centrism. The historically laissez-faire UNP came into power in 1977 determined to open Sri Lanka's economy, and that in turn entailed friendlier policies toward the West. Both were ideologically compatible with the UNP's past. But pursuing friendly relations with India was also a long-standing UNP policy, despite various UNP leaders' suspicions of Indian hegemonic designs. The UNP's post-1977 structural adjustment program and the escalating rebel movement in the Northern Province influenced Jayewardene and the party to further expand their pro-Western foreign policy, however, given that the government's legitimacy soon became tied to the economic reforms being successful. For example, besides disregarding Third World sentiments and siding with the West on a number of international issues (e.g., supporting the United Kingdom in the Falklands War and opposing the Soviet invasion of Afghanistan), the government also tried to join ASEAN; claimed that a defense pact reached with Britain just before independence was still in force—a claim that, while technically correct, showed a blatant attempt to move away from India's influence; sought to lease the strategically situated Trincomalee oil farm to an American concern; and reached agreement with the Americans to host a powerful Voice of America station, which the Indians believed could be used for surveillance purposes. Furthermore, the government contracted with Israeli intelligence agencies—Shin Beth and Mossad—and ex-SAS (Special Air Service) commandos from Britain to train its soldiers, thereby providing these agencies with a strategic presence in the island. The frosty relations between Jayewardene and Indira Gandhi also convinced some that Sri Lanka's actions were designed to spite Mrs. Gandhi and deliberately undermine India's regional security interests, and ultimately all this provided ample fodder for the Indian government to retaliate by trying to destabilize Sri Lanka's politics.[35] With the Tamils in Tamil Nadu demanding that the Indian central government intervene and help Sri Lanka's Tamils, with the ruling Congress Party dependant on Tamil Nadu's vote base, and with Sri Lanka's foreign policy considered intransigent and truculent, India's leading external intelligence agency, the Research and Analysis Wing (RAW), began to arm, train, and financially support the Tamil rebels. India was never intent on seeing Sri Lanka dismembered, because that would have encouraged certain secessionist groups within India itself, but RAW nonetheless gave the rebels a life buoy, and it is clear that Tamil separatism would never have reached its present deadly stage without this initial support.

There is a significant Sri Lankan Tamil diaspora in numerous Western countries, which soon began supporting the rebels financially as well. As the number of Tamils fleeing Sri Lanka increased, so did the diaspora support for the rebels. These diaspora groups soon began lobbying legislatures in Washington, D.C., Ottawa, Canberra, London, and many Western European countries, creating a well-funded, well-organized, and highly sophisticated transnational movement whose sole goal was to create a separate Tamil state in Sri Lanka. By the time the Indians, under Rajiv Gandhi, decided to halt their support for the rebels and instead impose an agreement between the Sri Lankan government and the LTTE, the latter, which had turned out to be the dominant group in the Tamil resistance, was well on its way to being able to support itself by relying on its business dealings, both legal and illegal, and on the Tamil diaspora (see chapter 7).

The Sinhala-Only Policy and Ethnic Conflict

The year 1983 is rightly seen as the beginning of Sri Lanka's savage ethnic conflict, but only an overly simplistic explanation would claim that that year's worst-ever anti-Tamil riots were the cause of the conflict. While economic rivalry and ethnic jealousies partly lay behind the 1983 riots, the major reasons were the Sinhala-only language policy and the culture of ethnic outbidding and the institutional decay that the language issue initiated, enculturated, and legitimated. It was the Official Language Act and the blatant discrimination that it imposed on the Tamils over two decades that led to the Tamil quest for *eelam*. This determination to attain Tamil nationhood was exemplified by Suntharalingam, who, despite mocking S. J. V. Chelvanayakam's quest for federalism, claimed in 1957 that "if the Sinhalese will not agree to federation the Tamils will have a fully autonomous Tamil linguistic State by whatever means they can get it, by all the methods of history—rebellion, guerilla warfare or anything you please."[36] As we have seen, such warnings were not only disregarded, but successive Sinhalese governments continued their ethnic outbidding to consistently deny the Tamils their language rights. That the Tamil quest for *eelam* is thus rooted in the discriminatory Official Language Act is overlooked, because scholars have failed to recognize the degree to which the Sinhala-only policy influenced the ethnic conflict.

Most scholars evaluate the Sinhala-only movement and the 1956 riots without adequate assessment of their effect. David Laitin has even suggested, remarkably, that the Sinhalese-Tamil "language conflict was one of the factors that worked to *ameliorate* violence [emphasis added], but other factors outweighed the language issue to drive Sri Lanka into large-scale ethnic war."[37] This argument is based on the belief that ethnic violence is unrelated to linguistic differences between groups and state language policies. The preceding discussion makes it clear, however, that Sri Lanka's discriminatory language policy was the catalyst for the island's civil war. While other factors certainly accentuated Sinhalese-Tamil differences, they hardly "outweighed the language issue."

The fact is that the Sirimavo Bandaranaike governments were so successful in favoring the Sinhalese and implementing the Sinhala-only policy that it was soon the majority community that was disproportionately overrepresented in the bureaucracy. For example, while Tamils constituted 40 percent of the General Clerical Service during independence, their numbers had dropped to under 6 percent in 1981. And according to the Public and Semi Government Services census conducted in 1994, the Sinhalese, who made up nearly 74 percent of the population, held 91.2

percent of the jobs, while the Tamils (12.5 percent), Indian Tamils (5.6 percent), and Moors (8 percent) held only 5.2 percent, 0.2 percent, and 2.7 percent respectively.[38] This in a country with 700,000 public servants, which makes it the Asian state with the highest ratio of civil servants to citizens.

As soon as the Sinhala-only legislation was enacted, Bandaranaike issued Gazette Notification No. 10,949, declaring that any languages hitherto used were to be continued until the requisite changes were implemented. The Gazette Notification itself ensured there would be no immediate switchover to a Sinhala-only milieu.[39] The fact, however, is that the legislation, coupled with its anti-Tamil rhetoric and ethnic outbidding, in turn influenced pro-Sinhalese state employment and educational policies at a time when the state was the largest employer and university education was viewed as a sure road to socioeconomic progress.

An utter disregard for Tamil ensued soon after the Official Language Act was passed in the House, so that less than a month later (and before the act had passed the Senate), Tamil senators were complaining that all the signs in the Ministry of Education were in Sinhala only.[40] Barely three months later, Tamil legislators also complained that most official invitations were extended in English or Sinhala but not Tamil, and that some government departments were corresponding with Tamils in Sinhala, despite their not knowing the language.[41] While all electoral registers for the 1956 election were prepared in Sinhala, Tamil, and English, the registers in Colombo's parliamentary electorates for the March 1960 election were in Sinhala and English only, and this despite Colombo's large Tamil and Muslim population. By the end of 1960, Tamil politicians complained that while numerous Sinhalese textbooks had been published, Tamil versions were not,[42] and that the Official Language Department,[43] which replaced the National Languages Department soon after the Official Language Act was passed, was obstructing the work done by the section overseeing Tamil affairs.[44] This disregard for Tamil was so pervasive by 1968 that there were 129 government departments and corporations with no Tamil translators, 122 government departments and corporations with no Tamils typists, and 68 government departments and corporations with no Tamil typewriters (with the Governor-General's Office, Prime Minister's Office, Cabinet Office, Office of the Leader of the House of Representatives, the Army, the Royal Ceylon Air Force, the Police Department, and the Department of Immigration and Emigration included in the first two categories, and most of them also included in the third category).[45] By the late 1960s, even individuals' transfers and promotions to governmental departments were being debated in parliament along ethnic lines.[46] All this had led Sinhalese panjandrums, many of whom were given sinecures to make the government look good in the eyes of the majority community, to develop a superiority complex vis-à-vis Tamils especially.

The Official Language Act and the anti-Tamil milieu it spawned encouraged an increasingly Sinhalized police, military, and civil service to heap indignities on Tamils, which constantly reminded even the most peace-loving Tamils that, rather than dealing with dispassionate bodies, they were being dominated by partial and hostile institutions representing an ethnocentric state. The FP's Naganathan noted: "[W]hen a Sinhalese man says that Tamils cannot have Tamil, Burghers cannot have English and Muslims cannot have Tamil, that they must have Sinhala only, that is not democracy. That is not a mandate. That is tyranny."[47]

What ought to be obvious by now is that the Official Language Act was not just another piece of legislation, which is why Tamils never ceased to praise their language, defend it, and clamor for linguistic parity. Indeed, their quest for linguistic parity was their most consistent demand, together with the consistent promise that they would never rest until their language was given its due recognition. At very least, they demanded official status for Tamil in the Northern and Eastern Provinces, because they saw their language as inextricably connected to their very livelihoods. And the FP never ceased to emphasize this, because the Tamil language remained the party's most comprehensive national symbol, given "the multi-religious confluence of the Tamils."[48] Consequently, in 1960, Naganathan passionately proclaimed: "What is the history of the Tamils? What is the history of our language? Our language, the Tamil language, is one of the most ancient classical languages in the world. Latin is dead, Sanskrit is dead, Pali is dead and classical Greek is dead. Classical Tamil alone lives today."[49] And Amirthalingam noted in July 1964: "The Sinhala only policy . . . means not merely the elimination of the Tamil language from its due place in the public life of this country but the shutting out of the Tamil-speaking people of this country from the political, economic and cultural life of Ceylon."[50] These Tamil politicians and their colleagues fully realized that the Official Language Act was the mechanism used by successive Sinhalese governments to ensure the socioeconomic dominance of the Sinhalese, and they consequently made recognition of their language a nonnegotiable demand.

There can be little doubt that Tamils' attempts to get the Official Language Act revoked also exacerbated anti-Tamil sentiments and further radicalized Sinhalese nationalists. These nationalists had fought hard to get the Sinhala-only policy implemented, and they did not hesitate to retaliate when they felt that Tamil pressure might force politicians to abrogate the Sinhala-only legislation. The Indian National Congress, by mobilizing nonviolent protests, had clearly shown how satyagraha campaigns could engender revolutionary transformations, and the lesson was not lost on the radical Sinhalese, who feared that the Tamils were resorting to similar tactics to undermine their community's gains. Nationalist groups and opposition parties constantly argued likewise when resorting to ethnic outbidding, with the UNP and SLFP taking turns claiming that the other had made a secret pact with the FP that would reverse the Sinhala-only policy. Consequently, even those Sinhalese who had favored some compromise in June 1956 soon thereafter adopted an uncompromising stand when dealing with the Tamils.

Communalism had been part of the island's politics starting around the beginning of the twentieth century, but it was the Official Language Act that made it a malevolent force. As N. M. Perera noted in June 1957, "never was there so much communal tension outside as today. Never was there that. The Federal Party existed for nine years. . . . But there was no such feeling of this disunity, of communal clashes, of the possibility of communal clashes of this type until the Sinhala Only Act was passed and the consequences which arose therefrom."[51] For nearly two decades, the Tamils too kept reiterating that it was the MEP's Sinhala-only legislation that was responsible for the severe downturn in Sinhalese-Tamils relations and the subsequent violence, and this is clear to anyone who peruses the parliamentary record or the newspapers covering the 1956–77 period. Chelvanayakam, for example, said: "The threat to communal amity, or rather the killing of communal amity, was carried out by the Government by its language policy."[52] And even after the Tamil Language (Special Provisions) Act had passed, Suntharalingam argued that "there can be no communal peace in this country as long as my Friend's nefarious Sinhala only Official Language Act continues to remain on the statute-book."[53] Amirthalingam likewise averred: "You will never have normal communal relations in this country as long as the obnoxious Sinhala Only Act remains on the statute book," because that act had "resulted in the creation of Herrenvolk—to use Hitler's term—in this country, making of the Tamil people a subject race dependent on the mercy of the hoodlums and the looters of the South."[54] In April 1960, when both the UNP and the SLFP under Mrs. Bandaranaike were resorting to the most despicable anti-Tamil rhetoric, S. M. Rasamanickam, the Tamil representative for Paddiruppu, observed that "the moment the Sinhala Only Act was passed in this country," the island had become unalterably "divided into the Sinhalese-speaking people and the Tamil-speaking people. . . . It is a worse division than the division envisaged under a federal set-up."[55] And in the mid-1960s, Naganathan could still say: "If we submit to the imposition of Sinhala in our areas, we are accepting for ever Sinhala domination, Sinhala supremacy, Sinhala rule, which is a substitute for colonial rule. . . . Today the language question has become a question of freedom."[56] With the 1956 riots having erupted the day the Official Language Act was introduced in parliament, and the 1958 riots having followed on the heels of the "anti-*sri*" campaign, the Tamils were fully aware that the Sinhala-only policy was responsible for all the anti-Tamil violence. The fundamental question that should be addressed when seeking to explain Sri Lanka's ethnic conflict is this: Why is extensive Sinhalese-Tamil violence a post-1956 phenomenon? The answer lies in the Sinhala-only movement and the Sinhala-only language policy.

It is clear that colonization and resource allocation played a major role in Sinhalese-Tamil hostilities, but the fact is that Tamils came to resent colonization principally after the Sinhala-only movement gathered momentum. Government-sponsored colonization was instituted in the early 1930s and intensified after independence, primarily because of the high unemployment and population density in the Western and Southern Provinces. But just as the Federal Party gained popularity after the Sinhala-only movement gained momentum, the protests over colonization heightened once Tamils came to view Sinhalese resettlement as a calculated attempt to vitiate the Federal Party's call for a linguistically based federal structure.[57] Indeed, the FP, despite being organized in December 1949 and having mobilized in the Tamil areas since then, won only two of seven seats it contested in the 1952 election. Even Chelvanayakam failed to win a parliamentary seat during the 1952 election. On the other hand, the FP won ten seats in the 1956 election, and the party and Chelvanayakam solidified their positions as the Tamil nation's main representatives. This was clear from how the party fared in subsequent elections, when it won fifteen seats in March 1960, sixteen seats in July 1960, fourteen seats in 1965, and thirteen seats in 1970. That linguistic nationalism was the key to the FP's success is well expressed by A. Jeyaratnam Wilson:

An oft-repeated refrain of the FP was about the dangers of Sinhala state-aided colonisation. But this did not catch on. While the Ceylon Tamils became increasingly conscious of the discrimination being practiced against them by the Sinhala-dominated state, they had not yet established the connection between language and territory. That only became a live issue after the language riots of 1956 and 1958 and after the enactment of the Sinhala Only Act in 1956.[58]

The Federal Party's calls for federalism and an end to Sinhalese colonization merged into its larger goal of obtaining a Tamil-speaking state. This was made clear on a number of occasions, as when the party's Working Committee adopted a resolution, soon after the Official

Language Act was passed, that encouraged the Tamils "to establish an autonomous Tamil linguistic state within a Federal form of government which would allow the Tamil language, traditions and homeland to be preserved inviolate." Emphasizing the importance of language, the party further called on the Tamils to

Refuse to transact any business with the government in Sinhalese; parents, school authorities and teachers should refuse to teach in Sinhalese; Tamil public servants should refuse to study in Sinhalese even if compelled to do so; and all local bodies, community centers and semi-official bodies should communicate with the government in Tamil or English.[59]

The language issue thus permeated all considerations, among both the Sinhalese and Tamils, and linguistic nationalism galvanized interethnic relations in the post-1956 era. K. M. de Silva rightly observes:

Up to the early 1950s the Tamils' concept of nationalism lacked coherence and cohesion despite all their talk of a linguistic, religious and cultural separateness from the Sinhalese. As with the Sinhalese, it was language that provided the sharp cutting edge of a new national self-consciousness. Indeed, the Federal Party's crucial contribution to Tamil politics was its emphasis on the role of language as the determinant of nationhood."[60]

It was Sinhalese, however, who turned the Tamil language into a nationalistic identity construct. Tamil nationalism might have been indefeasible, but it had remained torpid. When it did erupt, it represented a reactive nationalism, influenced by the Sinhala-only policy and its attendant ethnic outbidding, as opposed to a proactive nationalism. As Nigel Harris has aptly noted:

Successive [Sinhalese] governments were more preoccupied with securing their own base among the Sinhalese . . . at virtually any cost—or rather, in the political auction, preventing themselves being pushed out by their rivals. If the Tamils had not existed, Colombo would have had to invent them. And, in an important sense, it did. It was Colombo that forced the inhabitants of the north to become different, to cease to be Sri Lankan and become exclusively Tamil.[61]

The Official Language Act was the mechanism that achieved this. Sinhalese and Tamils had maintained their distinct ethnic differences over the centuries and still, in the main, coexisted peacefully. The communalistic rhetoric G. G. Ponnambalam unleashed during the 1930s and 1940s over the "fifty-fifty" campaign certainly frayed ethnic ties, but relations between the groups, and especially their political elites, remained commendably strong, Sinhalese and Tamils united to seek independence from the British, and Ponnambalam and Suntharalingam became cabinet ministers in the island's first postindependence government. Rather than conciliating the Tamils, satisfying some of their rightful desires, and thereby building on this unity, the Official Language Act created a chasm between the communities. As Nigel Harris observed, "if the gods had wished to destroy, the madness of Sri Lanka's rulers gave them every opportunity."[62]

Post-1977 Linguistic Accommodation: Too Little, Too Late

"The official Language of Sri Lanka shall be Sinhala," the island's 1978 constitution declared; and it added that "the official language shall be the language of administration throughout Sri Lanka," even while recognizing Tamil as a national language to be used for all transactions in the Northern and Eastern Provinces. It also gave "Buddhism the foremost place" and mandated that "it shall be the duty of the state to protect and foster the Buddha *Sasana* [Buddhist institutions and religion]."

The Language of the Courts (Special Provisions) Law, which enabled the use of Tamil in the Northern and Eastern Provinces, was enacted in 1973 to overcome the linguistic difficulties imposed by the Language of the Courts Act No. 3 of 1961. The 1978 constitution declared that "no citizen shall suffer any disability by reason of language" and guaranteed the use of Tamil in courthouses throughout the island. It further incorporated the Tamil Language Special Provisions Act No. 28 of 1958 as a permanent feature of the constitution. To compensate for the desultory functioning of the Department of Official Languages that was created under the Ministry of Finance in 1955, the UNP government also recreated an Official Language Department in 1978. If all this meant sudden progress for the Tamil language, it was merely progress on paper, however, for it became clear to many that "Sinhalese chauvinists in the government and the ruling party had thwarted attempts to enlarge dramatically the official use of Tamil."[63] Successive governments nevertheless continued in their quest to, at least on paper, make the Tamil language equal to Sinhalese. Subsequently, in line with the July 1987 Indo-Lanka Peace Accords, the Thirteenth Amendment to the constitution made Tamil an official language in November 1987, while the Sixteenth Amendment solidified this position by declaring both Sinhala and Tamil to be national languages for administrative purposes. Under the Official Language Commission Act No. 18 of 1991, another UNP government further created an Official Languages Commission to implement language policy. That nearly a decade later, at the beginning of the twenty-first century, when Tamils continue to experience difficulties when dealing with some government institutions that demand interactions in Sinhala; when certain courts conduct proceedings in Sinhala to prosecute Tamils not fluent in Sinhala; when the destination boards on buses and signs in hospitals, police stations, and post offices rarely include Tamil; when Tamil students, especially in rural areas, are deprived of equal educational opportunities mainly as a result of thousands of Tamil teaching positions not being filled; when government-produced Tamil school texts are replete with mistakes; and when it is Sinhalese and Buddhist history that dominates such texts, while the minorities' religious and cultural heritage is disregarded,[64] it would appear that this Official Languages Commission has hardly succeeded in its mandate.

One reason that the commission failed was that it was not given adequate authority to deal with those discriminating against the Tamil language. For example, the Official Languages Commission Act No. 18 of 1991 prohibits prosecuting anyone unless it can be proven the violator deliberately sought to avoid using Tamil. And even then the commission must have the attorney general's permission to carry out the prosecution. In a government dominated by Sinhalese who, in the main, do not speak and write Tamil, and where resources such as Tamil typewriters and typists are a rarity, it is almost impossible to prove that a Sinhalese official was deliberately avoiding using Tamil. Ultimately, the facts that the 1978 constitution did not address the long-standing Tamil claim for autonomy and that the Tamil language was afforded equal status only after Tamil youths mobilized militarily seeking *eelam* further suggest that the J. R. Jayewardene government's accommodative language policies were too little too late.

Under Chandrika Kumaratunga, the government continued to support the use of Tamil. The constitution allows for Tamil to be used for administrative purposes in any divisional secretariat divisions where Tamil speakers number one-fifth of the population, and in December 1999, the Kumaratunga government preened itself on proclaiming that this was to be permitted in the Nuwara Eliya and Badulla districts. The fact that such action had not been taken before, despite Tamils and Muslims demanding that the constitutional provision be honored, and the fact that similar status was not afforded to the Colombo divisional secretariat division, goes to show how little the Tamil language has been accommodated. Indeed, the chairman of the Official Languages Commission himself has pointed out that not one of the fourteen police stations within Colombo's city limits has a single constable who knows Tamil, despite the fact that nearly 60 percent of the residents speak Tamil![65] The situation is no different in the various bureaucracies, where Sinhalese bureaucrats disregard rules and instructions and continue to communicate with Tamils in Sinhala.[66] Indeed, such occurrences are so pervasive that the manifesto of the Tamil National Alliance (the four-party alliance that contested the December 2001 parliamentary elections) bemoaned, "The Sinhala language is yet the only language used even in some parts of the Tamil homeland."

In the meantime, over a hundred so-called international schools have opened, especially in Colombo, catering in English only to the rich and upper middle classes, even as the government seeks ways to introduce English in a more substantive fashion in all educational institutions throughout the island. Indeed, even some rabid nationalists in the Sinhala Urumaya (Sinhala Heritage) now advocate using English as a medium of instruction. The government has consequently proposed allowing advanced level students (those between grades eleven and thirteen) in the sciences to study in English, claimed it wants English to be introduced as a medium in all schools by 2003, and established an English and Foreign Languages Unit in the Ministry of Education. Advocating policies is easily done; implementing those policies, on the other hand, can present numerous hurdles. Especially given the dearth of qualified English teachers, it is debatable whether the government's ambitious agenda is realizable. One also wonders to what extent such policies would further marginalize rural students, and the socioeconomic and political impact this may have in the future.

The irony in all this is that while the Official Language Act unleashed ethnic outbidding and contributed to the Sinhalese-Tamil conflict, it failed to empower fully those Sinhalese the act targeted. Thus, a government-owned publication lamented that "[t]he social recognition that the Sinhala language enjoyed in the post-1956 era has waned. There is even a reincarnation of the spirit of contempt . . . [with] which the colonial masters" used to look "down upon the Sinhala educated,"[67] and an English weekly could recently note that although S. W. R. D. Bandaranaike's "idiotic 'Sinhala only' policy sought to dismantle the influence of the country's English-speaking elite, . . . the effect was entirely the opposite." According to the newspaper,

Today, this very elite has a monopoly on industry and commerce. Non-English speakers have been entirely disenfranchised, and the country has been inherited by the very minority Bandaranaike sought to disable. The rich kids who are today being educated at the tutories passing off as "international schools" in Colombo have the advantage of competing only amongst themselves: the vast majority of Sri Lanka's youth cannot ever match them. Thanks be to SWRD!"[68]

7

THE LIBERATION TIGERS OF TAMIL
EELAM AND ETHNIC CONFLICT

Some perspicacious Sinhalese and Tamils had warned that the Sinhala-only policy might radicalize the latter and encourage secession, but none could have dreamed that the quest for *eelam* would become so violent. The Sinhalese had no reason to believe the Tamils would embrace such insensate violence, because two decades of satyagraha campaigns and fasts had suggested Sinhalese preferences could be instituted without any adverse Tamil backlash. For the Tamils, on the other hand, the idea that their youth could resort to terrorism was inconceivable. Indeed, the beliefs that Sinhalese and Tamils held about themselves and the stereotypes they entertained about each other made it clear that neither considered the Tamils to be violent. Studies conducted soon after independence indicate some interesting perceptions: Sinhalese thought Tamils were arrogant, kind, cunning, thrifty, proud, clever, and clannish; Tamils thought Sinhalese were proud, lazy, and bold; Sinhalese children especially considered their kin to be bold, but neither group attributed violence or boldness to the Tamils.[1] The violence the Tamil rebel groups unleashed on the Sri Lankan state and on one another has altered that perception, and this is evident in the way Sri Lankans of all backgrounds perceive the LTTE's quest for *eelam*. The preceding chapters have shown how Sinhalese ethnocentrism transformed pacific Tamils into terrorists. We now turn to the rise of the Liberation Tigers of Tamil Eelam and the question of why the government has failed to defeat or tame them and end the ethnic conflict.

The Rise of Tamil Militarism

As we have already noted, Sirimavo Bandaranaike's utter disregard for Tamils' legitimate grievances especially radicalized Tamil youth. Tamil politicians may have partly designed the Vaddukoddai Resolution to pressure the government and appease the restive youth, but it is also clear that the 1972 constitution influenced some Tamils who had once advocated compromise to rethink the chances of achieving *eelam*. Thus, just before his death, S. J. V. Chelvanayakam made it clear that the FP had moved beyond demanding a federal constitution, even while maintaining that the separate state he envisioned would be attained through peaceful means. Speaking in parliament, he said: "We have abandoned the demand for a federal constitution. Our movement will be all nonviolent. . . . We know that the Sinhalese people will one day grant our demand and that we will be able to establish a separate state from the rest of the island."[2] When asked how this would eventuate, he responded: "We [Tamils] would make such a nuisance of ourselves that they [the Sinhalese] would throw us out."[3] The "nuisance" that lay in store for Sri Lankans would, however, arguably be the world's deadliest separatist struggle.

The May 1976 Vaddukoddai Resolution and the July 1977 TULF election manifesto could be read as jeremiads justifying the need for *eelam* and were released when Tamil nationalism, especially among the youth, was at a boil. The Official Language Act and the anti-Tamil riots of 1956 and 1958; the language policy's influence on state employment; the military's ham-handed occupation of the Northern Province and the soldiers' humiliating treatment of Tamils; the racist anti-Tamil rhetoric emanating especially from SLFP members and Sinhalese extremists; continued colonization of Tamil lands, coupled with a calibrated policy that prevented resources being allocated to Tamil areas; the attack by government forces during the International Tamil Conference in January 1974, which killed nine Tamils; discriminatory university policies; and an ethnocentric constitution had all coalesced to encourage Tamil militarism. The 1972 constitution especially had a profound psychological impact on Tamils, because while Sinhalese ethnocentrism had hitherto been advocated through rhetoric, parliamentary bills (which could always be changed by majority vote), and selective practices within the bureaucracies, that ethnocentrism was now constitutionalized. As already noted, a country's constitution is also its most important institution, and the 1972 constitution explicitly relegated the island's minorities to second-class status.

Chelvanayakam died in March 1977, just four months before Jayewardene's UNP came to power. Tamils had by then lost almost all confidence that the Sri Lankan state would treat them fairly, if not equally. The UNP's campaign promises and massive electoral victory in July allowed for some hope, but the anti-Tamil riots that followed in August, coupled with the racism displayed by leading UNP members, raised doubts as to whether the government was fully committed to promoting ethnic harmony. Jayewardene was determined to maintain the unitary state, and it soon became clear that he too was bound to disregard Tamils' grievances. Indeed, Sinhalese were so committed to the notion of the unitary state that Jayewardene and his government, rather than using their vast majority in parliament to push for a credible devolutionary arrangement that would have appeased the Tamils, introduced an ineffective District Development Councils (DDC) system. The TULF contested the DDC elections in 1981, notwithstanding its call for a separate Tamil state in the Vaddukoddai Resolution and the 1977 election manifesto, perhaps to indicate that the party was willing to operate within a united Sri Lanka.[4] It was clear to all, however, that Jayewardene and the UNP meant to maintain the DDCs as impotent local branches, designed to be controlled by the center, and this convinced those Tamils who had placed a modicum of faith in Jayewardene that there was no Sinhalese leader they could trust to give them a fair deal. While he later, in a rare admission, conceded that his "own lack of intelligence, lack of foresight and courage were to blame" for not accommodating the Tamils,[5] it was also clear that Jayewardene preferred to see the Tamil problem fester, since, he believed, that enabled him to maintain an iron grip on the polity and institute his preferences. Jayewardene was thus no different from the postindependence leaders who preceded him: enslaved to perpetuating his political career and wielding absolute power, he too deliberately exacerbated the island's ethnic relations for personal political gain. Indeed, one could argue that Jayewardene was the most perfidious of all, because it was abundantly clear when he came to office that the Tamil rebels were getting out of hand, and he, unlike his predecessors, had arrogated to himself all the necessary powers to rectify the problem politically. His clumsy handling of the situation merely radicalized and legitimized the rebels.

The Liberation Tigers of Tamil Eelam

There had been some minor altercations between the Sri Lankan military and Tamil youth in the Northern Province prior to 1970, but what transpired subsequently was full-fledged rebellion. In 1970, Tamil youths had formed the Tamil Students' Federation, which was rechristened the Tamil New Tigers soon thereafter and then renamed the Liberation Tigers of Tamil Eelam under Vellupillai Prabhakaran in 1976. A split within the LTTE led to Uma Maheshwaran forming the People's Liberation Organization of Tamil Eelam (PLOTE) in 1980. There were also three other groups that played significant roles in fighting for a separate Tamil state: the Tamil Eelam Liberation Organization (TELO), headed by Sri

Sabaratnam; the Eelam Revolutionary Organization of Students (EROS), headed by Velupillai Balakumar; and the Eelam People's Revolutionary Liberation Front (EPRLF), headed by K. Padmanabha. There was little agreement among the numerous rebel groups, which at one time may have numbered nearly forty. The LTTE eventually eradicated TELO and marginalized the others, and it is now the only group fighting for a separate state.

In the early 1970s, Tamil youths began robbing state-owned banks to support their insurrection and killing policemen (who were often Tamil) and Tamil politicians colluding with the UNP and SLFP. The militant youth were called "the boys," and many Tamils justified their actions by juxtaposing them with the looting, arson, murder, and rape perpetrated by Sinhalese mobs and the security forces. The first prominent assassination that stunned the northeast took place in July 1975, when a twenty-year-old named Vellupillai Prabhakaran killed Jaffna's mayor, Alfred Duraiappah. The mayor belonged to the SLFP, and the youth and many others considered him a traitor for being so unabashedly loyal to Sirimavo Bandaranaike.[6]

Prabhakaran, the youngest of four children, had been born just two years before the Official Language Act was passed and was consequently exposed to successive governments' anti-Tamil actions at an early age.[7] He quit school at sixteen and, together with seven others, organized a militant group to fight the Sinhalese army. The unnamed group had no weapons and initially relied on crude homemade guns and bombs to rob banks and attack the police. In 1976, Prabhakaran formed the LTTE. Two years later, the group identified itself by claiming responsibility for eleven high profile killings.

By the early 1980s, the LTTE and other Tamil groups had become more daring in their attacks against police and military personnel, whose colleagues retaliated by attacking Tamil civilians. While the military authorities initially sought to discipline soldiers who reacted with excessive violence, doing so demoralized the forces. On the other hand, attacking innocent civilians further radicalized average Tamils and generated fresh recruits for the rebel groups. On July 23, 1983, the LTTE ambushed an army patrol and killed thirteen Sinhalese soldiers in Tinneveli. The army retaliated by going on a killing spree in the Northern Peninsula in which nearly sixty Tamils died, but only the LTTE attack was made public. When the soldiers' bodies were brought to Colombo, Sri Lanka's worst-ever anti-Tamil riots spread throughout the country. The rioting has already been discussed in the previous chapter, but what bears repeating is that these riots led to a Tamil exodus to the Northern and Eastern Provinces that saw the various rebel groups, none of which had over fifty cadres,[8] increase their membership by the hundreds and thousands.[9] Equally important, the Jayewardene government introduced the Sixth Amendment to the constitution in August 1983, which required all parliamentarians to swear an oath proclaiming loyalty to the island's constitution. The TULF refused to do so, since the constitution upheld the unitary state structure, and boycotted parliament. That in turn further legitimized the militants, who were now determined to fully marginalize the moderates and violently pursue *eelam*.

While all the other major rebel groups had some Marxist-Leninist leanings, the LTTE, from its inception, most ardently embraced Tamil nationalism.[10] The LTTE's chief spokesman and ideologue, Anton Balasingham, initially used Marxist rhetoric to justify the need for *eelam*, but now all Tigers stick to Tamil nationalism and socialism when discussing the future Tamil state. Interestingly, while they have vilified the TULF and Tamil moderates, the LTTE consider their organization to be Chelvanayakam's only true successor.[11] The irony here is that Chelvanayakam was almost Gandhian in his nonviolent approach to life and politics, while the LTTE is one of the most violent separatist groups of the twentieth century.

There can be no doubt that the Tigers are arguably the most disciplined, dedicated, and ruthless guerrilla organization in the world.[12] The group's men and women cadres abstain from premarital and extramarital sexual activities and eschew alcohol and drugs. All LTTE fighters take an oath of loyalty to Prabhakaran. Since Prabhakaran believes that anyone will eventually succumb if tortured hard enough, LTTE fighters carry a cyanide capsule to commit suicide if threatened with capture. Many have done just that. In fact, the cyanide capsule has come to symbolize the LTTE's determination to create *eelam*.

It appears that while Prabhakaran consults with his political and military advisers, he alone makes the major decisions.[13] He has consequently been portrayed both as a murderous megalomaniac and as a brilliant strategist.[14] The LTTE has a Central Committee that basically approves Prabhakaran's dictates and political and military wings that ensure that those dictates are implemented. While the political wing covers areas such as the courts, economic development, health care, education, and the arts and culture, the military wing oversees policing, recruitment, finance, intelligence gathering, and special operations.[15] In wartime, the LTTE's regional leaders are permitted to use their discretion when attacking the Sri Lankan forces and are also encouraged to carry out at least one mission every day against government interests. The group thus combines an autocratic politico-military structure with some operational latitude.

The LTTE and the other Tamil groups were initially trained by India's external intelligence agency, the Research and Analysis Wing, which sought to undermine the Sri Lankan government, because India was upset over J. R. Jayewardene's post-1977 pro-Western policies, but some rebels were also trained elsewhere.[16] The training the RAW imparted, coupled with the camps the rebels built in Tamil Nadu, laid the foundation for challenging Sri Lanka's sovereignty. The LTTE was not one of the RAW's favorite organizations, and it was arguably the first to realize that the Tamils were being used to further India's regional designs.[17] Indian support for the secessionists was no doubt partly influenced by the Indian central government's alliance with Tamil Nadu's ruling party, the All India Anna Dravida Munnetra Kazhagam, whose leader, M. G. Ramachandran, and millions of India's Tamils sympathized with their fellow Tamils in Sri Lanka. But it is also clear that the RAW felt cocky about controlling the rebels and believed it could terminate the Tamil uprising in Sri Lanka's northeast whenever it suited India. This turned out to be one of the biggest miscalculations the RAW ever made.[18]

By the mid-1980s, both the rebel groups and the military were massacring people with abandon. The rebels killed security personnel and innocent Sinhalese in the border areas, while the security forces retaliated by burning Tamils' property, raping Tamil women, and often systematically killing civilians. It was difficult to distinguish between the rebels and civilians who were uninvolved, and no mercy was shown young Tamils by the military, which rounded them up by the dozen and imprisoned them under the Prevention of Terrorism Act. These prisoners were often tortured and then disappeared. The madness was taken to new heights when the LTTE went to Anuradhapura, a city sacred to Buddhists the world over, and massacred 146 civilians and worshipers. Soon thereafter the Indian government arranged for Sri Lankan government representatives to meet rebel leaders in Thimpu, Bhutan, and forced the Tamil groups to send representatives to the discussions.

The rebels made four principal demands at the Thimpu meeting: the Tamils of Sri Lanka should be recognized as a distinct nation; the northeast should be recognized as their historical homeland; they should be allowed the right of self-determination; and all Tamils should be granted Sri Lankan citizenship. The last demand was designed to benefit the many Indian Tamils who were denied citizenship by the Sri Lankan state. The talks collapsed when the government refused to meet these conditions, and violence between the rebels and the security forces continued despite an ongoing truce. The demands made in Thimpu have continued to form the bases for all the LTTE's subsequent negotiations with successive Sri Lankan governments.

The 1983 riots had driven thousands of Tamils to seek refuge in India and various Western countries, and by the late 1980s, many among them organized to create a well-financed and efficient international movement whose sole goal was to somehow create a separate state for Sri Lanka's Tamils.[19] The contributions the diaspora collected to support Tamil *eelam* were initially voluntary, but they were just as likely to be extorted.[20] The diaspora's contributions allowed the LTTE to invest abroad in gas stations, restaurants, grocery stores, farms, real estate, stock and money markets, finance companies, phone card companies, the gold trade, export-import businesses, and nearly a dozen ships, which, while mostly engaged in legal trade, are used to transport arms.[21] The group also bought newspapers, radio stations, and television networks to keep the Tamil diaspora informed about the war. Battlefield successes were often accompanied by large-scale voluntary donations, and the LTTE's video crews filmed all major battles and distributed the film abroad.[22] Reports, never fully substantiated, also suggest that the LTTE uses its ships to smuggle drugs. All in all, the LTTE collected approximately $80 million per year during the 1990s,[23] but that figure went down after the group was proscribed, especially in the United States, Canada, Australia, and the United Kingdom, and the post–September 11, 2001, milieu led to increased scrutiny of money transfers to terrorist organizations.

The LTTE's fighting prowess was especially evidenced when it took on the Indian Peacekeeping Force (IPKF) between 1987 and 1990. India's prime minister, Rajiv Gandhi, had intervened to stop a Sri Lankan economic embargo in the Tamil areas and a military operation, code-named Operation Liberation, against the rebels in May 1987. He thereafter imposed the Indo-Lanka Peace Accord on Sri Lanka and the LTTE. The agreement principally called for the Sri Lankan government to devolve power and conduct a referendum on merging the Northern and Eastern Provinces, the Tigers to surrender their weapons, and the Indians to station a peacekeeping force of 6,000 soldiers in Sri Lanka. The LTTE was never consulted in the drafting of the agreement, which Prabhakaran was forced to sign while in India. The accord caused massive protests among the Sinhalese and led the SLFP, many Buddhist clergy, and the People's Liberation Front to criticize the Sri Lankan government. What was not publicized was Gandhi's promise to Jayewardene that if the LTTE refused to disarm, the IPKF would intervene militarily to ensure that the agreement was adhered to.

In October 1987, the Sri Lankan navy intercepted a boat carrying seventeen LTTE members. When the Sri Lankan authorities disregarded IPKF and LTTE requests not to transfer the rebels to Colombo, the latter bit into their cyanide capsules and twelve of them died. The LTTE retaliated by assassinating a number of soldiers and innocent Sinhalese civilians. Soon thereafter, the LTTE attacked the IPKF, leading to ferocious fighting. The Indians code-named the assault on the LTTE "Operation Pawan [Wind]." Little did they realize that they were headed into a deadly quagmire, in which 1,157 Indian troops would lose their lives and nearly 3,000 would be wounded, in India's longest war.

Ranasinghe Premadasa, as prime minister in the Jayewardene government, strongly opposed the Indo-Lanka Accords, and he asked the Indians to leave Sri Lanka after becoming president in December 1988. Premadasa feared that the Indians planned to maintain an indefinite strategic presence in the island, and he consequently reached a cease-fire with the LTTE in April 1989 and even armed the group to fight the IPKF. The IPKF would likely have finished off the LTTE if allowed to stay on in Sri Lanka. But with strong opposition to the war among Tamils in the northeast and in Tamil Nadu, and Indian troops suffering severe losses, a different Indian government withdrew the IPKF from Sri Lanka in March 1990. The LTTE lost its best fighters during the war against the IPKF, but its leaders also realized that the women's wing, the so-called Freedom Birds or Birds of Independence, could be effective fighters. Consequently, women fighters are now represented in all of the LTTE's forces.

The IPKF, which was initially warmly welcomed in Jaffna, was not only humiliated by the LTTE but ended up committing numerous atrocities, including murders, rapes, and pillage, besmirching whatever reputation the Indian military had had when it landed. The IPKF had trained a Tamil National Army to replace it in the northeast, but the LTTE eradicated this force in no time. In June 1990, just three months after the IPKF left, talks between the LTTE and the government foundered, and civil war broke out again.

Chandrika Bandaranaike Kumaratunga was elected president of Sri Lanka in December 1994 amid great optimism, and the LTTE and the new government agreed to a cease-fire in January 1995. The peace was short-lived, however, and the two parties resorted to war again in April that year.[24] When the government security forces overran Jaffna and the Northern Peninsula in December 1995, the LTTE fighters fled into the eastern jungles, from where they waged a guerrilla war. The rebels forced thousands of civilians to flee with them, which merely contributed to the horrors endured by the Jaffna Tamils.

Assassinations, Suicide Bombings, and Child Soldiers

The LTTE refuses to be marginalized and it has consequently intimidated and assassinated opponents to ensure it alone represents the Tamils.[25] The systematic killing of those working with the Sri Lankan regime began in May 1983, when the LTTE demanded that everyone in the Jaffna

Peninsula boycott the local government elections. Nearly 90 percent of the population heeded the LTTE's demand, which clearly indicated that the Tamil extremists had now taken over from the moderates.

The LTTE has since killed numerous Tamil moderates. The more prominent casualties include V. Dharmalingam, representative for Manipay, in September 1985; K. Alalasunderam, representative for Kopay, in September 1985; A. Amirthalingam, TULF and opposition leader, in July 1989; V. Yogeswaran, representative for Jaffna, in July 1989; Sam Tambimuttu, representative for Batticaloa, in May 1990; V. Yogasandari, representative for Batticaloa, in June 1990; K. Kanaga-ratnam, representative for Pottuvil, in July 1990; Sarojini Yogeshwaran, mayor of Jaffna, in May 1998; P. Sivapalan, mayor of Jaffna, in September 1998; and Neelan Tiruchelvam, TULF parliamentarian, in July 1999. These assassinations have actually paid off, because few Tamils now dare oppose the Tigers publicly. Indeed, the LTTE's tactics have succeeded so well that almost all Tamil parties that participated in the December 2001 parliamentary elections did so only after acknowledging that the LTTE was the Tamils' main representative organization.

The LTTE has also not hesitated to assassinate prominent military and political figures whenever its leaders believed that they might act against it. Thus, for example, a suicide bomber assassinated Rajiv Gandhi during an election campaign in May 1991 when the LTTE feared that a victorious Gandhi might redeploy India's military against it. The UNP's Gamini Dissanayake, who strongly favored the Indo-Lanka Peace Accord, was also assassinated, at a campaign rally in September 1994, when it was thought that he would lobby for renewed Indian involvement. A suicide bomber killed President Ranasinghe Premadasa during a May Day rally in 1993, and President Chandrika Kumaratunga narrowly escaped being similarly assassinated during a campaign meeting in December 1999. Among the other Sri Lankan ministers the LTTE has assassinated are Ranjan Wijeratna, deputy minister of defense, who promised publicly to destroy the LTTE, in March 1991; Lalith Athulathmudali, the minister of education and one-time minister of defense, who forcefully advocated a military solution to the ethnic conflict, in April 1993; and C. V. Goonaratne, minister for industries, who was leading a group investigating a way to assassinate Prabhakaran, in June 2000.

The LTTE has perfected the way suicide bombings are conducted. Prabhakaran was supposedly influenced into using suicide bombers by watching a Hollywood movie that depicted a woman blowing herself up and assassinating a world leader. The suicide squad Prabhakaran has since created is among the most dedicated to the *eelam* cause, and these "Black Tigers" compete among themselves to go on suicide missions. The

Tigers claim that they are forced to use suicide bombers because they are pitted against a more numerous and militarily powerful foe.[26] The LTTE disapproves of the term "suicide bombers," however, because it claims that there is a clear distinction between "killing yourself" (*thatkolai*) and "giving yourself" (*thatkodai*) and says that the Black Tigers voluntarily do the latter.[27] It appears that most Black Tigers are recruited principally because they are disciplined, skilled, and battle-tested. Unlike groups like Hamas and Islamic Jihad, who use suicide bombers within days after they have volunteered, the LTTE supposedly rejects many applicants and informs others that they will be notified if the need arises. Prabhakaran is said to go over the written applications personally before inducting members into the Black Tiger squad, after which they are put through rigorous physical and psychological training.[28] Most Black Tigers will not have seen Prabhakaran until they are allowed to have dinner with him the day before they depart on their missions. If the suicidal culture exemplified by the Black Tigers epitomizes the group's capacity to perpetrate terrorism, it also shows its determination to achieve *eelam*.

The LTTE has also developed an effective naval capability, and the Sea Tigers, which include both men and women, have also resorted to suicide missions against Sri Lankan naval craft. The LTTE sees suicide bombers as just another means of attaining its ultimate goal.[29] Indeed, out of the top twelve groups engaged worldwide in suicide bombings between 1983 and 2000, the LTTE was responsible for 171 attacks, while the next eleven groups combined perpetrated a total of 115 attacks.[30] The LTTE's suicide attacks have primarily had two aims: to target those the group finds threatening, and to terrorize and destabilize the predominantly Sinhalese south. According to the LTTE's political leader, S. Thamilchelvam, suicide attacks "ensure maximum damage done with minimum loss of life."[31] The upshot is that these suicide attacks have killed over 1,500 innocent civilians and hardened Sinhalese opinion against the Tamils' demand for more devolution. That noted, it is also clear that the discussion of devolution by some Sinhalese politicians would hardly have taken place had the LTTE not been so ruthless.[32]

The LTTE has also detonated car and truck bombs in predominantly Sinhalese areas. Tamils in the northeast have suffered the most from the separatist war,[33] and these explosions were designed to bring the war to the Sinhalese and spread terror in the south, while others were intended to hurt the island's economy. The group's January 1998 suicide attack on the Temple of the Tooth, which is said to hold a tooth of Lord Buddha, may have also been staged to instigate a Sinhalese backlash against Tamils living in the south and thereby embarrass the government and further destabilize the country. "Terrorism is violence used in order to create fear; but it is aimed at creating fear in order that the fear, in turn, will lead somebody else—not the terrorist—to embark on some quite different program of action that will accomplish whatever it is the terrorist really desires," David Fromkin observes. Often the desired goal is "brutal police repression that . . . will lead to political conditions propitious to revolutionary agitation."[34] It is unknown whether such logic propelled the LTTE's July 1983 attack against the army convoy at Tinneveli, which led to the infamous 1983 anti-Tamil riots and swelled the rebel forces, but if the group sought similar consequences by attacking the Temple of the Tooth, it failed to generate a Sinhalese backlash.

The most daring and damaging suicide attack took place in July 2001, when suicide bombers infiltrated the Katunayake air force base and the island's only international airport and caused nearly U.S. $1 billion in damage. Such acts have caused a number of countries to proscribe the LTTE as a terrorist group. India banned the LTTE soon after Rajiv Gandhi's assassination, and Sri Lanka did likewise after the attack on the Temple of the Tooth.[35]

Prabhakaran has justified the LTTE's violent struggle as follows:

There are two dimensions in political violence. Firstly, there is the violence of the oppressor. Secondly, there is the violence of the oppressed. In most cases the oppressor belongs to the ruling elites, yields [sic] state authority and commands the armed forces. The oppressed are always the ruled, the minority nationalities, the exploited and the poor. The violence of the first category can be designated as state violence. The second category can be termed . . . violence against state violence. Since state violence is a form of repressive violence of the oppressor, it is unjust. The reactive violence of the oppressed is just since it is undertaken with the motive of obtaining justice. It is within the context of this distinction that the violent modes of political struggles of the oppressed find legitimacy.[36]

With many Tamils having fled the fighting in the northeast, the Tamil population has dwindled, which has caused recruitment problems for the LTTE.[37] The group has consequently abducted and forcibly recruited children, and it has been severely criticized by human rights organizations, Western governments, and the United Nations for doing so. This does not faze the LTTE, which simply promises not to recruit children but does exactly the opposite. Prabhakaran was merely sixteen years old when he became a Tamil militant, technically speaking a "child soldier,"[38] and he most likely has no qualms about inducting children into the LTTE. Estimates based on rebels killed during battle suggest that from 55 to 60 percent of the LTTE's fighters are under eighteen. Using child soldiers, known as the Baby Brigade,[39] is merely another means to achieve *eelam.*[40]

Illusions of Peace?

The LTTE initiated a cease-fire when a new UNP government under J. R. Jayewardene's nephew, Ranil Wickremesinghe, came to power in December 2001, and the parties reached a Memorandum of Understanding (MoU) as a precursor to talks on talks in February 2002. The government and the LTTE thereafter held talks on numerous occasions. The country was divided, however, as to whether these were really a first step toward resolving the conflict or merely an LTTE strategy to regroup and rearm. The LTTE is known to use cease-fires for purposes of regrouping, and it resorted to both forcible and voluntary recruitment to build up its forces and capabilities after the MoU was signed. It did likewise when engaged in peace talks with Presidents Premadasa and Kumaratunga, in 1989-90 and 1994-95, respectively.[41]

In the upshot, the February 2002 MoU was a boon for the Tigers. It enabled them to begin fresh recruitment and even opened up government-controlled areas that were hitherto closed for this purpose. Other benefits included the right to travel freely into government-controlled territories and promote the LTTE's political stance; recognition, among most parties, as the Tamils' sole representative in the northeast; strengthening its administration of LTTE-controlled areas; fortifying defenses and stockpiling supplies, while providing fresh cadres with the requisite training; getting the government to disarm Tamil paramilitary groups, and thereby eliminating whatever residual Tamil resistance remained in the northeast; recasting itself as an organization committed to reason and accommodation; and impeding the government's attempt to further marginalize the LTTE around the world. The government also agreed that the MoU would not be applied in the Mullaitivu and Killinochchi Districts, both controlled exclusively by the LTTE, and that the group's operatives were to be allowed access to government-controlled areas for political work, notwithstanding that the government's political activists were barred from LTTE areas. Both these concessions further bolstered the LTTE's recruiting and espionage activities, leading to the group's cadre base rising from between 5,000-6,000 in December 2001 to approximately 20,000 nearly two years later.

In the months preceding the signing of the MoU, an army intelligence unit called the Long Range Reconnaissance Patrol (LRRP) assassinated a number of Tiger leaders without ever being detected. The LRRP supposedly consisted of anti-LTTE Tamil rebels and one-time LTTE cadres. The latter were loyal to the former LTTE leader Mahattaya and became turncoats after Mahattaya communicated with the RAW and Prabhakaran ordered him killed.[42] The LRRP's success clearly showed that the LTTE lacked the cadre base to fully protect the territory it controlled, and the MoU with the government and the subsequent recruitment spree allowed the group to rectify this. Soon after the cease-fire was signed, the Tigers also went about systematically assassinating dozens of Tamil informants, and this further strengthened the leadership's security.

It is debatable whether the LTTE will ever settle for anything short of *eelam*,[43] and Sinhalese nationalists, who oppose the cease-fire agreement between the LTTE and the government argue that the UNF merely gave the LTTE a lifeline, and that the rebels would now be even harder to defeat.[44] When the Indo-Lanka Accord was imposed on the LTTE, Prabhakaran asked a reporter, "Is it for this that all of them died?"[45] Many thousands more Tamils and LTTE soldiers have died since the Indo-Lanka Accord was signed, and one must assume that Prabhakaran's determination to achieve *eelam* is now stronger than ever.[46] He has, for example, told his cadres that they can shoot him the day he backtracks on *eelam*. On the other hand, LTTE leaders have also suggested that they might settle for a Canadian-style federal setup that guarantees the Tamil areas widespread autonomy. "There must be a political solution," the LTTE's second-in-command, Thamilchelvam, has said. "The name is immaterial. Federation, confederation, northeast council, autonomous region, we can accept any of these solutions as long as we are guaranteed our equal rights, our dignity and justice. We don't want a lifestyle decided by Buddhist monks in Colombo."[47] And Prabhakaran, in his 2002 Heroes' Day address, said: "We are prepared to consider favourably a political framework that offers substantial regional autonomy and self-government in our homeland on the basis of our right to internal self-determination. But if our people's right to self-determination is denied and our demand for regional self-rule is rejected we have no alternative other than to secede and form an independent state."[48] The LTTE uses the term "self-determination" as often as it refers to *eelam*. Since self-determination can be attained without resorting to secession, it is possible that the LTTE might settle for an arrangement in which the Northern and Eastern Provinces are merged, given widespread autonomy, and placed under LTTE administration.[49] That said, merging the Northern Province with the Eastern Province is now all the more difficult to do, given the large numbers of Sinhalese and Muslims settled in the latter.[50] Indeed, Muslims in the Eastern Province are hostile to the idea of being under an LTTE administration, and they now demand autonomy for those enclaves where they are a plurality. They are angry that the LTTE taxes, harasses, and extorts from their community, and their youths have used Middle Eastern funds to set up makeshift training camps in an attempt to retaliate against the Tigers. Ominously, these youths have joined groups that operate under names such as Al Queda, Mujahideen, Osama, and Jehadi. Ultimately, while it is clear is that there will likely be no settlement to the civil war unless the LTTE is allowed widespread control over the territory and resources of the northeast, it is also clear that Muslim and Sinhalese concerns will need to be accommodated in any future northeastern merger.

One could argue that the LTTE was serious about negotiating a solution to the civil war after the UNF came to power, for four reasons.[51] First, the Norwegian government facilitated the cease-fire,[52] and many other countries, including the United States, closely monitored the progress being made. Second, both parties agreed to specific details (e.g., enabling border crossings, clearing land mines, and halting raids and ambushes) and, in the main, complied with them, notwithstanding the LTTE assassination of informants and former cadres and the Sri Lankan Navy sinking two LTTE ships smuggling arms to the rebels in 2003.[53] Third, the LTTE realized there was no support for a renewed war anywhere in Sri Lanka, and that some leading lights in the Tamil diaspora now also preferred a peaceful resolution to the conflict.[54] Finally, the September 11, 2001, terrorist attacks on the United States cornered those groups branded terrorist, and the Tigers, proscribed as such by the United States and other countries, were eager to be recast as a liberation force engaged in a legitimate freedom struggle.[55]

On the other hand, the LTTE's demands are inconsistent with its public pronouncements supporting federalism. For example, in July 2003, the UNF government proposed a Provisional Administrative Structure for the northeast that would have allowed the Tigers to oversee all development-related issues. The LTTE replied with counterproposals (see appendix H) that partly call for a Tiger-led Interim Self-Governing Authority to be set up with powers over development, rehabilitation, resettlement, reconstruction, land issues, and administrative structures in the northeast (e.g., courts and police). The LTTE also wants authority to disburse all foreign aid going to the northeast, solicit loans from foreign states and international financial institutions, control the region's natural resources, and control access to two-thirds of the island's coastal areas bordering the Tamil homeland. The group's proposals go beyond any federal arrangement and are structurally more confederal in nature. Indeed, the LTTE would be able to create a de facto statelet if most of its proposals were met. It is normal for parties anticipating difficult negotiations to make maximalist demands, and this may be the case with the LTTE's proposals. But they nevertheless call into question the group's sincerity about being willing to settle for a federal solution. This is the first time that the LTTE has specified in writing what it would take to bring about conflict resolution, and the proposals mark an important turning point in the Sinhalese-Tamil imbroglio, because they will henceforth form the bases for all future negotiations over devolution.

Prabhakaran has made it clear he does not believe in multiparty democracy. In a 1986 interview, he said: "The government of Ilam will be a socialist government; there will be only one party supported by the people; I do not want a multi-party democracy. Under a one-party government Tamil Ilam can develop and change much faster. In a socialist constitution the needs of the people will have priority."[56] It is doubtful whether his views on this score have changed,[57] and should the LTTE gain control over the northeast through a peace deal, the region will most likely be governed in an authoritarian and fascist fashion. It is puzzling to think how this would juxtapose with Sri Lanka's illiberal yet vibrant democracy. LTTE literature also portrays Prabhakaran as the *sooriya thevan* (sun god), and it is even more confounding to think what such deification might mean for a Tamil province in a united Sri Lanka. Does all this suggest that peace can only be achieved in the context of a one-country, two-systems solution? If so, how different would the area controlled by the LTTE be from the rest of the country, and could Sri Lankans tolerate such a setup? Even more important, does the LTTE have the capacity to transform itself into a political party—even one that is not democratic?

Those who have met Prabhakaran say he is both dogmatic and practical. It is possible that the latter trait may influence him to settle for a solution short of a separate state. Even assuming he did so, however, it is questionable whether he would be able to persuade his battle-hardened cadres to follow him. The Tigers consist of three generations. The first includes older Tamils like Anton Balasingham, who have cohabited with Sinhalese, may speak some Sinhala, and realize that the two ethnic groups can coexist provided that the Tamils are allowed broad devolution. The second generation includes those of Prabhakaran's age group, who are reaching middle age and may be mellowing in their separatist views. It is remotely possible that this group, too, could be persuaded to settle for a settlement short of dividing the country. The last generation, however, consists of young fighters who have known nothing but war and destruction. Having been indoctrinated to hate Sinhalese by the LTTE and suffered persecution by the Sri Lankan armed forces, this group may be the most violently committed to pursuing *eelam*.[58]

Many Tamils detest Prabhakaran for his autocratic policies. They likewise resent the LTTE for all the hardships imposed on them, and for assassinating hundreds of their fellow Tamils. Consequently, many Tamils, especially in the Eastern Province, would prefer never to come under the

LTTE's jurisdiction.[59] On the other hand, numerous Tamils, when interviewed, also claimed that if they were destined to live a subjugated life, they would rather do so under the LTTE than under a Sinhalese government.[60] These contradictory views are understandable, given that both the LTTE and the government have perpetrated manifold atrocities against innocent civilians and contributed to their now bleak plight. Tamils, especially in the north, are well aware that the fanatical LTTE has rarely considered the Tamil population's best interests when fighting for *eelam,* and that it has abducted and enslaved children to wage war, extorted money from fellow Tamils, resorted to torture and murder against Tamil opponents, and used Tamil civilians as shields when fighting the Sri Lankan military. But they have also suffered the atrocities committed by successive Sri Lankan governments and the military. As Scott Pegg has noted:

The government's ledger includes such things as indiscriminate shelling of civilian areas; torture; arbitrary arrest; disappearances; reprisal attacks on civilians that have included burning, looting, raping, and mass killings; and the use of so-called barrel bombs or "poor man's napalm"—drums of fuel with strips of rubber placed inside which are thrown from aircraft. Upon impact, the fuel explodes, sending forth burning pieces of rubber which can then attach themselves to a person's skin.[61]

Many have suffered in the course of Sri Lanka's two decades of civil war, but no one as terribly as the Tamils of the northeast. The circumstances suggest, moreover, that it is likely to be a long time before their lot changes for the better.

Whither Conflict Resolution?

The LTTE and the Sri Lankan military have both experienced spectacular gains and losses over the past few years, with neither being able to decisively defeat the other. The government's capture of Jaffna in December 1995 has been the military's biggest triumph to date. The subsequent military debacles were mainly precipitated by irresponsible campaigns designed to promote the Kumaratunga government's political agenda as opposed to gaining strategic advantage. This was the case with "Operation Jayasikuru" (Victory Assured), a military campaign initiated in May 1997 to recapture part of the A-9 highway from the rebels and open a land route to the Jaffna Peninsula. It was originally due to be completed within six months, but the military gave up after eighteen months when it failed to overcome the LTTE's counteroffensive, named "Sei Allathu Sethu Madi" (Do or Die). Over 3,700 rebels and troops were killed, and the A-9 became known as the "Highway of Death." The military also suffered heavy casualties when the LTTE attacked the Mullaitivu army camp and killed over 1,200 soldiers in July 1996 and when a similar assault on Killinochchi in September 1998 killed nearly 1,700 soldiers.[62]

The government also suffered a string of humiliating defeats in November 1999 when the LTTE launched "Operation Oyatha Alaigal III" (Unceasing Waves III) and in five days recaptured nine army camps and all the territory the army had won over during the preceding nineteen months.[63] The situation was not much different in April 2000 when the LTTE took control of the Elephant Pass military complex, which even U.S. Special Forces had considered impregnable. Elephant Pass is the key to controlling the Jaffna Peninsula, and it was only the LTTE's small cadre base (and rapid military assistance to the government from China, Pakistan, and other countries) that prevented it from taking over Jaffna.

Studies of conflict resolution suggest that conflict is least likely to revive if one combatant has decisively defeated its opponent.[64] Neither the LTTE nor the government has been able decisively to alter the distribution of power and dislodge the other, and the ensuing stalemate, in the main, explains why resolving Sri Lanka's ethnic imbroglio has been so intractable. What is surprising, however, is why the government, with its manifold resources, international support, and superior numbers, has been unable to defeat the Tigers. Poor political leadership, lack of political consensus between the major parties and the attendant ethnic outbidding, widespread corruption and divisions among politicians and the military, support for the war among certain constituencies, and the understandable distrust between the government and the LTTE are major reasons for the stalemate, but Vellupillai Prabhakaran's single-mindedness and the deadly organization he has fashioned are also an important part of the explanation.

Poor Leadership and Ongoing Ethnic Outbidding

Ethnic outbidding has continued among Sri Lanka's main political parties, which does not bode well for securing a lasting peace. For example, between March and July 2000, President Kumaratunga and the leader of the opposition, Ranil Wickremesinghe, met over fifteen times and agreed to a draft constitution that would have allowed the Tamils some devolution. The agreement was so watered down from the draft constitution the government had introduced in October 1997 that the mainstream Tamil parties, which were part of the president's People's Alliance (PA) coalition and had previously supported the Constitution Bill, opposed it. If the Tamil legislators opposed the bill because it did not go far enough, the extremist Buddhist monks and Sinhalese nationalists, including some from Kumaratunga's own party, opposed it because it would have breached Sri Lanka's unitary status. Monks resorted to extensive hunger strikes to protest against the bill, contending that devolution was the first step to Sri Lanka's dismemberment. This has been their mantra since the Bandaranaike-Chelvanayakam Pact was attempted, and subsequent events, rather than highlighting the necessity for devolution, have only made the monks and nationalists shriller in their opposition to devolution. The monks' opposition led Wickremesinghe to say that the UNP would oppose any bill that was not approved by the Buddhist clergy. Trying to outdo his opponent, the People's Alliance prime minister at the time, Ratnasiri Wickremanayake, proclaimed: "We will seek the views of the Mahanayake Theras [Buddhist leadership] on each and every paragraph of the draft constitution, so that they could correct us where we have gone wrong,"[65] thereby indicating that ethnic outbidding continued to be rife in Sri Lanka. This was increasingly evident during the parliamentary elections in October 2000 and December 2001.[66]

The United National Front (UNF), headed by the UNP, won the December 2001 parliamentary elections, but Chandrika Kumaratunga is slated to remain as president until December 2005. The call for cohabitation notwithstanding, the president and the UNF cabinet have operated at loggerheads. The president threatened to sack the cabinet; the cabinet and the UNF government threatened to resign and call for new elections; and the UNF also threatened to impeach Kumaratunga, whose presidential powers allow her to suspend parliament for one year after the last parliamentary elections unless impeachment proceedings are in progress. Such interparty politicking influenced the PA opposition to use the ethnic conflict to discredit the UNP. Consequently, Kumaratunga complained that the UNP had given away too much to the LTTE, even though she had once proposed conceding the Northern Province to the LTTE for ten years as a precursor to a devolutionary agreement. Kumaratunga even joined with the jingoistic JVP in 2001 to maintain the PA's majority in parliament, and the SLFP and JVP also conducted discussions in 2003 over a possible electoral alliance to agitate against the MoU and defeat the UNP at the next election. The JVP is among the Sinhalese groups most devoted to the principle of a unitary state. Kumaratunga, on the other hand, supports some devolution. The JVP was also responsible for assassinating Kumaratunga's husband in February 1988. That Kumaratunga could disregard all this and seek and alliance with the JVP to undermine the government shows that Sri Lanka's leaders continue to place political opportunism above the national interest.

In early November 2003, Kumaratunga proved once again how deepseated ethnic outbidding is and how opportunistic Sri Lanka's politicians can be when she suspended parliament for two weeks and cavalierly took over from UNF ministers the defense, internal affairs, and communication ministries, claiming that the UNF government's negotiations with the Tigers were undermining the country's sovereignty and territorial integrity. What was widely considered a power grab or constitutional coup was conducted just hours before Prime Minister Wickremesinghe met with President George W. Bush in Washington, D.C. Kumaratunga placed the security forces on high alert and replaced those heading the state media with her supporters, who immediately began singing paeans to the president, while underemphasizing all happenings concerning the prime minister and the UNF. She thereafter imposed a state of emergency, although this was, amid great confusion, rescinded after the international community, headed by India and the United States, put pressure on the president. A state of emergency allows the security forces to enter homes without warrants and to imprison suspected subversives without trial for lengthy periods, and Tamils especially feared that this would enable the military to begin targeting them all over again.

Kumaratunga had refused to sign the MoU between the government and the LTTE and was right to criticize the way the Tigers were using the cease-fire to strengthen their forces. According to Sri Lanka's constitution, the president is the commander-in-chief of the armed forces; she is the head of state, government, and cabinet; she can head multiple cabinet ministries; and she can summon, suspend, and dissolve parliament. The president's actions were thus constitutional. That said, they were crassly opportunistic and unprincipled, because Kumaratunga used the country's security situation as a cover to try and dethrone the UNF and enthrone her PA in parliament. Kumaratunga loathes the prime minister and is especially angry that she, despite bringing in the Norwegians to facilitate the peace process, has been sidelined since the MoU was signed. As the *Financial Times* noted in an editorial, "It is hard to escape the conclusion that Mrs Kumaratunga could not bear to see her bitter rival Ranil Wickremesinghe . . . succeeding where she had failed."[67]

Soon after the ministries were taken over, the president and PA party leaders sought to bribe UNF politicians to switch parties so that the latter would lose its majority in parliament, but none of the UNF parliamentarians crossed party lines. It appears that the president also wanted to make sure that she would have the military, police, and the government-controlled media on her side if she was unable to entice enough opposition members to join the PA, and was therefore forced to call new elections. The PA is unlikely to triumph over the UNF in free and fair elections, but the elections conducted in Sri Lanka since the PA came to power in 1994 have been unusually violent, with the security forces usually pandering to the governing party's illegal and fraudulent demands. It is thus highly likely that the president will try to resolve the constitutional crisis that she has unleashed by calling another sanguinary parliamentary election, which otherwise need not be held until December 2007. New parliamentary elections, which would be the third since October 2000, will most likely see the PA form an alliance with the prowar, anti-devolution, anti-Norway, and hypernationalist JVP, which would certainly bode ill for the current peace process.

The constitution prevents Kumaratunga from running for a third term as president once her second term ends in December 2005, and it would not be surprising if she tried somehow to introduce a constitutional amendment to change that, bring in a new constitution that would end the presidential system and thus allow her to occupy the helm in a different capacity (e.g., as prime minister), or postpone presidential elections (just as her mother postponed parliamentary elections from 1975 to 1977) by using the security situation as an excuse. That one can consider such scenarios as distinct possibilities makes clear the political decay facing Sri Lanka and the extent to which Sri Lanka's opportunistic leaders may go to see their selfish personal interests triumph over the island's national interest.

Sri Lanka's economy was showing strong signs of growth in late 2003, which many attributed to the ongoing peace process, but the island's stock market lost 20 percent of its value within two days after the president declared an emergency. This and international pressure forced the president to modify her blunderbuss tactics, and she claimed that she supported the peace process (despite having repeatedly called it "illegal") and said that she wanted the Norwegians to continue to play a part in it (notwithstanding that she had been hypercritical of their involvement, and that members of her party had referred to them as "salmon-eating busybodies"). She also encouraged the UNF government to continue negotiating with the LTTE; suggested that she might consider the LTTE's counterproposals as a basis for negotiations (despite having justified the takeover of the three ministries on the grounds that the UNF was giving away too much to the Tigers); and called for a national government that would include members of her party (although simultaneously entertaining an alliance with the JVP to topple the government). At the time of writing (in mid-November 2003), the prime minister has refused to proceed with the peace process unless the ministries are returned to UNF control, and he has asked the president to take over negotiations with the Tigers. For their part, the Tigers have made it known that they do not trust the president and are averse to conducting peace talks with her or the PA. And the Norwegians, citing the confusing political situation in the country, have decided to suspend their involvement in the peace process until it is clear who is in charge of peace talks in the south. The ethnic outbidding and the attendant destabilization of the situation was best captured by Prabhakaran, who laughingly told the Norwegian peace brokers that they ought now to begin another peace process to deal with intra-Sinhalese rivalries. And the *Financial Times* opined that "Mrs Kumaratunga has stopped the [peace] process in its tracks, perhaps because she believes she is the right person to strike the deal [with the LTTE]. Her capricious actions show that she is not."[68]

This power-at-any-cost mentality, long evidenced among the Sinhalese parties, and the attendant ethnic outbidding prevents the Tigers from moderating their views. The LTTE consequently feels justified in further arming itself and increasing its numbers, thereby magnifying Sinhalese distrust and providing grist for the mill of Sinhalese extremists who advocate a military solution to the conflict. Many Sinhalese extremists have demanded that the Tigers decommission their weapons before any peace agreement is reached, and Kumaratunga, as part of her outbidding strategy after the MoU was signed, did likewise. The LTTE leaders are well aware that it is the Tigers' military prowess that has forced the government to discuss ways to accommodate the Tamils' grievances, and they will not decommission their weapons. Indeed, the LTTE is unlikely to fully decommission its weapons even if an agreement, negotiated between the government and the LTTE and/or sponsored and overseen by the international community, is reached. This is because agreements reached between the Sinhalese and Tamils since the mid-1950s have either been abrogated or not implemented by the former. The LTTE will consequently hold on to its weapons, and this will further contribute to the hostility and mistrust between the parties.

Many Sinhalese genuinely believe that the LTTE will not deviate from the quest for *eelam*, and this generally colors Sinhalese perceptions when discussing resolution of the conflict. The LTTE leaders, on the other hand, are also convinced that over fifty years of ethnic politics has taught that Tamils can never trust the Sinhalese to address their legitimate grievances, and that only force, as mastered by the LTTE, will get the Tamils what they want. The discussions between the UNF government and the LTTE only catalyzed such perceptions, with the LTTE claiming that the government had disregarded the February 2002 cease-fire agreement by not reducing the Tamils' hardships in the northeast, and the government and, especially, the opposition claiming that the LTTE had repeatedly violated the clauses of the MoU.[69] However, the LTTE was most responsible for violating the agreement, given that the group continued to smuggle in weapons, forcibly conscripted child soldiers, assassinated Tamil rivals, and extorted money from Tamil and Muslim civilians. In light also of the LTTE's proposals, made as part of the interim self-governing authority document and the creation of its own banks, courthouses, prisons, police force, tax collection apparatus, and civil service, one can see why many Sri Lankans have doubts about the Tigers giving up their separatist agenda.

Widespread Corruption and War Gains

Support for the war in the predominantly Sinhalese south, widespread corruption among the armed forces and politicians, and nepotism and cronyism are also responsible for the government's inability to defeat the LTTE. For example, government ministers, businessmen, and army personnel have enriched themselves by knowingly procuring dilapidated military equipment and skimming off hefty commissions; some military officers have even been accused of smuggling for the LTTE. In short, many politicians and military officials consider the war a boon to their careers, and there is consequently a powerful lobby favoring continued war. Even President Kumaratunga has noted that widespread corruption within the government and military is what prevents the state from defeating the LTTE. Corruption is so rampant that one newspaper reported "the public belief is that corrupt officers within the armed forces deliberately bungle operations in order to keep the war going so that they may grow richer."[70]

Political considerations have also led to nepotism and cronyism, and this has seen some of the most qualified and successful generals marginalized. This contrasts with LTTE policy that awards responsibilities to its cadres based solely on performance, not seniority. For example, Sri Lanka's former deputy defense minister, who is also the president's uncle, was promoted from reserve lieutenant colonel to three-star general despite having launched numerous failed campaigns that led to thousands of soldiers being killed, and although coalition members opposed his renomination to the defense ministry post, President Kumaratunga gave him his old portfolio after the government was reelected in October 2000. Compounding the army's problems is the fact that Sri Lanka's soldiers are primarily socioeconomically marginalized village youths for whom the army has become the only gainful source of employment. As the *Sunday Leader* observed: "By and large, ours is a mercenary army. Impoverished lads are paid to die while the middle classes grumble over cocktails."[71] It is thus not surprising that nearly 58,000 army soldiers have deserted, with 8,000 absconding during the first year after the MoU was signed.[72]

Indeed, the southern region, which is among the country's poorest—and most hawkish—might be said to have benefited from the war the most, which is one major reason why the Kumaratunga government in particular was able to escalate the conflict. The war created a demand for nearly 150,000 security guards, who are mostly recruited from among the poor. Supplying goods and services to the military and the alternate opportunities for producing goods previously produced in the war-torn Northern and Eastern Provinces have further contributed to the southern war economy.[73] "In all, the war may be thanked for about 400,000 new jobs," the *Economist* noted, a figure "not to be sniffed at" in an island with nineteen million people.[74] Thus, while the vast majority of people in Sri Lanka want to see the war end, powerful constituencies and individuals dictate otherwise, and this is another reason for the prolonged conflict.

Eelam War IV?

Those close to President Kumaratunga say she is utterly convinced that there never will be a permanent solution to Sri Lanka's ethnic conflict as long as Prabhakaran is alive.[75] It was evidently this conviction, coupled with a near-death experience when the LTTE tried to assassinate her in December 1999, that prompted Kumaratunga to endorse a plan in February 2000 to kill Prabhakaran.[76] The plan called for locating Prabhakaran by triangulating the signal generated when he used a cellular phone and then bombing the location. The plan, if carried out, would have cost approximately $130 million and required U.S. and Indian assistance. But it was shelved when the Americans refused to cooperate. The LTTE purportedly discovered the plot, and a suicide bomber assassinated one of its leaders, Minister of Industries C. V. Gooneratne, on June 7, 2000.[77]

The LTTE equally detests Kumaratunga, her uncle Anuruddha Ratwatte (a former deputy defense minister), and the former PA foreign minister, Lakshman Kadiragamar. Many Tamils loathe the Bandaranaikes for the anti-Tamil politics they and the SLFP have pursued since the mid-1950s, and the LTTE prefers to see Kumaratunga as another opportunistic Bandaranaike who, like her parents, is determined to subjugate the Tamils to further her political ends. It thereby conveniently overlooks the efforts the president made to seek a solution to the conflict soon after coming to office.[78] Given his loyalty to the president, the LTTE and most Tamils also see Kadiragamar, a fellow Tamil, as a traitor, and he was (and most likely still is) high on the LTTE's hit list. Kadiragamar is dapper, suave, and articulate, and the fact that such a Tamil could be so wedded to a Bandaranaike-led government offends his fellows.[79] All this, combined with the SLFP's propensity to cater to Sinhalese Buddhist nationalists, makes the LTTE much more hostile toward Kumaratunga than toward the present-day UNP.

This is not to say that the LTTE leadership trusts the UNP, or that those in the UNP fully trust the LTTE. If the LTTE leaders prefer dealing with the UNP-led UNF government, it is only because they believe that they stand to get more from the latter. Furthermore, having jilted the PA and undermined the cease-fire reached soon after Kumaratunga came to power, the LTTE has had little choice but keep the channels to the UNP open. This also means that the chances of Eelam War IV occurring are greater if the UNP is out of power.

Part of the problem facing the UNP, as it tries to sell a peace proposal to the masses, is that many of its own members are not convinced that the LTTE leaders are willing to coexist in a united Sri Lanka.[80] As already noted, such perceptions were bolstered after the MoU was signed and the government and the LTTE conducted numerous rounds of discussions in Thailand, Norway, Germany, and Japan. The upshot, then, is that no government will be able to craft a devolution package to satisfy the LTTE until there is a sea change in the way the average Sinhalese views the LTTE. But this very hostility toward the LTTE and the Sinhalese aversion to supporting increased devolution is what partly motivates the rebels to pursue strategies that further undermine their image with the majority community. The Sri Lankan peace process has consequently led to a stage where each party's negative preconceptions about the other keep getting reinforced.

Sri Lanka's media have also contributed to distrust of the LTTE, with the state-owned media portraying the LTTE and Prabhakaran as both barbaric and rational, depending on the LTTE-government relationship at the time. Thus, for example, soon after the LTTE captured and destroyed the Elephant Pass military complex, the *Daily News* noted that "a special place we are sure has been reserved in the Devil's cemetery for Velupillai Prabhakaran, the Devil incarnate" and claimed that "Prabhakaran is making his last efforts and it is time that the South gives him the thorough beating he deserves."[81] Yet the newspaper portrayed Prabhakaran and the LTTE as partners in peace after the government and the LTTE agreed to the MoU in February 2002. The English-language *Island* newspaper has especially been critical of the peace process, and Tamil newspapers consistently emphasize how the war and Sinhalese politics adversely affect Tamils; meanwhile, Sinhala newspapers sympathize with the military and innocent Sinhalese victims of LTTE attacks.[82] The upshot is that the media too have contributed to exacerbating the enmity between the parties and, especially in the case of the Sinhalese, inculcated the belief that there is unlikely to be a settlement to the conflict unless Prabhakaran is killed and the LTTE eradicated.

The Prabhakaran Factor

Vellupillai Prabhakaran is neither an accident nor an aberration. Rather, he is the product of long-standing Sinhalese ethnocentrism, Tamil grievances, and the country's institutional decadence. As Sri Lanka's Prime Minister Ranil Wickremesinghe has noted, "Prabhakaran is the outcome of Sri Lanka's politics of the 20th century."[83] Having grown up amid all the injustices, indignities, and terror perpetrated by successive Sinhalese governments and the military, Prabhakaran and the LTTE have inflicted their own brand of terror upon the Sinhalese. Were it not for the thousands of innocent Sinhalese and Tamil civilians who have lost their lives and been crippled and maimed, the LTTE's terrorism might be characterized as condign retribution for the atrocities successive Sinhalese leaders and the island's undisciplined military have unleashed on the minorities in trying to create a Sinhalese ethnocracy.

In mid-1964, the moderate Tamil politician A. Amirthalingam warned:

Every year the development of events in the South leads us to the irresistible conclusion that the hopes of union are receding further and further. If the leaders of the Sinhalese people persist in this attitude, I will say, when you will be advocating federalism, we will rather choose to have a division of this country even at the cost of several lives and, if it be necessary, even our lives. We will rather have a division of this country than surrender as a nation without self-respect and be eternal slaves in this country."[84]

The quest for that division has now reached high tide, with the Sri Lankan government and the LTTE at a standoff in their savage war. Prabhakaran has repeatedly noted that Sinhalese politicians alone will determine whether the Tamils can coexist in a united Sri Lanka. This is true, provided he and the LTTE are willing to settle for a solution short of secession. With no guarantee that this is the case, Prabhakaran and the LTTE now also determine Sri Lanka's destiny and promise.

8

CONCLUSION

The account provided here makes it clear that the Official Language Act and the ethnic outbidding culture it unleashed were what led to widespread institutional decay in Sri Lanka, the Tamil quest for separatism, and the current bleak impasse that has made conflict resolution seem almost intractable. The Sri Lankan case also exemplifies the negative consequences that can ensue whenever ethnic outbidding is resorted to. But why do politicians indulge in ethnic outbidding and seek to impose ethnocentric policies when it is often obvious that doing so may undermine polyethnic coexistence? There are at least three reasons.

First, they may do so because minority guarantees are superficial or nonexistent and the political structure thereby facilitates ethnic outbidding. Politicians are by nature ambitious, but ambition is rarely accompanied by patience. Consequently, politicians are predisposed to taking the shortest road to attaining power. This means that if the political structure allows elites to profit by practicing outbidding and ethnocentrism, they will most likely do so. Even decent men and women can thus quickly be led astray, and this is perhaps nowhere more clearly evident than in Sri Lanka. In short, the governmental structure represents the single most important opportunity and constraint with regard to facilitating and encouraging ethnic outbidding and ethnocentric policies. Even assuming that some politicians were principled enough to eschew ethnic outbidding, there would be no assurance that their competitors would adopt a similarly principled stand if there were no constitutionally mandated minority guarantees. And even if opposing parties agreed not to use outbidding, there would still be no effective way to preclude extremist parties from incorporating outbidding into their manifestos if no clear-cut constitutional guarantees protecting minority interests have been institutionalized. Indeed, the evidence suggests that it is aspiring elites or elites in the opposition who would like to trade places with ruling politicians who are most susceptible to resorting to ethnic outbidding. As Ghia Nodia notes, "History shows that . . . nationalism is usually championed by *alternative* rather than *ruling* elites."[1] Yet once the outbidding process is under way, ruling politicians may feel that they have little choice but to follow suit, unless clearly defined constitutional constraints mandate otherwise.

Majoritarian democracies, which are fashioned to enable those in power to rule unfettered until they are defeated at the next election, usually preclude opposing parties from influencing governmental policy, and this is unproblematic if the societal divisions are ideological and not ethnic or racial.[2] But more often than not, polyethnic societies represent ethnic and racial divisions, and this is especially the case if the groups concerned are territorially based. When one incorporates ethnic outbidding into this mix, it becomes clear that a polyethnic society with a majoritarian system may allow parties from a particular ethnicity to dominate and thereby marginalize ethnic minorities.

If the majoritarian principle, in the main, justifies one-party rule with little input from those in the opposition, then the consensus principle promotes multiple outlets for power to be disbursed, checks and balances for ensuring a more impartial decision-making process, and the capacity for a larger proportion of interests to be aggregated and represented. When combined with the fact that proportional voting models, as opposed to majoritarian models, encourage more governmental policies closer to median voters' preferences,[3] it appears that polyethnic societies are better off adopting political structures that distribute, as opposed to concentrate, power. Although Sri Lanka's constitutional structure was changed in 1978, and it in the process also adopted a convoluted proportional representation system, rather than enabling consensus politics, this encouraged governance smacking of dictatorship. Thus, from a polyethnic standpoint, the governmental structure and the rules electing representatives may have changed, but that had no impact on the governing process itself, because the opposition parties and minorities continued to have little say on how the country was governed.

Emphasizing the importance of structural factors should not, however, absolve elites from their responsibility of governing effectively, and political opportunism is a second major reason for ethnic outbidding and ethnocentrism. It takes political elites to resort to outbidding, and these very same elites might just as well structure institutions that preclude outbidding. This is why institutions influence but do not determine outcomes. In Sri Lanka's case, Sinhalese elites have had numerous opportunities to restructure their political institutions, but in every instance, they have reconfigured them for the worse. Their actions stand out as being all the more egregious given that the two postindependence constitutions, which might have been fashioned to sufficiently incorporate minority grievances, actually disregarded Tamils' major concerns at the time. Not only is ambition accompanied by impatience, it is also myopic. Consequently, politicians are prone to calculate immediate benefits and disregard long-term consequences. In doing so, they also place their personal preferences above the national interest, which is what Sinhalese politicians have done consistently. It is then hardly surprising that ethnic outbidding continues in the island.

Leading politicians in Sri Lanka today acknowledge that the Tamils have been wronged, and that the malpractice of successive governments is responsible for the ethnic conflict. President Kumaratunga has repeatedly noted that Sri Lanka "has failed in the essential task of nation building"[4] because successive governments "failed to address the issue of building a truly pluralist nation-state."[5] She added: "It is Sinhalese racism that has become the greatest strength of the Tamil racism [practiced by the LTTE leader Vellupillai Prabhakaran]."[6] Prime Minister Ranil Wickremesinghe, during a visit to the United States, also noted: "The Tamils tried peaceful protest which soon degenerated into violence. With the underlying grievances being unattended the stage was set for terrorist groups to emerge. Whatever the cause, the reality became the Liberation Tigers of Tamil Eelam."[7] Both acknowledge that Sinhalese chauvinism was responsible for Tamil militarism, and that the country's constitutional structure needs to be redesigned to allow Tamils more political autonomy. Yet when faced with serious political contests, both Kumaratunga and Wickremesinghe resorted to petty politicking, pandered to Sinhalese hardliners, and practiced ethnic outbidding. Chapter 7 has shown how Wickremesinghe, despite meeting with Kumaratunga on numerous occasions to design a draft constitution that would have given the Tamil regions some autonomy, caved into the extremist Buddhist clergy and refused to support any parliamentary bill that did not have the monks' imprimatur. And Kumaratunga, when faced with a tough reelection challenge in December 1999, embraced a hawkish position on the war and accommodated hardliners from opposition parties to ensure getting reelected. As one knowledgeable observer noted, "the fact that she [Kumaratunga] accommodated these Sinhala hardliners in her camp affected her credibility as a genuine non-racist Sinhala leader."[8] As already noted, in 2001, she formed an alliance with the nationalist JVP to prevent the UNP from gaining a majority in parliament, and in 2003, she agreed to discuss an alliance with the JVP to undermine the UNF-LTTE Memorandum of Understanding and defeat the UNP at the next election.[9] She has also been disingenuous and equivocal when supporting the peace process, suggesting that just like her predecessors, she is incapable of putting the country's interest before her political career. Sri Lanka's politicians thus prolong the conflict and contribute to political decay in two ways: they use the threat of the LTTE to outbid their Sinhalese political opponents, and they resort to ugly rhetoric and violence to undermine the opposition.[10]

Underestimating the consequences of their actions is a major reason elites resort to ethnic outbidding and ethnocentric practices. There is simply no way to specify in advance the exact outcome of a particular piece of legislation or policy, for all such endeavors carry unintended consequences. The best one can hope for is that whatever ensues is manageable. Overconfidence may, conversely, encourage extremism, and it is therefore easy enough to envision those in power adopting controversial and destabilizing policies, whether because they are deluded by a temporary sense of omnipotence or because they are overconfident about their capacity to maintain stability, believing they are well equipped to handle the fallout. Consequently, while there were prescient warnings made regarding the Official Language Act and the discriminatory policies that attended it, Sinhalese politicians, in the main, believed that they could effectively negotiate the adverse consequences. Simply put, they believed that they could get away with outbidding and ethnocentrism. This was especially true in the case of S. W. R. D. Bandaranaike. It was also true in the case of his wife, Sirimavo, who was utterly insensitive to the suffering she imposed on the Tamils.

Finally, a defanged minority also encourages ethnic outbidding, and one may argue that some Sinhalese elites felt that there was little the Tamils could do to counter their discriminatory tactics. A number of things contributed to such thinking: Sri Lanka is a small island, ill suited to division into two separate states; Sinhalese stereotypes had long portrayed the Tamils as passive, and no violent retaliation was thus anticipated; Tamils' numbers in the Eastern Province were dwindling relative to Sinhalese (and Muslim) numbers, given out-migration and successful colonization programs, which were bound to make Tamil claims that the province was part of the Tamil homeland untenable; those Tamils who were thriving economically were mostly doing so outside the Northern Province, and they consequently had every reason to ensure that Tamil extremism was avoided and that Tamils protested peacefully; and the Tamils were a minority compared to the large Sinhalese majority and if need be, it was believed, could easily be put in their place. The Sinhalese elites thus had ample reasons to think that Tamil politicians' threats of secession were mere bluster, designed to placate their constituents, and that they had nothing to lose and much to gain by practicing ethnic outbid-

ding. In believing that the Tamils' options were limited, Sinhalese politicians failed to realize the extents to which their ethnocentrism would undermine the country's institutions and radicalize the Tamils, thereby influencing this hitherto passive minority to mobilize militarily and
challenge the government's sovereignty.[11]

It is understandable why a majority community that comprised nearly
76 percent of the population would feel that it had a right to dominate
the political process. And such domination is perhaps feasible, provided
the majority community legitimizes itself as an ethnic hegemon. This
would require the dominant community to take measures that limit its
power, even as it gets the country's minorities to acknowledge its dominant status and guarantees them fair, if not equal, access to the state's resources. By crafting operating principles that limited what it could do
with its dominant status and ensuring that these principles were institutionalized, the dominant community might be able to entice all the state's
citizens to willingly participate in the system, thereby legitimizing its ethnic hegemonic status and ensuring stable and predictable interactions
among the communities. There is no reason why the Sinhalese could not
have been the island's hegemonic ethnic group if they had accommodated
the Tamils and other minorities. But by pursuing ethnocentric policies
and trying to subjugate the minorities, they became a superordinating
ethnic group and thereby lost all hegemonic legitimacy.[12] Sri Lanka's military has played a major part in reinforcing this superordination and humiliating the Tamils, and the manifesto issued by the four-party Tamil
National Alliance in December 2001 noted that the Sri Lankan army continues to be responsible for the disappearances of "Tamil youth in their
thousands and frequent sexual assault against Tamil females."[13]

It is axiomatic that those who are marginalized will do their best to demand reforms. Typically, they will initially mobilize politically to have the
unfair and partial rules changed. The political agitation that is bound to
follow may be tamed if the majority/dominant group seeks to accommodate the marginalized group's grievances, or if the latter is marginalized
in just one sphere (e.g., politically but not economically, as is the case
with Malaysia's and Indonesia's Chinese and Fiji's Indians). But if marginalization takes place across the board, so as to smack of ethnocentrism, then the institutions representing the state will cease to interact
with all citizens in an impartial fashion, minority confidence in the state
will be undermined, and those feeling subjugated will begin to fight back
more passionately. This will especially be the case if the minority is a territorial one. In a real sense, when it comes to evaluating why some polyethnic societies experience secessionist movements, what transpired in Sri
Lanka is typical. Those feeling betrayed, victimized, and subjugated look

to their politicians—who more often than not tend to be moderates clamoring for peaceful change—until the latter disappoint them. The longer it takes the moderates to obtain face-saving changes, the more those marginalized lose confidence in the state's capacity to treat them impartially, and the easier it becomes for extremist elements to gain legitimacy. Impassioned rhetoric, accompanied by minor skirmishes between the state authorities and the extremists, leads to the latter becoming radicalized. The more the extremists challenge the state, the more pressured its authorities will feel to strike back, believing that accommodation and conciliation would smack of weakness, which is a mistake, because only they are likely to fully delegitimize the extremist forces and bolster the moderates. But the state's heavy-handed policies inevitably lead to atrocities, with innocent civilians being targeted, which only further compromises the state in the eyes of the marginalized community and adds to the extremists' numbers. Soon political mobilization will have turned to military mobilization, which leads to a spiral of violence, with each violent episode emboldening, justifying, and legitimating further violence. The end result will likely be ethnic conflict. This is what happened in Kosovo in the 1990s. It continues to take place in Chechnya.[14] It is also the story in Kashmir to a great degree. It was fortunately avoided in Macedonia. This process played out nowhere more typically than in Sri Lanka.

In the Sri Lankan case, the mechanism used to initially undermine minority confidence in the state's institutions was language. Few observers, if any, however, draw an explicit causal link between linguistic nationalism and the civil war. A major reason the Official Language Act's impact on the ethnic conflict has been underappreciated is because scholars working on Sri Lanka have failed to realize sufficiently that the act, while influenced by the extant political structure, also helped transform the political structure over a period of time. From the standpoint of polyethnic coexistence, the changes were for the worse. Changes by themselves mean little, however, unless they impact the institutional setup, and the Official Language Act helped drastically transform the way institutions dealing with economic and educational issues in particular affected the Sinhalese and Tamils. It was the first major ethnocentric law that was passed, and all the other laws, rules, and policies that were thereafter crafted to ensure its implementation and fulfill its promise systematically undermined impartial interactions between the country's institutions and the minorities. It is only by analyzing how the act influenced the country's institutions over time, and how those institutions in turn gradually regressed toward an ethnocracy, that one can fully appreciate how and why Sri Lanka became mired in civil war.

Primordialism no doubt provides some historical context for the

Sinhalese-Tamil rivalry, but it lacks robustness as an explanation for the conflict itself. After all, assuming one buys into the various myths of origin, Sinhalese and Tamils have coexisted more or less peacefully for over a millennium. Why the ferocious conflict now? The constructivist arguments rest on firmer ground, because there is ample evidence that colonialism and modern infrastructure did encourage more competitive notions of ethnic identity. Yet the constructivist project in Sri Lanka had been going on for some time (especially among the Sinhalese), and it does not explain the post-1956 interethnic violence. Certainly, the pressures stemming from modernization influenced ethnonationalism and the competition for scarce resources, and this would be part of the constructivist explanation. However, evaluating the competition for scarce resources without analyzing the institutional structure provides for only a limited account. Likewise, rational choice accounts, while useful when describing elite machinations, fail to recognize the sociocultural and historical influences motivating elites. Ethnic entrepreneurs, like all actors, are predisposed to maximizing their preferences, but this does not mean that they have no appreciation of, or allegiance or commitment to, their community's national projects, whatever those projects may be. Indeed, a greater appreciation for the historical and social contexts may further the rational choice approach by helping to explain somewhat where actors' preferences come from, which is something rational choice scholarship is typically inept at explaining. For example, some Sinhalese torched the very businesses they worked at (and thereby became unemployed) during the 1983 anti-Tamil riots, simply because the establishments were owned by Tamils. And dozens of Black Tigers compete for the chance to blow themselves up, even though their families do not benefit from their actions and they are under no illusion that martyrdom generates heavenly rewards, unlike in the case of the suicide bombers dispatched by Hamas and Islamic Jihad. Such acts are perhaps better explained using an ethnopsychological or values-driven explanation than one based on pure rationality.[15] The account presented here makes clear how the political structure encouraged ethnic outbidding, even as it constrained certain elites' rational preferences geared toward ethnic accommodation, which further suggests that institutionalist accounts are perhaps better suited to explaining ethnic relations and conflict.

The upshot, then, is that postindependence Sri Lankan institutions failed to justify the trust the country's minorities reposed in them. Unlike India, which has, for the most part, successfully dealt with numerous minority communities, or Canada, which has striven to accommodate the Québécois, the Sri Lankan state, beginning with the Official Language Act, gradually jettisoned the meritocracy and liberal democracy the is-

land was respected for and instead instituted an ethnic outbidding culture, which generated a pernicious ethnocracy. The institutional decay
that encompassed the state over the next two decades led to Tamil mobilization to create a separate state. Indeed, this decay was so acute that
even the island's vibrant civil society was relegated to the margins, while
uncivil elements triumphed.[16]

The Tamils' relationship with the postindependence Sri Lankan state
may be broken down into four distinct periods. The period between 1948
and 1956 can be labeled "ethnic cohabitation," with Sinhalese and Tamil
elites mainly cooperating to ensure that the newly independent state continued to be a viable democracy. The years between 1956 and 1972 saw
a movement seeking autonomy, with the Federal Party and S. J. V. Chelvanayakam holding sway. Aversion to the 1972 constitution, which influenced the call for an ethnic divorce in the Vaddukoddai Resolution
and the TULF's 1977 election manifesto, led to the period between 1972
and 1983 being one of "soft separatism." During this time, Tamil politicians talked openly about attaining a separate state, even as they continued to operate within the government seeking devolution. Finally, the
post-1983 period has been one of ethnic conflict. The process thus followed the sequence: ethnic cohabitation (1948–56)→ autonomy (1956–
72)→ soft separatism (1972–83)→ ethnic conflict (1983–present).

Sinhalese and Tamils will likely never enjoy their old camaraderie
again, but the tenuous ethnic accommodation countries like Macedonia
and Spain have achieved suggests that Sri Lanka too could revive peaceful ethnic coexistence. This would, however, require that the island's
Sinhalese elites in particular jettison ethnic outbidding and seriously try
to address Tamils' legitimate grievances and aspirations.

The continuation of ethnic scapegoating and ethnic particularism, coupled with the increasingly prosperous Tamil diaspora's support for *eelam*,
the LTTE's tenacity, and extremist Sinhalese politics may contribute to a
long-drawn-out conflict. Any lasting solution to the civil war will need to
be preceded by radically taming, if not eradicating, ethnic outbidding;
pursuing policies that encourage impartial interactions with all ethnic
groups; and restructuring the country's institutions.

Lessons Learned: A Case for Devolution

Sri Lanka's institutional decay and the subsequent civil war afford numerous lessons. First, they indicate how easily ethnonationalism is stoked
whenever particularistic linguistic policies are introduced. Second, the Sri
Lankan case specifically highlights how language policies in a polyethnic
society are related to education and to individuals' and groups' socioeco-

nomic upward mobility and the blowback that can ensue when those marginalized retaliate. Third, and especially when compared to India, the Sri Lankan case suggests that it may be easier to pursue accommodative linguistic policies in multilingual societies than in bilingual ones. Since multilingual societies generate more crosscutting cleavages and also prevent a single ethnic group from excessive dominance (because other groups could band together against it), they may be more likely to promote linguistic accommodation.

Consequently, a fourth lesson stemming from the Sri Lankan case is that ethnic animosities and conflict are much more easily escalated than deescalated. This is especially the case when the minority group is a territorial one and such animosities stem from linguistic differences, for nothing cements a group's cultural inheritance and consciousness as does language.

A fifth lesson stemming from the Sri Lankan case is the importance of timing. Thus with ethnic animosities stemming from linguistic discrimination becoming ingrained over time and grievances aggravated, solutions that might have satisfied the Tamils in the 1950s, 1960s, and even 1970s are now seen as too little, too late. For example, if the Sinhalese had conceded linguistic parity in the 1950s, it is unlikely that the Tamils would have clamored as strongly for federalism and devolution. Likewise, if devolution had been conceded in the 1978 constitution or soon thereafter, it is highly unlikely that Sri Lanka would be embroiled in its current ethnic conflict. One need only read the LTTE's proposals (appendix H) to realize how moderate the Tamils' initial demands were. That Sri Lanka's leaders failed to take advantage of the numerous windows of opportunity to modify the political structure in the 1950s, 1960s, and 1970s testifies to both their ineptitude and their pathological placing of petty personal and party ambitions above the national interest.

A sixth lesson the Sri Lankan case teaches is that institutions are easier to break down than to build up, and that promoting ethnic accommodation and dispassionate governance may be the most effective confidence-building measure in polyethnic societies. Governance based on ethnic impartiality strengthens minorities' belief that they will not be marginalized, habituates a culture of tolerance, conciliation, and inclusiveness, and ultimately institutes norms conducive to polyethnic coexistence. The longer these norms are embedded, the more confidence the minority communities will have in the state's institutions. Discriminatory treatment conversely undermines confidence in the state and leads territorially based groups in particular to mobilize.

Seventh, the Sri Lankan case nicely highlights how informal state actors can influence governance in a flawed democracy for the worse, and how the dynamic between formal and informal state actors, if not carefully tended, can have baneful consequences. The actions perpetrated by the Sinhalese nationalist forces and extremists in the Sangha have only exacerbated the damage already done by the country's political elites. In a real sense, these groups feed off one another, especially when it comes to imposing pressure on the political party (typically the governing party) trying to accommodate the Tamils.[17]

Eight, the Sri Lankan case indicates how outbidding and ethnocentrism could become embedded and path-dependent, which is to say that so many Sinhalese have become accustomed to profiting so much from successive governments' ethnocentric policies that they now find a change to consensus politics threatening.

Ninth, with no resolution in the offing after two decades of conflict, nearly 70,000 killed, and a million innocent Sinhalese and Tamil civilians displaced, the Sri Lankan case also proves that violent quests for secession rarely end in secession. Although the end of the Cold War saw ethnonationalism play a role in creating some new states, the fact remains that secession rarely offers an answer to complicated ethnic issues.[18] It is understandable that Tamil youth felt the urge to rebel, but it is also clear that the quest for *eelam* has worsened the average Tamil's plight and made a complicated problem nearly intractable.

The Need for Devolution

Given the military stalemate, granting the Tamils widespread autonomy is clearly the best way to resolve the conflict. Indeed, the Sri Lankan case makes it clear that autonomy or decentralization may be better suited than unitary structures to avoiding ethnic instability in polyethnic societies. John Stuart Mill pessimistically declared: "Free institutions are next to impossible in a country made up of different nationalities."[19] Yet the world is replete with polyethnic communities that have come together to fashion stable institutions, especially on federal principles. Decentralization in which minority groups are given some self-government may consequently be more effective when a state includes territorially based minorities. In the mid-1920s, some Kandyan Sinhalese and S. W. R. D. Bandaranaike, for different reasons, called for a federal structure, but Bandaranaike, as was his wont, backed off when Sinhalese nationalists pressed for a unitary state. In retrospect, it is hard to believe that a federal structure would not have better served the island. Even the Bandaranaike-Chelvanayakam Pact or the Senanayake-Chelvanayakam Pact, if implemented, would have gone a long way to assuaging Tamil concerns, especially regarding language and colonization, and would have contained the Tamils' grievances within their regional or district councils.

But the emphasis on centralization made successive governments responsible for all Tamil affairs, a charge Sri Lanka's ethnic entrepreneurs were woefully inept at undertaking.

The evidence clearly suggests that even if federalism and devolution do pose risks, "every single longstanding democracy in a multilingual and multinational polity is a federal state."[20] If Sri Lanka can be proud of having at least maintained a flawed democracy since independence, there can nevertheless be little doubt that a federal arrangement that addressed the Tamils' linguistic demands would largely have prevented the ethnic conflict and repression that occurred. A unitary state cannot, and an independent Tamil entity (that includes the Eastern Province and is headed by the LTTE) would not, generate the impartial governance required to promote stability and polyethnic coexistence. Consequently, the only peaceful option remaining to Sri Lanka's elites is to grant the Tamils sufficient devolution to attain self-determination.

While fears that devolution and self-determination may eventually lead to secession are understandable, they are mostly exaggerated. Indeed, there is no causal relationship between devolution and secession. On the contrary, what the causal arrow suggests is that irrespective of their constitutional structures and electoral systems, states tend to be confronted with separatist movements when majority groups in polyethnic societies eschew conciliation, accommodation, and compromise. "[A]utonomy and federation are better solutions than usually considered, if they are honestly applied and carefully tended," William Zartman contends.[21] Dismemberment is in this view likely to occur only if the devolutionary agreement is not "honestly applied."

Extremist Sinhalese parties like the JVP and Sinhala Urumaya (SU) would no doubt violently oppose any attempt at accommodation. The once-Maoist JVP is now nationalist. And since nation and religion are easily conflated with the Sinhalese Buddhists, the party is exceedingly pro-Buddhist as well. It consequently melds religion and nationalism and puts the UNP and SLFP on the defensive. Most important, it opposes any attempt to accommodate the minorities and is hostile to devolution or a negotiated settlement to the ethnic conflict. The JVP rails against any cease-fire between the government and the LTTE, since it wants a military solution to the conflict. It has thus demanded that the civil war be prosecuted more forcefully. Indeed, the JVP has even been accused of taking bribes from arms dealers who want to keep the conflict going.[22] The JVP, in a real sense, apes Sri Lanka's earlier postindependence politicians, because its primary objective is to attain and hold on to power. To do so, it will manipulate whatever issue is available, be it opposing the IPKF or the LTTE or embracing chauvinism.

The SU, on the other hand, which was organized in April 2000 under the pretense that Sinhalese economic and political fortunes were endangered, is patently a racist party. The party's founders justified its creation by arguing that while the Sri Lankan Tamils, Indian Tamils, and Muslims all had political parties along ethnic lines, the Sinhalese alone did not.[23] Party leaders claimed that they were forced to organize "to prevent the ultimate betrayal of the Sinhalese people," and they have promised to ensure that the "aspirations of the majority Sinhalese . . . [will] take precedence over . . . minorities such as the Tamils."[24] During the December 2001 parliamentary elections, the SU also claimed that if elected, it would ensure that all males under eighteen years of age were ordained into the Buddhist priesthood, leading some to wonder if Sri Lanka was witnessing the birth pangs of a Sinhalese Buddhist Taliban. If Sinhalese ethnocentrism and the military's ham-handed policies in the Northern Province legitimated Tamil militarism, it appears that Tamil militarism has in turn legitimized extremists in organizations like the SU. On the other hand, one can also argue that groups like the SU merely continue an extremist Sinhalese tradition that has existed in the island since the 1950s. The fact that the UNP and SLFP continue to get the vast majority of votes in elections suggests that Sri Lankans have little confidence that such extremist parties can solve the ethnic conflict. But it is clear that parties like the JVP and SU are trying to outbid the UNP and SLFP (or PA) on the ethnic conflict, just as the latter are playing the same game with each other.

Extremist Tamils are perhaps justified in arguing that the LTTE commands the moral authority to fight for separatism as long as opportunistic politicians, chauvinistic nationalists, and purblind academics continue their infatuation with the extant unitary state and oppose devolution. This has also been the LTTE's claim, but there is no reason to believe that a separate Tamil state would be secure, stable, and viable. A credible autonomy proposal must therefore be viewed as the sine qua non for future Sinhalese-Tamil coexistence.[25]

The government undoubtedly needs to defang the various nationalist organizations if it is successfully to reintroduce polyethnic coexistence. However, these groups clearly need not exert themselves too much, given that politicians are always eager to submit to their dictates. J. R. Jayewardene bluntly claimed, for example, that Cyril Mathew was required in his cabinet because his bigotry helped counter Mrs. Bandaranaike's anti-Tamil rhetoric.[26] President Kumaratunga similarly picked the nationalist Ratnasiri Wickremanayake as prime minister because doing so gave her some cover against the nationalist factions. And as we have seen, despite twenty years of civil war, ethnic outbidding continues to be eagerly practiced in Sri Lanka. It is imperative that it be contained, if not eradicated, and a more consensus-oriented political order formulated, if a climate conducive to peace is to be facilitated. This means that the power to induce a true and lasting peace lies primarily in Sinhalese hands.

It is possible that the LTTE has not deviated from wanting to create a separate state, but that can only be proven when Sinhalese leaders call the LTTE's bluff and institute a system that mainstream Tamils and the international community would endorse as fair. What Sinhalese hardliners need to realize is that the international community is averse to creating new states (especially when a territorial divorce is not amicable). In any case, India and the rest of South Asia, the United States and other leading powers, and the United Nations and the dominant international organizations would not recognize an LTTE-led state as an independent entity. To do so, especially in the post–September 2001 era, would suggest that terrorism does pay off. Thus even if the Tigers were to administer the north or the northeast as a de facto statelet, such an entity would be dependent on the Sri Lankan government and the international community for sustenance. This was indeed the case when the LTTE controlled the Jaffna Peninsula between 1990 and 1995. But if the Sri Lankan state does not devolve power sufficiently for Tamils in the northeast to live dignified and secure lives, then the international community may have no choice but turn a blind eye to the LTTE's actions. With the Sri Lankan civil war internationalized as never before, the state's inability or unwillingness to provide sufficient devolution to the northeast would also prove to the world that it is the petty politicking of the Sinhalese, and not so much the LTTE's intransigence, that is mainly responsible for the failure to resolve the conflict.

With Sinhalese preferences institutionalized and constitutionalized, the nationalists, especially those in the jingoistic JVP and SU, now claim that the country faces a terrorist problem, not an ethnic problem. While Tamils are sensitive to the carnage the LTTE has unleashed, they nevertheless realize that some leading Sinhalese politicians consider devolution seriously only because the rebels threaten Sri Lanka's sovereignty and territorial integrity. Consequently, the anti-Tamil climate has taken a new turn, because extremist Sinhalese politicians now conveniently vilify Tamil terrorism, while not overtly clamoring for Tamils' marginalization, as was the case from the 1950s to the 1980s. Then the Tamil quest for federalism on a linguistic basis was deliberately misconstrued as an attempt to dismember the country. Now that the LTTE has fought to create a Tamil state, these same forces feign sympathy for the Tamils, even while using the LTTE to justify anti-Tamil rhetoric and actions. The nationalists, and Sinhalese in general, obviously loathe the LTTE. The irony is that it was the extremist Sinhalese who facilitated and legitimated the extremist LTTE.

The events that have overcome Sri Lanka in the past fifty years are a tragedy by any measure. For of all the countries that gained independence and transited to democracy in the post–World War II period, Sri Lanka was said to have the best chance of building a prosperous polyethnic democratic polity. The country's leaders believed this too. For example, S. W. R. D. Bandaranaike thought that the island was uniquely poised to be a beacon for all of Asia. "Ceylon amongst all countries of Asia is best fitted to make a success of democracy," he told the Sinhala Maha Sabha in 1948. "In doing so we can not only benefit ourselves but [also] encourage the whole democratic movement in Asia, and in fact prove to be a valuable link between East and West."[27] Little did Bandaranaike realize at the time that in his quest to become prime minister, he would, less than a decade later, unleash enmity between Sinhalese and Tamils, and that the policies he, his spouse, and their progeny advocated would undermine liberal democracy, install and perpetuate an ethnocracy, and threaten to divide the country.

In hindsight, it is clear that the Official Language Act and the nationalism surrounding the Sinhala-only issue were what led to the current violent crescendo. The violence the Sinhala-only policy promoted left indelible scars and emboldened both sides to perpetrate further destruction. Sri Lanka's horrifying postindependence ethnic saga is thus a classic case of how a majority group's ethnolinguistic malpractices undermined the accommodation, conciliation, and compromise so essential to ensuring interethnic stability, thereby precluded impartial institutional interactions and delegitimized the state from a minority standpoint, and ultimately radicalized those marginalized to seek a separate existence.

REFERENCE MATTER

Appendixes

A. The Official Language Act, No. 33 of 1956

An Act to prescribe the Sinhala Language as the One Official Language of Ceylon and to enable certain transitory provisions to be made.

Be it enacted by the Queen's Most Excellent majesty by and with the advice and consent of the Senate and the House of Representatives of Ceylon in this present Parliament assembled, and by the authority of the same, as follows:—

Short Title

1. This Act may be cited as the Official Language Act, No. 33 of 1956.

Sinhala Language to Be the One Official Language

2. The Sinhala language shall be the one official language of Ceylon:
Provided that where the Minister considers it impracticable to commence the use of only the Sinhala language for any official purpose immediately on the coming into force of this Act, the language or languages hitherto used for that purpose may be continued to be so used until the necessary change is effected as early as possible before the expiry of the thirty-first of December, 1960, and, if such change cannot be effected by administrative order, regulations may be made under this Act to effect such change.

Regulations

3. (1) The Minister may make regulations in respect of all matters for which regulations are authorized by this Act to be made and generally for the purpose of giving effect to the principles and provisions of this Act.
(2) No regulations made under sub-section (1) shall have effect until it is approved by the Senate and the House of Representatives and notification of such approval is published in the *Gazette*.

B. Resolutions Passed at the Fifth (Special) National
Convention of the Federal Party (1957)

Held at Batticaloa on July 28, 1957.

Resolution No. 1

This special session of the National Convention of the Ilankai Tamil Arasu Kadchi assembled at the Town Hall Batticaloa on the 28th of July 1957 having considered the agreement reached between the representatives of the Federal Party on the one hand and the Prime Minister on the other and having reviewed the report of the negotiations submitted to it by its representatives reiterates its unalterable determination to achieve

(1) An Autonomous Tamil linguistic state or states within the framework of a Federal Union of Ceylon.

(2) Parity of status for the Tamil language with Sinhalese throughout Ceylon and,

(3) The revision and reorientation of the present unnatural and undemocratic citizenship laws of Ceylon to ensure the recognition of the right of every Tamil speaking individual who has made Ceylon his home to full citizenship.

This convention having regard to the fact that by the agreement *inter alia*,

(a) state-aided Sinhalese colonisation of the Northern and Eastern provinces will be effectively stopped forthwith.

(b) that the Tamil language is given official recognition as the language of a National Minority,

(c) that Tamil shall be the language of administration of the Northern and Eastern provinces,

(d) that the right of every Tamil speaking person in every part of the country to transact all affairs with government in Tamil and to educate and nurture his children in the Tamil language and culture is secured,

(e) and further in consideration of the large measure of regional self-government granted to the people under the proposed Regional Councils Act. "Resolves to accept the agreement as an interim adjustment and hereby ratifies the decision to withdraw the Satyagraha which was scheduled to commence on the 20th August 1957.

This convention further calls upon the Government to implement expeditiously the terms of the agreement reached between the Prime Minister and the Federal Party expeditiously in good faith and in the spirit in which it was entered into.

Resolution No. 2

This special session of the National Convention of the Illankai Tamil Arasu Kadchi calls upon the Tamil speaking people who are struggling for the attainment of full freedom and self respect solemnly to resolve to work for the regeneration and unification of the Tamil speaking people by undertaking immediate action for the removal of all forms of social inequalities and injustices, in particular that of untouchability which still exists among a section of the people and towards this end to organize a campaign of self purification if necessary by Ahimsa and Satyagraha for the achievement of this goal without which the Tamil speaking Nation in Ceylon cannot and never will realise its fundamental object of attaining Political and Cultural freedom for the Tamil speaking people of Ceylon by the establishment of a Tamil linguistic state or states within the frame work of the Federal Union of Ceylon.

C. The "Bandaranaike-Chelvanayakam Pact" (1957)

The text of the joint statements by the prime minister and representatives of the Federal Party on July 26, 1957.

Statement on the general principles of the Agreement between the Prime Minister and the Federal Party

Representatives of the Federal Party have had a series of discussions with the Prime Minister in an effort to resolve the differences of opinion that had been growing and creating tension.

At an early stage of these conversations it became evident that it was not possible for the Prime Minister to accede to some of the demands of the Federal Party.

The Prime Minister stated that from the point of view of the Government he was not in a position to discuss the setting up of a federal constitution or regional autonomy or any step which would abrogate the Official Language Act. The question then arose whether it was possible to explore the possibility of an adjustment without the Federal Party abandoning or surrendering any of its fundamental principles and objectives.

At this stage the Prime Minister suggested an examination of the Government's draft Regional Councils Bill to see whether provision could be made under it to meet reasonably some of the matters in this regard which the Federal Party had in view.

The agreements so reached are embodied in a separate document.

Regarding the language issue the Federal Party reiterated its stand for parity, but in view of the position of the Prime Minister in this matter they came to an agreement by way of an adjustment. They pointed out that it was important for them that there should be a recognition of Tamil as a national language and that the administrative work in the Northern and Eastern Provinces should be done in Tamil.

The Prime Minister stated that as mentioned by him earlier it was not possible for him to take any step which would abrogate the Official Language Act.

[*Use of Tamil*] After discussions it was agreed that the proposed legislation should contain recognition of Tamil as the language of a national minority of Ceylon, and that the four points mentioned by the Prime Minister should include provision that, without infringing on the position of the Official Language Act, the language of administration in the Northern and Eastern Provinces should be Tamil and that any necessary provision be made for the non-Tamil speaking minorities in the Northern and Eastern Provinces.

Regarding the question of Ceylon citizenship for people of Indian descent and revision of the Citizenship Act, the representatives of the Federal Party put forward their views to the Prime Minister and pressed for an early settlement.

The Prime Minister indicated that this problem would receive early consideration.

In view of these conclusions the Federal party stated that they were withdrawing their proposed satyagraha.

Joint Statement by the Prime Minister and Representatives of the Federal Party on Regional Councils

(A) Regional areas to be defined in the Bill itself by embodying them in a schedule thereto.

(B) That the Northern Province is to form one Regional area whilst the Eastern Province is to be divided into two or more Regional areas.

(C) Provision is to be made in the Bill to enable two or more regions to amalgamate even beyond provincial limits; and for one region to divide itself subject to ratification by Parliament. Further provision is to be made in the Bill for two or more regions to collaborate for specific purposes of common interest.

[*Direct Elections*] (D) Provision is to be made for direct election of regional councilors. Provision is to be made for a delimitation Commission of Commissions for carving out electorates. The question of M.P.'s representing districts falling within regional areas to be eligible to function as chairmen is to be considered. The question of Government Agents being Regional Commissioners is to be considered. The question of supervisory functions over larger towns, strategic towns and municipalities is to be looked into.

[*Special Powers*] (E) Parliament is to delegate powers and to specify them in the Act. It was agreed that Regional Councils should have powers over specified subjects including agriculture, co-operatives, lands and land development, colonization, education, health, industries and fisheries, housing and social services, electricity, water schemes and roads. Requisite definition of powers will be made in the Bill.

[*Colonisation Schemes*] (F) It was agreed that in the matter of colonization schemes the powers of the Regional Councils shall include the power to select allottees to whom lands within their area of authority shall be alienated and also power to select personnel to be employed for work on such schemes. The position regarding the area at present administered by the Gal Oya Board in this matter requires consideration.

[*Taxation, Borrowing*] (G) The powers in regard to the Regional Councils vested in the Minister of Local Government in the draft bill to be revised with a view to vesting control in Parliament wherever necessary.

(H) The Central Government will provide block grants to all Regional Councils. The principles on which the grants will be computed will be gone into. The Regional Councils shall have powers of taxation and borrowing.

D. The Tamil Language (Special Provisions) Act, No. 28 of 1958

An Act to make provision for the use of the Tamil language and to provide for matters connected therewith or identical thereto.

Whereas the Sinhala language has been declared by the Official Language Act, No. 33 of 1956, to be the one official language of Ceylon:

And whereas it is expedient to make provision for the use of the Tamil language without conflicting with the provisions of the aforesaid Act:

Be it enacted by the Queen's Most Excellent majesty, by and with the advice and consent of the Senate and the House of Representatives of Ceylon in this present Parliament assembled, and by the authority of the same, as follows:—

Short Title

1. This Act may be cited as the Tamil Language (Special Provisions) Act, No. 28 of 1958.

Tamil language as a medium of instruction

2. (1) A Tamil pupil in a Government school or an Assisted school shall be entitled to be instructed through the medium of the Tamil language in accordance with such regulations under the Education Ordinance, No. 31 of 1939, relating to the medium of instruction as are in force or may hereafter be brought into force.

(2) When the Sinhala language is made a medium of instruction in the University of Ceylon, the Tamil language shall, in accordance with the provisions of the Ceylon University Ordinance, No. 20 of 1942, and of the Statutes, Acts and Regulations made thereunder, be made a medium of instruction in such University for students who, prior to their admission to such University, have been educated through the medium of the Tamil language.

Tamil language as a medium of examination for admission to the Public Service

3. A person educated through the medium of the Tamil language shall be entitled to be examined through such medium at any examination for the admissions of persons to the Public Service, subject to the condition that he shall, according as regulations made under this Act in that behalf may require,—

(a) have a sufficient of the official language of Ceylon, or

(b) acquire such knowledge within a specified time after admission to the Public Service:

Provided that, when the Government is satisfied that there are sufficient facilities for the teaching of the Sinhala language in schools in which the Tamil language is a medium of instruction and that the annulment of clause (b) of the preceding provisions of this section will not cause undue hardship, provision may be made by regulation made under this Act that such clause shall cease to be in force.

Use of Tamil language for correspondence

1. Correspondence between persons, other than officials in their official ca-

pacity, educated through the medium of the Tamil language and any official in his official capacity or between any local authority in the Northern or Eastern Province and any official in his official capacity may, as prescribed, be in the Tamil language.

Use of the Tamil language for prescribed administrative purposes in the Northern and Eastern Provinces

2. In the Northern and Eastern Provinces the Tamil language may be used for prescribed administrative purposes, in addition to the purposes for which that language may be used in accordance with the other provisions of this Act, without prejudice to the use of the official language of Ceylon in respect of those prescribed administrative purposes.

Regulations

3. (1) The Minister may make regulations to give effect to the principles and provisions of this Act.

(2) No regulation made under sub-section (1) shall have effect until it is approved by the Senate and the House of Representatives and notification of such approval is published in the Gazette.

This Act to be subject to measures adopted or to be adopted under the proviso to section 2 of Act No. 33 of 1956

4. This Act shall have effect subject to such measures as may have been or may be adopted under the proviso to section 2 of the Official Language Act, No. 33, of 1956, during the period ending on the thirty-first day of December, 1960.

Interpretation

5. In this Act unless the context otherwise requires—

6. "Assisted school" and "Government school" shall have the same meaning as in the Education Ordinance, No. 31 of 1939; "local authority" means any Municipal Council, Urban Council, Town Council, or Village Committee; "official" means the Governor-General, or any Minister, Parliamentary Secretary or officer of the Public Service; and "prescribed" means prescribed by regulation made under this Act.

E. The Agreement Between Dudley Senanayake and S. J. V. Chelvanayakam (1965)

"Mr. Dudley Senanayake [UNP] and Mr. S. J. V. Chelvanayakam [Federal Party] met on the 24.3.1965 and discussed matters relating to some problems over which the Tamil-speaking people were concerned, and Mr. Senanayake agreed that action on the following lines would be taken by him to ensure a stable Government."

1. Action will be taken early under the Tamil Language Special Provisions Act to make provision for the use of Tamil as the language of administration and of record in the Northern and Eastern provinces.

2. Mr. Senanayake stated that it was the policy of his Party to amend the Language of the Courts Act to provide for legal proceedings in the Northern and Eastern Provinces to be conducted and recorded in Tamil.

3. Action will be taken to establish District Councils in Ceylon vested with

powers over subjects to be mutually agreed upon between the two leaders. It was agreed, however, that the Government should have power under the law to give directions to such Councils in the national interest.

4. The Land Development Ordinance will be amended. Mr. Senanayake further agreed that in the granting of land under colonisation schemes the following priorities be observed in the Northern and Eastern Provinces.

(a) Land in the Northern and Eastern Provinces should in the first instance be granted to landless persons in the District.

(b) Secondly—to Tamil-speaking persons resident in the Northern and Eastern Provinces, and

(c) Thirdly—to other citizens in Ceylon, preference being given to Tamil citizens in the rest of the Island.

Sgd/ Dudley Senanayake 24. 3. 1965.

Sgd/ S. J. V. Chelvanayakam 24. 3. 1965

F. The Tamil Language (Special Provisions) Regulations (1966)

1. These regulations may be cited as the Tamil Language (Special Provisions) Regulations, 1966.

2. Without prejudice to the operation of the Official Language Act No. 33 of 1956, which declared the Sinhala language to be the one official language of Ceylon, the Tamil language shall also be used—

(a) In the Northern and Eastern Provinces for the transaction of all Government and public business and the maintenance of public records whether such business is conducted in or by a department or institution of the Government, a public corporation or a statutory institution; and

(b) For all correspondence between persons other than officials in their official capacity, educated through the medium of the Tamil language and any official in his official capacity, or between any local authority in the Northern and Eastern Provinces which conducts its business in the Tamil language and any official in his official capacity.

3. For the purpose of giving full force and effect to the principles and provisions of the Tamil Language (Special Provisions) Act, No. 28 of 1958, and these regulations all Ordinances and Acts, and all Orders, Proclamation[s], rules, by-laws, regulations and notifications made or issued under any written law, the Government Gazette and all other official publications, circulars and forms issued or used by the Government, public corporations or statutory institutions, shall be translated and published in the Tamil language also.

G. The Vaddukoddai Resolution (1976)

Political Resolution Unanimously Adopted at the 1st National Convention of the Tamil United Liberation Front Held at Pannakam (Vaddukoddai Constituency) on 14-5-76, Presided over by Mr. Chelvanayakam, Q.C., M.P.

Whereas throughout the centuries from the dawn of history the Sinhalese and Tamil nations have divided between them the possession of Ceylon, the Sinhalese inhabiting the interior of the country in its Southern and Western parts from the river Walawe to that of Chilaw and the Tamils possessing the Northern and Eastern districts;

And whereas the Tamil Kingdom was overthrown in war and conquered by the Portuguese in 1619 and from them by the Dutch and the British in turn independent of the Sinhalese Kingdoms;

And whereas the British Colonists who ruled the territories of the Sinhalese and Tamil Kingdoms separately joined under compulsion the territories of the Sinhalese Kingdoms for purposes of administrative convenience on the recommendation of the Colebrooke Commission in 1833;

And whereas the Tamil Leaders were in the forefront of the Freedom movement to rid Ceylon of colonial bondage which ultimately led to the grant of independence to Ceylon in 1948;

And whereas the foregoing facts of history were completely overlooked and power was transferred to the Sinhalese nation over the entire country on the basis of a numerical majority thereby reducing the Tamil nation to the position of subject people;

And whereas successive Sinhalese governments since independence have always encouraged and fostered the aggressive nationalism of the Sinhalese people and have used their political power to the detriment of the Tamils by—

(a) Depriving one half of the Tamil people of their citizenship and franchise rights thereby reducing Tamil representation in Parliament,

(b) Making serious inroads into the territories of the former Tamil Kingdom by a system of planned and state-aided Sinhalese colonization and large scale regularization of recently encouraged Sinhalese encroachments calculated to make the Tamils a minority in their own homeland,

(c) Making Sinhala the only official language throughout Ceylon thereby placing the stamp of inferiority on the Tamils and the Tamil language,

(d) Giving the foremost place to Buddhism under the Republican constitution thereby reducing the Hindus, Christians, and Muslims to second class status in this Country,

(e) Denying to the Tamils equality of opportunity in the spheres of employment, education, land alienation and economic life in general and starving Tamil areas of large scale industries and development schemes thereby seriously endangering their very existence in Ceylon,

(f) Systematically cutting them off from the main-stream of Tamil cultures in South-India while denying them opportunities of developing their language and culture in Ceylon thereby working inexorably towards the cultural genocide of the Tamils,

(g) Permitting and unleashing communal violence and intimidation against the Tamil speaking people as happened in Amparai and Colombo in 1956; all over the country in 1958; army reign of terror in the Northern and Eastern Provinces in 1961; Police violence at the International Tamil Research Conference in 1974 resulting in the death of nine persons in Jaffna; Police and communal violence against Tamil speaking Muslims at Puttalam and various other parts of Ceylon in 1976—all these calculated to instill terror in the minds of the Tamil speaking people thereby breaking their spirit and the will to resist injustices heaped on them,

(h) By terrorizing, torturing, and imprisoning Tamil youth without trial for long periods on the flimsiest grounds,

(i) Capping it all by imposing on the Tamil Nation a constitution drafted under conditions of emergency without opportunities for free discussion by a constituent assembly elected on the basis of the Soulbury Constitution distorted by the Citizenship laws resulting in weightage in representation to the Sinhalese majority thereby depriving the Tamils of even the remnants of safeguards they had under the earlier constitution,

And whereas all attempts by various Tamil political parties to win their rights by co-operating with the governments, by parliamentary and extra-parliamentary agitations, by entering into pacts and understandings with successive Prime Ministers in order to achieve the bare minimum of political rights consistent with the self-respect of the Tamil people have proved to be futile;

And whereas the efforts of the All Ceylon Tamil Congress to ensure non-denomination of the minorities by the majority by the adoption of a scheme of balanced representation in a Unitary Constitution have failed and even the meager safeguards provided in article 29 of the Soulbury Constitution against discriminatory legislation have been removed by the Republican Constitution;

And whereas the proposals submitted to the Constituent Assembly by the Ilankai Thamil Arasu Kadchi for maintaining the unity of the country while preserving the integrity of the Tamil people by the establishment of an autonomous Tamil State within the framework of a Federal Republic of Ceylon were summarily and totally rejected without even the courtesy of a consideration of its merits;

And whereas the amendments to the basic resolutions intended to ensure the minimum of safeguards to the Tamil people moved on the basis of the nine point demands formulated at the conference of all Tamil Political parties at Valvettithurai on 7th February 1971 and by individual parties and Tamil members of Parliament including those now in the government party were rejected in total by the government and Constituent Assembly;

And whereas even amendments to the draft proposals relating to language, religion, and fundamental-rights including one calculated to ensure that at least the provisions of the Tamil Language (Special Provisions) Regulations of 1956 be included in the Constitution were defeated resulting in the boycott of the Constituent Assembly by a large majority of the Tamil members of Parliament;

And whereas the Tamil United Liberation Front, after rejecting the Republican Constitution adopted on the 22nd of May, 1972 presented a six point demand to the Prime Minister and the Government on 25th June, 1972 and gave three months time within which the Government was called upon to take meaningful steps to amend the Constitution so as to meet the aspirations of the Tamil Nation on the basis of the six points and informed the Government that if it failed to do so the Tamil United Liberation Front would launch a non-violent direct action against the Government in order to win the freedom and the rights of the Tamil Nation on the basis of the right of self-determination;

And whereas this last attempt by the Tamil United Liberation Front to win Constitutional recognition of the rights of the Tamil Nation without jeopardizing the unity of the country was callously ignored by the Prime Minister and the Government;

And whereas the opportunity provided by the Tamil United Liberation leader to vindicate the Government's contention that their constitution had the backing of the Tamil people, by resigning from his membership of the National State Assembly and creating a by-election was deliberately put off for over two years in utter disregard of the democratic right of the Tamil voters of Kankensanthurai, and

Whereas in the by-election held on the 6th February 1975 the voters of Kankensanthurai by a preponderant majority not only rejected the Republican Constitution imposed on them by the Sinhalese Government but also gave a mandate to Mr. S. J.V. Chelvanayakam, Q.C. and through him to the Tamil United Liberation Front for the restoration and reconstruction of the Free, Sovereign, Secular, Socialist State of TAMIL EELAM.

The first National Convention of the Tamil United Liberation Front meeting at Pannakam (Vaddukoddai Constituency) on the 14th day of May, 1976 hereby declares that the Tamils of Ceylon by virtue of their great language, their religion, their separate culture and heritage, their history of independent existence as a separate state over a distinct territory for several centuries till they were conquered by the armed might of the European invaders and above all by their will to exist as a separate entity ruling themselves in their own territory, are a nation distinct and apart from Sinhalese and this Convention announces to the world that the Republican Constitution of 1972 has made the Tamils a slave nation ruled by the new colonial masters the Sinhalese who are using the power they have wrongly usurped to deprive the Tamil Nation of its territory, language, citizenship, economic life, opportunities of employment and education thereby destroying all the attributes of nationhood of the Tamil people.

And therefore, while taking note of the reservations in relation to its commitment to the setting up of a separated state of TAMIL EELAM expressed by the Ceylon Workers Congress as a Trade Union of the Plantation Workers, the majority of whom live and work outside the Northern and Eastern areas,

This convention resolves that restoration and reconstitution of the Free, Sovereign, Secular Socialist State of TAMIL EELAM based on the right of self-determination inherent to every nation has become inevitable in order to safeguard the very existence of the Tamil Nation in this Country.

This Convention further declares—

(a) that the state of TAMIL EELAM shall consist of the people of the Northern and Eastern provinces and shall also ensure full and equal rights of citizenship of the State of TAMIL EELAM to all Tamil speaking people living in any part of Ceylon and to Tamils of EELAM origin living in any part of the world who may opt for citizenship of TAMIL EELAM.

(b) that the constitution of TAMIL EELAM shall be based on the principle of democratic decentralization so as to ensure the non-domination of any religious or territorial community of TAMIL EELAM by any other section.

(c) that in the State of TAMIL EELAM caste shall be abolished and the observance of the pernicious practice of untouchability or inequality of any type based on birth shall be totally eradicated and its observance in any form punished by law.

(d) that TAMIL EELAM shall be a secular state giving equal protection and assistance to all religions to which the people of the state may belong.

(e) that Tamil shall be the language of the State but the rights of the Sinhalese speaking minorities in TAMIL EELAM to education and transaction of business in their language shall be protected on a reciprocal basis with the Tamil speaking minorities in the Sinhala State.

(f) that TAMIL EELAM shall be a Socialist State wherein the exploitation of man by man shall be forbidden, the dignity of labor shall be recognized, the means of production and distribution shall be subject to public ownership and control while permitting private enterprise in these branches within limits prescribed by law, economic development shall be on the basis of socialist planning and there shall be a ceiling on the total wealth that any individual or family may require.

This Convention directs the Action Committee of the TAMIL UNITED LIBERATION FRONT to formulate a plan of action and launch without undue delay the struggle for winning the sovereignty and freedom of the Tamil Nation;

And this Convention calls upon the Tamil Nation in general and the Tamil youth in particular to come forward to throw themselves fully in the sacred fight for freedom and to flinch not till the goal of a sovereign state of TAMIL EELAM is reached.

H. The LTTE Proposal for an Interim Self-Governing Authority for the Northeast (2003)

Proposal by the Liberation Tigers of Tamil Eelam on Behalf of the Tamil People for an Agreement to Establish an Interim Self-Governing Authority for the Northeast of the Island of Sri Lanka.

Consistent with the principles of the rule of law, the human rights and equality of all persons, and the right to self-determination of Peoples,

Determined to bring lasting peace to all persons of the island of Sri Lanka,

Acknowledging with appreciation the services of the Royal Norwegian Government, the Norwegian People, and the international community in attempting to bring peace to the island,

Recognizing that a peaceful resolution is a real possibility, despite the challenging history of the peace between the Tamil people and the Sinhala people,

Determined to establish an interim self-governing authority for the NorthEast region and to provide for the urgent needs of the people of the NorthEast by formulating laws and policies and, effectively and expeditiously executing all resettlement, rehabilitation, reconstruction, and development in the NorthEast, while the process for reaching a final settlement remains ongoing,

Being aware that the history of the relations between the Tamil People and the Sinhala People has been a process of broken promises and unilateral abrogation, by successive governments of Sri Lanka, of pacts and agreements solemnly entered into between the government of Sri Lanka (GOSL) and the elected representatives of the Tamil People,

Bearing in mind that successive Governments of Sri Lanka have perpetrated persecution, discrimination, State violence and State-orchestrated violence against the Tamil People,

Noting that the Tamil people mandated their elected representatives to establish an independent sovereign, secular State for the Tamil people in the elections subsequent to the Vaddukoddai Resolution of 1976,

Bearing in mind that the Tamil armed struggle as a measure of self-defense and as a means for the realisation of the Tamil right to self-determination arose only after more than four decades of non-violent and peaceful constitutional struggle proved to be futile and due to the absence of means to resolve the conflict peacefully,

Recalling that the Liberation Tigers of Tamil Eelam (LTTE) first took measures towards peace by unilaterally declaring the ceasefire in December, 2000 and again in December, 2001, opening highways, facilitating trade and the free movement of people, and entering into peace negotiations in good faith in the hope of creating an environment conducive to the return of normalcy and a just resolution of the conflict,

Taking Note of the political courage of the present GOSL in reciprocating to the 2001 ceasefire,

Realising that the war in the island of Sri Lanka was principally confined to the NorthEast, resulting in the destruction of the social, economic, administrative, and physical infrastructure of that area, and that the NorthEast still remains the region in the island of Sri Lanka affected by war,

Recognising that the majority of the Tamil People in the NorthEast, by their actions in the general elections held in the year 2000, gave their mandate acknowledging the LTTE as their authentic representative,

Knowing that the LTTE exercises effective control and jurisdiction over the majority of the NorthEast area of the island of Sri Lanka,

Realising that reaching a final negotiated settlement and the implementation thereof is expected to be a long process,

Affirming the necessity for the safe and free return of all refugees and displaced persons and their urgent need for unimpeded access to their homes and secure livelihoods at land and sea in the North East,

Mindful that institutions and services provided by the GOSL have proved to be inadequate to meet the urgent needs of the people of the North East,

Recognising the failure of the Sub-committee on Immediate Humanitarian and Rehabilitation Needs (SIHRN) and other Sub-Committees formed during the peace negotiations, which failure was due to the composition of such Sub-Committees, which repeatedly led to inaction,

Acknowledging the recognition by the GOSL of the necessity for an Interim Authority, as mentioned in its 2000 election manifesto,

Realising that maintenance of law and order is an essential pre-requisite for a just and free society,

Recognising that need for raising revenue to meet the urgent needs for the Resettlement, Rehabilitation, Reconstruction and Development of the NorthEast region, which has been devastated by war, and for the carrying out of any function of Government,

Recognising the importance of control over land in resettlement, rehabilitation, reconstruction and development,

Mindful that the Tamils did not participate in the making of the 1972 and 1978 constitutions, which institutionalized discrimination and denied them an effective role in the decision-making process,

Noting the practice in international relations over the last decade of solving conflicts between Peoples through agreement between the parties to the conflict on terms of equality and through innovative and imaginative measures,

Relying on international precedents for establishing interim governing arrangements in war torn countries having the force of law based solely on pacts or agreement between the warring parties recognized by the international community,

Noting that measures such as the Ceasefire Agreement, including the role of the Sri Lanka Monitoring Mission (SLMM), and, the establishment of the SIHRN and the North East Reconstruction Fund (NERF) constitute valid precedents for making such arrangements,

Wherefore, the Parties, namely the Liberation Tigers of Tamil Eelam and the Government of Sri Lanka, hereby agree to the following provisions:

1. Interim Self-Governing Authority

An Interim Self-Governing Authority (ISGA) shall be established comprised of the eight districts namely: Amparai, Batticaloa, Jaffna, Kilinochchi, Mannar, Mullaitivu, Trincomalee and Vavuniya in the NorthEast, until a final negotiated settlement is reached and implemented.

Representatives of the Muslim community have the right to participate in formulation of their role in the ISGA.

2. Composition of the ISGA

2.1. The ISGA shall consist of such number of members as may be determined by the Parties to this Agreement.

2.2. The composition of the ISGA shall be:
    2.2.a. Members appointed by the LTTE,
    2.2.b. Members appointed by the GOSL, and
    2.2.c. Members appointed by the Muslim community in the NorthEast.

2.3. The number of members will be determined to ensure:
    2.3.a. An absolute majority of the LTTE appointees in the ISGA.
    2.3.b. Subject to (a) above, the Muslim and Sinhala Communities in the NorthEast shall have representation in the ISGA.

2.4. The Chairperson shall be elected by a majority vote of the ISGA and shall serve as the Chief Executive of the ISGA.

2.5. The Chairperson shall appoint the Chief Administrator for the NorthEast and such other officers as may be required to assist in the performance of his/her duties. The Chairperson shall have the powers to suspend or terminate any such appointment.

3. Elections

The provisions of Clauses 2.2 and 2.3 shall continue until elections for the ISGA are held. Such elections shall be held at the expiry of five years of the coming into force of this Agreement, if no final settlement has been reached and implemented by the end of the said period of five years. An independent Election Commission, appointed by the ISGA, shall conduct free and fair elections in accordance with international democratic principles and standards under international observation.

4. Human Rights

The people of the NorthEast shall be accorded all rights as are provided under international human rights law. Every law, regulation, rule, order or decision of the ISGA shall conform to internationally accepted standards of human rights protection. There shall be an independent Human Rights Commission, appointed by the ISGA, which shall ensure the compliance with all such human rights obligations. The Commission will seek the assistance of international human rights bodies to facilitate the rapid establishment of an effective regime for protecting human rights. The Commission shall be entitled to receive petitions from any individual person, award compensation to any such affected person, and ensure that such person's rights are restored.

5. Secularism

No religion shall be given the foremost place in the NorthEast.

6. Prohibition against Discrimination

The ISGA shall ensure that there is no discrimination on grounds of religion, race, caste, national or regional origin, age or gender in the NorthEast.

7. Prevention of Bribery and Corruption

The ISGA shall ensure that no bribery or corruption is permitted in or under its administration.

8. Protection of All Communities

No law, regulation, rule, order or decision that confers a privilege or imposes a disability on any community, which is not conferred or imposed on any other community, shall be made concerning culture or religion.

9. Jurisdiction of the ISGA

9.1. The ISGA shall have plenary power for the governance of the NorthEast including powers in relation to resettlement, rehabilitation, reconstruction and development, including improvement and upgrading of existing services and facilities (hereinafter referred to as RRRD), raising revenue including imposition of taxes, revenue, levies and duties, law and order, and over land.

These powers shall include all powers and functions in relation to regional administration exercised by the GOSL in and for the NorthEast.

9.2. The detailed modalities for the exercise of such powers and the performance of such functions shall be subject to further discussion by the parties to this agreement.

10. Separation of Powers

Separate institutions for the administration of justice shall be established for the NorthEast, and judicial powers shall be vested in such institutions. The ISGA shall take appropriate measures to ensure the independence of the judges.

Subject to Clauses 4 (Human Rights) and 22 (Settlement of Disputes), of this Agreement, the institutions created under this clause shall have sole and exclusive jurisdiction to resolve all disputes concerning the interpretation and implementation of this agreement and any other disputes arising in or under this agreement or any provision thereof.

11. Finance

The ISGA shall prepare an annual budget.

There shall be a Financial Commission consisting of members appointed by the ISGA. The members should have distinguished themselves or held high office in the fields of finance, administration or business. This Commission shall make recommendations as to the amount out of the Consolidated Fund to be allocated to the NorthEast. The GOSL shall make its good faith efforts to implement the recommendation.

The ISGA will, giving due consideration to an equitable distribution, determine the use of funds placed at its disposal. These funds shall include the NorthEast General Fund, the NorthEast Reconstruction Fund (NERF) and the Special Fund.

The GOSL agrees that any and all of its expenditures in or for the NorthEast shall be subject to the control of the ISGA.

11.1. NorthEast General Fund

The NorthEast General Fund shall be under the control of ISGA and shall consist of:

11.1.a. The proceeds of all grants and loans made by the GOSL to the ISGA and the proceeds of all other loans made to the ISGA.

11.1.b. All allocations by the GOSL from agreements with states, institutions and/or other organizations earmarked in any such agreements for the NorthEast.

11.1.c. All other receipts of the ISGA, other than the funds specified below.

11.2. NorthEast Reconstruction Fund

The NERF shall continue to exist in its present form except that control over it will be transferred to the ISGA.

All grants given for the reconstruction of the NorthEast, will be received through the NERF. Utilization of resources from NERF will be directly determined and supervised by the ISGA.

11.3. Special Fund

All loans and any grants which cannot be channeled through the NERF for the specific purpose of RRRD will be received into the Special Fund. As in the case of other Funds, the ISGA shall control the Special Fund.

12. Powers to Borrow, Receive Aid and Trade

The ISGA shall have powers to borrow internally and externally, provide guarantees and indemnities, receive aid directly, and engage in or regulate internal and external trade.

13. Accounting and Auditing of Funds

13.1.The ISGA shall appoint an Auditor General.

13.2. All funds referred to in this Agreement shall be operated, maintained and audited in accordance with internationally accepted accounting and auditing standards. The accounts will be audited by the Auditor General. The auditing of all moneys received from international sources shall be subjected to approval by an internationally-reputed firm appointed by the ISGA.

14. District Committees

14.1. In the effective exercise of its legislative and executive powers, the ISGA may create District Committees to carry out administration in the districts and delegate to such Committees, such powers as the ISGA may determine. The Chairpersons of such committees shall be appointed by the ISGA from amongst its members in order to serve as a liaison between the ISGA and the Committees.

14.2. The other members of the Committees shall also be appointed by the ISGA, which shall have the powers to suspend or terminate any such appointment. In appointing such members, due consideration shall be given to ensure representation of all communities.

14.3. The Committees will function directly under the ISGA.

14.4. The Chief Administrator of the ISGA shall appoint Principal Executive Officers in the districts, who shall also function as the Secretaries to the Committees. The Chief Administrator shall have the powers to suspend or terminate any such appointment.

14.5. All activities and functions of the Committees shall be coordinated through the respective Secretaries to the Committees.

14.6. Sub-committees may also be appointed to facilitate administration.

15. Administration

As part of the exercise of its executive powers the ISGA shall have direction and control over any and all administrative structures and personnel in the NorthEast pertaining to the powers set out in Clause 9 of this Agreement.

The ISGA may, at its discretion, create expert advisory committees in necessary areas. These areas will include but are not limited to Economic Affairs, Financial Affairs, Judicial Affairs, Resettlement and Rehabilitation Affairs, Development of Infrastructure, and Essential Services.

16. Administration of Land

Since land is vital to the exercise of the powers set out in Clause 9 (jurisdiction of the ISGA), the ISGA shall have the power to alienate and determine the appropriate use of all land in the NorthEast that is not privately owned.

The ISGA shall appoint a Special Commission on Administration of Land to inquire into and report on the rights of dispossessed people over land and land subject to encroachment, notwithstanding the lapse of any time relating to prescription.

The ISGA shall determine the term of competencies of the Special Commission.

17. Resettlement of Occupied Lands

The occupation of land by the armed forces of the GOSL, and the denial to the rightful civilian owners of unfettered access to such land, is a violation of the norms of international law. Such land must be immediately vacated and restored to the possession of the previous owners. The GOSL must also compensate the owners for the past dispossession of their land.

The ISGA shall be responsible for the resettlement and rehabilitation of displaced civilians and refugees in such lands.

18. Marine and Off-shore Resources

The ISGA shall have control over the marine and offshore resources of the adjacent seas and the power to regulate access thereto.

19. Natural Resources

The ISGA will have control over the natural resources in the NorthEast region. Existing agreements relating to any such natural resources will continue in force. The GOSL shall ensure that all monies due under such agreements are paid to the ISGA. Any future changes to such existing agreements should be made with the concurrence of the ISGA. Future agreements shall be entered into with the ISGA.

20. Water Use

Upper riparian users of river systems have a duty to ensure that there is a fair, equitable and reasonable use of water resources by lower riparian users. The GOSL and the ISGA shall ensure that this internationally recognized principle is followed in the use of water resources.

21. Agreements and Contracts

All future agreements concerning matters under the jurisdiction of the ISGA shall be made with the ISGA. Existing agreements will continue, but the GOSL shall ensure that all proceeds under such agreements are paid to the ISGA. Any changes to such existing agreements should be made with the concurrence of the ISGA.

22. Settlement of Disputes

Where a dispute arises between the Parties to this Agreement as to its interpretation or implementation, and it cannot be resolved by any other means acceptable to the Parties including conciliation by the Royal Norwegian Government, there shall be an arbitration before a tribunal consisting of three members, two of whom shall be appointed by each Party. The third member, who shall be the Chairperson of the tribunal, shall be appointed jointly by the Parties concerned. In the event of any disagreement over the appointment of the Chairperson, the Parties shall ask the President of the International Court of Justice to appoint the Chairperson.

In the determination of any dispute the arbitrators shall ensure the parity of status of the LTTE and the GOSL and shall resolve disputes by reference only to the provisions of this Agreement.

The decision of the arbitrators shall be final and conclusive and it shall be binding on the Parties to the dispute.

23. Operational Period

This Agreement shall continue until a new Government for the NorthEast, pursuant to a permanent negotiated settlement, is established. The Parties will negotiate in good faith to reach such a settlement as early as possible.

Provided, however, that at the end of four years if no final agreement has been reached between the Parties to this agreement, both Parties shall engage in negotiations in good faith for the purpose of adding, clarifying, and strengthening the terms of this Agreement.

Notes

1. An Overview

1. An ethnocracy ensues when the dominant ethnic group eschews accommodation, conciliation, and compromise with the state's minorities and instead seeks to institutionalize and constitutionalize its preferences, so that it alone controls the levers of power.

2. "Ethnic outbidding" refers to the auctionlike process whereby politicians create platforms and programs to "outbid" their opponents on the anti-minority stance adopted. See Rabushka and Shepsle 1972; Horowitz 1985; DeVotta 2002.

3. The argument is influenced by Huntington 1968; Ganguly 1997; Kohli 1991. It was first applied to Sri Lanka, albeit in a preliminary fashion, in DeVotta 2000.

4. "Ethnic entrepreneurs" are political—and sometimes business and religious—elites who promote ethnic polarization in attempts to accrue resources and power.

5. Huntington 1968, 11.

6. Snyder 1993, 12.

7. See, e.g., Dharmadasa 1992a.

8. Politicians and journalists especially tend to suggest that the 1983 riots caused the ethnic conflict. "[T]he present economic difficulties are due to the war, which in turn is the result of the 1983 riots," Sri Lanka's minister for ethnic affairs is quoted as saying, for example, in the *Lanka Academic*, June 14, 2001, at http://www.theacademic.org/. Accessed June 14, 2001. It appears that the media have also played a significant role in creating the belief that the 1983 riots caused the ethnic conflict. See Kandiah et al. 2001, 23.

9. Laitin 2000.

10. See Steinmo 1989; Steinmo et al. 1992; Immergut 1992.

11. Koelble 1995, 232. See also Ikenberry 1988, 222–23. For the distinctions between the so-called "new institutionalisms," see ibid., 231–43; Hall and Taylor 1996; Immergut 1998. For explications of rational choice institutionalism, see Weingast 1996; Shepsle 1989; North 1990; Bates 1989.

12. Immergut 1998, 26.

13. Steinmo 1989, 502.

14. Wickremeratne 1995; B. L. Smith 1978; Little 1994.

15. Wickramasinghe 1995; K. M. de Silva 1973.

16. Russell 1982a; Spencer 1990; Pfaffenberger 1984; Ellison 1987.

17. Nithiyanandan 1987, 124.

18. Wriggins 1961, 316; Kearney 1967, 72–73; Tambiah 1967, 230; Roberts 1978, 368; Phadnis 1989, 191–92.

19. Horowitz 1985, 140.

20. Horowitz 1991, 98.

21. According to the 1995 census, Malaysia's ethnic breakdown was as follows: Malays 62 percent, Chinese 27 percent, Indians 8 percent. See *Seventh Malaysia Plan, 1996–2000* (Kuala Lumpur: Government of Malaysia, 1996), 105.

22. Wriggins 1961, 314. See also Horowitz 1990, 459–61.

23. Jupp 1978; Tambiah 1986; Wilson 1988; Sivarajah 1996.

24. Huntington 1968; Horowitz 1985; Ganguly 1997; Zartman 1998; Snyder 2000.

25. See, e.g., Krishna 1999.

26. Hobsbawm 1990, 105–6.

27. The seminal literature dealing with traditional communities, modern societies, and linguistic nationalism in general will inevitably include Deutsch 1966a, 1966b; Brass 1974; Das Gupta 1970. For other useful accounts, see Yapp 1979; Brass 1979.

28. O'Neill 2000, 114.

29. See Laitin 1998.

30. See Swamy 1994; Ponnambalam 1983; Tambiah 1986; DeVotta 2000.

31. See Arasaratnam 1979, 507; Wilson 1966.

32. Those Tamils who came to the island in the nineteenth century to primarily work on tea plantations are called Indian Tamils and are not involved in the separatist violence. Chapter 2 elaborates on these Indian Tamils and other groups.

33. Horowitz 1991

34. Rabushka and Shepsle 1972, 83.

35. Horowitz 1985, 358.

36. Brown 1996, 575. For a horrifying account of how bad leadership has influenced ethnic conflict in Africa, see Berkeley 2001.

37. David A. Lake and Donald Rothchild, "Spreading Fear: The Genesis of Transnational Ethnic Conflict," in Lake and Rothchild 1998, 20.

38. Gagnon 1994–95.

39. Quoted in Carter 1995, 96.

40. See Geertz 1963; Shils 1957.

41. See van den Berghe [1967] 1978, 1996.

42. See Posen 1993; Gellner 1983; Deutsch 1966a; Anderson 1991.

43. See A. D. Smith 1986; Armstrong 1982.

44. Brass 1991.

45. Breton et al. 1995; Banton 1994; Hechter 1995, 1986.

46. Hechter 1986, 268.
47. Bates 1997, 699; J. Scott 1997.
48. David A. Lake and Donald Rothchild, "Ethnic Fears and Global Engagement," in Lake and Rothchild 1998, 344.
49. See Powell and DiMaggio 1991.
50. Harty 2001, 194.
51. March and Olsen 1989, 38; Hall 1986, 19.
52. Rothstein 1996, 138.
53. O'Neil 1996, 582.
54. Ostrom 1995, 175. See also Goldstein 1988.
55. Deutsch 1966a, 97; Kedourie 1966, 15; Stalin 1972; Brass 1974, 8–9; Anderson 1991, 6.
56. Barrington 1997, 713; Hass 1986, 736.
57. Deutsch 1996b, 10–11.
58. Brass 1974, 43.
59. Gagnon 1994–95, 131.
60. See Waldron 1985, 427.
61. Burton et al. 1992, 8.

2. Ethnic Identities and Politics Before Independence

1. Berlin 1972, 17.
2. See V. S. Sambandan, "A Tough Presidential Race," *Frontline* 16, no. 26 (Dec. 11–24, 1999): 124. Over 800,000 Tamils have fled to India and numerous Western countries since the 1983 anti-Tamil riots. The statistics presented here do not appear to take this hegira into account. Indeed, current estimates suggest that 15,000–18,000 refugees continue to leave Sri Lanka on a yearly basis. See "Blood and Money," *Economist*, Aug. 8, 1998, 38. See also V. S. Sambandan, "Shrinking Numbers in Jaffna," *Frontline* 16, no. 10 (May 8–21, 1999) at http://flonnet. com/fl1610/16100590.htm. Accessed July 21, 2002.
3. The Sinhalese chronicles do not dispute that authochthonous peoples were present when Vijaya and his entourage disembarked. But these peoples are portrayed as subhuman and "man-eating," suggesting the Sinhalese were the first civilized humans to reach the island. See Paranavitana 1959, 84.
4. Succinct accounts of this rich myth include Mendis 1965; Basham 1952.
5. As quoted by a prominent monk in the *Ceylon Daily News* [hereafter cited as *CDN*], "Vijaya Only a Pirate Not Ancestor of Sinhalese," *CDN*, Jan. 4, 1955, 5.
6. Quoted in Hobsbawm 1990, 12.
7. The discovery of Arlington Woman in Santa Rosa, an island off the California coast, strongly suggests that the first settlers of the Americas used a maritime route even before the Bering Strait was passable. See William Booth, "The Theory of the Really Ancient Mariner," *Washington Post National Weekly*, Sept. 27, 1999, 35; John Noble Wilford, "New Answers to an Old Question: Who Got Here First?" *New York Times*, Nov. 9, 1999, D1, 4.
8. See Basham 1952, 167. See also C. R. de Silva 1997, 18–19; Mendis 1985, 16.

9. Ponnambalam 1983, 20.

10. Ceylon, Senate, *Debates*, vol. 10, col. 541. Tambiah 1986, 5, similarly asserts that "it would not be a distortion to say that if it were possible to trace the present-day Sinhalese population's ancestry far enough, all lines would in major part lead back to South India."

11. Tambiah 1986, 6. See also Mendis 1985, 16; K. M. de Silva 1981, 13; Kearney 1967, 11; Manor 1989, 132–33; Jupp 1978, 27–28.

12. South Asians are obsessed with skin color, and it is common to hear Sinhalese especially claim that they are fairer and the Tamils darker in complexion. There is simply no evident basis for such a claim; or, if there is, it may be because the Sinhalese have, over the centuries, resorted to more miscegenation than the Tamils. As a Sri Lankan weekly somewhat facetiously noted, "With regular and not insignificant contributions from the Dutch and the British, the gene-pool that is now called Sinhala has been shandied by an army of Robert Knoxes [Knox was an Englishman imprisoned on the island for nearly two decades in the mid seventeenth century], making us a good deal lighter-skinned than our Tamil brethren. Good Sinhala mothers still shower talcum powder on their brats in the hope that they will look even more like the itinerant progenitors to whom they owe their complexion." *Sunday Leader*, "Suicidal Heritage," May 4, 2003, at http://www.thesundayleader.lk/20030504/editorial.htm. Accessed May 4, 2003.

13. Rogers 1994, 17.

14. Jennings 1950, pt. 1, 73.

15. K. M. de Silva 1981, 15.

16. There were intermittent south Indian invasions that led to wars with the island's kingdoms prior to European colonization. The Dutthagamani story was reiterated during such wars to galvanize the Buddhists against the Shaivite invaders, but it was manipulated to cause communal divisions only in the nineteenth and twentieth centuries. The Dutthagamani story has consequently had a powerful impact on the modern Sinhalese Buddhist psyche. As Gananath Obeyesekere has noted, "the general message that emerges [from the story] is everywhere the same: 'The Sinhalese kings are the defenders of the secular realm and the *sasana* [Buddhism]; their opponents are the Tamils'" (Obeyesekere 1979, 286). With democratically elected leaders having replaced kings, Sinhalese ethnic entrepreneurs have often appealed to the story's divisive emotions to portray themselves as defenders of Buddhism and the Sinhalese race.

17. Rahula 1956, 79.

18. K. M. de Silva 1981, 15. See also Gunawardana 1990, 78.

19. For a useful account along these lines, see Gunawardana 1990, 45–86. Dharmadasa 1992b challenges Gunawardana's "modernist" argument; Gunawardana 1995 responds; and Dharmadasa 1996 replies.

20. Vijayavardhana 1953, 3.

21. See Schwarz 1988, 5.

22. Gunawardana 1990, 70.

23. Malalgoda 1976, 35.

24. Ibid.

25. On this issue and its consequences, both for Buddhists and Buddhist-Christian relations, see ibid.

26. Hardy 1860, 430.

27. Ibid., 430, 311–12, and 366.

28. See esp. Bond 1992, 45–74. Obeyesekere 1970, 46–47, calls this anti-Christian Buddhist revival "Protestant Buddhism"; contra this concept, see Holt 1990, 1–8.

29. Tambiah 1996, 51. For a provocative and contemporary account of the riots, see Ramanathan 1916.

30. A. D. Smith 1999, 336–37. See also van der Veer 1999.

31. Guruge 1965, 481.

32. Ibid., 484.

33. Ibid., 510.

34. Ibid., 207.

35. Ibid., 735.

36. Dharmadasa 1992a, 231.

37. Ibid., 231–32.

38. See Roberts 1978, 368; Wriggins 1961, 316; Phadnis 1989, 191–92; K. M. de Silva 1981, 513–14; Kearney 1967, 72–73; Tambiah 1967, 230.

39. Guruge 1965, 479.

40. Ibid., 717.

41. Ibid., 530.

42. Seneviratne 1999 argues that there were two sides to Dharmapala's rhetoric: the moral/economic side that sought to encourage rural development, and the ethnocentric and chauvinistic side that clamored for Sinhalese superordination. Unfortunately, it was the latter that won out. Indeed, the Sinhala-only issue played a major role in ensuring that the ethnocentric faction triumphed.

43. See Dharmadasa 1992a, 138.

44. Ibid., 540.

45. See Tambiah 1996, 56–81. And see also G. M. Scott 1989.

46. Price 1924, 153.

47. K. M. de Silva 1981, 369; Tambiah 1967, 224.

48. Tambiah 1986, 69.

49. Rajan 1995, 20–21.

50. Jennings 1950, pt. 1, 79.

51. This is not to trivialize the efforts headed by Munidasa Kumaratunge, a prominent Sinhalese who sought to resuscitate a form of "pure" Sinhala. He and the secondary school English teachers associated with him were strongly opposed by the liberal and pro-English political elites.

52. Pieris 1956, 169–79. See also Ryan 1961, 463–76.

53. Great Britain, *Ceylon: Report of the Special Commission on the Constitution*, Cmd. 3131 (London: His Majesty's Stationery Office, 1928), 13–16. This document is hereafter cited as Donoughmore Report.

54. Broomfield 1968, 23.

55. Jayawardene 1972, 71.

56. Roberts 1982, 169–70.

57. Quoted in Jayawardene 1972, 196.

58. Donoughmore Report, 99.

59. The fifty-fifty campaign is often referred to as a Tamil demand for equal

representation, but this was hardly the case. Tamils, headed by G. G. Ponnambalam, were its most vociferous supporters, but the scheme was designed so that all minorities combined, including the Tamils, shared half the legislative representation. It thus undermined the one person, one vote principle, and the Soulbury commissioners correctly pointed out that it discouraged "a healthy and progressive advance towards parliamentary self-government." And as Jane Russell observed, the fifty-fifty plan would have "conferred a minority supremacy amounting to virtual minority rule. It was, in effect, a denial of the democratic principle" (Russell 1982a, 311). For the quotation from the Soulbury commissioners, see Great Britain, *Ceylon: Report of the Commission on Constitutional Reform* (London: His Majesty's Stationery Office, 1945; repr., Colombo: Ceylon Government Press, 1969), 93. This document is hereafter cited as Soulbury Report.

60. Soulbury Report, 98–99.
61. Namasivayam 1953, 79.
62. Weerawardana 1960, 87.
63. Dahl 1970, 89. Zimbabwe adopted temporarily this strategy in 1980, when the constitution allowed whites, who were barely 2 percent of the population, to hold 20 percent of the parliamentary seats for seven years. The policy was thus terminated in 1987, but doing so gradually marginalized the whites and has encouraged President Robert Mugabe into pursuing divisive policies that have undermined Zimbabwe's racial coexistence and economic viability.
64. C. R. de Silva 1997, 207.
65. In 1924, only 204,997 voters were registered, even though the 1921 census placed the population at 4,498,605. See Donoughmore Report, 80, 82.
66. K. M. de Silva 1981, 385.
67. Donoughmore Report, 19.
68. Soulbury Report, 74.
69. Jennings 1950, pt. 3, 201. See also Barron 1988, 147–57.
70. Ibid.
71. Namasivayam 1953, 78 n. 3.
72. Weerawardana 1950, 88.

3. From Linguistic Parity to Sinhala-Only

1. Gunawardana 1995, 10.
2. Ibid.
3. Kearney 1967 provides a concise and useful account of Sri Lanka's language issue. See also Dharmadasa 1992a; K. M. de Silva 1996, 11–48.
4. Ponnambalam 1981, 8.
5. Ibid., 15–18.
6. Ibid., 16.
7. Murdoch and Nicholson 1868, v.
8. Quoted in Wickremeratne 1973, 181.
9. Ceylon, House of Representatives, *Debates*, vol. 20, col. 2057.
10. See "Shortage of English School Teachers," *CDN*, Jan. 28, 1944, 1.

11. Ceylon, Department of Census and Statistics 1959, 33.

12. Based on figures obtained in Ceylon, Department of Census and Statistics 1957, 192, 196.

13. Vittachi 1958, 17.

14. See Denham 1912, 399.

15. From a talk given in parliament on Sept. 1, 1953, in Bandaranaike 1961, 927.

16. *Sinhalese and Tamil as Official Languages* (Sessional Paper XXII, 1946), 10.

17. Ibid., 11.

18. Kearney 1967, 59.

19. Ceylon, State Council, *Debates*, May 24, 1944, 758.

20. Manor 1989, 229, 219.

21. The first *"swabasha* telegram" was sent to the prime minister, Sir John Kotelawala, and its message did not augur well for polyethnic coexistence. Dictated by the minister of posts and broadcasting, the message stated: "Today is an auspicious day for our mother tongue. May Sinhalese prosper till the end of time. May you, our nation and our language be victorious." See "Swabasha 'Wires' Were Popular in a Few Hours," *CDN*, Mar. 15, 1956, 1.

22. Ceylon, Legislative Council, *Debates*, 1926, 317.

23. Ceylon, State Council, *Debates*, 1932, 3118.

24. Ibid., 3220.

25. Ibid., 1936, 881.

26. Russell 1982b, 50.

27. Denham 1912, 434.

28. C. R. de Silva 1984a, 116.

29. Great Britain 1938, 20.

30. Denham 1912, 401.

31. Ceylon, *Census Report, 1921,* vol. 1, pt. 2, 29.

32. Ceylon, State Council, *Debates*, May 24, 1944, 760.

33. "New Official Language Proposed," *CDN*, May 25, 1944, 1. The newspaper article further observed that Jayewardene's "un-English [national] dress seemed to give an added punch to the theories he expounded" and wondered "whether the exposition of powerful ideas like these can do more than tickle the throats of members of the House."

34. Jayewardene's resolution is reproduced in Ceylon, State Council, *Debates*, May 24, 1944, 745. A useful account on the 1944 language debates is Russell 1982c.

35. Ceylon, State Council, *Debates*, May 25, 1944, 807.

36. Ibid., 748.

37. "National Language," *CDN*, May 25, 1944, 2.

38. Ceylon, State Council, *Debates*, May 24, 1944, 769.

39. Ibid., 751.

40. Ibid., May 25, 1944, 809.

41. Ibid., 810.

42. Ibid., May 24, 1944, 755.

43. Ibid., 754.

44. Ibid., 764.

45. Ibid., 765.

46. Ibid., 767–68.

47. Ibid., 749–50.

48. Ibid., May 25, 1944, 813.

49. Ceylon, House of Representatives, *Debates*, vol. 20, col. 2077.

50. Ceylon, State Council, *Debates*, May 24, 1944, 746.

51. Ibid., May 25, 1944, 813.

52. Ibid., May 24, 1944, 752.

53. Ceylon, Official Languages Commission, *The Final Report of the Official Languages Commission* (Sessional Paper XXII, 1953), 26.

54. "P.M.'s Statement on Languages Condemned," *CDN*, Oct. 6, 1954, 3.

55. "P.M.: 'I Will Carry Out All My Promises,'" *CDN*, Oct. 20, 1954, 3.

56. Ceylon, House of Representatives, *Debates*, vol. 20, col. 1408.

57. "SWABASHA Now or Never, Is Their Cry," *CDN*, Jan. 22, 1955, 1.

58. Ceylon, House of Representatives, *Debates*, vol. 21, col. 430.

59. Ibid., col. 443.

60. Ibid., col. 445.

61. Ibid., col. 447.

62. "One State Language Proposal Affirmed," *CDN*, Aug. 19, 1955, 1.

63. "Tamil United Front Will Function Soon," *CDN*, Sept. 2, 1955, 5.

64. "'Restore Kataragama to the Buddhists,'" *CDN*, May 9, 1955, 3.

65. "Sinhalese Language in Peril, Says Monk," *CDN*, Sept. 15, 1955, 6.

66. "The Government Is Accused of Delay in Deciding," *CDN*, Oct. 12, 1955, 6.

67. "Sinhalese 'Death-Knell' if Language Solution Failed," *CDN*, Nov. 23, 1955, 6.

68. Ceylon, House of Representatives, *Debates*, vol. 30, col. 1275.

69. Ibid., vol. 22, col. 1755.

70. G. P. Malalasekera, "One Language Helps Develop a Political, Cultural Entity," *CDN*, Oct. 10, 1955, 8.

71. G. P. Malalasekera, "Article 29 Does Not Preclude One State Language," *CDN*, Oct. 12, 1955, 4.

72. "Mr. Ponnambalam Prefers English," *CDN*, June 3, 1955, 1.

73. Ceylon, House of Representatives, *Debates*, vol. 30, col. 1280.

74. Ibid., vol. 23, cols. 572–73.

75. Ibid., cols. 596, 598.

76. Ibid., col. 600.

77. Ibid., col. 622.

78. Ibid., col. 626.

79. Ibid., col. 651.

80. "Parity Impracticable—Dudley Senanayake," *CDN*, Nov. 15, 1955, 5.

81. "If Sinhalese is State Language Tamils Will Form Own State," *CDN*, Nov. 5, 1955, 3.

82. Quoted in Ceylon, Senate, *Debates*, vol. 10, col. 593.

83. "Tamilnad Motion For the UNP," *CDN*, Nov. 24, 1955, 1.

84. "'My Well Whole World,' Sir John Retorts," *CDN*, Mar. 16, 1956, 5.

85. Part of Bandaranaike's complaint was that the UNP government had not worked hard and fast enough to replace English with the vernacular languages.

86. See Gooneratne 1986, 3–6. Bandaranaike's progeny have found the family's Hindu ancestry, coupled with subsequent miscegenation, embarrassing to their present Sinhalese Buddhist credentials, which partly shows how acceptance of racially hybridized Sri Lankans has been vitiated by interethnic hostilities. See James T. Rutnam's article "Bandaranaike Family Tree," first published in 1957 and reproduced in the *Sunday Leader*, Oct. 18, 1998 at http://lanka.net/sundayleader/1998/october/18th/politics.html#politics12. Accessed Oct. 20, 1998.

87. Quoted in Ceylon, House of Representatives, *Debates*, vol. 20, col. 2083.

88. Quoted in S. Nadesan, "Equality Between Majority and Minority Is Cornerstone of Democracy," *CDN*, Oct. 12, 1955, 8.

89. Jennings 1954, 344.

90. Ibid., 342–43.

91. Namasivayam 1953, 79.

92. Manor 1989, 231.

93. Ceylon, House of Representatives, *Debates*, vol. 20, cols. 640–41.

94. Ceylon, State Council, *Debates*, May 25, 1944, 810–11.

95. Ibid.

96. Quoted in Ceylon, Senate, *Debates*, vol. 10, col. 593.

97. See "Press for a 'Sinhalese Only' Pronouncement—SWRD," *CDN*, Nov. 28, 1955, 6.

98. "Parity Means Disaster to Sinhalese—SWRD," *CDN*, Nov. 24, 1955, 7.

99. "Sinhalese Fade-Out With Parity Predicted," *CDN*, Jan. 4, 1956, 5.

100. See "Leftist Leader Assailed at Language Meeting," *CDN*, Nov. 28, 1955, 5; "'Parity Will Be Undemocratic,' Says Bhikkhu," *CDN*, Oct. 12, 1955, 5; "Sinhalese 'Death-Knell' if Language Solution Failed," *CDN*, Nov. 23, 1955, 6; "Parity 'Disgraceful, Unjust,'" *CDN*, Nov. 25, 1955, 6.

101. "Language 'Mix-Up' Is Opposed," *CDN*, Jan. 4, 1956, 5.

102. Rahula 1974, 132.

103. Ibid., 21. With the chief monks of the three Buddhist sects demanding a military, as opposed to a political, solution to the ethnic conflict, Rahula's line of thinking continues to hold sway. Consequently, even the government-owned *Sunday Observer* could note that "it is frightening to observe the insouciance with which the most revered prelates of the Maha Sangha talk of a recourse to arms." See "The Maha Sangha and the Nation," Mar. 19, 2000 at http://www.sundayobserver.lk/2000/03/19/. Accessed Mar. 20, 2000.

104. Vittachi 1958, 19.

105. Successive governments implemented all these demands. The Sunday holiday was later reinstated for practical reasons even as Poya day continued to be celebrated as a national holiday.

106. Ceylon, House of Representatives, *Debates*, vol. 21, col. 485.

107. Ibid., vol. 23, col. 652.

108. Ibid., vol. 21, cols. 486–87.

109. Quoted ibid., vol. 22, cols. 1753–54.

110. "Sinhalese Only—If the UNP Gets 68 Seats or Less," *CDN*, Mar. 15, 1956, 5.

111. "Premier Pinpoints Three Dangers to Nation," *CDN*, Mar. 19, 1956, 5.

112. Weerawardana 1960, 127–28.

113. "Tamil M.P.'s to Work for Tamilnad," *CDN*, Jan. 21, 1956, 7.

114. Manor 1989, 231. Some, however, saw Buddhism as playing the more important role. For example, in a letter to the *New York Times*, G. P. Malalasekera claimed that "[t]he [1956] Ceylon elections were decided on a few very clear-cut issues. The chief of these was the Buddhist issue." See "Voting in Ceylon," *New York Times*, May 6, 1956, E8.

115. K. M. de Silva 1981, 518.

116. See DeVotta 2001.

117. See, e.g., Deutsch 1966a; Das Gupta 1970; Gellner 1983.

118. Jennings 1950, pt. 1, 71.

119. Ceylon, Department of Census and Statistics 1950, 186.

120. Unattributed quotation in K. M. de Silva 1981, 413.

121. Jayaweera 1973, 466.

122. Roberts 1973, 273.

123. Ceylon, Department of Census and Statistics 1950, 225.

124. Jennings 1950, pt. 1, 71.

125. Bandaranaike even said that he had erred in suggesting that he needed twenty-four hours to make Sinhala the official language, given that he could actually do so in twenty-four minutes. But in typical doublespeak, he also noted; "Of course, it would take about six months before the whole conversation got into its stride, but the start would not take more than 24 minutes." See "'I'll Do It in 24 Minutes' Now Says Mr. Bandaranaike," *CDN*, Jan. 15, 1955, 5.

4. The Official Language Act of 1956

1. Immergut 1998, 9.

2. Quoted in C. V. Vivekananthan, "Let's Go Back to English," *Sunday Times*, Feb. 22, 2003, at http://www.sundaytimes.lk.030223/columns/cv.html. Accessed Feb. 22, 2003.

3. Jennings 1950, pt. 3, 202.

4. Quoted in Ceylon, Senate, *Debates*, vol. 10, col. 600.

5. Ibid.

6. Ibid., col. 603.

7. Ibid., col. 604.

8. See Jennings 1949, 176.

9. Ceylon, House of Representatives, *Debates*, vol. 24, cols. 944–45.

10. "Regional Councils to Solve Language Problem," *CDN*, May 10, 1956, 1.

11. "Sinhala Bill Draft Accepted," *CDN*, May 23, 1956, 1.

12. Ibid., 1.

13. "Premier's First Press Conference," *CDN*, Apr. 26, 1956, 3.

14. "Mettananda Drafts a Sinhala Bill and Explains It," *CDN*, May 16, 1956, 1.

15. Ceylon, House of Representatives, *Debates*, vol. 24, col. 326.
16. Ibid., vol. 25, cols. 747–48.
17. "Death-Fast Lecturer Issues Two Statements," *CDN*, May 25, 1956, 3.
18. Ibid.
19. "Premier on Lecturer's Somersault," *CDN*, May 26, 1956, 1.
20. Some Tamils interpreted Bandaranaike's actions as another slight against their community, given that one Thambu Ratnam had been on a similar fast for a number of weeks in the Northern Province to protest the Sinhala-only bill and the prime minister and his government had done nothing to placate or appease him.
21. Ceylon, House of Representatives, *Debates*, vol. 28, col. 178.
22. "Tamils Urged to Resist Change," *CDN*, May 1, 1956, 1.
23. "Fighting Speeches by Tamil MPs," *CDN*, May 19, 1956, 3.
24. Ceylon, House of Representatives, *Debates*, vol. 24, col. 142.
25. Ibid., col. 330.
26. Ibid., col. 144.
27. Quoted ibid., vol. 47, col. 189.
28. Ibid., vol. 24, col. 1790.
29. "Mettananda on Counter-Boycott," *CDN*, June 4, 1956, 1.
30. Ceylon, House of Representatives, *Debates*, vol. 24, col. 770. See also ibid., vol. 28, cols. 177–78; Ceylon, Senate, *Debates*, vol. 10, col. 368.
31. On the last incident, see Ceylon, House of Representatives, *Debates*, vol. 41, col. 1700.
32. "Satyagraha—P.M. Appeals for Calm," *CDN*, June 6, 1956, 1.
33. "'I Will Show How Firm I Can Be,' Says Premier," *CDN*, June 6, 1956, 1.
34. Manor 1989, 261–62.
35. Ceylon, House of Representatives, *Debates*, vol. 24, col. 874.
36. Ibid., col. 938.
37. Ceylon, Senate, *Debates*, vol. 10, col. 383.
38. Ceylon, House of Representatives, *Debates*, vol. 24, col. 739.
39. Vittachi 1958, 20. The government officially claimed that only twenty-six people were killed (fourteen Sinhalese, ten Tamils, and two unidentified persons). See Ceylon, House of Representatives, *Debates*, vol. 27, col. 2177.
40. Ceylon, House of Representatives, *Debates*, vol. 24, col. 214.
41. Ibid., col. 740.
42. Ceylon, Senate, *Debates*, vol. 10, col. 426.
43. Vossler 1932, 132. Senator Nadesan used this same quotation during the language debate in the Senate, which partly goes to show that many Tamils who defended their language at this time empathized with Vossler's words. Their own words certainly emphasize spirit, passion, and defiance.
44. Ceylon, House of Representatives, *Debates*, vol. 24, col. 1797.
45. Ceylon, Senate, *Debates*, vol. 10, col. 172.
46. Ibid., col. 487.
47. Ceylon, House of Representatives, *Debates*, vol. 24, col. 939.
48. Ibid., vol. 10, col. 33.
49. Ibid., col. 536.
50. Ibid., col. 501.

51. Ceylon, House of Representatives, *Debates*, vol. 24, cols. 211–12.
52. Ibid., col. 1275.
53. Ibid., cols. 982–83.
54. Ibid., col. 988.
55. Ibid., col. 1872. A number of Tamil politicians reiterated this throughout the next few years. For example, four years later, M. Balasunderam, the representative for Kopai, observed that "in the willingness to understand our brethren in the South, we compulsorily taught the Sinhalese language to our children. It was only after 1956, when the Government, without any kind of provocation, very gratuitously insulted and humiliated the Tamil people, then and then only, that we said we shall not have the Sinhalese language in the Northern and Eastern Provinces" (ibid., vol. 41, col. 4427). And the Tamil representative for Kayts, V. A. Kandiah, likewise noted: "Did we not study Tamil in the Northern and Eastern Provinces before 1956? Why was it necessary for us to stop doing this? So long as we felt that it was the language of our brother we studied it with pleasure. . . . But the moment the Government said that Sinhala is going to be the language of the ruler we stopped studying it and said to ourselves: 'To hell with the language of our rulers'" (ibid., col. 4155). Over ten years later, the Federal Party's E. M. V. Naganathan said: "Before the Sinhala Only Bill was brought into being in 1956, there were many schools, especially the better organized schools, in which Sinhala was also taught. The people learned Sinhalese very willingly not because Sinhala was the Official Language or because they would be able to get jobs if they learnt Sinhala, but because they wanted to enjoy a sense of comradeship and unity with their Sinhalese brothers in the country. When the Sinhala Only Act came into force there was an attack on our language. Our language was sought to be degraded and destroyed. Naturally, it was to us, therefore, a question of honour to resist the Sinhala Only Act" (ibid., vol. 69, col. 2948).
56. Ibid., vol. 24, col. 988.
57. Ibid., col. 1189.
58. Ibid., col. 1221.
59. Ceylon, Senate, *Debates*, vol. 10, col. 37.
60. Ibid., col. 504.
61. Ibid., col. 130.
62. Ceylon, House of Representatives, *Debates*, vol. 24, col. 1275.
63. Ibid., col. 1878.
64. "Mettananda Says He Is Sure of Sinhala Bill," CDN, May 5, 1956, 5.
65. Sartori 1966, 158.
66. "UNP on the Sinhala Bill," CDN, July 18, 1956, 3.
67. "Race Tensions Could Have Been Avoided, Says J. R.," CDN, July 16, 1956, 3.
68. Ceylon, House of Representatives, *Debates*, vol. 24, col. 1917.
69. Ibid., col. 1711.
70. Ibid., col. 1939.

5. Institutional Decay

1. Quoted in Harrison 1956, 621.
2. Laitin et al. 1994, 5.
3. Gellner 1973, 11.
4. A. D. Smith 1979, 29.
5. Brass 1974, 422.
6. See Swamy 1994; DeVotta 2000.
7. See "Day of Mourning in North," *CDN*, June 7, 1956, 1.
8. "Dr. Naganathan Adjures Tamils to Be Peaceful," *CDN*, June 7, 1956, 3.
9. "PM Will Look After Interests of Tamil and Minorities," *CDN*, June 22, 1956, 5.
10. "Sinhala Bill Called 'Policy of Apartheid,'" *CDN*, July 2, 1956, 5.
11. "The Reasonable Use of Tamil," *CDN*, Apr. 24, 1957, 4.
12. "Sir John Kotelawala . . . spoke first and thought afterwards. . . . Bandaranaike speaks first and also speaks afterwards," a Tamil member of the House noted (E. M. V. Naganathan, "The Reasonable Use of Tamil," *CDN*, Apr. 24, 1957, 4).
13. "The Only Resolution," *CDN*, Aug. 20, 1956, 3.
14. Wilson 1994, 18.
15. "Reactions to F.P. Ultimatum," *CDN*, Aug. 21, 1956, 3.
16. "Ceylon 'on Downward Path,' Says Sir John," *CDN*, Mar. 27, 1956, 3.
17. See Jennings 1954, 347.
18. Ceylon, House of Representatives, *Debates*, vol. 33, col. 1747.
19. "Sinhala Only Act an Eye Wash—JR," *CDN*, May 3, 1957, 3.
20. "Suntharalingam on Language Policy," *CDN*, May 30, 1957, 5.
21. Ceylon, House of Representatives, *Debates*, vol. 28, col. 206.
22. "Suntharalingam on Language Policy," *CDN*, May 30, 1957, 5.
23. "Federal Party Has Ignored a Million Tamils," *CDN*, May 5, 1957, 5.
24. Quoted in Wilson 1994, 17–18.
25. Quoted in Ceylon, House of Representatives, *Debates*, vol. 79, cols. 740–41.
26. "'No Concessions to Federalists'—J. R.," *CDN*, June 13, 1957, 10.
27. "'Think of the Other Man, Too' Says Premier," *CDN*, June 13, 1957, 5.
28. Ceylon, House of Representatives, *Debates*, vol. 28, col. 125.
29. "Federal Party's Political Session," *CDN*, July 29, 1957, 3.
30. "Open Letter to the Premier," *CDN*, Aug. 2, 1957, 4.
31. "'Reasonable Use of Tamil Is Not Contrary to Sinhala Only Policy': PM," *CDN*, Sept. 16, 1957, 3.
32. "P.M. Calls Pact with F.P. Greatest Single Feat in 100 Years," *CDN*, Sept. 26, 1957, 7.
33. "'PM Deserves Nobel Prize for Preventing the Satyagraha,'" *CDN*, Aug. 8, 1957, 11.
34. "Premier Averted National Disaster, Says Dahanayake," *CDN*, Aug. 30, 1957, 7.

35. "Political Leaders Comment on PM's Statement No. 1," *CDN*, Aug. 14, 1957, 7.

36. "More Reactions to the Outcome of P.M.–F.P. Talks," *CDN*, July 27, 1957, 3.

37. "Tamils Duped, Says Ponnambalam," *CDN*, Sept. 23, 1957, 7.

38. "F.P. Acceptance of Sinhala Act Ignominious," *CDN*, Sept. 4, 1957, 11.

39. "Vavuniya M.P. to F.P. Leader," *CDN*, July 30, 1957, 4.

40. "Political Leaders Comment on PM's Statement No. 1," *CDN*, Aug. 14, 1957, 7.

41. Ceylon, House of Representatives, *Debates*, vol. 30, col. 1271.

42. This exchange is taken from ibid., cols. 1391–92.

43. Quoted in Manor 1989, 256.

44. Ceylon, House of Representatives, *Debates*, vol. 30, col. 1515.

45. Ibid., vol. 28, col. 206.

46. Ibid., vol. 23, col. 684.

47. "Foundation of Goodwill," *CDN*, Aug. 22, 1957, 6.

48. "Satyagraha Threat from Another Quarter," *CDN*, Aug. 5, 1957, 1.

49. "Pact a Racial Division of Ceylon, Says Dudley," *CDN*, Aug. 12, 1957, 7.

50. Ceylon, State Council, *Debates*, May 25, 1944, 815.

51. Ibid., May 24, 1944, 748.

52. Ibid.

53. Ceylon, House of Representatives, *Parliamentary Debates*, vol. 20, col. 1708.

54. "J. R. Jayewardene On Sinhale [*sic*] Bill," *CDN*, June 4, 1956, 5.

55. Jayewardene's march to Kandy was called off at Imbulgoda, approximately fourteen miles from Colombo, when opponents blocked the marchers' passage with two motor vehicles and threatened violence, but the anti-Tamil message the enterprise evoked merely emboldened those determined to undermine the B-C Pact. The chief protagonist who halted the march was the member of parliament for Gampaha, S. D. Bandaranayake, who also prostrated himself on the road. The prime minister and the MEP thereafter proclaimed him the "Imbulgoda *weeraya* [hero]." For J. R. Jayewardene's account on this, see Ceylon, House of Representatives, *Debates*, vol. 41, cols. 1447–50.

56. "Mixed Reception," *CDN*, July 27, 1957, 1.

57. "Sinhalese Told: Be Watchful," *CDN*, Sept. 17, 1957, 3.

58. "Theros and Mettananda Condemn Agreement," *CDN*, Aug. 12, 1957, 5.

59. Arasaratnam 1986, 32.

60. Ceylon, House of Representatives, *Debates*, vol. 30, pt. 2, col. 4598.

61. "Send Unregistered Buses to the North and East," *CDN*, Mar. 20, 1958, 5.

62. Ceylon, House of Representatives, *Debates*, vol. 30, pt. 2, col. 4575.

63. Ibid., cols. 4583–84.

64. "It Went On Till Late at Night," *CDN*, Apr. 2, 1958, 1.

65. Vittachi 1958, 25.

66. Ceylon, House of Representatives, *Debates*, vol. 31, col. 148.

67. Ibid., vol. 30, pt. 2, col. 4610.

68. Swamy 1994, 12.

69. "Leftist M.P.'s Opinion of U.N.P. 'Rebel,'" *CDN*, Apr. 7, 1948, 5.
70. Ceylon, Senate, *Debates*, vol. 10, col. 29.
71. Manor 1989, 256.
72. "Move to End Sri Numbers," *CDN*, May 15, 1958, 10.
73. "Vavuniya M.P. to F.P. Leader," *CDN*, July 30, 1957, 4.
74. Ibid.
75. "Views of Party Leaders," *CDN*, Apr. 11, 1958, 3.
76. The 1958 race riots are best described in Vittachi 1958.
77. Horowitz 2001.
78. Vittachi 1958, 38.
79. Ibid., 7.
80. Ceylon, House of Representatives, *Debates*, vol. 31, col. 80.
81. Ibid., col. 56.
82. Ceylon, State Council, *Debates*, May 24, 1944, 750.
83. Vittachi 1958, 103.
84. Ibid., 42.
85. As quoted by N. M. Perera in Ceylon, House of Representatives, *Debates*, vol. 31, col. 31.
86. Ibid., col. 812.
87. For a longer list, see ibid., cols. 490–91.
88. Taken from the account presented in the House, ibid., col. 500.
89. Vittachi 1958, 63.
90. Ceylon, House of Representatives, *Debates*, vol. 31, col. 27.
91. Ibid., col. 11.
92. Ibid., vol. 32, col. 88.
93. Ibid., col. 124.
94. Ibid., vol. 31, col. 163.
95. See, e.g., ibid., vol. 48, col. 1335.
96. See Wriggins 1960, 268.
97. "Premier Assures Peace in His Term," *CDN*, Sept. 22, 1958, 3.
98. Ceylon, House of Representatives, *Debates*, vol. 31, col. 839.
99. Ibid., col. 787.
100. Ibid., vol. 33, col. 509.
101. Ibid., col. 1973.
102. Ibid., vol. 41, col. 1700.
103. See Gooneratne 1986, 160.
104. Sivanayagam 1991, 40.
105. Bradman Weerakoon, who worked as private secretary to both S. W. R. D. and Sirimavo Bandaranaike, recalled that the former was very "anguished" when he was told during the 1956 anti-Tamil riots that a Tamil man had been tied to a tree and burned alive. Author interview, Prime Minister's Office, Colombo, Jan. 4, 2003. It is noteworthy that while those who knew Mrs. Bandaranaike referred to her as "decent" and "honest," none of them said that she had been similarly disturbed over any of the subsequent riots and the Tamils who were injured and killed.
106. "Ceylon: Tearful Ruler," *Time*, Aug. 1, 1960, 28.

107. "Not Even for a Crown, Says Dudley," *CDN*, May 12, 1960, 5.
108. Kearney 1962, 21.
109. Ceylon, House of Representatives, *Debates*, vol. 79, col. 821.
110. Ibid., vol. 56, col. 343.
111. Ponnambalam 1983, 142.

112. Sri Lanka's Sinhalese and Tamils alike have looked up to India for religio-cultural reasons, and the Tamils have also maintained close ties to Tamil Nadu for the same reasons. Mrs. Bandaranaike's insensitivity in this respect is all the more glaring when compared to the attitude of Jawaharlal Nehru, who observed: "[Indian] Muslims can certainly look to Arabia as the country which was the fountain-head of their religion. That is natural. But politically the citizens of each country look to that [their] country and not to another. Christians, no doubt, look to Jerusalem as a city connected with the founder of their religion, but politically and culturally they look to their own countries. There is no conflict between these two approaches." Quoted in A. G. Noorani, "Nehru and Linguistic States," *Frontline* 19, no. 6 (Aug. 3–16, 2002), at http://flonnet.com/fl1916/19160760.htm. Accessed Aug. 10, 2002.

113. Ceylon, House of Representatives, *Debates*, vol. 56, col. 251.
114. Ibid., vol. 41, col. 4423.
115. Ibid., col. 4571.
116. Ibid., col. 4747.
117. Phadnis 1979, 348.
118. Ceylon, House of Representatives, *Debates*, vol. 56, col. 337.
119. Ibid., col. 253.

120. M. Balasunderam, the Tamil representative for Kopai, ridiculed Felix Dias Bandaranaike, saying, "a petty little dictator hiding behind the voluminous saree of the innocuous Prime Minister is going about talking of little doses of totalitarianism." Ceylon, House of Representatives, *Debates*, vol. 45, cols. 1862–63.

121. "Ceylon: Tearful Ruler," *Time*, Aug. 1, 1960, 28.
122. Ceylon, House of Representatives, *Debates*, vol. 31, col. 782.
123. Ibid., vol. 57, col. 664.
124. Ibid., vol. 56, col. 254.
125. Ibid., col. 254.
126. See Horowitz 1980.
127. Ceylon, House of Representatives, *Debates*, vol. 41, col. 1698.
128. Ibid., col. 1699.
129. Soulbury Report, 98.
130. Ceylon, House of Representatives, *Debates*, vol. 56, col. 246.
131. Soulbury Report, 98.
132. Ceylon, House of Representatives, *Debates*, vol. 56, cols. 727–28.
133. Ibid., col. 246.

134. See Tiruchelvam 1984a; Matthews 1986, 33; Peebles 1990; Shastri 1990, 56–77.

135. Roberts 1978, 367.
136. Ceylon, House of Representatives, *Debates*, vol. 60, col. 717.

137. Ibid., vol. 61, col. 1922.

138. Ibid., vol. 79, col. 818.

139. See Wilson 1994, 103–4.

140. Ibid., 104.

141. Ceylon, House of Representatives, *Debates*, vol. 61, col. 1931.

142. Ibid., col. 1932.

143. "The Tamils 'Will Soon Overrun Ceylon'—Mrs. B," *CDN*, Oct. 5, 1965, 6.

144. Ceylon, House of Representatives, *Debates*, vol. 79, col. 820.

145. Hardgrave 1965, 399. See also King 1997.

146. Ceylon, House of Representatives, *Debates*, vol. 79, col. 821.

147. Ibid., vol. 60, col. 1023.

148. "Ceylon: Miss Willis Regrets," *Time*, Aug. 3, 1962, 19.

149. Wilson 1994, 115.

150. It is significant that over 76 percent of those involved in the 1971 JVP insurrection were between 16–25 years old. Almost 94 percent were Buddhists. Tamils and Muslims accounted for less than 1.5 percent of those arrested. See Kearney and Jiggins 1975, 44.

151. Phadnis 1979, 337.

152. Wilson 2000, 99. Wilson considers "full-fledged Tamil nationalism" as related to the second Sirimavo Bandaranaike government's policies dealing with state sector employment and university enrollment during the early 1970s (ibid., 102, 182). There is no gainsaying that the standardization and quota systems used to decrease Tamils' enrollment in the universities coupled with the government's successful attempts at restricting Tamils' employment in the state sector exacerbated the grievances many young Tamils harbored, but I argue that it was the milieu created by the Sinhala-only movement that legitimized and even necessitated such discriminatory actions. Indeed, many young Tamils had mobilized militarily and resorted to assassinations by the time Mrs. Bandaranaike's second government embarked on trying to stuff the universities and state sector with Sinhalese.

153. The term "youth bulge," used with reference to Sri Lanka, is from Fuller 1995, 154. The population figures are from Ceylon, Department of Census and Statistics 1979, 23; Sri Lanka, Department of Census and Statistics 1972, 1.

154. Kearney and Jiggins 1975, 46.

155. Mapp 1972, 73–96; Hargrove 1970, 473–99; Katzenstein 1979, 63–81.

156. C. R. de Silva 1984b, 137. Tamil test graders were even accused of inflating their students' scores so as to ensure university entrance, although this allegation was never proved true.

157. Ibid., 138, 140.7.

158. Phadnis 1979, 336.

159. Nithiyanandan 1987, 100–170.

160. See Wilson 2000, 107.

161. Ceylon, House of Representatives, *Debates*, vol. 24, col. 1888.

162. Author interview with M. D. D. Pieris, July 8, 2003, World Trade Center, Colombo. This argument is also presented in Pieris 2002, 251.

163. Thornton 1977, 136.

164. Ceylon, House of Representatives, *Debates*, vol. 41, col. 1700.

165. Ibid., vol. 33, col. 1165.

166. The TUF was formed after the 1972 constitution was introduced, and the group made six demands: the Tamil language should be recognized; Sri Lanka should be a secular state; the northeast should be granted autonomy; the new constitution should guarantee minorities certain fundamental rights; the caste system should be abolished; citizenship should be granted to all people living in Sri Lanka. The Sirimavo Bandaranaike government disdainfully disregarded all of them.

167. Wilson 2000, 105.

168. "What's Up in the North?" *CDN*, July 10, 1972, 6.

169. Ceylon, House of Representatives, *Debates*, vol. 79, col. 815.

170. Tiruchelvam 1984b, 198.

171. Dissanayake 1983, 29.

172. Seneviratne 1999, 204.

6. From Linguistic Nationalism to Civil War

1. Zakaria 1997, 22–43; Plattner 1999, 121–34.

2. Snyder 2000.

3. Huntington 1991, 266–67.

4. See Diamond 1994, 4–17; Schedler 1998, 91–107.

5. DeVotta 2002.

6. For more detailed accounts along these lines, see Obeyesekere, 1984, 153–74; Senaratne 1997, 34–43; Tambiah 1986.

7. "J. R. on the Future of Democracy in Ceylon," *CDN*, Nov. 12, 1957, 5.

8. See DeVotta 2003a, 115–42.

9. See Oberst 1984.

10. As a Communist Party member quoted in Hyndman 1988, 117, noted during a parliamentary debate in September 1983: "We know one thing, that at the end of the day when the two-third majority is necessary the entire voting machine of the Government will be here. Whether they have heard the arguments, whether they are convinced of the arguments, or not, they will be here because if they are not here their letters of resignation will [be sent in] . . . and they will cease to be Members of Parliament."

11. "J. R. On Opposition's Role in a Democracy," *CDN*, Sept. 8, 1956, 6.

12. Quoted in Samarakone 1984, 86.

13. Kemper 1990, 191.

14. See *Report of the Presidential Commission of Inquiry into the Incidents Which Took Place between 13th August and 15th September 1977*, 121–23, 130.

15. Manor 1984, 12–13.

16. Manogaran 1994, 84–125.

17. This is clear from an incident that took place soon after Jayewardene and the UNP came to power in July 1977. When a group of businessmen who had advised Jayewardene and his party and helped them win the elections went to see him in November 1977 to discuss the anti-Tamil riots that had erupted in August

that year, Jayewardene told Bunty Zoyza: "You are a lawyer; I am a politician. I need this [Tamil] problem for the survival of my party." Author interview with Godwin Fernando, who was among those who went to see Jayewardene, Jan. 1, 2003, Dehiwala.

18. This was a scheme designed to promote limited devolution throughout the country.

19. Obeyesekere 1984, 163.

20. Gunasinghe 1984, 199.

21. Even simple economic competition, lacking any major transition, can encourage an ethnic or racist stance if those competing belong to different groups. Horowitz 1971, 175, notes, e.g., that some Sinhalese small businessmen who believed they were competing against "disproportionate Tamil influence" readily supported the Jathika Vimukthi Peramuna (National Liberation Front), an extremist Sinhalese organization.

22. "Sri Lanka Puts a Torch to Its Future," *Economist*, Aug. 6, 1983.

23. "Ergophobia," *Economist*, Aug. 13, 1983, 29.

24. Hyndman 1988, 26.

25. The official death toll was 400, but unofficial figures placed the number killed as high as 2,000. See ibid.

26. "Sri Lanka Puts a Torch to Its Future," *Economist*, Aug. 6, 1983, 25.

27. Ibid.

28. Quoted in Obeyesekere 1984, 167.

29. S. W. R. D. Bandaranaike and Jayewardene were also indecisive at different points of the decision-making process: Bandaranaike was notorious for vacillating after he had reached agreements (especially with the Tamils), while Jayewardene vacillated prior to making any major decisions, since he sought to ensure that he sided with the most popular (as opposed to the most principled) position. Interviews with numerous persons close to Jayewardene all indicated that he was loath to admit he had erred.

30. The parties banned were the Maoist Janatha Vimukthi Peramuna (People's Liberation Front), which is not to be confused with the Jathika Vimukthi Peramuna (National Liberation Front) that created a splash during the 1950s; the Nava Sama Samaja Party (New Equal Society Party), an insignificant group that was created when the LSSP split; and the pro-Moscow Communist Party.

31. Quoted in Hyndman 1988, 43. It is noteworthy that when Jayewardene fired Cyril Mathew from the cabinet in December 1984, it was because of the latter's intransigence toward the government's All Party Conference meetings and not due to the anti-Tamil propaganda and carnage he had facilitated.

32. Quoted in Bullion 1995, 31.

33. K. M. de Silva 1993, 362.

34. Ceylon, House of Representatives, *Debates*, vol. 41, col. 4014.

35. See DeVotta 1998.

36. Ceylon, House of Representatives, *Debates*, vol. 30, col. 1271.

37. Laitin 2000, 125. See also K. M. de Silva 1996, 36.

38. See G. L. Peiris, "New Equal Opportunity Bill in the Offing," *Sunday Observer*, Sept. 12, 1999, at http://www.lanka.net/lakehouse/1999/09/12/fea25.htm. Accessed Sept. 28, 1999.

39. On how the Sinhala-only policy was implemented, see Gunasekera 1996; Samarasinghe 1996.

40. Ceylon, Senate, *Debates*, vol. 10, cols. 575–76.

41. See Ceylon, House of Representatives, *Debates*, vol. 27, cols. 298, 685–86.

42. Ibid., vol. 41, cols. 2126–28.

43. The change to the singular indicated that the department's hitherto multi-lingual responsibilities were now monolingual.

44. Ceylon, House of Representatives, *Debates*, vol. 41, cols. 4051–52.

45. Ibid., vol. 77, cols. 30–39.

46. See, e.g., ibid., vol. 61, cols. 347–58.

47. Ibid., vol. 41, col. 4014.

48. Phadnis 1979, 335.

49. Ceylon, House of Representatives, *Debates*, vol. 41, col. 2131.

50. Ibid., vol. 56, col. 247.

51. Ibid., vol. 28, col. 390.

52. Ibid., col. 120.

53. Ibid., vol. 33, col. 1695.

54. Ibid., cols. 1728–29.

55. Ibid., vol. 38, col. 559.

56. Ibid., vol. 56, col. 727.

57. See Weerawardana 1960, 181; Wriggins 1960, 266.

58. Wilson 1994, 72.

59. "Federalists Appeal to Tamilnad," *CDN*, June 25, 1956, 1.

60. K. M. de Silva 1981, 513.

61. Harris 1990, 221.

62. Ibid., 222.

63. Manor 1984, 10.

64. Tamil complaints along such lines often appear in the Tamil press. For a good account, see Rajan 1995, 82–123.

65. M. C. M. Iqbal, "Securing Language Rights," *CDN*, June 8, 2002, at http://www.dailynews.lk/2002/06/08/fea01.html. Accessed June 13, 2002. This claim is perhaps an exaggeration, for some Colombo police stations do have one or two Tamil-speaking officers.

66. For example, the president of the Ceylon Tamil Teachers' Union recently complained: "The Minister of Human Resources, Development, Education and Cultural Affairs directed the relevant officials in his ministry to correspond with Tamil medium schools in Tamil or English. But education officials still correspond only in the Sinhala language." Quoted in TamilNet, "Teachers' Union Deplores Correspondence in Sinhala," July 30, 2002, at http://www.tamilnet.com/reports/. Accessed July 30, 2002.

67. "Use and Misuse of Sinhala," *Observer*, Mar. 3, 2000, at http://www.lanka.net/lakehouse/2000/03/04/obsedito.htm. Accessed Mar. 4, 2000.

68. "Enlightening the Masses," *Sunday Leader*, Feb. 20, 2000, at http://www.is.lk/is/spot/spo433/clip6/htm. Accessed Feb. 24, 2000.

7. The Liberation Tigers of Tamil Eelam
and Ethnic Conflict

1. Sivanayagam 1991, 30.

2. Quoted in Wilson 1994, 129.

3. Wilson 2000, 110.

4. Gunatilleke 2001, 27. It was during this election campaign that military personnel and government-sponsored thugs burned the public library in Jaffna.

5. Jayewardene quoted in Mary Anne Weaver, "The Gods and the Stars," *New Yorker*, Mar. 21, 1988, 79.

6. The dragnet that followed Duraiappah's killing led to many youths being tortured for long periods. These tortured youths "were to be the indispensable forward troops of the future militant Tamil insurgency," Wilson, 1994, 126, notes.

7. Swamy 1994, 50–51. Prabhakaran's "national sentiment arose from a determination to resist Sinhala racist oppression that aims at the destruction of his people. In other words, the racism of the Sinhala state made him a fierce patriot, a passionate lover of his oppressed nation," according to Adele Balasingham, the wife of the LTTE's chief spokesman, Anton Balasingham (Adele Balasingham 2001, 335).There is no doubt a whiff of propaganda associated with such statements, although it should be clear by now that Tamil militarism was influenced by ethnocentric Sinhalese policies.

8. Swamy 1994, 104.

9. Johnson 1962 has shown, for example, how the Japanese army of occupation so brutalized Chinese peasants that the survivors felt compelled to join the Chinese Communist Party, which they saw as the only force that could resist the invader. The savagery the 1983 anti-Tamil riots unleashed likewise drove Tamil youth to the rebel groups, since they were the only ones willing to resist Sinhalese tyranny.

10. For accounts of the other leading rebel groups, see Hellmann-Rajanayagam 1994b; Swamy 1994.

11. Hellmann-Rajanayagam 1994a, 171.

12. See, e.g., Pratap 2001, 21–22.

13. It is commonly thought that Prabhakaran makes the major decisions alone, but a few Tamils who have interacted with Prabhakaran and the LTTE's chief spokesperson, Anton Balasingham, note that Prabhakaran may be dependent on Balasingham for political advice, since he usually prefers not to discuss political matters until consulting the latter. It should be noted, however, that Balasingham has not played a leading role in the organization since mid-2003.

14. President Premadasa, for example, regarded Prabhakaran to be "a demigod of military strategy" and used to say that he would gladly have made the LTTE leader a general in the Sri Lankan army. Author interview with the secretary to President Premadasa, Bradman Weerakoon, Prime Minister's Office, Colombo, Jan. 4, 2003.

15. Norell 2000, 113.

16. Some EROS members went to Lebanon to train with the Palestinian

Liberation Organization in the late 1970s. Author interview with Suresh Prema-chandra, secretary-general of EPRLF, Colombo, Jan. 6, 2003.

17. Interviews with former rebel leaders, many of whom are now part of the political mainstream, confirm this.

18. On RAW's involvement in Sri Lanka, see Muni 1993.

19. The diaspora's commitment combined with the LTTE's ideology endowed the Tamils with the necessary "prerequisites" to pursue separatism. According to Barany 2002, 281, these prerequisites are: (1) political opportunity; (2) ethnic identity and its formation; (3) leadership; (4) organizational capacity; (5) ideology, profile, and program; (6) financial resources; (7) communication; and (8) symbols.

20. Author interviews and discussions with various Tamils in Ontario, Canada, make it clear that extortion continues to occur.

21. See, e.g., Raymond Bonner, "Tamil Guerrillas in Sri Lanka: How They Build Their Arsenal," *New York Times*, Mar. 7, 1998, A1, 5.

22. Many in the Tamil diaspora and the LTTE leadership admire the way Israel has prospered despite being a small country. All male Israelis serve in the military for two and a half years after they turn eighteen, and then for one month a year until they are fifty-two; women serve for two years at eighteen and may be called into the reserves. Some accounts claim that Prabhakaran would like the future Tamil *eelam* state to replicate Israel's military policy. Many in the Tamil diaspora are also impressed by Jews' munificence toward Israel. "It was the efforts of the Jewish diaspora that made Israel a free country. Why shouldn't Tamils do that?" one Canadian Tamil is quoted as saying in Somini Sengupta, "Canada's Tamils Work for a Homeland from Afar," *New York Times*, July 16, 2000, A3.

23. "The War the World Is Missing," *Economist*, Oct. 7, 2000, 32.

24. It is fairly assumed that the LTTE may never have been serious about peace talks and may have agreed to the cease-fire merely to strengthen its forces and capabilities. Thus it is accepted that the war was renewed when the LTTE violated the cease-fire. However, it is also questionable whether the Chandrika Kumaratunga government was serious about pursuing a peaceful strategy, given that the government vacillated in implementing many of the conditions the parties had agreed to in the cease-fire. This is especially evident when one reads the letters exchanged between the government and the LTTE. See Anton Balasingham 2000.

25. Brass 1991, 49, asserts that it is important that "one political organization be dominant in representing the demands of the ethnic group against its rivals," and one may argue that the Tamils failed when negotiating with the Sinhalese leadership in the 1950s and 1960s because they lacked a cohesive front. The LTTE no doubt believes this as well, but its incapacity or unwillingness to put up with any form of dissent offends and troubles most people.

26. See Martin Regg Cohn, "Destination: Hope," *Toronto Star*, Oct. 27, 2002, B5.

27. See Amy Waldman, "Masters of Suicide Bombing," *New York Times*, Jan. 14, 2003, A8.

28. Ibid.

29. For an account of LTTE ideology that justifies suicide bombings, see Schalk 1997, 61–83.

30. Sprinzak 2000, 69. In July 2001, the LTTE claimed that 217 suicide bombers had died for the movement and that 59 of them were women.

31. Quoted in Amy Waldman, "Masters of Suicide Bombing: Tamil Guerrillas of Sri Lanka," *New York Times*, Jan. 14, 2003, A8.

32. Just prior to the December 2001 parliamentary elections, a number of Tamil political parties agreed that the LTTE was the sole representative of the Tamils, but the TULF's leader later reversed his position, and the Tigers responded by demanding that he be replaced. The mainstream parties have all acknowledged that the LTTE's military prowess ensures that it is likely to get the best deal from the Sri Lankan government. This was also a view voiced by Dharmalingam Sithadthan, president of PLOTE and the Democratic People's Liberation Front. Sithadthan has never agreed that the LTTE is the Tamils' sole representative, but he too has made it clear that he does not oppose the government conducting negotiations with the Tigers and has said that he and PLOTE are willing to accept any agreement reached between the government and the LTTE. Author interview, Colombo, Jan. 2, 2003.

33. See, e.g., Hoole et al. 1990; Somasundaram 1998.

34. Fromkin 1975, 693.

35. Sri Lanka dropped its ban when the UNP-led United National Front government and the LTTE reached a Memorandum of Understanding in February 2002.

36. This is part of the Heroes' Day speech delivered by Prabhakaran on November 27, 2001, accessible through the pro-LTTE website *TamilNet*. See "LTTE Leader Makes Special Plea to the Sinhalese: 'Reject Racist Forces, Offer Justice to the Tamils,'" Nov. 27, 2001, at http://www.tamilnet.com/reports/2001/11/2701.html. Accessed Aug. 1, 2002.

37. The Sri Lankan Tamil population is officially said to be approximately 13 percent of the total population, but some estimates suggest that it may not be more than 8 percent. It is instructive that the LTTE insisted that the government's 2001 census should not be conducted in Tamil areas.

38. See Adele Balasingham 2001, 334.

39. The Baby Brigade needs to be distinguished from the Leopard Brigade, which is made up of children taken from orphanages run by the LTTE. These child soldiers are said to be among the LTTE's most dedicated fighters.

40. The LTTE, of course, is not the only group using child soldiers. According to human rights groups, child soldiers are used in forty-one countries. See Nicol Degli Innocenti, "About 800,000 Children 'Being Used as Soldiers Worldwide,'" *Financial Times*, June 13, 2001, 5. For an account of LTTE child soldiers, see Nirupama Subramanian, "The LTTE's 'Baby Brigade,'" *Frontline* 18, no. 24 (Nov. 14–Dec. 7, 2001), at http://flonnet.com/fl1824/18240700.htm. Accessed Nov. 24, 2001.

41. In keeping with the successive cease-fires, Sri Lanka's civil war has thus far had three stages: *Eelam* War I, which began after the July 1983 riots, ended when the Premadasa government reached a cease-fire with the LTTE in April

1989; *Eelam* War II lasted from September 1990 to January 1995, when Chandrika Kumaratunga came to power; and *Eelam* War III, which began in April 1995, was concluded when the LTTE declared its unilateral cease-fire in December 2001. Failure to reach a peace agreement between the LTTE and the Wickremesinghe government could unleash *Eelam* War IV.

42. Author interview with a former rebel leader, Colombo, Dec. 2002. Many who discussed the LRRP acknowledge that Sinhalese soldiers from the south were unfamiliar with the terrain in the LTTE-controlled Wanni and could therefore not have played a major role in the LRRP.

43. This is all the more evident when one analyzes LTTE propaganda among the diaspora, because such propaganda typically does not appear to explain why the Tigers are pursuing peace; it instead seeks to argue that the peace process is part of the Tamil struggle.

44. When this question was posed to G. L. Peiris, minister of industrial development, cabinet spokesman, and one of the government negotiators talking with the LTTE, he retorted, "Those who say so must send their own children to fight the war." Author interview at "Visumpaya," Colombo, Jan. 1, 2003.

45. Quoted in Ram 1991, 29.

46. According to the LTTE, 17,211 rebels have died fighting for *eelam* as of November 2001.

47. Quoted in Marie Colvin, "Fighting Tigers Talk of Peace Deal," *Sunday Times*, Apr. 15, 2001, at http://www.sunday-times.co.uk/news/pages/Sunday-Times/stifgnasio2001.html. Accessed Apr. 16, 2001.

48. "LTTE Leader Calls for Autonomy and Self-Government for Tamil Homeland," Nov. 27, 2002, at http://news.tamilnet.com/art.html. Accessed Nov. 27, 2002.

49. Self-determination is not to be confused with separatism. The latter, obviously, refers to territorial dismemberment and new state creation, while the former may be "viewed as entitling a people to choose its political allegiance, to influence the political order under which it lives, and to preserve its cultural, ethnic, historical, or territorial identity. Often, although not always, these objectives can be achieved with less than full independence." See Halperin et al. 1992, 47.

50. Some Muslims now want an autonomous Muslim region created in the east if the Northern and Eastern Provinces are merged to satisfy the Tamil minority. On Muslims and minority rights in Sri Lanka, see also Uyangoda 2001.

51. These are also sentiments shared by those coordinating the peace process since the UNF came to power. Author interview with John Gooneratne, director (research), Secretariat for Co-ordinating the Peace Process, Colombo, Dec. 20, 2002.

52. For Norway's involvement in the peace process, see Bullion 2001.

53. While these assassinations understandably create doubts about the LTTE's intentions, there is no reason automatically to assume that they signify LTTE insincerity about the peace process, since they could be revenge killings. Furthermore, given that there is no guarantee that the peace process will succeed, the assassinations might also be seen as a rational strategy to ensure that the LTTE faces as little opposition as possible in a future conflict. Just because the

LTTE seeks an advantage in a potential future conflict does not mean that it is planning to wage a future conflict.

54. Interviews with Tamil politicians made clear that this was especially the case in the northeast.

55. There were, however, certain former non-LTTE rebel leaders who claimed that the post–September 2001 milieu had nothing to do with the LTTE pursuing a cease-fire. According to them, the LTTE sought the cease-fire merely to regroup and strengthen its forces.

56. Quoted in Hellmann-Rajanayagam 1994b, 65.

57. This is an opinion held by many Sinhalese and Tamil politicians and, for that matter, most Sri Lankans.

58. This argument is partly influenced by a discussion with Professor Siri Hettige at the University of Colombo.

59. A Tamil parliamentarian who insisted that he would only talk about anti-LTTE sentiments among the Tamils provided he would not be identified further confirmed this.

60. For some evidence along these lines, see also Pamela Constable, "Enduring Civil War Defaces Picture of Sri Lankan Serenity," *Washington Post*, Jan. 30, 2000, A18, 20. This is also a sentiment voiced among many in the Tamil diaspora, who can afford such bluster, ensconced as they are in Western countries.

61. Pegg 1997, 101.

62. The Mullaitivu army camp was captured and demolished during "Operation Oyatha Alaigal I" (Unceasing Waves I) and the Killinochchi military base was destroyed as part of Operation Unceasing Waves II. The number of Sri Lankan government soldiers said to have been killed in the latter battle varies. The figure adopted here is from Sugeeswara Senadhira, "Security Council Reviews War Stalemate," *India Abroad*, Nov. 6, 1998, 20. It should be noted that the battle of Pooneryn in November 1993 saw nearly 1,000 government soldiers killed within twenty-four hours.

63. The LTTE claimed that it killed and buried over 1,400 government soldiers during Operation Unceasing Waves III, a figure vehemently denied by the government, which claimed that only 101 soldiers were killed, whereas over 150 LTTE cadres lost their lives. It is now standard for both sides to provide differing casualty figures. While it appears that the LTTE, in the main, tends to report its casualties with a semblance of accuracy, it is clear that the government prevaricates. It may do so for political reasons and to maintain the military's morale, but some speculate that underreporting military casualties is part of a government scheme to avoid paying the dead soldiers' families reparations. The claim is plausible, given that some figures suggest as many as 10,000 soldiers are missing in action. As of August 2002, the Sri Lankan Army admitted that over 3,300 soldiers were missing in action, and that over 18,000 had been killed and 16,600 disabled in the war with the LTTE. See Sanjeevi Jayasuriya, "Officers and Men Missing in Action in North-East Exceed 3,300," *Island*, Aug. 29, 2002, at http://www.island.lk/2002/08/29/news01.html. Accessed Aug. 29, 2002.

64. See, e.g., Licklider 1995, 684.

65. See "New Draft Constitution Only After Consulting Mahanayake

Theras—PM," *Island*, Aug. 13, 2000, at www.island.lk/2000/08/13/news01.html. Accessed Sept. 20, 2000.

66. See DeVotta 2003a.

67. *Financial Times*, "Crisis in Colombo," Nov. 6, 2003, 12.

68. Ibid.

69. The events that transpired soon after the MoU was signed are detailed in Dissanayaka 2002.

70. "Corruption Still the Bane of the Armed Forces," *Island*, Sept. 1, 2002, at http://www.island.lk/2002/09/01/defenco1.html. Accessed Sept. 2, 2002.

71. Quoted in Dayan Candappa, "Sri Lanka War Losses Prompt Soul-Searching," May 1, 2000, at slnet-news@lacnet.org. Accessed May 1, 2000.

72. The air force and navy, in contrast, had 3,000 and 500 deserters, respectively. See Ranil Wijayapala, "Discharge Certificates for Army Deserters," *Daily News*, Mar. 5, 2003, at http://www.dailynews.lk/2003/03/05/newo1.html. Accessed Mar. 5, 2003; Ramani Kangaraarachchi, "Fear Losing Skilled Personnel: Navy, Air Force Defer Deserter Amnesty," *Sunday Observer*, Mar. 9, 2003, at http://www.sundayobserver.lk/2003/03/09/newo1.html. Accessed Mar. 9, 2003.

73. "The Costs of the War," *Weekend Express*, Feb. 10–11, 2001, at http://www.is.lk/is/spot/spo531/clip2.html. Accessed Feb. 14, 2001.

74. "Blood and Money," *Economist*, Aug. 8, 1998, 38.

75. This is also a view shared by some former non-LTTE rebels.

76. The information in this paragraph was provided by a leading participant in the plan to assassinate Prabhakaran and is based on discussions conducted in May 2002 and January 2003.

77. In May 2000, U.S. Under Secretary of State for Political Affairs Thomas Pickering told President Kumaratunga that America would not help assassinate Prabhakaran. Explaining why the United States could not support such an action, a high-ranking American diplomat in Colombo is quoted as having said: "Even Prabhakaran has human rights." Pickering stopped in New Delhi on his way to Sri Lanka, and those in the know say he briefed or updated the Indians about the plan to kill Prabhakaran. It is also suggested that India's Research and Analysis Wing informed the LTTE about the plot, but the reasons for the RAW doing so are based on conjecture. One plausible suggestion was that there are elements within the RAW that consider the perpetuation of Sri Lanka's ethnic conflict to be in India's interest, and that this was why the LTTE was notified.

78. Some, perhaps justifiably, prefer to see Kumaratunga as an undisciplined, dilatory, and incompetent virago, but soon after coming to power in 1994, she single-handedly castigated those she considered racist and worked hard to fashion a draft constitution that, if implemented, would have gone a long way toward addressing the Tamils' grievances. Tamils in fact voted for Kumaratunga in large numbers in 1994, because they saw her as a fresh face, notwithstanding that she was a Bandaranaike. That the UNP opposed her tooth and nail and that she compromised her own position to stay on in power says as much about Sri Lanka's political structure as it does about the island's unprincipled politicians.

79. This is especially so with Tamils in the diaspora, and it is common to hear how, when it comes to opposing Tamils' aspirations, the "Sinhalized" Kadiragamar is just as dangerous as the Sinhalese extremists.

80. One reason for this is because the UNP, as a pro-commerce party that is more comfortable dealing with urban business interests and the educated classes, has not done a good job keeping its grassroots base abreast of the ongoing developments with the LTTE. For example, only eleven out of eighty local UNP politicians participating in a National Peace Council workshop in 2002 in the southern city of Matara had read the MoU signed between their party and the LTTE, claiming that this was because the UNP leadership had failed to send them the document. Author interview with Sathivale Balakrishnan, programs director for the National Peace Council, Colombo, Jan. 9, 2003.

81. "Unite to Fight Terrorism," *Daily News,* Apr. 25, 2000, at http://www.lanka.net/lakehouse/2000/04/25/edito.htm. Accessed Apr. 25, 2000.

82. The rare exception is the Tamil paper *Thinakaran*, which is state-owned and therefore follows the government's dictates. See Kandiah et al. 2001.

83. Quoted in Anthony Spaeth, "Ranil Wickremesinghe the Peacemaker," *Time Asia,* Apr. 28, 2003, at http://www.time.com/time/asia/2003/heroes/ranilwickremesinghe.html. Accessed May 10, 2003.

84. Ceylon, House of Representatives, *Debates*, vol. 56, cols. 255–56.

8. Conclusion

1. Nodia 2000, 171. Emphasis in original.
2. Lijphart 1999.
3. See, e.g., the arguments made by Powell 2000.
4. Quoted in Sugeeswara Senadhira, "Ethnic Strife Overshadows Freedom Jubilee," *India Abroad*, Feb. 15, 1998, 24. President Kumaratunga repeated the remark when she addressed the UN's 53rd Annual General Assembly.
5. Quoted in "Sri Lanka President Says Neglect Led to Ethnic War," Apr. 23, 2002, at http://in.news.yahoo.com/020423/64/1mdgz.html. Accessed Apr. 23, 2002.
6. Quoted in "Massacre a Conspiracy by LTTE: Chandrika," *The Hindu*, Nov. 1, 2000 at wysiwyg://36/http://www.the-hindu.com/holnus/03011801/htm. Accessed Nov. 2, 2000. Kumaratunga's former foreign minister Lakshman Kadirgamar has similarly said: "We must openly recognize the fact that we have made mistakes. We have made collective mistakes. Some of our mistakes have been compounded by further mistakes." Quoted in V. S. Sambandan, "Chandrika Starts Ethnic Reconciliation," *The Hindu*, July 27, 2002, at http://www.hinduonnet.com/stories/2002072702381200.htm. Accessed July 27, 2002.
7. Quoted in "Our Approach for a Better Tomorrow Free from Terrorism," *Daily News*, July 25, 2002, at http://www.dailynews.lk/2002/07/25/fea01.html. Accessed July 25, 2002.
8. V. S. Sambandan, "A Second Chance for Kumaratunga," *Frontline*, Jan. 21, 2000, 30.
9. For details of the draft constitution and PA-JVP pact, see DeVotta 2003a.
10. See ibid.
11. Thangarajah 2003, 15–36.
12. Arguments dealing with liberal hegemony in the international relations literature influence the discussion in this paragraph. See, e.g., Ikenberry 1999, 123–45.

13. The four parties that formed the Tamil National Alliance are the TULF, the All Ceylon Tamil Congress, the Tamil Eelam Liberation Organization, and the Eelam People's Revolutionary Liberation Front.

14. "The most appalling thing is that, by their actions, the soldiers swell the ranks of the [Chechen] militants," Russia's human rights ombudsman is quoted as saying in Robert Cottrell, "Russian Roulette," *Financial Times*, Aug. 28, 2002, 12.

15. See, e.g., Connor 1994; Varshney 2003.

16. See DeVotta 2003b.

17. Sinhalese Buddhists understandably protest whenever the Sangha is portrayed as intolerant and violent, yet such a portrayal hardly contradicts Sri Lanka's historiography. Uyangoda 1996, 129 n. 5, observes: "Sinhalese Buddhism has made no significant contribution to the evolution of a non-violent social ideology. On the contrary, the Sinhalese Buddhist historiographical tradition and ideology inherent in it supports ethnic political violence."

18. See Horowitz 2003.

19. Mill [1861] 1991, 310.

20. Stepan 1999, 19. And as Gurr 2000, 56, aptly notes: "In very few contemporary instances did negotiated autonomy lead to independence. Sometimes an autonomous regional government pushes hard for greater authority, as the Basques have done in Spain. But the ethnic statelets that won de facto independence in the 1990s—Somaliland, Abkhazia, the Trans-Dniester Republic, and Iraqi Kurdistan—did so in the absence of negotiations, not because of them. Those truly looking to reduce ethnic bloodshed should embrace autonomy, not fear it."

21. Zartman 1998, 324. See also Horowitz 2003.

22. "Why Ranil Must Deproscribe Now," *Sunday Leader*, May 5, 2002, at http://origin.thesundayleader.lk/20020505/politics.htm. Accessed May 6, 2002.

23. This, of course, is countered by the fact that the major parties pandered to Sinhalese Buddhist sentiments and practiced ethnic outbidding to such an extent that that there was no need for an ethnic Sinhalese party to perform this role.

24. See "Sihala Urumaya Not Racist," *Island*, Sept. 17, 2000, at http://www.island.lk/2000/09/17/featur04.html. Accessed July 25, 2002.

25. Sri Lankans have, especially over the past decade, debated whether a future devolutionary arrangement should provide all regions with similar powers or if the Tamil regions should be given preferential powers. This debate on symmetrical versus asymmetrical devolution is useful only provided there is a consensus among the major parties on the need to devolve power. The challenge is to convince the radicals that providing the Tamils (and perhaps the Muslims in the Eastern Province) with some form of autonomy is the best way to ensure a united Sri Lanka. Absent such consensus, it is premature to engage the issue of symmetrical versus asymmetrical devolution.

26. See Wilson 2000, 143.

27. Quoted in "Today is 43rd Death Anniversary of Former Sri Lankan Premier," *Daily News*, Sept. 26, 2002, at http://www.dailynews.lk/2002/09/26/fea03.html. Accessed Sept. 27, 2002.

REFERENCES

Anderson, Benedict. 1991. *Imagined communities: Reflections on the origin and spread of nationalism*. 2d rev. ed. London: Verso.

Arasaratnam, Sinnappah. 1979. Nationalism in Sri Lanka and Tamils. In *Collective identities, nationalisms, and protest in modern Sri Lanka*, ed. Michael Roberts, 500–518. Colombo: Marga Institute.

———. 1986. *Sri Lanka after independence: Nationalism, communalism and nation building*. Madras: University of Madras.

Armstrong, John A. 1982. *Nations before nationalism*. Chapel Hill: University of North Carolina Press.

Balasingham, Adele. 2001. *The will to freedom: An inside view of Tamil resistance*. Mitcham, UK: Fairmax.

Balasingham, Anton. 2000. *The politics of duplicity: Re-visiting the Jaffna peace talks*. Mitcham, UK: Fairmax.

Bandaranaike, S. W. R. D., ed. 1928. *The handbook of the Ceylon National Congress 1919–1928*. Colombo: H. W. Cave.

———. 1961. *Towards a new era*. Colombo: Department of Information.

Banton, Michael. 1994. Modeling ethnic and national relations. *Ethnic and Racial Studies* 17, no. 1 (Jan.): 1–20.

Barany, Zoltan. 2002. Ethnic mobilization without prerequisites: The East European Gypsies. *World Politics* 54, no. 3 (Apr.): 277–307.

Barrington, Lowell W. 1997. "Nation" and "nationalism": The misuse of key concepts in political science. *PS: Political Science and Politics* 30, no. 4 (Dec.): 712–16.

Barron, T. J. 1988. The Donoughmore Commission and Ceylon's national identity. *Journal of Commonwealth and Comparative Politics* 26, no. 2 (July): 147–57.

Basham, A. L. 1952. Prince Vijaya and the aryanization of Ceylon. *Ceylon Historical Journal* 1, no. 3 (Jan.): 163–71.

Bates, Robert H. 1989. *Beyond the miracle of the market: The political economy of agrarian development in rural Kenya*. Cambridge: Cambridge University Press.

———. 1997. Comparative politics and rational choice: A review essay. *American Political Science Review* 91, no. 3 (Sept.): 699–704.

Berkeley, Bill. 2001. *The graves are not yet full: Race, tribe and power in the heart of Africa.* New York: Basic Books.

Berlin, Isaiah. 1972. The bent twig: A note on nationalism. *Foreign Affairs* 51, no. 1 (Oct.): 11–30.

Bond, George D. 1992. *The Buddhist revival in Sri Lanka: Religious tradition, reinterpretation, and response.* 1st Indian ed. Delhi: Motilal Banarsidass.

Brass, Paul, R. 1974. *Language, religion and politics in North India.* New York: Cambridge University Press.

———. 1979. Elite groups, symbol manipulation and ethnic identity among the Muslims of South Asia. In *Political identity in South Asia*, ed. David Taylor and Malcolm Yapp, 35–77. London: Curzon Press.

———. 1991. *Ethnicity and nationalism: Theory and comparison.* New Delhi: Sage Publications.

Breton, Albert, Gianluigi Galeotti, Pierre Salmon, and Ronald Wintrobe, eds. 1995. *Nationalism and rationality.* Cambridge: Cambridge University Press.

Broomfield, J. H. 1968. *Elite conflict in a plural society: Twentieth-century Bengal.* Berkeley: University of California Press.

Brown, Michael E. 1996. The causes and regional dimensions of internal conflict. In *The international dimensions of internal conflict*, ed. Michael E. Brown, 571–601. Cambridge, Mass.: MIT Press.

Bullion, Alan. 1995. *India, Sri Lanka and the Tamil crisis 1976–1994: An international perspective.* London: Pinter.

———. 2001. Norway and the peace process in Sri Lanka. *Civil Wars* 4, no. 3 (Autumn): 70–92.

Burton, Michael, Richard Gunther, and John Higley. 1992. Introduction: Elite transformations and democratic regimes. In *Elites and democratic consolidation in Latin America and Southern Europe*, ed. John Higley and Richard Gunther, 1–37. Cambridge: Cambridge University Press.

Carter, Dan T. 1995. *The politics of rage: George Wallace, the origins of the new conservatism, and the transformation of American politics.* New York: Simon & Schuster.

Ceylon [see also Sri Lanka]. 1923–26. Census publications. Colombo: Government Press.

———. 1950. *Census of Ceylon, 1946.* Vol. 1, pt. 1. Colombo: Department of Census and Statistics.

———. 1957. *Census of Ceylon, 1953.* Vol. 1. Colombo: Government Press.

———. 1959. *Ceylon Year Book, 1958.* Colombo: Government Press.

———. 1979. *Statistical Pocket Book of Ceylon, 1970.* Colombo: Department of Census and Statistics.

Connor, Walker. 1994. *Ethnonationalism: The quest for understanding.* Princeton, N.J.: Princeton University Press.

Dahl, Robert A. 1970. *After the revolution.* New Haven, Conn.: Yale University Press.

Das Gupta, Jyotirindra. 1970. *Language conflict and national development.* Berkeley: University of California Press.

Denham, E. B. 1912. *Ceylon at the Census of 1911.* Colombo: Government Printer.

De Silva, Chandra Richard. 1977. Education. In *Sri Lanka: A survey,* ed. K. M. de Silva, 403–33. London: C. Hurst.

———. 1978. The politics of university admissions: A review of some aspects of the admission policy in Sri Lanka, 1971–1978. *Sri Lanka Journal of Social Sciences,* 4, no. 2 (Dec.): 85–123.

———. 1984a. Sinhala-Tamil ethnic rivalry: The background. In *From independence to Statehood: Managing ethnic conflict in five African and Asian states,* ed. Robert B. Goldman and A. Jeyaratnam Wilson, 111–24. New York: St. Martin's Press.

———. 1984b. Sinhala-Tamil relations and education in Sri Lanka: The university admissions issue—The first phase, 1971–77. In *From independence to Statehood: Managing ethnic conflict in five African and Asian states,* ed. Robert B. Goldman and A. Jeyaratnam Wilson, 125–46. New York: St. Martin's Press.

———. 1997. *Sri Lanka: A history.* 2d rev. ed. New Delhi: Vikas.

De Silva, K. M., ed. 1973. *History of Ceylon,* vol. 3: *From the beginning of the nineteenth century to 1948.* Peradeniya: University of Ceylon Press Board.

———. 1981. *A history of Sri Lanka.* Delhi: Oxford University Press.

———. 1993. The police and armed services. In *Sri Lanka: Problems of governance,* ed. K. M. de Silva, 347–71. New Delhi: Konark.

———. 1996. Coming full circle: The politics of language in Sri Lanka, 1943–1996. *Ethnic Studies Report* 14, no. 1 (Jan.): 11–48.

Deutsch, Karl W. 1966a. *Nationalism and social communication: An inquiry into the foundations of nationality.* 2d ed. Cambridge, Mass.: MIT Press.

———. 1966b. *The nerves of government: Models of political communication and control.* New York: Free Press.

DeVotta, Neil. 1998. Sri Lanka's structural adjustment program and its impact on Indo-Lanka relations. *Asian Survey* 38, no. 5 (May): 457–73.

———. 2000. Control democracy, institutional decay, and the quest for *eelam:* Explaining ethnic conflict in Sri Lanka. *Pacific Affairs* 73, no. 1 (Spring): 55–76.

———. 2001. The utilisation of religio-linguistic identities by the Sinhalese and Bengalis: Towards a general explanation. *Journal of Commonwealth and Comparative Politics* 39, no. 1 (Mar.): 66–95.

———. 2002. Illiberalism and ethnic conflict in Sri Lanka. *Journal of Democracy* 13, no. 1 (Jan.): 84–98.

———. 2003a. Sri Lanka's political decay: Analysing the October 2000 and December 2001 parliamentary elections. *Commonwealth and Comparative Politics* 41, no. 2 (July): 115–42.

———. 2003b. *Uncivil groups, unsocial capital: Whither civil society and liberal democracy in Sri Lanka?* Middleberry College Working Paper Series, No. 8: 1–51. Middleberry, Vt.: Rohatyn Center for International Affairs.

Dharmadasa, K. N. O. 1992a. *Language, religion, and ethnic assertiveness: The growth of Sinhalese nationalism in Sri Lanka.* Ann Arbor: University of Michigan Press.

————. 1992b. "The people of the lion": Ethnic identity, ideology and historical revisionism in contemporary Sri Lanka. *Ethnic Studies Report* 10, no. 1 (Jan.): 37–59.

————. 1996. The roots of the Sinhala ethnic identity in Sri Lanka: The debate on the "people of the lion" continued. *Ethnic Studies Report* 14, no. 2 (July): 137–70.

Diamond, Larry. 1994. Rethinking civil society: Toward democratic consolidation. *Journal of Democracy* 5, no. 3 (July): 4–17.

Dissanayake, T. D. S. A. 1983. *The agony of Sri Lanka: An in-depth account of the racial riots of 1983*. Colombo: Swastika.

————. 2002. *The quest for peace: War and peace in Sri Lanka*. Vol. 3. Colombo: Swastika.

Ellison, Christopher G. 1987. Elites, competition, and ethnic mobilization: Tamil politics in Sri Lanka, 1947–77. *Journal of Political and Military Sociology* 15, no. 2 (Fall): 213–28.

Fromkin, David. 1975. The strategy of terrorism. *Foreign Affairs* 53, no. 4 (July): 683–98.

Fuller, Gary. 1995. The demographic backdrop to ethnic conflict: A geographic overview. In *The challenge of ethnic conflict to national and international order in the 1990s: Geographic perspectives*, 151–54. RTT 95–10039. Washington, D.C.: Central Intelligence Agency.

Gagnon, V. P. 1994–95. Ethnic nationalism and international conflict: The case of Serbia. *International Security* 19, no. 3 (Winter): 130–66.

Ganguly, Sumit. 1997. *The crisis in Kashmir: Portents of war, hopes of peace*. Woodrow Wilson Center Series. Cambridge: Cambridge University Press.

Geertz, Clifford, ed. 1963. *Old societies and new states: The quest for modernity in Asia and Africa*. New York: Free Press.

Gellner, Ernest. 1973. Scale and nation. *Philosophy of the Social Sciences* 3, no. 1 (Mar.): 1–17.

————. 1983. *Nations and nationalism*. Oxford: Basil Blackwell.

Goldstein, Judith. 1988. Ideas, institutions, and American trade policy. In *The state and American foreign economic policy*, ed. G. John Ikenberry, David Lake, and Michael Mastanduno, 179–217. Ithaca, N.Y.: Cornell University Press.

Gooneratne, Yasmine. 1986. *Relative merits: A personal memoir of the Bandaranaike family of Sri Lanka*. London: C. Hurst.

Great Britain. 1928. *Ceylon: Report of the Special Commission on the Constitution*. Cmd. 3131. London: His Majesty's Stationery Office. Cited as Donoughmore Report.

————. 1938. *Correspondence Relating to the Constitution of Ceylon*. Cmd. 5910. London: His Majesty's Stationery Office.

————. 1945. *Ceylon: Report of the Commission on Constitutional Reform* London: His Majesty's Stationery Office. Reprint. Colombo: Ceylon Government Press, 1969. Cited as Soulbury Report.

Gunasekera, R. G. G. Olcott. 1996. The implementation of the official language policy, 1956–70. In *National language policy in Sri Lanka 1956 to 1996:*

Three studies in its implementation, ed. K. N. O. Dharmadasa, 17–77. Kandy: International Center for Ethnic Studies.

Gunasinghe, Newton. 1984. The open market and its impact on ethnic relations in Sri Lanka. In Committee for Rational Development, *Sri Lanka: The ethnic conflict: Myths, realities, and perspectives*, 197–214. New Delhi: Navrang.

Gunatilleke, Godfrey. 2001. *Negotiation for the resolution of the ethnic conflict.* Colombo: Marga Institute.

Gunawardana, R. A. L. H. 1990. The people of the lion: The Sinhala identity and ideology in history and historiography. In *Sri Lanka: History and the roots of conflict*, ed. Jonathan Spencer, 45–86. London: Routledge.

———. 1995. *Historiography in a time of ethnic conflict: Construction of the past in contemporary Sri Lanka.* Colombo: Social Scientists' Association.

Gurr, Ted Robert. 2000. Ethnic warfare on the wane. *Foreign Affairs* 79, no. 3 (May–June): 52–64.

Guruge, Ananda. 1965. *Return to righteousness: A collection of speeches, essays and letters of the Anagarike Dharmapala.* Colombo: Ministry of Education and Cultural Affairs.

Hall, Peter A. 1986. *Governing the economy: The politics of state intervention in Britain and France.* New York: Oxford University Press.

Hall, Peter A., and Rosemary Taylor. 1996. Political science and the three new institutionalisms. *Political Studies* 44, no. 5 (Dec.): 936–57.

Halperin, Morton, David Scheffer, and Patricia Small. 1992. *Self-determination in the new world order.* Washington, D.C.: Carnegie Endowment for International Peace.

Hardgrave, Robert L., Jr. 1965. The riots in Tamil Nadu: Problems and prospects of India's language crisis. *Asian Survey* 5, no. 8 (Aug.): 399–407.

Hardy, Robert. 1860. *Eastern monachism: An account of the origin, laws, discipline, sacred writings, mysterious rites, religious ceremonies, and present circumstances, of the order of mendicants founded by Gótama Budha. . . .* London: Partridge & Oakey, 1850. Reprint. London: Williams & Norgate.

Hargrove, Ervin C. 1970. Nationality, values, and change: Young elites in French Canada. *Comparative Politics* 2, no. 1 (Apr.): 473–99.

Harris, Nigel. 1990. *National liberation.* London: I. B. Tauris.

Harrison, Selig S. 1956. The challenge to Indian nationalism. *Foreign Affairs* 34, no. 4 (July): 620–36.

Hass, Ernst. 1986. What is nationalism and why should we study it? *International Organization* 40, no. 3 (Summer): 707–44.

Harty, Siobhan. 2001. The institutional foundations of substate national movements. *Comparative Politics* 33, no. 2 (Jan.): 191–210.

Hechter, Michael. 1986. Rational choice theory and the study of race and ethnic relations. In *Theories of race and ethnic relations*, ed. David Mason and John Rex, 264–79. Cambridge: Cambridge University Press.

———. 1995. Explaining nationalist violence. *Nations and Nationalism* 1, no. 1 (Mar.): 53–68.

Hellmann-Rajanayagam, Dagmar. 1994a. The "groups" and the rise of militant secessionism. In *The Sri Lankan Tamils: Ethnicity and identity*, ed.

Chelvadurai Manogaran and Bryan Pfaffenberger, 169–207. Boulder, Colo.: Westview Press.

———. 1994b. *The Tamil tigers: Armed struggle for identity.* Stuttgart: Franz Steiner.

Hobsbawm, E. J. [1990] 1992. *Nations and nationalism since 1780: Programme, myth, reality.* 2d ed. Cambridge: Cambridge University Press.

Holt, John. 1990. Sri Lanka's Protestant Buddhism? *Ethnic Studies Report* 8, no. 2 (July): 1–8.

Hoole, Rajan, et al. 1990. *The broken palmyra: The Tamil crisis in Sri Lanka—An inside account.* Claremont, Calif.: Sri Lanka Studies Institute.

Horowitz, Donald L. 1971. Multiracial politics in the new states: Toward a theory of conflict. In *Issues in comparative politics,* eds. Robert J. Jackson and Michael B. Stein, 164–80. New York: St. Martin's Press.

———. 1980. *Coup theories and officers' motives: Sri Lanka in comparative perspective.* Princeton, N.J.: Princeton University Press.

———. 1985. *Ethnic groups in conflict.* Berkeley: University of California Press.

———. 1990. Making moderation pay: The comparative politics of ethnic conflict management. In *Conflict and peacekeeping in multiethnic societies,* ed. Joseph V. Montville, 451–75. Lexington, Mass.: D. C. Heath.

———. 1991. *A democratic South Africa? Constitutional engineering in a divided society.* Berkeley: University of California Press.

———. 2001. *The deadly ethnic riot.* Berkeley: University of California Press.

———. 2003. The cracked foundations of the right to secede. *Journal of Democracy* 14, no. 2 (Apr.): 5–17.

Huntington, Samuel P. 1968. *Political order in changing societies.* New Haven, Conn.: Yale University Press.

———. 1991. *The third wave: Democratization in the late twentieth century.* Norman, Okla.: University of Oklahoma Press.

Hyndman, Patricia. 1988. *Sri Lanka: Serendipity under siege.* Nottingham, UK: Spokesman.

Ikenberry, G. John. 1988. Conclusion: An institutional approach to American foreign economic policy. In *The state and American foreign economic policy,* ed. G. John Ikenberry, David Lake, and Michael Mastanduno, 219–43. Ithaca, N.Y.: Cornell University Press.

———. 1999. Liberal hegemony and the future of American postwar order. In *International order and the future of world politics,* ed. T. V. Paul and John A. Hall, 123–45. Cambridge: Cambridge University Press.

Immergut, Ellen M. 1992. *Health politics: Interests and institutions in Western Europe.* New York: Cambridge University Press.

———. 1998. The theoretical core of the new institutionalism. *Politics and Society* 26, no. 1 (Mar.): 5–34.

Jayawardene, Kumari. 1972. *The rise of the labor movement in Ceylon.* Durham, N.C.: Duke University Press.

Jayaweera, Swarna. 1973. Education policy in the early twentieth century. In *History of Ceylon,* vol. 3: *From the beginning of the nineteenth century to*

1948, ed. K. M. de Silva, 461–75. Peradeniya: University of Ceylon Press Board.

Jennings, Ivor. 1949. *The constitution of Ceylon.* London: Oxford University Press.

———. 1950. *Nationalism and political development in Ceylon: The background of self-government* (parts 1, 2, & 3). New York: Institute of Pacific Relations.

———. 1954. Politics in Ceylon since 1952. *Pacific Affairs* 27, no. 4 (Dec.): 338–52.

Johnson, Chalmers A. 1962. *Peasant nationalism and communist power: The emergence of revolutionary China.* Stanford: Stanford University Press.

Jupp, James. 1978. *Sri Lanka: Third World democracy.* Studies in Commonwealth Politics and History No. 6. London: Frank Cass.

Kandiah, Thiru, et al. 2001. *The media and the ethnic conflict in Sri Lanka.* Marga Monograph Serices on Ethnic Reconciliation, No. 19. Colombo: Marga Institute.

Katzenstein, Mary. 1979. *Ethnicity and equality: The Shiv Sena party and preferential policies in Bombay.* Ithaca, N.Y.: Cornell University Press.

Kearney, Robert N. 1962. The new political crisis of Ceylon. *Asian Survey* 2, no. 4 (June): 19–27.

———. 1967. *Communalism and language in the politics of Ceylon.* Durham, N.C.: Duke University Press.

Kearney, Robert N., and Janice Jiggins. 1975. The Ceylon insurrection of 1971. *Journal of Commonwealth and Comparative Politics* 13, no. 1 (Mar.): 40–64.

Kedourie, Elie. 1966. *Nationalism.* 3d ed. London: Hutchinson.

Kemper, Steven. 1990. J. R. Jayewardene: Righteousness and realpolitik. In *Sri Lanka: History and the roots of conflict,* ed. Jonathan Spencer, 187–204. London: Routledge.

King, Robert D. 1997. *Nehru and the language politics of India.* Delhi: Oxford University Press.

Koelble, Thomas A. 1995. The new institutionalism in political science and sociology. *Comparative Politics* 27, no. 2 (Jan.): 231–43.

Kohli, Atul. 1991. *Democracy and discontent: India's growing crisis of governability.* Cambridge: Cambridge University Press.

Krishna, Sankaran. 1999. *Postcolonial insecurities: India, Sri Lanka, and the question of nationhood.* Minneapolis: University of Minnesota Press.

Laitin, David. 1998. *Identity in formation: The Russian-speaking populations in the near abroad.* Ithaca, N.Y.: Cornell University Press.

———. 2000. Language conflict and violence: The straw that strengthens the camel's back. *European Journal of Sociology* 41, no. 1: 97–137.

Laitin, David, Carlotta Sole, and Stathis N. Kalyvas. 1994. Language and the construction of states: The case of Catalonia in Spain. *Politics and Society* 22, no. 1 (Mar.): 5–29.

Lake, David A., and Donald Rothchild, eds. 1998. *The international spread of ethnic conflict: Fear, diffusion, and escalation.* Princeton, N.J.: Princeton University Press.

Licklider, Roy. 1995. The consequences of negotiated settlements in civil wars, 1945–1993. *American Political Science Review* 89, no. 3 (Sept.): 681–90.

Lijphart, Arend. 1999. *Patterns of democracy: Government forms and performance in thirty-six countries.* New Haven, Conn.: Yale University Press.

Little, David. 1994. *Sri Lanka: The invention of enmity.* Series on religion, nationalism, and intolerance. Washington, D.C.: United States Institute of Peace Press.

Malalgoda, Kitsiri. 1976. *Buddhism in Sinhalese society 1750–1900: A study of religious revival and change.* Berkeley: University of California Press.

Manogaran, Chelvadurai. 1994. Colonization as politics: Political use of space in Sri Lanka's ethnic conflict. In *The Sri Lankan Tamils: Ethnicity and identity,* ed. Chelvadurai Manogaran and Bryan Pfaffenberger, 84–125. Boulder, Colo.: Westview Press.

Manor, James. 1984. Introduction. In *Sri Lanka in change and crisis,* ed. James Manor, 1–31. London: Croom Helm.

———. 1989. *The expedient utopian: Bandaranaike and Ceylon.* Durham, N.C.: Duke University Press.

Mapp, Roberta E. 1972. Cross-national dimensions of ethnocentrism. *Canadian Journal of African Studies* 6, no. 1 (Winter): 73–96.

March, James G., and Johan P. Olsen. 1989. *Rediscovering institutions: The organizational basis of politics.* New York: Free Press.

Matthews, Bruce. 1986. Radical conflict and the rationalization of violence in Sri Lanka. *Pacific Affairs* 59, no. 2 (Spring): 28–44.

Mendis, G. C. 1965. The Vijaya legend. In *Paranavitana felicitation volume,* ed. N. A. Jayawickrama, 263–92. Colombo: M. D. Gunasena.

———. 1985. *The early history of Ceylon and its history with India and other foreign countries.* New Delhi: Asian Educational Services.

Mill, John Stuart. [1861] 1991. *Considerations on representative government.* Amherst, N.Y.: Prometheus Books.

Muni, S. D. 1993. *Pangs of proximity: India's and Sri Lanka's ethnic crisis.* New Delhi: Sage Publications.

Murdoch, John, and James Nicholson. 1868. *Classified catalogue of printed tracts and books in Singhalese.* Madras: Christian Vernacular Education Society.

Namasivayam, S. 1953. Aspects of Ceylonese parliamentary government. *Pacific Affairs* 26, no. 1 (Mar.): 76–83.

Nithiyanandan, V. 1987. An analysis of economic factors behind the origin and development of Tamil nationalism in Sri Lanka. In *Facets of Ethnicity in Sri Lanka,* ed. Charles Abeysekera and Newton Gunasinghe, 100–170. Colombo: Social Scientists Association.

Nodia, Ghia. 2000. Nurturing nationalism. *Journal of Democracy* 11, no. 4 (Oct.): 169–73.

Norell, Magnus. 2000. Is peace possible? The case of Sri Lanka. *Civil Wars* 3, no. 4 (Winter): 105–18.

North, Douglas C. 1990. *Institutions, institutional change, and economic performance.* Cambridge: Cambridge University Press.

Oberst, Robert. 1984. Proportional representation and electoral system change in Sri Lanka. In *Sri Lanka in change and crisis*, ed. James Manor, 118–33. London: Croom Helm.

Obeyesekere, Gananath. 1970. Religious symbolism and political change in Ceylon. *Modern Ceylon Studies* 1, no. 1 (Jan.): 43–63.

———. 1979. The vicissitudes of Sinhala-Buddhist identity through time and change. In *Collective identities nationalisms and protest in modern Sri Lanka*, ed. Michael Roberts, 279–313. Colombo: Marga Institute.

———. 1984. The origins and institutionalisation of political violence. In *Sri Lanka in change and crisis*, ed. James Manor, 153–74. London: Croom Helm.

O'Neil, Patrick H. 1996. Revolution from within: Institutional analysis, transitions from authoritarianism, and the case of Hungary. *World Politics* 48, no. 4 (July): 579–603.

O'Neill, Michael. 2000. Belgium: Language, ethnicity, and nationality. *Parliamentary Affairs* 53, no. 1 (Jan.): 114–34.

Ostrom, Elinor. 1995. New horizons in institutional analysis. *American Political Science Review* 89, no. 1 (Mar.): 174–78.

Paranavitana, S. 1959. Aryan settlements: The Sinhalese. In *History of Ceylon*, vol. 1: *From the earliest times to 1505*, ed. S. Paranavitana, 82–97. Colombo: Ceylon University Press.

Peebles, Patrick. 1990. Colonization and ethnic conflict in the Dry Zone of Sri Lanka. *Journal of Asian Studies* 49, no. 1 (Feb.): 30–55.

Pegg, Scott M. 1997. On the margins: International society and the de facto state. Ph.D. diss., University of British Columbia.

Pfaffenberger, Bryan. 1984. Fourth world colonialism, indigenous minorities and Tamil separatism in Sri Lanka. *Bulletin of Concerned Asian Scholars* 16, no. 1 (Jan.–Mar.): 17–21.

Phadnis, Urmila. 1979. Ethnicity and nation-building in South Asia: A case study of Sri Lanka. *India Quarterly* 35, no. 3 (July–Sept.): 329–50.

———. 1989. *Ethnicity and nation-building in South Asia*. New Delhi: Sage Publications.

Pieris, M. D. D. 2002. *In the Pursuit of Governance: A Memoir of over Three and a Half Decades in the Public Service of Sri Lanka*. Pannipitiya: Stamford Lake (Pvt) Ltd.

Pieris, R. 1956. *Sinhalese social organizations: The Kandyan period*. Colombo: Ceylon University Press.

Plattner, Marc F. 1999. From liberalism to liberal democracy. *Journal of Democracy* 10, no. 3 (July): 121–34.

Ponnambalam, Satchi. 1981. *Dependent capitalism in crisis: The Sri Lankan economy, 1948–1980*. London: Zed Press.

———. 1983. *Sri Lanka: The national question and the Tamil liberation struggle*. Thornton Heath, Surrey: Tamil Information Centre.

Posen, Barry R. 1993. Nationalism, the mass army, and military powers. *International Security* 18, no. 2 (Fall): 80–124.

Powell, G. Bingham, Jr. 2000. *Elections as instruments of democracy: Majoritarian and proportional views*. New Haven, Conn.: Yale University Press.

Powell, Walter, and Paul DiMaggio, eds. 1991. *The new institutionalism in organizational analysis.* Chicago: University of Chicago Press.

Pratap, Anita. 2001. *Island of blood: Frontline reports from Sri Lanka, Afghanistan and other South Asian flashpoints.* New Delhi: Penguin Books India.

Price, Maurice T. 1924. *Christian missions and oriental civilizations: A study in culture contact.* Shanghai: private printing.

Rabushka, Alvin, and Kenneth A. Shepsle. 1972. *Politics in plural societies: A theory of democratic instability.* Columbus: Charles E. Merrill.

Rahula, Walpola. 1956. *History of Buddhism in Ceylon: The Anuradhapura period, 3d century BC –10th century AC.* Colombo: M. D. Gunasena.

———. 1974. *The heritage of the bhikkhu: A short history of the bhikkhu in educational, cultural, social, and political life.* New York: Grove Press.

Rajan, A. Theva. 1995. *Tamil as official language: Retrospect and prospect.* Colombo: International Center for Ethnic Studies.

Ram, N. 1991. Understanding Prabakaran's LTTE. In Sri Lanka's crisis and India's response, ed. V. Suryanarayan, 25–29. New Delhi: Patriot Publishers.

Ramanathan, Ponnambalam. 1916. *Riots and martial law in Ceylon, 1915.* London: St. Martin's Press.

Roberts, Michael. 1973. Elite formation and elites, 1832–1931. In *History of Ceylon*, vol. 3: *From the beginning of the nineteenth century to 1948*, ed. K. M. de Silva, 263–84. Peradeniya: University of Ceylon Press Board.

———. 1978. Ethnic conflict in Sri Lanka and Sinhalese perspectives: Barriers to accommodation. *Modern Asian Studies* 12, no. 3 (July): 353–76.

———. 1982. *Caste conflict and elite formation: The rise of a Karava elite in Sri Lanka, 1500–1931.* Cambridge: Cambridge University Press.

Rogers, John D. 1994. Post-orientalism and the interpretation of premodern and modern political identities: The case of Sri Lanka. *Journal of Asian Studies* 53, no. 1 (Feb.): 10–23.

Rothstein, Bo. 1996. Political institutions: An overview. In *A New Handbook of Political Science*, ed. Robert E. Goodin and Hans-Dieter Klingemann, 133–66. New York: Oxford University Press.

Russell, Jane. 1982a. *Communal politics under the Donoughmore constitution, 1931–47. Ceylon Historical Journal* 26. Dehiwala: Tisara Prakasakayo.

———. 1982b. The dance of the turkey cock—The Jaffna boycott of 1931. *Ceylon Journal of Historical and Social Studies* 8, no. 1: 47–67.

———. 1982c. Language, education and nationalism—the language debate of 1944. *Ceylon Journal of Historical and Social Studies* 8, no. 2: 38–64.

Ryan, Bruce. 1961. Status, achievement, and education in Ceylon: An historical perspective. *Journal of Asian Studies* 20, no. 4 (Aug.): 463–76.

Samarakone, Priya. 1984. The conduct of the referendum. In *Sri Lanka in change and crisis*, ed. James Manor, 84–117. London: Croom Helm.

Samarasinghe, S. G. 1996. Language policy in public administration, 1956–1994: An implementor's perspective. In *National language policy in Sri Lanka 1956 to 1996: Three studies in its implementation*, ed. K. N. O. Dharmadasa, 79–111. Kandy: International Center for Ethnic Studies.

Sartori, Giovanni. 1966. European political parties: The case of polarized plural-ism. In *Political Parties and Political Development*, ed. Joseph LaPalombara and Myron Weiner, 137–76. Princeton, N.J.: Princeton University Press.

Schalk, Peter. 1997. Resistance and martyrdom in the process of state formation of Tamililam. In *Martyrdom and political resistance: Essays from Asia and Europe*, ed. Joyce Pettigrew, 61–83. Comparative Asian Studies 18. Amsterdam: VU University Press.

Schedler, Andreas. 1998. What is democratic consolidation? *Journal of Democracy* 9, no. 2 (Apr.): 91–107.

Schwarz, Walter. 1988. *The Tamils of Sri Lanka*. 4th rev. ed. Minority Rights Group Report No. 25. London: Minority Rights Group.

Scott, George M., Jr. 1989. The economic bases of Sinhalese-Muslim ethno-reli-gious conflicts in twentieth-century Sri Lanka. *Ethnic Studies Report* 7, no. 1 (Jan.): 20–35.

Scott, Jim. "Futures of Asian Studies." *Asian Studies Newsletter*, Summer 1997, 7.

Senaratne, Jagath P. 1997. *Political violence in Sri Lanka, 1977–1990: Riots, in-surrections, counterinsurgencies, foreign intervention*. Amsterdam: VU University Press.

Seneviratne, H. L. 1999. *The work of kings: The new Buddhism in Sri Lanka*. Chicago: University of Chicago Press.

Shastri, Amita. 1990. The material bases for separatism: The Tamil eelam move-ment in Sri Lanka. *Journal of Asian Studies* 49 (Feb.): 56–77.

Shepsle, Kenneth. 1989. Studying institutions: Some lessons from the rational choice approach. *Journal of Theoretical Politics* 1, no. 2 (Apr.): 131–47.

Shils, Edward. 1957. Primordial, personal, sacred and civil ties: Some particular observations on the relationships of sociological research and theory. *British Journal of Sociology* 8, no. 2 (June): 130–45.

Sivanayagam, S. 1991. The phenomenon of Tamil militancy. In *Sri Lankan crisis and India's Response*, ed. V. Suryanarayan, 30–47. New Delhi: Patriot Publishers.

Sivarajah, Ambalavanar. 1996. *Politics of Tamil nationalism in Sri Lanka*. New Delhi: South Asian Publishers.

Smith, Anthony D. 1979. Towards a theory of ethnic separatism. *Ethnic and Racial Studies* 2, no. 1 (Jan.): 21–37.

———. 1986. *The ethnic origins of nations*. Oxford: Blackwell.

———. 1999. Ethnic election and national destiny: Some religious origins of na-tionalist ideals. *Nations and Nationalism* 5, no. 3 (July): 331–55.

Smith, Bardwell L., ed. 1978. *Religion and legitimation of power in Sri Lanka*. Chambersburg, Pa.: Anima Books.

Snyder, Jack. 1993. Nationalism and the crisis of the post-Soviet state. *Survival* 35 (Spring): 5–26.

———. 2000. *From voting to violence: Democratization and nationalist conflict*. New York: Norton.

Somasundaram, Daya. 1998. *Scarred minds: The psychological impact of war on Sri Lankan Tamils*. New Delhi: Sage Publications.

Spencer, Jonathan, ed. 1990. *Sri Lanka: History and the roots of conflict.* London: Routledge.

Sprinzak, Ehud. 2000. Rational fanatics. *Foreign Policy,* Sept.–Oct.: 66–73.

Sri Lanka [see also Ceylon]. Department of Census and Statistics. 1972. *Census of Population, 1971: Preliminary Release No. 2.* Colombo: Department of Census and Statistics.

Stalin, Joseph V. 1972. Marxism and the national question. In *The essential Stalin: Major theoretical writings, 1905–52,* ed. Bruce Franklin, 54–84. New York: Anchor Books.

Steinmo, Sven. 1989. Political institutions and tax policy in the United States, Sweden, and Britain. *World Politics* 41, no. 4 (July): 500–535.

Steinmo, Sven, Kathleen Thelen, and Frank Longstreth, eds. 1992. *Structuring politics: Historical institutionalism in comparative analysis.* Cambridge: Cambridge University Press.

Stepan, Alfred. 1999. Federalism and democracy: Beyond the U.S. model. *Journal of Democracy* 10, no. 4 (Oct.): 19–34.

Swamy, M. R. Narayan. 1994. *Tigers of Lanka: From boys to guerrillas.* Delhi: Konark.

Tambiah, Stanley J. 1967. The politics of language in India and Ceylon. *Modern Asian Studies* 1, no. 3 (July): 215–40.

———. 1986. *Sri Lanka: Ethnic fratricide and the dismantling of democracy.* Chicago: University of Chicago Press.

———. 1996. *Leveling crowds: Ethnonationalist conflicts and collective violence in South Asia.* Berkeley: University of California Press.

Thangarajah, Yuvi. 2003. Ethnicization of the devolution debate and the militarization of civil society in north-eastern Sri Lanka. In *Building local capacities for peace: Rethinking conflict and development in Sri Lanka,* ed. Markus Mayer, Darini Rajasingham-Senanayake, and Yuvi Thangarajah, 13–36. Delhi: Macmillan India.

Thornton, A. P. 1977. *Imperialism in the twentieth century.* Minneapolis: University of Minnesota Press.

Tiruchelvam, Neelan. 1984a. Ethnicity and resource allocation. In *From independence to statehood: Managing ethnic conflict in five African and Asian states,* ed. Robert B. Goldman and A. Jeyaratnam Wilson, 185–95. New York: St. Martin's Press.

———. 1984b. The politics of decentralization and devolution: Competing conceptions of district development councils in Sri Lanka. In *From independence to statehood: Managing ethnic conflict in five African and Asian states,* ed. Robert B. Goldman and A. Jeyaratnam Wilson, 196–209. New York: St. Martin's Press.

Uyangoda, Jayadeva. 1996. Militarization, violent state, violent society: Sri Lanka. In *Internal conflicts in South Asia,* ed. Kumar Rupesinghe and Khawar Mumtaz, 118–30. London: Sage Publications.

———. 2001. *Questions of Sri Lanka's minority rights.* Minority Protection in South Asia Series, No. 2. Colombo: International Center for Ethnic Studies.

Van den Berghe, Pierre L. [1967] 1978. *Race and racism: A comparative perspective*. New York: Wiley.

———. 1996. Does race matter? In *Ethnicity*, ed. John Hutchinson and Anthony D. Smith, 57–63. Oxford: Oxford University Press.

Van der Veer, Peter. 1999. Hindus: A superior race. *Nations and Nationalism* 5, no. 3 (July): 419–30.

Varshney, Ashutosh. 2003. Nationalism, ethnic conflict, and rationality. *Perspectives on Politics* 1, no. 1 (Mar.): 85–99.

Vijayavardhana, D. C. 1953. *The revolt in the temple*. Colombo: Sinha Publications.

Vittachi, Tarzie. 1958. *Emergency '58: The story of the Ceylon race riots*. London: André Deutsch.

Vossler, Karl. 1932. *The spirit of language in civilization*. Translated by Oscar Oeser. New York: Harcourt, Brace.

Waldron, Arthur N. 1985. Theories of nationalism and historical explanation. *World Politics* 37, no. 3 (Apr.): 416–33.

Weerawardana, I. D. S. 1960. *Ceylon general election 1956*. Colombo: M. D. Sunasena.

Weingast, Barry R. 1996. Political institutions: Rational choice perspectives. In *A New Handbook of Political Science*, ed. Robert E. Goodin and Hans-Dieter Klingemann, 167–90. New York: Oxford University Press.

Wickramasinghe, Nira. 1995. *Ethnic politics of colonial Sri Lanka, 1927–47*. New Delhi: Vikas.

Wickremeratne, Ananda. 1973. Education and social change, 1832 to c. 1900. In *History of Ceylon*, vol. 3: *From the beginning of the nineteenth century to 1948*, ed. K. M. de Silva, 165–86. Peradeniya: University of Ceylon Press Board.

———. 1995. *Buddhism and ethnicity in Sri Lanka: A historical analysis*. New Delhi: Vikas.

Wilson, A. Jeyaratnam. 1966. The Tamil Federal Party in Ceylon politics. *Journal of Commonwealth Political Studies* 4, no. 2 (July): 117–37.

———. 1988. *The break-up of Sri Lanka: The Sinhalese-Tamil conflict*. Honolulu: University of Hawaii Press.

———. 1994. *S. J. V. Chelvanayakam and the crisis of Sri Lankan Tamil nationalism, 1947–1977*. Honolulu: University of Hawaii Press.

———. 2000. *Sri Lankan Tamil nationalism: Its origins and development in the nineteenth and twentieth centuries*. Vancouver: University of British Columbia Press.

Wriggins, Howard. 1960. *Ceylon: Dilemmas of a new nation*. Princeton, N.J.: Princeton University Press.

———. 1961. Impediments to unity in new nations: The case of Ceylon. *American Political Science Review* 55, no. 2 (June): 313–20.

Yapp, Malcolm. 1979. Language, religion and political identity: A general framework. In *Political identity in South Asia*, ed. David Taylor and Malcolm Yapp, 1–34. London: Curzon Press.

Zakaria, Fareed. 1997. The rise of illiberal democracy. *Foreign Affairs* 76, no. 6 (Nov.–Dec.): 22–43.

Zartman, William I. 1998. Putting Humpty Dumpty together again. In *The international spread of ethnic conflict: Fear, diffusion, and escalation*, ed. David Lake and Donald Rothchild, 317–36. Princeton, N.J.: Princeton University Press.

INDEX

In this index an "f" after a number indicates a separate reference on the next page, and an "ff" indicates separate references on the next two pages. A continuous discussion over two or more pages is indicated by a span of page numbers, e.g., "57–59."